MW01382845

THE FAMILY LEGACY OF HENRY CLAY

Topics in Kentucky History

James C. Klotter, SERIES EDITOR

Books in the Series

THE FAMILY LEGACY OF
HENRY CLAY

In the Shadow of a Kentucky Patriarch

For Jonathan
Hope you enjoy!
Lindsey Apple

Lindsey Apple

THE UNIVERSITY PRESS OF KENTUCKY

Copyright © 2011 by The University Press of Kentucky

Scholarly publisher for the Commonwealth,
serving Bellarmine University, Berea College, Centre
College of Kentucky, Eastern Kentucky University,
The Filson Historical Society, Georgetown College,
Kentucky Historical Society, Kentucky State University,
Morehead State University, Murray State University,
Northern Kentucky University, Transylvania University,
University of Kentucky, University of Louisville,
and Western Kentucky University.
All rights reserved.

Editorial and Sales Offices: The University Press of Kentucky
663 South Limestone Street, Lexington, Kentucky 40508-4008
www.kentuckypress.com

15 14 13 12 11   5 4 3 2 1

Library of Congress Cataloging-in-Publication Data

Apple, Lindsey.
  The family legacy of Henry Clay : in the shadow of a Kentucky patriarch / Lindsey
Apple.
      p. cm.
  Includes bibliographical references and index.
  ISBN 978-0-8131-3410-9 (hardcover : alk. paper)
  ISBN 978-0-8131-3411-6 (ebook)
  1. Clay, Henry, 1777–1852. 2. Clay, Henry, 1777–1852—Family. 3. Clay family.
4. Clay, Henry, 1777–1852—Influence. 5. Kentucky—Biography. 6. Statesmen—United
States—Biography. 7. Legislators—United States—Biography. 8. United States. Congress.
Senate—Biography. I. Title.
  E340.C6A67 2011
  328.092—dc23
  [B]
                                          2011019756

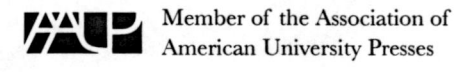

For Brian, Elizabeth, Andrew, and Gabrielle

CONTENTS

ILLUSTRATIONS

CAST OF CHARACTERS

Alice Dudley McDowell: 1913–1985, sixth generation; Henry Clay Jr. branch; became a professional dancer and created her own dance company. As a child, she added excitement to Ashland.

Anne Brown Clay Erwin: 1807–1835, second generation; married James Erwin; bright, charming, much like her father.

Anne Clay McDowell: 1837–1917, third generation; Henry Clay Jr. branch; married H. C. McDowell and returned to Ashland, making her family the third Clay family to live there. Died of tuberculosis.

Anne Clay McDowell Stucky: 1891–1966, fifth generation; favorite of her grandmother, for whom she was named.

Annie Green Clay Gibson: fourth generation; Thomas H. Clay branch; remained in Pennsylvania when her family moved back to Kentucky, but helped Glyndon Van Deusen and other historians. As a young girl, she kept scrapbooks about the family and about European nobility.

Charles Donald Clay Sr.: 1857–1935, third generation; James Clay branch; retired colonel, served in three wars; held very traditional values that restricted his children.

Charles (Charley) Donald Clay Jr.: 1899–1922, fourth generation; James Clay branch; the epitome of Clay honor, expelled from West Point; committed suicide or was murdered at Fort Snelling, Minnesota.

Charles Edward Erwin: 1835–1860, third generation; Erwin branch; impulsive, a spendthrift; died young of tuberculosis.

Eliza (Elizabeth Hart) Clay: 1813–1825, second generation; died in Lebanon, Ohio, on the way to Washington, D.C.

Elizabeth Clay Blanford: 1904–1999, fourth generation; James Clay branch; epitomized the genteel values expected of a Clay woman late into the twentieth century; recorded aspects of the family history in short character sketches.

Eugene Erwin: 1830–1863, third generation; Erwin branch; capable and courageous; Confederate officer; died at Vicksburg.

Eugenia Erwin: 1864–1864, fourth generation; Erwin branch; posthumous child of Eugene; died as an infant, probably as a result of the stress of the Civil War on her mother.

George Hudson Clay: 1858–1934, third generation; James Clay branch; melancholy and impulsive, excellent breeder of horses, joked about family heritage.

Goodloe McDowell: 1895–1974, fifth generation; Henry Clay Jr. branch; veteran of World War I, sold the McDowell stable of horses, ran the Phoenix Hotel in Lexington.

Harry (Henry) Boyle Clay: 1840–1919, third generation; Thomas H. Clay branch; Confederate officer; married and moved to Rogersville, Tennessee.

Harry Boyle Clay Jr.: 1864–1917, fourth generation; Thomas H. Clay branch; in business with his father; died of tuberculosis.

Harry (Henry) Independence Clay: 1849–1884, third generation; James Clay branch; compared favorably to Henry Clay; Arctic explorer, Louisville politician; murdered by a Louisville saloon keeper.

Henrietta Clay: 1800–1801; first child of the Clays, she died as an infant.

Henrietta Clay: d. 1975, fourth generation; Thomas H. Clay branch; business woman, left papers to Transylvania University.

Henry Clay: 1777–1852; patriarch.

Henry Clay Jr.: 1811–1847, second generation; lawyer, politician; died in the Mexican War.

Henry (Hart) Clay III: 1833–1862, third generation; Henry Clay Jr. branch; intelligent, energetic, but ill-disciplined, he was expelled from West Point. Died of disease as a Union officer during the Civil War.

Henry Clay Anderson: 1891–1959, fifth generation; Erwin branch; professor of physics at Western Kentucky University; considered a black sheep in the family.

Henry Clay Duralde: 1824–1850, third generation; Duralde branch; charming, gregarious, but reckless and prone to bad habits, his grandmother Lucretia banned him from Ashland. He died in a swimming accident.

Henry Clay Erwin: 1827–1859, third generation; Erwin branch; intelligent but impulsive, drank heavily; died young of tuberculosis.

Henry Clay List: 1950–, seventh generation; Erwin branch; served in Kentucky state legislature, businessman.

Henry Clay McDowell Sr.: 1832–1899, third generation; married to Anne Clay of Henry Clay Jr. branch; successful businessman and breeder of horses.

Henry Clay McDowell Jr.: 1861–1933, fourth generation; Henry Clay Jr. branch; lawyer, businessman, federal judge. Considered for Supreme Court and as potential vice presidential candidate.

Henry Clay Simpson Sr.: 1896–1986, fifth generation; Erwin branch; Lexington businessman, active in support of Ashland, the Henry Clay Estate.

Henry Clay Simpson Jr.: 1938–, sixth generation; Erwin branch; banker, family historian.

Henry McDowell Bullock: 1893–1976, fifth generation; Henry Clay Jr. branch; eccentric and in poor health, he was the last Clay descendant to live at Ashland. Because of his antics, the Ashland Foundation moved him away from the estate.

James Brown Clay: 1817–1864, second generation; businessman, lawyer, Confederate.

James Brown Clay Jr.: 1846–1906, third generation; James Clay branch; Confederate veteran; excellent horseman but cantankerous and addicted to alcohol.

James Erwin: d. 1851, second generation; husband of Anne Clay, business partner of Henry.

James Erwin Jr.: 1828–1848, third generation; Erwin branch; considered promising; committed suicide after a night of drinking and gambling.

John C. J. Clay: 1847–1872, third generation; James Clay branch; showed promise but died young of typhoid fever.

John Morrison Clay: 1821–1887, second generation; excellent horseman, suffered bouts of insanity.

Josephine Russell Erwin Clay: 1835–1920, third generation; married a grandson, then a son of Henry Clay. Novelist and premiere horsewoman, she became a stronger member of the family than many blood relatives.

Julia Erwin: 1825–1828, third generation; Erwin branch; daughter of Anne Clay and James Erwin; died as a child.

Julia McDowell Brock: 1970–, seventh generation; Henry Clay Jr. branch; family researcher, active at Ashland and in the Clay Family Society.

Julia Prather Clay: 1813–1840, second generation; wife of Henry Clay Jr.

Julia Prather McDowell Brock: 1868–1942, fourth generation; Henry Clay Jr. branch; married William B. Brock.

Kenneth Bynum Kenner: 1893–1954, fifth generation; Thomas H. Clay branch; military veteran, community leader; murdered in Rogersville, Tennessee.

Laura Clay: 1816–1817, second generation; died of whooping cough after grueling trip to Washington, D.C.

Louis William (Bill) List: 1945–1998, seventh generation; Erwin branch; served in Vietnam as a helicopter pilot.

Lucretia Hart Clay: 1781–1864; matriarch.

Lucretia Hart Clay: 1809–1823, second generation; died of tuberculosis.

Lucretia (Teetee) Hart Clay: 1851–1923, third generation; James Clay branch; enforcer of the family values, she wrote novels, family biographies, and works of theology; active in the Daughters of the American Revolution and Confederate women's groups.

Lucretia Hart Clay Breckinridge: 1839–1860, third generation; Thomas H. Clay branch; married W. C. P. Breckinridge; died young in childbirth.

Lucretia Hart Erwin: 1829–1866, third generation; Erwin branch; impulsive, argumentative; nearly entered a convent.

Lucretia (Lula) Hart Erwin Simpson: 1854–1929, fourth generation; Erwin branch; married Minor Simpson.

Lucy Jacob Clay: 1844–1863, third generation; James Clay branch; invalid daughter, favorite of Henry Clay; died of diphtheria during the Civil War.

Lucy Starling Clay Boyajian: 1931–, fifth generation; James Clay branch; an example of current family members who appreciate the past but keep it in healthy perspective. She has supported Ashland, the Henry Clay Estate, and encouraged research on the family.

Madeline (Madge) McDowell Breckinridge: 1872–1920, fourth generation; Henry Clay Jr. branch; leading Progressive Era reformer and suffragist. She was perhaps the most outstanding member of Henry Clay's descendants. Suffered from tuberculosis of the bone but died young from a stroke.

Mariah (Ria) Pepper Clay: d. 1939, third generation; wife of Colonel Charles D. Clay.

Martin Duralde Jr.: d. 1848, second generation; husband of Susan Hart Clay.

Martin Duralde III: 1823–1846, third generation; Duralde branch; Henry Clay placed him in the navy; died young of tuberculosis.

Mary Ellyn LaBach Hutton: 1940–, seventh generation; Erwin branch; Woodrow Wilson scholar in college, lawyer, music critic for a Cincinnati newspaper.

Mary Erwin: 1832–1832, third generation; Erwin branch; one of several descendants to die in infancy.

Mary Lucretia Clay Kenner: 1867–1957, fourth generation; Thomas H. Clay branch; dominated Rogersville Clays after the death of her father, Harry Boyle Clay.

Mary (Marie) Mentelle Clay: 1806–1891, second generation; wife of Thomas Hart Clay, befriended Lucretia, her mother-in-law, and Susan, Thomas's sister-in-law; bulwark of the family.

Mary Webster Clay Erwin Anderson: 1861–1931, fourth generation; Erwin branch; married Matthew Anderson, a banker; enjoyed the risks associated with horse racing.

Minnie (Mary) Russell Clay: 1848–1892, third generation; Thomas H. Clay branch; remained single, taught piano lessons.

Nathaniel Hart Clay: 1861–1862, third generation; James Clay branch; died of diphtheria during the Civil War.

Ned Boyajian: 1964–, sixth generation; James Clay branch; businessman, able researcher in the family history.

Nettie (Nanette) McDowell Bullock: 1859–1948, fourth generation; Henry Clay Jr. branch; socialite, founder of Ashland as a house museum honoring Henry Clay and later family members.

Parker LaBach: 1943–, seventh generation; Erwin branch; left West Point to study medicine; prominent physician in Missouri.

Robert (Bob) Pepper Clay: 1903–1977, fourth generation; James Clay branch; West Point graduate and career soldier; struggled early with family restrictions but made similar demands of his children.

Robert Pepper Clay Jr.: 1941–1973, fifth generation; James Clay branch; the last Henry Clay descendant capable of continuing the Clay name; died while scuba diving.

Rose Victoire Clay: 1845–1878, third generation; Thomas H. Clay branch; married Garland Hale but died young without children.

Susan Hart Clay Duralde: 1805–1825, second generation; married Martin Duralde Jr. of New Orleans.

Susan Jacob Clay: 1855–1863, third generation; James Clay branch; died of diphtheria during the Civil War.

Susan Jacob Clay Sawitzky: 1897–1981; fourth generation; James Clay branch; poet who chronicled the struggle of a cautious rebel against traditional and family values.

Susan (Suzannah) Maria Jacob Clay: 1823–1905, second generation; married to James B. Clay; biographer and major mythmaker after the Civil War.

Theodore Wythe Clay: 1802–1870, second generation; named for George Wythe, Henry Clay's mentor; went insane.

Thomas Clay McDowell: 1866–1935, fourth generation; Henry Clay Jr. branch; bred and raced thoroughbred horses; known for his integrity.

Thomas Hart Clay: 1803–1871, second generation; troubled youth, suffered from depression throughout his life; served Lincoln as a diplomat and farmed Mansfield successfully.

Thomas Hart Clay Jr.: 1843–1907, third generation; Thomas H. Clay branch; editor of *Youth's Companion,* wrote a biography of his grandfather, active in philanthropic work.

Thomas Jacob Clay: 1853–1939, third generation; James Clay branch; soldier and respected horseman, active in Geronimo campaign; strong sense of Clay honor.

Thomas Julian Clay: 1840–1863, third generation; Henry Clay Jr. branch; Confederate officer, expressed his hatred of all things Yankee; died of disease during the Civil War.

Thomas S. Bullock: 1859–1929, fourth generation; married Nettie McDowell.

William Adair McDowell: 1863–1925, fourth generation; Henry Clay Jr. branch; prominent Lexington banker.

William Cochran McDowell: 1888–1936, fifth generation; Henry Clay Jr. branch; practiced progressive agricultural techniques at Ashland until the property was subdivided in the second decade of the twentieth century.

William Davis Kenner: 1943–, sixth generation; Thomas H. Clay branch; a psychiatrist, he has shared family papers and artifacts with the Tennessee Historical Society, the University of Kentucky, and Ashland, the Henry Clay Estate.

William LaBach: 1938–, seventh generation; Erwin branch; mathematician, lawyer, author, and family researcher.

William McDowell Stucky: 1916–1961, sixth generation; Henry Clay Jr. branch; commander in the navy during World War II and a journalist.

Wood Simpson: 1941–, sixth generation; Erwin branch.

CLAY FAMILY TREES

Henry Clay
Born: 12 Apr 1777
Died: 29 Jun 1852

Lucretia Hart Clay
Born: 18 Mar 1781
Died: 4 Apr 1864
Mar. 11 Apr 1799

Henrietta Clay	Theodore Wythe Clay	Thomas Hart Clay	Susan Hart Clay	Anne Brown Clay	Lucretia Hart Clay	Henry Clay Jr.	Elizabeth (Eliza) Hart Clay	Laura Clay	James Brown Clay	John Morrison Clay
b. 25 Jun 1800	b. 3 Jul 1802	b. 22 Sept 1803	b. 11 Feb 1805	b. 15 Apr 1807	b. Feb 1809	b. 10 Apr 1811	b. 5 Jul 1813	b. 16 Oct 1816	b. 9 Nov 1817	b. 21 Feb 1821
d. 4 Jun 1801	d. 5 May 1870	d. 8 Mar 1871	d. 18 Sep 1825	d. 10 Dec 1835	d. 18 Jun 1823	d. 23 Feb 1847	d. 11 Aug 1825	d. 5 Jan 1817	d. 26 Jan 1864	d. 10 Aug 1887

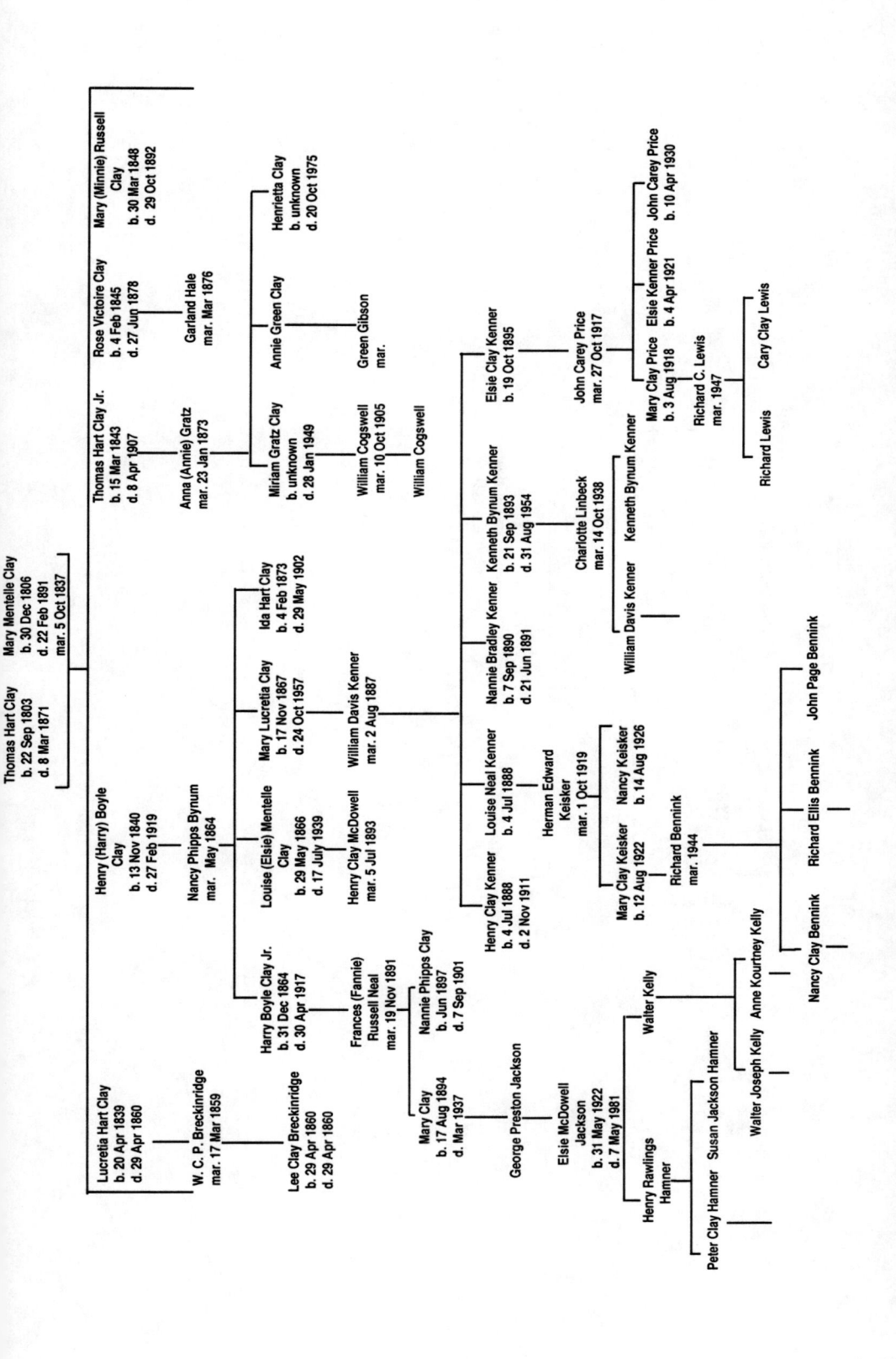

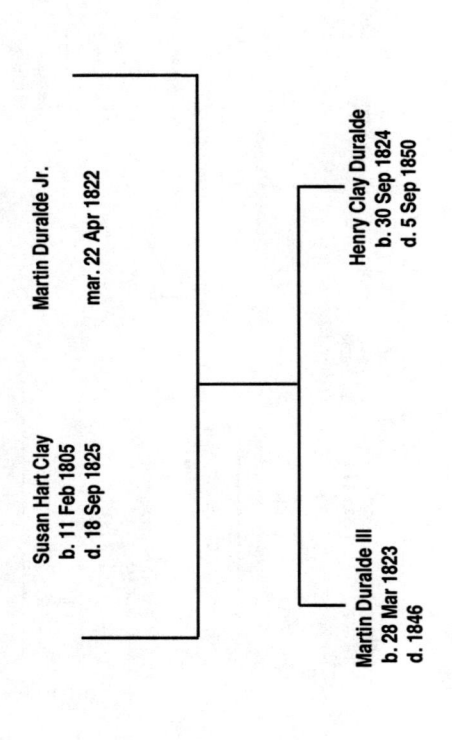

Susan Hart Clay
b. 11 Feb 1805
d. 18 Sep 1825

Martin Duralde Jr.

mar. 22 Apr 1822

Martin Duralde III
b. 28 Mar 1823
d. 1846

Henry Clay Duralde
b. 30 Sep 1824
d. 5 Sep 1850

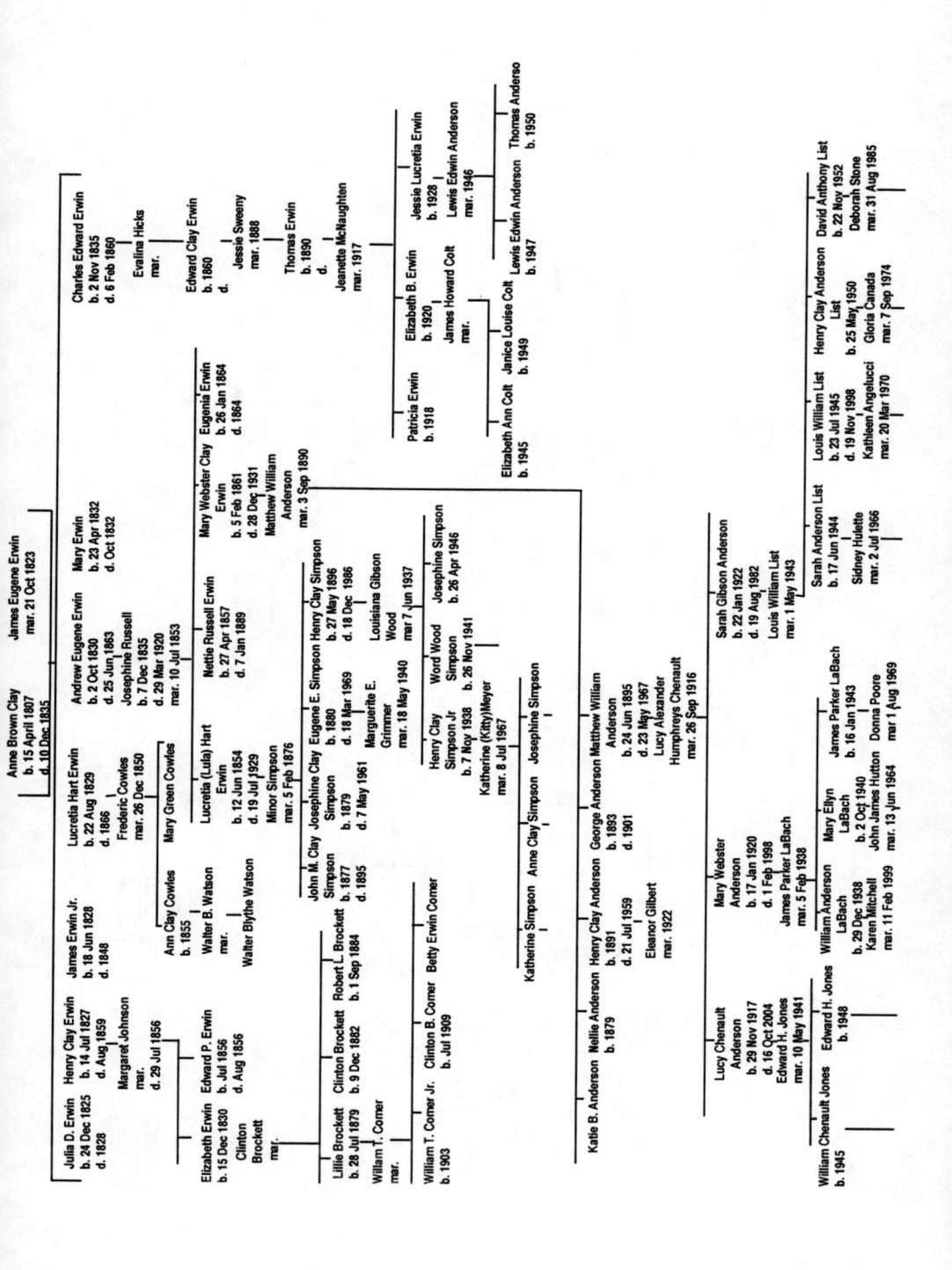

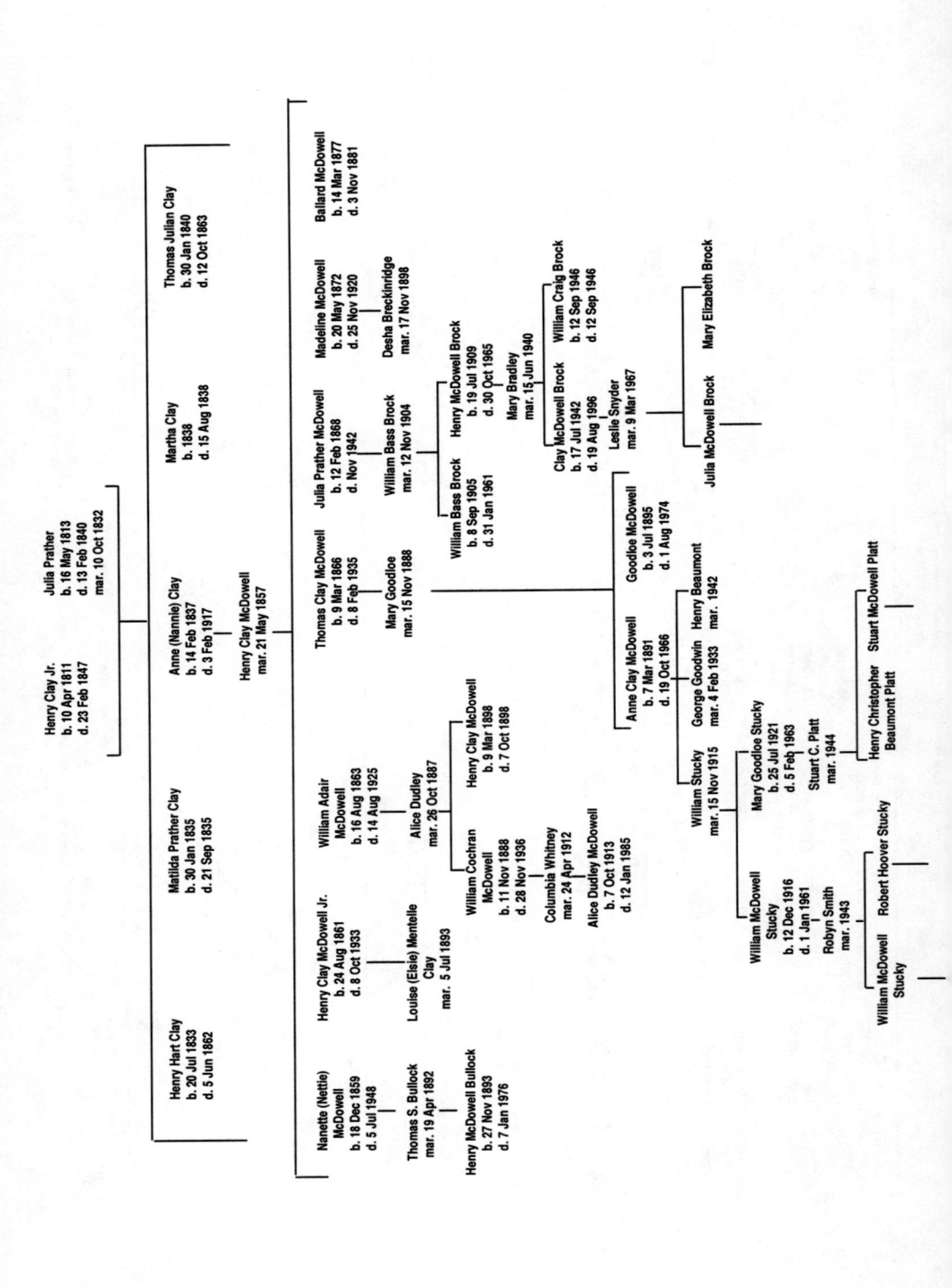

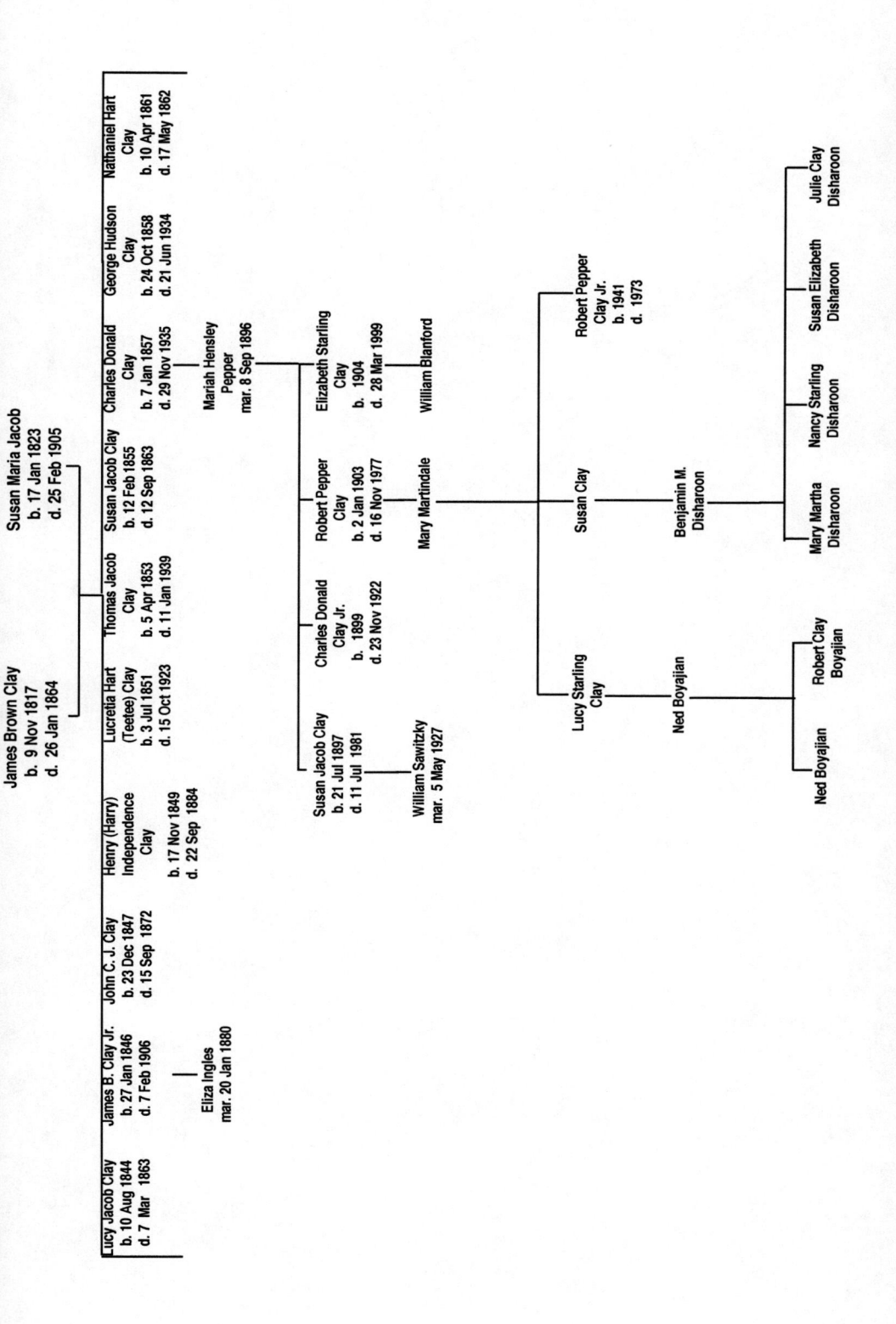

INTRODUCTION

In 1957 a senate committee chaired by future president John F. Kennedy chose five senators considered to be the most influential in the nation's history. Their portraits would hang in the Senate reception room. The first choice was Henry Clay of Kentucky. Studies have suggested that more than a century and a half after his death, Clay remains better known than many of those who served as president during his era. The historian Merrill Petersen included him in the second great triumvirate, along with Daniel Webster and John C. Calhoun, worthy successors to Washington, Adams, and Jefferson.[1] Clay created the position of Speaker of the House as one of consequence in American government. An ardent nationalist, he first provoked a war in 1812, then helped create a peace at Ghent that established a working relationship between the United States and Great Britain. He encouraged the growth of democracy not only in the United States but also in South America, Greece, and other areas struggling against tyranny. Daniel Walker Howe, historian of the Whig Party in American history, claims Clay was the only man in the antebellum era with a comprehensive vision for the nation.[2] Urging an "American System," he wanted to unite the country through commerce, industry, and transportation. Standing on the porch of his beloved estate, Ashland, in Lexington, Kentucky, Clay would today look toward the intersection of two interstate highways linking his community to the four regions of the country. One suspects he might be inclined to gloat. That was a part of his nature.

But Clay is best remembered as the Great Compromiser. Believing strongly that in a democracy, compromise had to be raised to the level of principle, he fashioned a series of compromises—largely over the slavery issue—that held the Union together during a critical period. Although Henry

Clay certainly did not realize it at the time, his compromises preserved the Union through a time when the South had its best chance to destroy it. By 1861 the type of growth Clay's American System had encouraged for the entire nation had made the North predominant. Henry Clay left an enduring legacy to the nation.

He also left a legacy to his family, one not yet studied. That legacy is important for two reasons. Henry Clay made serious political mistakes that explain in part his failure to win the presidency, but historians and biographers have suggested that his family life contributed significantly to that failure. Yet, the family life is appended to his story almost as an afterthought. Harriet Martineau, a British observer, described his family life as "melancholy," and that seems to be enough evidence for most historians and biographers. David Davis has argued that biography provides a key to the synthesis of culture and history by showing how cultural tensions may be internalized, struggled with, and resolved.[3] Henry Clay worked as diligently to influence, and save, his family as he did for the nation, and he could not escape the tragedy and sorrow that led Martineau to declare the family so sad. A study of his family does shed some light on why he did not win the presidency, just not necessarily in the way historians and moralists have traditionally implied.

These pages explain the legacy Clay bequeathed to his family and how it affected generation after generation of his descendants. Family life is the major means of transmitting important values to each new generation, and as such it too provides the key to understanding the synthesis Davis noted.[4] Family biography speaks to a general audience, but it can also satisfy scholars with sound historical interpretation. Biographies of the Adams, Lee, Stevenson, Breckinridge, and Percy families, among others, have revealed a great deal about how values and identities are transmitted.[5] The values of the individuals transmitting them, and the pressures on busy people—now women as well as men—who seek to combine parenting and profession, may also be revealed.

Some scholars express strong distaste for the study of powerful white men, including their families. They believe it is more important to study the masses. Edward Pessen, however, argues that we need to know all we can about both the masses and the classes, about groups and individuals.[6] That said, families who think they are, or may be, important are most likely to preserve their papers, the building blocks for any history. Henry Clay was born with the nation, became active politically at the beginning of the nineteenth century, and fathered his first child in 1800. He wrote thousands of letters. The published correspondence fills eleven volumes. The Clay family traverses the American experience, and its branches—Clays, Duraldes, Erwins, McDowells, Kenners, Simpsons, LaBachs, and others—continued to keep the record because the family legacy contained an appreciation for history and because the record would provide evidence if some member of the family again approached the level of Henry Clay's fame. The Clay family records document America's social history.

Henry Clay's descendants expected someone within the family to repeat the fame of the patriarch. With very few exceptions, his descendants have exhibited intelligence, creativity, and energy. The heritage provided each member with a great deal of confidence, at least at the outset of life, and a set of values that would help achieve his or her blood-centered potential. Every Clay had the genius of "Grandfather" in his or her veins. Much was believed possible, but much was also expected. In that sense, the Clays were exceptional; but no family, important patriarch or otherwise, arrives on history's stage with a crystal ball. The Clay family faced events like every other family or individual.

Admittedly, money and position may create advantages, but they also have disadvantages. If the child of a famous man succeeds, he or she is often accused of using the influence of his family name. Roosevelts and Kennedys come to mind, but the phenomenon is not limited to politicians. Whether a parent leads a Fortune 500 corporation or runs a small family business, sons and daughters have faced the charge. When they fail, they are accused of squandering a birthright. They also have to live with their predecessor's reputation and enemies.

The title of this book is taken from a note in the diary of Henry Clay Jr. "I attribute," he wrote, "much in the world to accident and fortune, but perhaps an opportunity will never occur of using even the qualities I possess. How difficult it is for a young tree to grow in the shade of an aged oak."[7] Adamses, Websters, Roosevelts, and Kennedys could relate to Henry Clay Jr.'s lament. Likewise, the sons and daughters of business leaders, ministers, plumbers, and pipe fitters might feel such pressure. Yet, the legacy also inspired confidence. According to Elizabeth Stone in *Black Sheep and Kissing Cousins,* most families have a grandfather or uncle who becomes the standard of values members of the next generation are encouraged to adopt. Bertram Wyatt-Brown, in *Southern Honor,* says that although the example might not be grand in poorer families, children are still urged to match the achievements of that ancestor.[8] The lesson can be a blessing or a curse.

The descendants of Henry Clay, particularly after the Civil War, created a myth, a collective memory, that explained both the blessings and the responsibilities of membership in the family. This myth created a shared identity that to a large degree motivated the actions of family members. W. Fitzhugh Brundage argues that we must learn how historical memory informs day-to-day life. This study speaks both to the transmission of such memories and to their impact. Equally important, the memory of Clay became inextricably bound to the post–Civil War tenets of the Lost Cause, thus providing evidence of the broader influence of selective memory.[9]

The most important value was loyalty to family. Henry Clay clearly exhibited the trait, and it evolved in the trauma of civil war and family need. Loyalty to family encompassed both the ability and the duty to contribute. It involved honor and the need to protect the name, both through proper conduct and through refutation of "unfair" assaults on it. It required the education of the children to family values and a family identity. In each branch and generation, family names were repeated. Although it provides evidence of family loyalty, such practice can be frustrating to the reader. There are just too many Henrys, Lucretias, Susans, and Thomases. Because of the potential for confusion given the large cast of characters (so many with the same names), this volume includes family trees and a glossary of family members.

Desire for the success of one's children and the teaching of family values know no class limitations. Each generation sought to prepare its children for the future. Henry Clay borrowed money for his sons' business ventures throughout his life, and that obligation extended beyond the nuclear family in later generations. He showed remarkable patience and great anxiety for sons who found it difficult to settle into a profession or an area of service. His parenting reflected clearly the family values of the Whig Party, but more important, his values paralleled those of the rising middle class in a market economy. He worked untiringly to establish his sons as solid members of an evolving society. He also mourned, like any father, at the death of each of six Clay daughters and other tragedies, extending into the third generation in his lifetime. His measure of sorrow would have destroyed many men.

Family values, by their very nature, are often more suited to the past than to the present. Clay's sons struggled with their father's issues as they sought to make their own political contributions. The Clay family also reflected the dilemma that characterized the American South as a result of the Civil War and the rapid change thereafter. The war brought such catastrophic change to the South that the people of the region took refuge in the past. Kentucky, a Union state throughout the war, became increasingly pro-South as the war progressed. The Clays epitomized the struggle of the border state. Mentally burying the disloyalty of some branches of the family, they emphasized Henry's loyalty to the Union. However, they also embraced the myth of the Lost Cause, the South's method of dealing with defeat, and molded the image of Henry Clay to suit the needs of their era. The new Henry Clay became to the Clays what Robert E. Lee represented for the American South.

Clay social values mixed the personal expectations of the Lost Cause myth and the Victorian values prominent among the northern middle class, certainly a reflection of a border-state family. Loyalty to family, masculinity, honor, and business acumen were emphasized for the males. For young women, although Barbara Welter's work has largely been relegated to the historiography of women's history, the "Cult of True Womanhood" continued to be a standard throughout the South. Those values proved particularly confining for Clay women. They inherited the "blood" of Henry Clay too. Their efforts to combine refinement, piety, and submissiveness with the inherited need to succeed add a special dimension to the history of women.

Clays also inherited a legacy of risk. Henry Clay's love of gambling is well documented by historians and Victorian moralists alike. The former, though not the latter, suggest he gained control over his love of the "fickle goddess." He channeled the love of risk into politics and business. Henry Clay rarely approached a new business opportunity without visions of immense profit. He created a sort of Clay Corporation that included his sons and occasionally other family members. For generations, the Clays continued to be successful businesspeople. Some continued to gamble— including one great-granddaughter who, according to the family, carried a pocketbook full of gold from track to track, betting on the horses—but most wagered on the breeding and selling of thoroughbreds, banking, and other business ventures.[10]

Most important, the Clays inherited a legacy of service. Given Henry Clay's loyalty to and love of the Union, it was the duty of his descendants to serve. Reluctant to seek national political office, Clays often chose the military as an avenue of service. There has been a descendant of Henry Clay serving in every American War from the Mexican War through Vietnam. The legacy of service evolved over time. With the emphasis on the importance of the family after the Civil War, it became a sense of noblesse oblige. Because the family had been blessed, they owed something back to the society at large. Paul Nagel, in *Descent from Glory,* implies that the Adams family descended from greatness. That overstates the situation for the Clays. No Clay reached the prominence of "Grandfather," but leadership is required at all levels of society. If few reached the halls of power in Washington, D.C., they would serve in Kentucky, Florida, Tennessee, Virginia, or New York. They would support the women's suffrage movement and progressive reform in Kentucky and the nation. They would "protect" African Americans from baser elements within society and intercede with the law when necessary. They would lead in the thoroughbred and trotting horse industries, in banking, in education. Lawyers and landowners, politicians and professors, physicians and soldiers, horsemen and -women, bankers and journalists, and even a priest and a ballerina, the Clays offered the "genius" of Henry Clay back to the state and nation.

They would also lend their support to the less fortunate. The heritage of the Clay family reflects the complicated contradictions of American society on the subject of race. Henry Clay's attitudes were tortured at best. From his youth, he consistently spoke and wrote of slavery as an evil, but he did not know how to end it. He supported emancipation and colonization, but he continued to own slaves and suggested to his son that he should not consider farming as a career if he remained opposed to owning slaves.[11] He offered a plan of gradual emancipation but could not sell his vision to the nation. Even on his own estate, kind treatment and manumission were mixed with slave unrest, runaways, and the sale of intransigent slaves. When the Civil War ended slavery, the Clays adopted most of the new and demeaning attitudes of the Lost Cause. Yet, their attitudes were as much a mixture of myth and reality as those of the patriarch. The lives of family members and their servants were closely linked. Clay children played with the children of black servants. They listened to the stories of the women in the kitchens, absorbing lessons of biblical morality and common decency. Elizabeth Clay Blanford, a great-granddaughter, preserved a series of those stories and proudly, and publicly, proclaimed herself a child of Millie Lawson, an uneducated but wise black servant. Though paternalistic, the relationship between family and servants was anything but segregated. It reflects the complexity of race in the American South, and perhaps in the nation.

A final legacy must be noted. Tragedy and the emotional distress derived from it know no class distinctions. Clays proved particularly susceptible to illness and disease. In the nineteenth century the death of wives and mothers in childbirth was nearly pandemic at all levels of society. Typhoid, diphtheria, cholera, and tuberculosis affected rich and poor alike. The Clays seemed to be attacked by every contagious illness that visited the region.[12] Death stalked families in America's wars and in accidents. Family history, particularly the Clay history, can speak to the impact of such losses. A newspaper article titled "Brilliant—but Short-Lived" noted the eerie trait of bright family members dying tragically young.[13] That shadow hung over the family well into the twentieth century.

The trauma of seeing promising lives cut short may also explain some of the depression, or melancholy, that plagued the family for generations. The Clays called themselves "high spirited." Their intelligence and energy led to solid societal contributions, but sometimes it crossed a line into reckless behavior, bad decision making, and mental illness. Mania and depression appeared frequently within the family. Daniel Walker Howe attributes Clay's pursuit of a politics of order to his quest for psychological order. His private struggle to "attain self-mastery mirrored a statecraft whose objective was the substitution of compromise and rationality for violence and passion."[14] Others have hinted at the issue, but few have explored it. Clay may have conquered his passions, but great emotional stress seemed to occur simultaneously with his most costly political mistakes. Family papers document the existence of depression, melancholy, low spirits, and "blue periods" in other family members. Suicides and nervous breakdowns, deaths due to reckless behavior, and alcohol addiction occurred too often. In the nineteenth century, issues of mental health were hidden as much as possible, but they were far more widespread than was thought until the late twentieth century. Even in a modern era, psychologists estimate that one in ten Americans suffers from some form of depression at some point in their lives. Paul Nagel's and Bertram Wyatt-Brown's studies of the John Adams and Walker Percy families emphasize the coexistence of melancholy and creativity. Kay Redfield Jamison, experiencing bipolar disorder herself, has discovered many artists, musicians, and writers who exhibited its characteristics.[15] Winston Churchill, Abraham and Mary Todd Lincoln, Teddy Roosevelt, even Norman Rockwell suffered from some variety of depression or melancholy. This study demonstrates similar patterns in the early generations of the Clay family. The Clays recognized "family eccentricities"; they could even laugh at their idiosyncrasies. But they also worried about them. Of course, not all members of the family suffered from these illnesses, and some suffered episodically. They struggled with and in most instances overcame "afflictions" to live good lives and to contribute more significantly than most, a factor that makes their story more compelling.

Perhaps most important, the Clay family reflects the resiliency of the American family, with a mixture of success and failure, strength and weakness. They had their black sheep and their prejudices, and they endured disease and tragedy, but they were also men and women who made solid contributions to their communities, to their professions, and to other people. The family history suggests that no Clay ever quit trying. Their history adds to our knowledge of Henry Clay, but it also illustrates the best of the American family across a wide expanse of American history.

Chapter 1

MARRIAGE

When Henry Clay rode into Lexington, Kentucky, in late November 1797, after what was certainly a long, tiring ride from Virginia, he no doubt urged his mount to a canter and stood tall in the saddle. There is no evidence of this, but from what is known of the future statesman and politician, he would have allowed no less a response. Barely twenty years old, he had been on his own for nearly six years. His mother and stepfather, Captain Henry Watkins, left him in Virginia as an apprentice in a drug store when they moved their new family to Kentucky. To Watkins's credit, he later secured his stepson a position as a deputy clerk in the Virginia High Court of Chancery. George Wythe, the chancellor of the court and one of the founding fathers, used the young Clay as his amanuensis, or secretary, and later arranged for him to study law with Robert Brooke, formerly governor and later attorney general of Virginia. Clay also joined the debating society of Richmond, where he honed the skills essential to young lawyers. He rode into Lexington with great confidence. He knew how to make friends. He knew how to impress people.

Lexington offered great opportunities for a young lawyer if he was good at his profession and knew the right people. Virginia had made a mess of the land laws in the state, so there was much litigation settling multiple claims to the same pieces of land. Despite the talk of religious freedom and other noble reasons for moving to Kentucky, most who did so came to make money. That too assured work for attorneys. Hardly a handsome man by most standards, Clay stood a little over six feet tall. Noticeably thin, everything about him seemed lithe and long, even gangly. In letters written over a fifty-year span, he repeatedly mentioned the need to "add flesh," for the sake of both appearance and health. His face was thin: high forehead, long, thin nose, and an angular chin. He had narrow lips that stretched the width of his face, and bright-blue eyes that expressed his moods. His were strong features; two hundred years later some descendants can still be identified by them.

Personality rather than physical features drew people to him. Friends and relatives complained in later years that no painter ever captured the true Henry Clay. That was probably because no one—except perhaps Lucretia, his wife for more than fifty-three years—ever saw him completely still. His demeanor was animated; he drew attention by his gesturing, by telling wild and always humorous stories, by the use of props—his cane, a snuff box. An energetic man, he epitomized Alexis de Tocqueville's new democratic personality: an anxious achiever, constantly striving.

His family called him high spirited. Others have called him passionate and even impetuous. Biographer Bernard Mayo characterized Clay as amiable, humorous, hot tempered yet warmhearted, capable of impulsive acts, sharp tongued but quick to apologize. Clay, Mayo said, craved excitement.[1] A daughter-in-law more given to praise than objectivity said in a moment of candor, "Mr. Clay's chief physical peculiarity, however, was in the structure of his nervous system. It was so delicately strung, a word, a touch, a memory would set it in motion."[2] A favorite story of biographers recounts a dinner party when Clay jumped on the dinner table and danced its sixty feet in length, kicking china and crystal in all directions. The story represents only one example of impulsive behavior.[3] Biographers accuse him of having consumed too much wine, but it would have been equally within his character to have been seized by the moment, leaving the consequences to worry about later. In Central Kentucky, such behavior has for generations been seen as characteristic of the various branches of the Clay family. The impulsive and reckless conduct of Cassius Marcellus Clay is legendary in that region.[4] Although he produced a rational argument for the abolition of slavery, the community knew him as a high-tempered street brawler and bowie-knife fighter. Historians and biographers have noted such moments of high spirit in Henry, but they have been less inclined to mention that he could also sink to great depths of despondency, especially when confronted by tragedy or political defeat. New ideas, projects, and opportunities excited him, and he entertained them confident of success. Perseverance was not always a strength. Daniel Walker Howe has argued that Clay, in good Whig fashion, gained control over his passions as he aged. Harriet Martineau claimed he did so "at the cost of prodigious self-denial on his own part." Margaret

Young Henry Clay. Courtesy
of the Elizabeth Clay Blanford
Collection.

Bayard Smith, for many years a family friend in Washington, D.C., made a similar argument, noting that the control exacted much from him.[5] Henry Clay may have learned to control the expression of his passions, high and low, but they remained always with him.

Charisma defined the personality of Henry Clay. Women, in particular, found him mesmerizing. Because of the attention women paid him, as well as the enjoyment he took from it, his political enemies would later accuse him of womanizing. But men were also drawn to him. Horace Greeley stated, "I have admired and trusted many statesmen: I loved profoundly Henry Clay."[6] Most scholars tell the tales of his "gamester" years—drinking, dueling, gambling—then suggest that such habits never affected his legal or political judgment. He changed with the times, but his adversaries, the Jacksonian Democrats, saw no reason to let him escape the label.

Clay spent those early years honing his skills at storytelling and public speaking. He first used these arts to sway Kentucky juries, later discovering they worked as well in Congress. He also had what contemporaries called a matchless voice. A great speech or legal argument is part evidence and part presentation. Technology allows the voices of Winston Churchill and

Franklin D. Roosevelt to be heard today; the voices of Clay and Webster are lost to the historian.

On his arrival in Kentucky, Clay joined a group of young lawyers who traveled from one county seat to another in search of cases. Robert Remini suggests that Clay lost some of his Virginia refinement, intentionally adopting the more rustic temperament of the frontier to be accepted by his peers.[7] Arguing legal cases by day, the young lawyers had long evenings to fill. They lingered over dinner to talk about their cases, or as young men of any historical period are inclined to do, they found other things to occupy their time: playing cards, drinking, or by word or deed, challenging one another. In the frontier South as in the West, the requirements of manhood demanded risk taking. Bertram Wyatt-Brown argues that it would have been difficult for any man in the antebellum South not to gamble at cards, and the ability to hold prodigious amounts of intoxicating drink and to brag about it the next day may be a timeless method of proving youthful manhood.[8] Clay chose to fit in, and he did.

Henry Clay was also ambitious. Scores of contemporaries, as well as later historians and biographers, have noted his ambition, usually as a fault; but few men who wanted to be president lacked ambition. Clay's early nemesis, John Quincy Adams, was certainly ambitious despite expressing his fear of the trait, and a later adversary, Andrew Jackson, was not lacking ambition either. Clay's ambition left little time for idleness, and he went to work immediately upon his arrival in Kentucky. Family legend said that when he arrived, he had in his saddlebag only his license to practice law. That qualifies more as myth than as reality. He had a rather wealthy mother and stepfather just outside Lexington. He also had contacts with noted attorneys. He had, as mentioned, begun the study of law under Robert Brooke, and George Wythe, for whom he served as amanuensis, was the tutor of Kentucky's first wave of gentleman lawyers, George Nicholas, John Breckinridge, and James Brown.[9]

Clay's ambition, however, went beyond politics. In Virginia he had been on the periphery of tidewater society, but he had known Brooke, Wythe, and at least by reputation, Thomas Jefferson and James Madison. He moved to Kentucky because it seemed to be a land of economic opportunity, a place where he might create an estate and a social standing like those he had known in Virginia. That was not an uncommon goal among the early settlers in Kentucky. According to John Adair, an early political leader in the state, Kentuckians were "as greedy after plunder as ever the old Romans were."[10] In fact, the leading families of the Kentucky Bluegrass seemed intent on creating a replica of the tidewater aristocracy.

Clay's goal also required a large family grounded in the social and economic life of the region. He sought to make a marriage that met these needs, and it did not take him long after arriving in Kentucky to find a suitable partner in the venture. He then pursued her, and her father, with businesslike efficiency. Lucretia Hart was the youngest daughter of Colonel Thomas Hart, veteran of the Revolutionary War and a member of the Transylvania Company, one of the early speculative land ventures in Kentucky. He had moved his family from Maryland to Kentucky in 1794, when Lucretia was fourteen years old. Colonel Hart came to Kentucky for many of the same reasons that drew Henry Clay westward. He brought with him titles to large amounts of land and quickly developed both mercantile and manufacturing interests that tied him to relatives in Pittsburgh and New Orleans. Family conglomerates were the rule rather than the exception, so the young Clay had many examples to follow. The Harts, the Januarys, the Johnsons, and the Craigs, to name just a few, worked as family units with the intention of building fortunes for all. Thomas Hart, one of the wealthiest men in Kentucky, had the influence within the business community that went with prosperity.[11]

As was fitting in the eighteenth century, Thomas Hart sought to marry his daughters into prominent families that might provide social stature, business opportunity, or both. Other Hart daughters married Thomas Marshall, the chief justice of the Kentucky Supreme Court; James Brown, a lawyer, diplomat, and later senator from Louisiana; and Dr. Richard Pindell, a prominent Louisville surgeon. Henry Clay seemed on the surface to be something of an exception, but his reputation must have offered enough promise to satisfy Colonel Hart. On April 11, 1799, one day before his twenty-second birthday, Clay married Lucretia and the Hart family.

Lucretia, born on March 18, 1781, was barely eighteen when she married Henry Clay, and she was his polar opposite in terms of personality. Descriptions of her appearance are not flattering. Robert Remini describes her as a "hard-featured woman." Glyndon Van Deusen has said she was neither "beautiful nor intellectual," and her own grandson suggested that she was rather plain, at least from the standpoint of physical appearance.[12] The fiftieth-anniversary daguerreotype of Henry and Lucretia, worthy as a model for Grant Wood's painting *American Gothic*, seals for most observers the unflattering image of her.

Henry and Lucretia Clay.
Courtesy of the Elizabeth Clay
Blanford Collection.

Through careful reconstruction of the existing record, a more accurate picture of Lucretia can be drawn. She may not have been a beautiful woman, but the popular image of her is far too harsh. Two portraits, one at Ashland, the Henry Clay Estate, and one in the possession of a descendant, suggest a pleasant-looking woman not unlike many women of the gentry.[13] Susan M. Clay described her as being at the time of her marriage a "slender, gracefully formed young girl, with beautiful hands and feet; her complexion fair, her features delicate, her eyes blue, and she had a wealth of beautiful auburn hair."[14] The trials of bearing and raising eleven children, being the wife of a politician who was loved and hated, and her own poor health would certainly take their toll, but at the time of her marriage, she was not as unattractive as has been suggested.

Lucretia did not appear to biographers to be a woman of deep thought or to share her husband's interest in politics. She preferred, they claim, to stay home in Lexington rather than go to Washington and support her husband. Henry's biographers have treated her as an extension of him, and frequently as a dark spot obscuring a brilliant star. Joseph Rogers,

Lucretia Hart Clay. Courtesy of
Dr. William D. Kenner.

Van Deusen, Remini, and scores of others suggest that Lucretia became a
liability for Clay during his political career.[15] This is the price Lucretia has
paid for her aversion to writing letters—in fact, her refusal to write them.
Historians prefer those who leave a record of their life. Because she left few
written records, some have even suggested that Lucretia was uneducated.
Many scholars have called her cold and impassionate. Most writers claim
that she disliked society, and Van Deusen suggests that Washington was
not a very enjoyable place for the Clays because of her aversion to people.[16]
In fact, the prevailing image, though never described directly, is that she
stayed in Lexington while Henry traveled the country or spent his time in
the nation's capital.

Emphasizing her practical nature, those who have written about Henry
have questioned Lucretia's intellectual depth. Lucretia never expressed
any interest in books or ideas. Then again, she never expressed anything
in writing. However, there is no reason to believe she was uneducated.
Thomas Hart educated his other daughters, why not Lucretia? Moving
from Maryland to Kentucky when Lucretia was fourteen years old may
have interrupted her formal education, but there is no indication that it
stopped altogether. There is ample evidence that she did know how to write.
Daughter-in-law Susan Clay noted in her biographical sketch that Lucretia

had received an education in Maryland, and James Brown, Lucretia's brother-in-law, mentioned in correspondence addressed to Henry both her hesitancy to write and a letter she had written to her sister Nancy Brown, his wife. Nancy "was delighted at finding that Lucretia had overcome her repugnance to writing, and by the next post replied to her letter. She begs me to press upon you the task of urging her to write more frequently." Lucretia's youngest son, John Morrison Clay, wrote to his brother Thomas in 1841, "Having written several times to mama since my arrival here, but without any expectation of receiving an answer, as she never writes, I address you now." Finally, Henry wrote matter-of-factly to his son James that "your mother never writes," made excuses for her, and even apologized to her for not writing more often, though she did not write at all. He wrote to Anna Mercer, for example, "She [Lucretia] is so out of the habit of writing that she now hardly writes to me, when I am from home, leaving other members of my family to perform that office."[17]

None of the letters suggests that Lucretia did not know how to write. Rather, they emphasize the fact that she had an aversion to writing that existed at least from 1804, when James Brown wrote to Henry. The letter she apparently wrote to her sister has not been found. However, several extant documents do bear her signature. The first, written on March 10, 1814, is a short letter to Henry, then a member of the diplomatic delegation at Ghent.[18] The others are legal documents written in the 1850s indicating that James, her son, had met, or owed, financial obligations to her. Though probably written by someone else, the documents include Lucretia's signature, one with a note that it is "grandma's signature." Three of the documents are located in the James O. Harrison Papers at the Library of Congress.[19] The letter written to Henry does not suggest great writing skills, but it appears to be the letter of a literate woman. The signatures on the mortgage notes seem almost juvenile, certainly unpracticed, but by the 1850s Lucretia had reached an advanced age. Most women of her social standing wrote in a much clearer, formal hand, an issue that may have been a source of embarrassment to her. The letters written by several members of later generations also suggest something like dyslexia—reversed letters and words, very poor spelling, and some grammatical errors.[20]

Lucretia apparently received some musical training, commonly a part of the education of a young woman of her social class. Glyndon Van Deusen says she played the piano. He cites Margaret Bayard Smith, but he may have learned the fact from discussions with family members. There was a piano in the Clay home; the Harts had one of the earliest pianos in Kentucky. Smith noted that Lucretia provided the music at parties the two women gave to entertain their children, but does not mention whether vocal or instrumental, or which instrument. However, Wilhelm Iucho, the organist at the Episcopal church Lucretia attended in Lexington, composed and dedicated "The Lexington Grand Waltz" to her.[21] All of this suggests a level of refinement often ignored by some of Henry's biographers.

Having created a picture of her as detrimental to Henry's career, some scholars even suggest Lucretia used her responsibilities at Ashland as an excuse to keep from joining her husband in Washington. Remini, Rogers, and others obligingly tell the local myth that portrayed Lucretia as a skilled farmer. In so doing, they have perpetuated a tale that is, by most accounts, false, and one that further robbed Lucretia of her status as a lady. Allegedly, a visitor to the region asked a local man whether Henry Clay was the best farmer in Fayette County. "No," the old man replied, "Mrs. Clay is." According to the myth, Lucretia remained at Ashland and cared for the farm while Henry sought fame in Washington. She allegedly cured hams and sold eggs to the Phoenix Hotel in Lexington, but Susan Clay, her daughter-in-law, refuted the notion that she raised eggs to sell. The anecdote also suggests that when Henry came home, Lucretia returned the money he had left her to run the farm with a profit. In her unpublished biographical sketch, Susan Clay stated emphatically, "Mrs. Clay is not a farmer." Refuting Rogers's account, she wrote, "Outside of a general knowledge of what was going on and a warm interest in it, she had absolutely nothing to do with the farm." Susan Clay stated that there was always an overseer to manage the farm "according to Mr. Clay's directions."[22]

The collected correspondence of Henry Clay supports that argument. In fact, Henry wrote to James Brown in 1831 that Lucretia's repugnance to country life might require them to move back to Lexington.[23] Clay frequently dealt with the problems of keeping a good overseer on task, but he also had sons to oversee the farm. He sent explicit instructions to whoever was in charge. When southern men claimed to "work," they generally meant overseeing the work of slaves or hired labor. Henry Clay directed the work of the farm, but despite his being called the "Farmer of Ashland," no accounts suggest that he got his hands dirty digging in the soil or mucking stalls. Susan Clay proposes the same for Lucretia. Additionally, for more than fifty years, an English woman—Sarah, or Sally, Hall—served as a housekeeper and companion, relieving Lucretia of duties for which "she had no taste." Lucretia enjoyed the orchards, gardens, and grounds about the house, and in 1835 Henry had a greenhouse constructed for her use. There seems little doubt that she offered suggestions, but a "competent white gardener, with efficient negro gardeners under him, kept every thing in the most perfect order."[24]

During his absences, Clay left money with Lucretia and frequently asked in his correspondence whether she needed anything. He also sent money to his sons for her use. Finally, if she was averse to asking her husband for money, the Clay papers indicate that her favorite son, John Morrison Clay, who never left home, was not. All of this suggests that Ashland did not keep Lucretia from traveling to Washington with her husband.

Perhaps the best description of Lucretia is derived from the account of the Clays' friend Margaret Bayard Smith. All major biographers cite her, albeit selectively. As is so often mentioned, she called Lucretia a "plain and unadmired woman" in issues of mind and matters, but she also described her as "kind, good, and above all, discreet, [so] that I do not think the many years she lived here she ever made an enemy." Smith also called her a woman of strong natural sense. Amos Kendall, who tutored the Clay children, became a bitter enemy of Henry, but he maintained great respect and appreciation for Mrs. Clay, perhaps even delaying his break with Clay because of her. Smith portrays Lucretia as an active and helpful woman, pragmatic, and happy to stay in the background supporting the ambitions of her husband. Certainly, a relationship between two dominant, charismatic personalities like Henry's would not have survived long. Lucretia did not want or need to be at the center of attention like her husband. Yet, over time, people came to admire and respect her. One admirer, James C. Johnston, sent the Clays a painting of the George Washington family, executed at his request, because he so admired Mrs. Clay. Despite being ill and unhappy due to problems at home, in 1831 Lucretia was received wherever she went, with "demonstrations of affection."[25] Echoing that description, as late as 1852 her son Thomas, tending to his dying father in Washington, wrote that Lucretia's friends had inquired about her.[26] Mrs. Clay had not been to Washington for seventeen years at the time.

Smith noted that Lucretia provided her with good advice about Washington and its social requirements, advising her on etiquette and inviting her to make social calls with her. She stated, "[Lucretia] often brings work of an evening into our room and in the morning I go to hers—We help each other dress and she always offers us seats in her carriage when we visit,—or go shopping, and her woman who has been nurse of all her children, attends to mine whenever I wish it." They helped mutual friends in time of need and comforted each other when tragedy struck within their families.[27]

Lucretia undoubtedly preferred a quiet life at home. Margaret Bayard Smith emphasized, again in bits and pieces, Lucretia's propensity for or acceptance of the domestic role assigned to women. Smith claimed Lucretia was "a thousand times better pleased sitting in the room with all her children round her, and a pile of work by her side, than in the most brilliant drawing room." Lucretia developed a strong relationship with her children, particularly her daughters. Susan and Anne, the two daughters who married, wrote to their mother about raising children as a shared experience. Lucretia's youngest was only two years older than Susan's first son, so there were immediate interests for mother and daughter to share. She was also very close to her daughters-in-law. It was Susan M. Clay, wife of son James, who wrote the spirited defense of her mother-in-law mentioned previously when historians and biographers questioned Lucretia's worthiness as Henry's wife. Furthermore, in a letter to Susan Clay, Mary Mentelle Clay, wife of son Thomas, praised Lucretia as "a second mother." Lucretia, Mary claimed, was kind and supportive, seeking to make all those around her contented. Her words were "never but those of goodness, never anything to wound in the least."[28]

Lucretia's preference for a simple life surrounded by children and work did not obscure for her the duty to support her husband. Contrary to what historians have said, she did accompany Henry to Washington regularly until 1835. She frequented the brilliant drawing rooms of early nineteenth-century America despite a preference otherwise. The Clays were frequent visitors to the president's soirees during James Madison's term, and when Clay served as secretary of state, the Clays alternated weekly social affairs with the president and Mrs. Adams. Smith said that Lucretia felt obliged to go to other people's parties whether sick or well, rather than give offense.[29] Lucretia was in Washington in 1813. Susan Clay recalled a story her mother-in-law told about the fear among Washington ladies of a British invasion. They frequently held their handkerchiefs into the wind to see in what direction it was blowing. If blowing from the sea, there was a danger the British could reach the shore. Henry went to Ghent, leaving Lucretia to get their children back to Kentucky. She returned with her husband in 1816 and gave birth in Washington to a son, James Brown Clay, in

November 1817. Henry Clay retired from Congress in 1820, but Lucretia joined him in Washington from 1825 to 1829, when he was secretary of state. According to Smith, Lucretia resided again in the capital between 1831 and 1834.[30] It should be noted that Lucretia buried two daughters because of the trips to Washington—one along the route in Ohio, a second in the congressional cemetery in Washington. Tragedy and responsibility within the family account in part for the fact that during the last seventeen years of his career, from 1835, Henry went to Washington alone.[31] Lucretia clearly supported her husband as the requirements of their time prescribed.

Henry and Lucretia Clay settled into a married life with clearly defined roles. Those roles were not unusual in the late eighteenth century. Historians of women have moved beyond the concept of separate spheres, but Aileen Kraditor could have been writing about Henry and Lucretia in her *Up from the Pedestal*. There were no limits to Henry's sphere; the world was literally his, and Lucretia was to provide a comforting home where he could recover from the harsh political world.[32] Their married life began in a small house on Lexington's Mill Street, an area that symbolized the city's rapid transition from frontier town to settled community. Two-story brick structures suggested permanency. It was there that Lucretia began to fulfill her primary obligation under the marriage contract. She gave birth to their first child, Henrietta, on June 25, 1800, a little over a year after her marriage. That began the two-year cycle of childbirth that characterized her life in the early years of marriage. Ultimately, she would give birth to eleven children over a period of twenty-one years.[33]

During the same period, Henry busied himself meeting his responsibilities under the marriage agreement. The small house on Mill Street would neither fit the family needs nor satisfy his ambition. He began as early as 1804 to purchase land that would become the Clay family home, Ashland. Parcels of land would be purchased until the estate comprised approximately six hundred acres. From the beginning, Henry Clay researched blooded stock of all descriptions and made Ashland a progressive farming operation. In 1806 he participated in one of the first syndications in America, purchasing with four other men the proven English thoroughbred Buzzard. As in all his ventures, he was literally off to the races. Clay's stable of horses grew quickly, and he was racing thoroughbreds by 1809. He built a private track on his growing estate and participated in the first Jockey Club in Lexington, where he shared information with men such as Abraham Buford and Dr. Elisha Warfield, founders of the thoroughbred industry in Kentucky. A few years later he began to import Hereford, Holderness, and Durham cattle as well.[34] With customary self-confidence, he later said, "I shall make a better farmer than statesman."[35]

Clay gave particular attention to the house, which would become the seat of his political and family life. The two-and-a-half-story federal-style structure faced west toward Lexington. The exterior was constructed of brick (in another impetuous moment he sought to save money by using less-than-prime brick—a mistake that would cause trouble later). The central portion of the house, designed to resemble homes found in the area of Virginia where he had grown up, was completed by 1809. Henry Clay Jr., born on April 10, 1811, professed to be the first child born at the estate. Indicating that construction was ongoing, he claimed to have been born in the dining room.[36]

Additional living space was provided by one-story wings to the north and south, added as the family grew. Benjamin Latrobe, the designer of the wings of the Capitol in Washington, has been credited with the design for the house. Although there are legitimate questions regarding his involvement in the original structure, he is certainly responsible for the design

Ashland. Courtesy of the Elizabeth Clay Blanford Collection.

of the wings. The main entrance, a fan doorway flanked by windows, faced west toward Lexington. A large hall with high ceiling served to greet guests but also provided access to the dining parlor and rooms in the wings. The first floor reflected Clay's political and social ambitions. Fixtures of Sheffield silver adorned doors and windows, and rich, polished wood framed the rooms. On the second floor, the family area, cheaper materials were used. The most striking room on the first floor was, perhaps, the library. Octagonal in shape with a domed ceiling, the room was paneled in walnut and ash.[37] Expressing the public and private nature of the man, access could be gained from every direction, yet the room could be closed off from the goings and comings of a large and boisterous family.

Grand lawns, formal gardens, and a variety of out-buildings with functions essential to the times and to a working farm surrounded the house. Native locust and cedar trees were in abundance, but there were also walks shaded by walnut, ash, and other trees that Henry had planted himself. Formal gardens and a tree-lined walk perhaps reminded him of the English gentry. They provided peace and solitude when he needed to restore his energy. Like everything about Henry Clay, the estate was a work in progress. He oversaw every aspect of the construction, and he enjoyed showing visitors the results of his efforts.

There was also a legal practice to build. Clay may have started his career as something of an itinerant lawyer, but Breckinridge, Brown, and Nicholas, the corps of Kentucky's lawyers, gave him cases they were too busy to handle. His marriage reinforced his career ambitions because of his father-in-law's connections with the merchant and landowning elite of the state. When George Nicholas died, Clay inherited his practice.[38] In addition to handling land claims, he gained a reputation as a criminal lawyer. Clay, much to his later embarrassment, defended Aaron Burr when the latter was charged with treason. But his real interest centered on politics. Writing letters to be published in the *Kentucky Gazette* and addressing crowds on the Alien and Sedition Acts, the young man was on a mission to make a name for himself. Although he spent most of his early years in the state legislature, the Kentucky legislature elected him in 1806 to fill the unexpired term of John Adair in the United States Senate, despite the fact that Clay had not reached the legal age for service in that body, and again in 1810 to complete the term of Buckner Thruston. In 1811 he became a member of the U.S. House of Representatives and was chosen as Speaker of the House. A War Hawk, he played a large role in forcing the president into the War of 1812, then served as a diplomat at the treaty negotiations. Remini says that when Clay returned to the United States in September 1815, he had ambitions of becoming president.[39]

Young Henry Clay was a busy man. In 1832 he coined the phrase "self-made man," but he was a living example of it from a much earlier age. His marriage was part of a larger plan. Little affection is apparent in Henry's letters to Lucretia until much later. He wrote about business, local news, and occasionally politics. He often asked about her health and the welfare of the children, but rarely did he express any intimacy. He sought intellectual stimulation from women other than his wife, perhaps fueling the charges of womanizing that political enemies threw at him. Henry Clay and Lucretia Hart formed a partnership that was more business than romance. They showed one another respect; affection developed over time and with shared experiences. Initially, each performed the functions they believed required by the definitions of marriage that had become a part of their values. Whether that was a mutual decision or one orchestrated by Henry can only be surmised.[40]

Chapter 2

PARENTING

If Lucretia has been criticized for not supporting her husband's career, Henry acquired a reputation as a poor husband and parent. Trying to meet the requirements of a young Kentucky lawyer, and male, Henry earned a reputation for heavy drinking, gambling, salty language, and being quick to defend his honor. A "gamester," John Quincy Adams called him, and a risk taker, because his personality and the code of male conduct required it.[1] Political opponents added the charge of womanizing when they saw how much he enjoyed the company of attractive and intelligent women and their appreciation of his attention. Modern scholars have suggested that many of the stories about him were exaggerated, and they note his efforts to control his "passions" as he and the nation matured. Nevertheless, the charges continued throughout his career because his opponents found them politically expedient. His wife and family were forced to endure the embarrassment of such public accusations.

The charge of bad parenting apparently began with Amos Kendall, a member of Andrew Jackson's Kitchen Cabinet, who as a young man briefly served as tutor to the oldest Clay children. He found the children unruly and undisciplined. That should come as no surprise. There were ten more after Henrietta. Theodore Wythe Clay, named for his father's legal mentor, was born barely thirteen months after Henrietta on July 3, 1802; he was followed by Thomas Hart on September 22, 1803; Susan Hart, February 11, 1805; Anne Brown, April 15, 1807; and Lucretia Hart, February 1809. After Henry Jr. (April 10, 1811) came Eliza, July 5, 1813; Laura, October 16, 1816; and finally, the "little boys," James Brown and John Morrison, who were born November 9, 1817, and February 21, 1821, respectively.

Kendall harbored animosity toward Clay, joining the Jackson forces after Clay refused what amounted to a bribe. However, his assessment of the children had some credibility. The children were all woefully uneducated, according to Kendall, and he placed the blame squarely on Henry. Frequently absent or absorbed in business and farming, Clay, Kendall charged, neglected his children. An assessment of the Clay family by Harriet Martineau, an English philosopher and reformer visiting in the United States, provided an additional blow. Citing instances of mental illness and tragedy, she described the condition of Henry Clay's family as "melancholy." Robert Remini goes so far as to call Henry a "wretched" father.[2]

It is not difficult to see why contemporaries and biographers would make such a charge. Kendall believed the Clay children were bright, but he described them as passionate; both terms were used frequently to describe Henry Clay.[3] Kendall found it difficult to keep them at their work. That too was probably characteristic of the father, although when intrigued by a project, his energy level was astounding. Kendall saw promise in the children but grew frustrated by their lack of perseverance.[4] Clay had to struggle to attain self-mastery, to achieve order.[5] There was a lot of Henry Clay in his children, and they did experience serious difficulties. The family history was indeed melancholy. Like good Victorians, historians have been inclined to blame the parents.

Clay's personality would appear to make consistent parenting difficult as well. Quick tempered, sharp tongued, impatient, self-centered, and demanding, he was the type of man who could easily overwhelm children. In politics he could be charming, complimentary, and amiable on one occasion and harsh and threatening on another. In parenting that could be disastrous. Clay made the additional mistake of appearing to enjoy himself too much when he was away from home. Abigail Adams expressed concern about her husband's absence and its effect on the children when he served as a diplomat, but John Adams had the good sense to record his worries as well. Henry, by contrast, cavalierly asked about the children and failed to conceal his enthusiasm for his adventures.

Kendall's account of the children and their upbringing raises a number of issues about the Clays and about his own views of raising children. Since he was brought up in the Northeast, the lax parenting practiced in the South created some culture shock. The antics of young children were tolerated, even valued, as signs of developing strength. Parents appreciated aggressiveness in young children; molding them would come later. Even in the North, parenthood was undergoing a transition. As men left the farms after the Revolutionary War to be involved in business or factory labor, they spent less time with their children. The revolution also led to the view that mothers could be the major nurturing force, particularly in the formative years.[6] After calling Clay a wretched father, Remini notes matter-of-factly that leaving young children in the care of their mother was not unusual at the time.[7]

In fact, Lucretia was primarily responsible for the children when they were young, and whether at Ashland or in Washington, D.C., she had ample help with her growing brood. One servant, for example, devoted her time to the children. Ashland also provided a number of other people to help a child grow. Older sisters took some of the burden off women, like Lucretia Clay, who birthed children at regular intervals. The letters of Anne Clay, written after she was an adult, suggest the attitude of a protective older sister regarding Henry Clay Jr., and she served as a second mother to James and John. The Clay children learned to ride horses early in life, and wherever they rode, servants and field-workers made sure they did not stray into too much danger. Visiting cousins and older slave children likewise served as playmates and protectors. Bertram Wyatt-Brown notes that children, including young girls, were given a great deal of freedom. They would be the leaders of a slave society, so they needed to develop confidence. Cowing a child was self-defeating. Advising a sister-in-law, George H. Clay, a lifelong bachelor, said the same thing in Kentucky terms: "Give the little filly her head, so she'll have spirit."[8]

Henry adapted easily to a "village" concept of education. Not only did it relieve him of some responsibility, but he had experienced a similar upbringing himself. His own father died when Henry was four years old, and his stepfather moved his mother and siblings when he was fourteen. Young Henry depended on the households of Robert Brooke and George Wythe, and a group of young men studying law, to be his extended family. Besides, it was characteristic of the southern style of life he was trying to carve out of the Kentucky wilderness. He saw nothing unusual about being an absent father.[9]

Kendall complained that the education of the children had been neglected because of Henry's absence. What he did not seem to grasp was that the very fact the Clays hired him as a tutor signaled dissatisfaction with the children's educational progress. Very much a part of that discussion, Clay was, in fact, actively involved in the lives of his children. Providing an education for his children was a major responsibility according to the code of the times, and he made a significant effort to fulfill it.[10]

That said, the education of the Clay daughters suggests a rather traditional view of women's education. He did educate them, but the sparse written record indicates this was accorded a low level of importance. Kendall taught the daughters as well as the sons. Given Clay's support for the family of Waldemar Mentelle, cultured and talented refugees from the French Revolution, the daughters probably attended Madame Mentelle's school for young ladies. Established in the last years of the eighteenth century, the school moved to Rose Hill, near Ashland, around 1820. Gifted in music, language, art, and manners, Mentelle offered a quality education for gentry daughters, including Mary Todd, the future wife of Abraham Lincoln. Daughter Lucretia attended the Lexington Female Academy, but no record exists of Eliza's schooling. To Henry's credit, he supported both the Mentelle school and the Lexington Female Academy, even recruiting students from New Orleans and Philadelphia. The letters written by Susan and Anne suggest their writers were intelligent young women. They expressed their thoughts correctly and confidently. Henry claimed that Anne was the child most like him, a considerable compliment coming from him, and he clearly enjoyed their correspondence and respected her judgment. According to the code of the time, however, the daughters would marry, and their husbands would provide for them. Susan married Martin Duralde Jr. of New Orleans when she was seventeen years old; Anne married James Erwin at sixteen.[11]

For Clay, the education of his sons formed the primary concern. He first hired a succession of tutors in the Lexington area, then each of his five sons attended Transylvania University, a school Clay helped to build a national reputation. Theodore and Thomas, the oldest sons, attended briefly before being sent to preparatory schools in the East. Henry Jr. entered the preparatory school at the age of ten in 1821, graduating in 1826. James and John attended several private schools before Henry sent them to Transylvania.[12]

Clay spent considerable energy and money to send his sons to preparatory schools in other parts of the country. In each case, the schools were led by educators with strong reputations. Both Theodore and Thomas attended the Bancel School in New York in 1816, and they later attended a school operated by Dr. James Carnahan in Washington, D.C. Carnahan served as president of Princeton College from 1823 to 1854. John Morrison attended a preparatory school in Princeton before entering the college. Clay wrote to Henry Jr. on one occasion that he was debating whether to send John Morrison to Transylvania or to a school operated by Dr. Benjamin Peers, who would later serve as acting president of Transylvania. He also wrote to Henry Jr. that he had considered sending James and John to a school in Northampton, Massachusetts, probably the Round Hill School founded by George Bancroft and Joseph Cogswell, but decided against it because of the distance and the expense. James attended Central Academy in Washington, D.C., for a year, probably so Henry could be close to him, but in 1826 he attended a preparatory school operated by Bishop Philander Chase, president of Kenyon College.[13]

Clay exhibited no less attentiveness to the second level of education. He secured appointments to the military academy at West Point for two of his sons. Thomas began his studies in the summer of 1821, and Henry Jr. was admitted in 1826. Henry's letters suggest that he believed the discipline would provide a strong learning opportunity. He sent Theodore to Harvard, and John Morrison, as mentioned, studied at Princeton, although neither completed his education. James received a classical education at Transylvania, but for reasons that are unclear, when he was only fifteen years old Henry secured a position for him in a Boston counting house rather than sending him for further education. In later correspondence, Henry spoke repeatedly of James's good business sense, so he clearly believed that was the best direction for his son.[14] All five sons also received training in law.

Ledger pages in the Clay papers indicate that the boys received adequate spending money and that Henry clothed them in the manner of young gentlemen. He planned their travel between home and school, often asking his friends to accompany them, and both he and Lucretia, traveling together or separately, scheduled visits to the boys.[15]

Henry wrote frequently to his sons, encouraging them to apply themselves to their work. He also played a strong role in their moral upbringing. The advice he gave would have surprised his political friends and foes. Alcohol and gambling were seductive goddesses. Choose friends wisely, he suggested. But his favorite warning was to avoid dissipation. Henry had good reason to warn his sons. Wyatt-Brown claims that nearly half the young men raised in the South were sooner or later ruined by dissipation. Henry's concern originated in his Jeffersonian past and his Whig values. He believed in the therapeutic and spiritual value of work. Through work one maintained control over one's life. Concerned about gaining control in his own life, he sought to give direction to the lives of his sons as well.[16]

Clay checked regularly with school officials about the academic standing and behavior of his sons. After a student protest against new disciplinary regulations at West Point, Henry wrote to see whether Thomas had been involved. A few years later, discussions with Sylvanus Thayer allowed Henry Jr. to remain at West Point after a show of temper nearly got him expelled. He sounded like a distinctly modern parent when he wrote to Enoch Wines, the headmaster of John's school, in 1835 to defend his youngest son. John had a public disagreement with one of his teachers and said things inappropriate by the standards of the day. Wines required him to apologize to the teacher before the entire school. Although John's comments were unfortunate, Clay said, such a public apology seemed excessive and potentially injurious to his full development.[17]

Involvement as a parent extended further than placing his children in schools. Clay's correspondence indicates that he invested enough time to know the individual strengths and weaknesses of all his sons. Historians have claimed that Henry Jr. was his favorite son. This conclusion is based on letters exchanged with Henry Jr. when he was a cadet at West Point, but historians have not put them into their proper context. Perhaps because of the authors' emphasis on Henry Clay's blinding ambition, they believed he chose Henry Jr. as the son who would follow in his footsteps. Other people said that, but not Henry. He wrote long, intimate letters expressing the importance he placed on his sons' success. He wrote letters to Henry Jr. and, much later, to James, urging them to work diligently for his sake, because they were his sons and his hopes rested on them. He also stated frequently how close he felt to Anne, how similar her thoughts were to his, and how he trusted her judgment. Henry Clay directed the education and offered advice based on what he perceived to be the individual needs of each of his children. He wrote to James in 1838, "I desire most ardently, my dear Son, your happiness and that of every child I have."[18] He did not always succeed, but it was not for want of trying or for lack of concern for any of them.

Clay's letters to Henry Jr. sought to help a young man who did not have a lot of confidence far away from home and in a difficult environment. Henry Jr. was a student at West Point from 1826 to 1830, the years when Henry was busy as secretary of state, suffered a painful loss in the presidential election, and sought to restore the productivity of his farm. Nevertheless, he wrote letters with warm, occasionally moving passages

Henry Clay Jr. Henry Clay
Memorial Foundation Collection.
Courtesy of University of Kentucky
Special Collections.

in them. Clay expressed his confidence in his son's abilities, praised his academic success, assured the young man of his affections, and offered advice in words that sounded more like those of a friend than a father. He even stated in one letter that he gave advice as "your father and friend."[19]

There is, however, a great deal more to the letters. Unfortunately, Clay's correspondence also placed enormous pressure on the young cadet. On November 14, 1828, he wrote, "And now, my dear Son, you are one of my greatest comforts. Indeed there is no object in life about which I have so much solicitude as your success in your studies which I believe to be so intimately connected with your welfare and future usefulness. I intreat you therefore by your love for me, and by your own good, to perservere [sic] and do as you have done."[20] In another letter, he revealed the same urgency and the reason for it. "I am more anxious about you," he wrote, "because I have not much hope left about my older sons. . . . If you too disappoint my anxious hopes a Constitution, never good, and now almost exhausted, would sink beneath the pressure. You bear my name. You are my son, and the hopes of all of us are turned with anxiety upon you."[21]

Throughout Henry Jr.'s four years at West Point, Theodore and Thomas, the older sons, were creating grave problems for their father.

Perhaps for the first time in his life, Henry could not fix the problem. Impulsively, he poured out his own frustration and placed a burden on his middle son. James and John were still young boys, so his immediate hopes centered on Henry Jr.

Amos Kendall had correctly recognized problems with Theodore and Thomas when they were still young boys. He considered all the children except Theodore to have fine minds, but their ungovernable tempers and "passionate" natures worried him. Theodore and Thomas fought with each other so frequently they had to be separated. Theodore, "swearing in great rage," threatened to stab one slave, and Thomas flew into such a rage that he threatened to kill several slaves at the same time.[22]

Exhibiting his knowledge of nineteenth-century child psychology, Kendall stated that he would curb their wills if he had to draw blood to do it. Behind their conduct was a more serious problem. Intelligent, even creative children, they could be charming and well mannered, but they frequently flew into uncontrollable fits of temper. High spirited like their father, their anger, or enthusiasm, led to impulsive and often destructive actions. Theodore and Thomas were boys of twelve and eleven when the incidents Kendall recorded occurred. On another occasion, Thomas, angered by Kendall, publicly called his tutor a "damned Yankee rascal." He later cried in embarrassment, apologized, and promised to improve his conduct in the future. Thomas made frequent promises. In a letter to Henry Jr., Clay noted, "Poor Thomas! He brought tears from me to behold him. . . . He promises, but there I fear the matter will end." At the writing, Thomas was twenty-four years old.[23]

Historians are generally extremely cautious about making psychological assessments. The nuances of psychological diagnoses are far too complicated. Symptoms vary within an individual and from one person to another. That the biological and chemical basis of mental illness remains a mystery makes it even more difficult to consider historical figures. Yet, authorities in the field note the existence of bipolar symptoms in many artists and political figures—such as Lord Byron, Norman Rockwell, Napoleon Bonaparte, and Winston Churchill—and of depression in both Abraham and Mary Todd Lincoln. Paul Nagel has written convincingly of the problems with forms of depression experienced by generations of the John Adams family, and Bertram Wyatt-Brown studied the inherited inclination to despondency and creativity in the family of southern novelist Walker Percy. Our knowledge of these historical figures and their contributions are richer for it. The struggle with depression has not been limited to great political figures and artists. According to J. Raymond DePaulo and Leslie Horvitz, authors of *Understanding Depression,* roughly one in ten Americans experience a clinical depression or manic-depressive episode during their lifetime. Alcoholism, self-destructive behavior, delusions of grandeur, irritability, accelerated speech, hyperexcitability, paranoia, and a tendency to blame others are only a few of the characteristics of the family of illnesses associated with mania and despondency. Manic behavior and depression also come in a variety of forms, some serious, some more an inconvenience. Such disorders run in families, but not all members experience them.[24]

Individual members of the Clay family suffered such symptoms over a period of four generations. The family "personality" at its best exhibited the creative, happy-go-lucky, fun-loving, and spontaneous qualities of Henry Clay. At its worst, however, it became manic or included risk taking to the point of reckless behavior that caused death or injury. As mentioned, the family referred to some members as high spirited. On the down side, there was depression; some episodes were quite severe, others typical, perhaps, of those suffered by so many Americans. Letters and diaries note melancholy, "blue periods," nervous breakdowns, and abject hopelessness. Historians have attributed family members' reckless behavior to excessive consumption of alcohol, but when viewed over generations, it clearly appears to have had other causes.[25] The five sons experienced varying degrees of mania or depression; they all had violent tempers that led to rash behavior. Although bouts of melancholy are generally more common in women, it was the men of the family who suffered from them most frequently.[26]

Despite their intellectual abilities, Theodore and Thomas Clay could not bring any project to completion. They made numerous beginnings, often exhibiting excitement or at least a willingness to try a new project, but they inevitably lost interest. As their father feared, they sank into dissipation. Theodore showed some promise as a young man, despite Kendall's early predictions. He inherited his father's quick wit and his gift for oratory. He wanted to follow in his father's footsteps, but he could not pay the price in time and effort. He learned quickly but found it difficult to apply himself to the kind of study required for intellectual depth. He adopted a bon vivant attitude and a confidence greater than the depth of thought behind his ideas. At times he wrote his father in very familiar terms, seeing himself perhaps as political ally and adviser. He thought in grandiose terms but lacked perseverance and focus.[27] He could not decide on a profession, looked for get-rich-quick schemes, and became something of a social dandy. Leaving Harvard without a degree, he studied law at Transylvania University. Once again, his passions overcame good sense; he was called before the board for "making a disturbance." Surprisingly, he became a lawyer, but he never practiced the profession seriously.[28]

Clay next tried to make Theodore a farmer. He first assigned him the task of overseeing the operations at Ashland. The healing power of land and labor, however, failed in the case of Theodore. His wit degenerated into cynicism: Henry painfully wrote that Theodore seemed "soured with all the world."[29] Showing his frustration, Clay bluntly proclaimed Theodore prone to indolence and dissipation, but he refused to give up on his son. He took him to Washington in 1824, but Theodore began to gamble heavily, losing $500 with David White, a young congressman from Kentucky. Given Henry's youthful habits, one can only surmise what he might have said had Theodore won. But losing money and failing to work brought out Clay's serious side. He sent Theodore home and refused to pay his gambling losses.[30]

In 1827 Clay tried to involve his son in public affairs again. Despite charges of nepotism from the Andrew Jackson camp, Clay used his position as secretary of state to name Theodore a bearer of dispatches to Mexico. His stated goal was to cure Theodore of "indolence and dissipation." Under strict supervision from his father, Theodore completed his assignment without embarrassment, but the young man seemed no closer to finding direction in his life.[31] In 1829 Clay sent his son to explore and evaluate twenty thousand acres owned by the estate of John Morrison, for which Henry was the executor. And a year later, he sent him on a mission through Indiana, Illinois, and Missouri to find land that he might farm or on which he could establish himself as a cotton planter. Clay was anxious to see Theodore settled "and doing something." Theodore made it to Saint Louis, where he spent several months wasting his time and his father's money.[32] The problem was more than that of a prodigal son. A year later, Theodore would be committed to the Lexington Lunatic Asylum. He believed a young woman to be in love with him. He stalked her by day and roamed the woods all night, cursing and shouting. He could neither sleep nor eat. He was a threat to himself and to others. Brandishing a weapon, he demanded that the father of the young woman allow them to marry. With the exception of a brief period, much to his father's pain and sadness, he would spend the rest of his life in the asylum.[33]

Clay worked as diligently with his second son. Amos Kendall had called Thomas an "admirable boy" despite his bad temper and lack of discipline. He also called him the laziest of the children, but as with Theodore, there was probably more to the problem. A pattern in his behavior developed early. He failed to prepare his lessons due to distraction or stubbornness. When reprimanded, he sulked or raged, then felt guilty. Apologies and promises of reform were made, only for him to repeat the cycle. When Clay sent him to the military academy, it may have been an attempt to provide some direction for an intelligent, but unfocused, young man.

Admitted to West Point in June 1821, Thomas was asked to leave in January 1822. Academy records indicate he was deficient in mathematics.[34] Henry's earlier fear that his son was involved in the student protest and Thomas's history suggest other reasons as well. Thomas compounded the problem by failing to inform his father of his dismissal. Henry learned the embarrassing news two weeks after it occurred. The problem grew larger because Thomas could not be found. Pieced together from the letters in the Clay papers, the account of an expelled and missing cadet is one of a son's feelings of guilt and a father's frustration. In a letter characterized more by frustration than concern about his missing son, Henry asked Thomas Morris, a New York friend, to help find Thomas. Convinced that he was somewhere in the city spending the money advanced to him for school expenses, Clay cautioned Morris to give his wayward son no additional funds. He also sent a letter to be given to Thomas, but this is not a part of the collection. The purging of embarrassing letters was not uncommon in the Victorian era, and in this instance, and others, it seems to be true of the Clay papers as well. As angry and frustrated as Henry was when he wrote to Morris, one can only guess what he must have said in his letter to Thomas. It certainly would not have portrayed the image of Clay later generations wished to see or to present to the public. He closed one letter to Morris, "The truth is, and I say it with definite pain, that I have lost all confidence in his stability." The remainder of the letter provides a clear example of bad parenting. He expressed no concern for the humiliation Thomas felt at being expelled from the academy, but repeatedly returned to the subject of the money Thomas had cost him: "I neither have the ability nor inclination to supply him with money to waste in dissipation and idleness in the Cities. He has cost me $500 since he left home in June last, and one half of it after he had made me a solemn promise to limit his expenses to his allowance as a Cadet."[35]

Morris found Thomas, apparently without money, because Henry sent him $100 upon the pledge of his honor that he would return home. Fearful of facing his father or deeply humiliated, Thomas expressed through Morris a desire for self-exile. He would join the Marine Corps or leave the country altogether, enlisting with the forces fighting for South American independence. Henry scoffed at both ideas: "The Marine Corps is full; and if it were not, I could not think of asking the public to take into its service, a son of mine, in whose firmness and consistency of conduct, I have so little confidence. In short, he fills me, my dear Sir, with inexpressible distress."[36]

Thomas's reaction throughout the episode suggests the humiliation he must have felt. First, he refused to go home, not even telling his father about his dismissal. Then, in a form of self-punishment, he would fight for a cause that was not his, although his father championed it, or join a branch of the military that would take him far from the home and family he had disgraced. The father, on the other hand, was embarrassed and frustrated. His letters to Morris expressed far more than one usually said publicly about family problems in the Victorian age. But Henry Clay sent another sixty dollars for Thomas to join him in Philadelphia, and from there they returned to Lexington.

Despite the tone of his letters, Clay immediately arranged for Thomas to study law with a personal friend, Judge John Boyle of Frankfort, Kentucky. Thomas entered his studies with some enthusiasm, and Boyle expressed confidence in his abilities. However, by the end of 1825, Boyle was hinting of trouble. Thomas had stayed away on Christmas break longer than he should have.[37] Then Thomas began to drink heavily, and he behaved badly, according to his father, in New York and Philadelphia. After some embarrassment, he renewed his efforts, only to fall again into the dissipation his father feared so greatly. Clay wrote to Henry Jr., "He [Thomas] begins to shew, at his early age, the effects of a dissipated life."[38]

Despite Henry's fears, Thomas completed his studies and was licensed to practice. In 1827 he moved briefly to Woodville, Mississippi, with the intention of establishing a law office.[39] The Mississippi venture, however, proved short lived. In February 1829 Thomas was arrested in Philadelphia for failure to pay a bill for lodging. Drinking heavily, Thomas had walked away from Hieskell's City Hotel without settling the bill. Thomas I.

Wharton interceded for Henry, and Thomas avoided going to jail. Henry sent $250 to pay the court costs and Thomas's expenses home.[40]

Although Clay had "little confidence" in Thomas, in 1829 he tried to make his son a farmer. There were patterns to Henry's actions. At various times, he sought to establish all five sons in business, law, and farming, though in a different order for different sons. He sent Thomas to Clay's Prairie, a farm of 137 acres along the Illinois side of the Wabash River. Clay hoped that Thomas would like it there, farm the land, and, no doubt, reap the moral values of working the soil. Thomas agreed, though it is impossible to know whether the agreement came under duress. No one questions Henry Clay's persuasiveness, but it is also possible that Thomas, too, with typical Clay enthusiasm, embraced the original proposal as the means to redeem himself. Henry supplied the land, seed, livestock, and equipment, and Thomas became a farmer. By December, however, Clay had received very bad accounts of Thomas's habits there. On a trip back to Ashland, Thomas became involved in what his father called two "debauches." According to Henry, one of them threatened his life, but he did not elaborate on the matter. Thomas returned to Illinois, but he remained despondent and again developed a drinking problem. Henry wrote, "Poor Tom, I fear, is irreclaimable."[41] By mid-1833 the Illinois farm was heavily in debt, so Clay decided to sell it and bring Thomas back to Lexington.[42]

Thomas seems clearly to have suffered from recurring bouts of depression accompanied by alcoholism. What triggered the episodes cannot be determined, but none of the brothers handled stress particularly well. The difficulty of being a famous man's son may have been a part of the problem. It would not have been the first or the last time in American history. Daniel Webster's son struggled with the dilemma, and Roosevelts, Kennedys, and Reagans of a more modern period have experienced similar difficulties. Henry Clay Jr. wrote in his diary, "How difficult it is for a young tree to grow in the shade of an aged oak." Many years later, having found religion, Thomas would note the requirement and the difficulty of always honoring father and mother.[43] Thomas reacted to pressure by becoming erratic or morose to the point that he could not cope. Henry eventually developed a farm and built a home for Thomas in Lexington, but he kept the deed and the decision making largely to himself.

Given such difficulties, it is little wonder that Henry wrote to Henry Jr. as he did. His two oldest sons had caused him "inexpressible pain." The two youngest were mere boys, so he pinned his hopes at the time on Henry

Thomas Hart Clay.
Courtesy of Dr. William D.
Kenner.

Jr.: "But when I turn to you, my dear son, I find relief and consolation. On you my hopes are chiefly encentrd."[44]

Henry Jr. gave his father reason to hope. He craved his father's praise and worked diligently to earn it. Physically, Henry Jr. looked a great deal like his father. He was thin and of delicate features. He had his father's long thin nose, wide mouth, and narrow chin. His eyes, at least in portrait, however, seemed those of a dreamer. There was less fire and more contemplation in them. He loved books and thought at one point of becoming a college professor or writer.[45] Interestingly, he said on one occasion to his father that his disposition was "naturally wild," but there is little evidence of it. He did not gamble or drink excessively, although he did have the Clay temper. Henry Clay Jr. graduated second in his class at West Point, and seemed, to the outside world, poised to follow in his father's footsteps.

Such praise did not mean that Henry was unaware that this son, too, had weaknesses. According to Harriet Martineau, Henry Jr. was "so jealous and irritable in his temper that there is no living with him."[46] In his letters to his father, he put himself above the excesses of his older brothers and the potential of the younger ones, and at times seemed to be in competition with his sister Anne. No politician as astute as Henry Clay could have missed the fact that Henry Jr. sought in virtually every letter to ingratiate himself. But Henry Jr. had other problems that his father addressed cautiously but knowingly. After arriving at West Point in May 1827 for early training, he was asked to leave the post because of an incident at the local post office. Attempting to post a letter, Henry Jr. gave a note that the clerk could not change. He left the note intending to recover the change later. When he returned, a new clerk knew nothing of the arrangement but agreed to look into it. Returning a third time, he learned that the clerk had done nothing, and Clay proceeded to remind him of his responsibilities. The clerk took exception, essentially reminding young Clay that he was sixteen years old. Clay struck him, and was tossed out of the post office. He then returned to his base to arm himself but was restrained by other cadets. Colonel Sylvanus Thayer, the commandant, sent him to Newburgh, New York, with letters of introduction until the incident could be resolved. Henry Jr. wrote that the decision whether he would enter the academy depended on Clay. He did become a cadet that June, so Clay obviously used his influence in the matter.[47]

Young Clay performed well at the academy. West Point records indicate he received only three demerits in his second year and none thereafter. He also became an assistant teacher in French in his fourth year, graduating second in his class behind Roswell Park, a cadet who held the first position throughout his career.[48] Despite his success, however, Henry Jr. had little confidence in his abilities or his father's appreciation of them, and he needed frequent encouragement. Preferring law to a military career, he believed his father had steered him toward the military because he was intellectually unfit for the practice of law. Henry immediately sought to reassure his son: "You are greatly mistaken my son in supposing that I entertain a low opinion of your talents. On the co[ntrary], I have thought very favorable of them, and I have [thought] that, by perserverance [sic] in that course of study and regu[larity], which has given me so much happiness, you can make yourself any thing you please." Henry went into great detail to explain to his son the benefits of the education he would receive at West Point and the opportunities it would open even if he chose another profession.[49]

As the young man struggled for perfection, he was inclined to blame others when anything less was achieved. Falling behind Roswell Park, Henry Jr. blamed his educational training. When he received a third place in mathematics, he suggested that he had been done an injustice by the professor because of politics, and on another occasion, he accused Colonel Thayer of catering to the Andrew Jackson crowd. Henry responded by expressing pride in his son's achievement and noting that Colonel Thayer had mentioned Henry Jr. favorably to himself and to others.[50] The father patiently encouraged his son, mixing words of caution and praise. A third place in mathematics was a respectable standing, and he should be proud of it. Then he cautioned that one of the easiest mistakes a man could make was to attempt judgment of his own merit. One might wonder whether Henry did not need to heed that lesson himself, but his next comments respected one he had clearly learned. Some men encouraged others to overstate their merits and complain about ill treatment only to laugh at them later. Consequently, one had to judge friends carefully. When Henry Jr. accused Thayer of Jacksonian bias, his father spoke more forcefully: "There is one feeling against which, my dear son, I would anxiously caution you, since it is often founded in mistake and is a source of much unhappiness. It is a feeling of distrust which prompts us to believe too readily that the world, or some particular individuals, do not render justice to our pretensions. Depend upon it that, in the general, the world justly distributes its praise and censure."[51]

Clay also recognized in his namesake an impetuousness that perhaps reminded him too much of himself. Many of their letters while Henry Jr. was a cadet discussed career options open to the son. Once he learned his father believed him intellectually fit for practicing law, Henry Jr. wanted to forget his class work and take up the reading of law. Henry cautioned him to stay focused on the requirements at West Point. Later, the son spoke of taking a trip to Europe. Rather than say no to a suggestion that was obviously inopportune, Henry encouraged postponement until his son's formal education was completed. After graduating from West Point, Henry Jr. studied law with another friend of his father's. Grandiose plans to practice in New Orleans, Lexington, and Louisville followed. Eventually, Henry Jr. took his turn as the overseer of Ashland as well. But Henry must have been most surprised when he received a letter in 1832 suddenly announcing that the young man planned to marry. The tone of Henry Jr.'s letter may indicate, at least in part, the reason Henry Clay received the news with some concern: "How changeable our dispositions! How unfixed our determinations! But yesterday, I was resolved upon a life of celibacy; today, I am almost equally resolved to propose a matrimonial union." Henry Clay found no fault in his son's bride-to-be, and he did not object when other sons chose to marry. Henry did not record his objections to Henry Jr.'s marriage other than to say it was "contrary to my wishes," but it seems that concern over his son's rapid mood shifts certainly played a role. Henry had written about despondency when his son was at West Point and had expressed concern to daughter Anne when Henry Jr. studied law in New Orleans. Henry worried about the young man's focus and the dark spirits that occasionally consumed him.[52]

Clay's greatest concern was to get his sons established in a profession that would hold their attention and keep them busy. Even in that regard, he often drew distinctions based on his perceptions of his sons' needs. More frequently than not, his assessments were correct. While he criticized Theodore and Thomas for laziness, he worried that the intensity Henry Jr. and James took to each new project risked mental strain. He frequently expressed his frustration with the lavish spending of Theodore and Thomas on social activities, but he urged Henry Jr. to take time for relaxation and reflection. He offered James the same advice.[53]

By the time Henry became aware of the "little boys," James and John, he had either mellowed or grown weary. Harriet Martineau had declared that at age seventeen and thirteen they did not show much promise. That was not the assessment of Henry or the Clay family. When Anne Clay Erwin returned in the summers from her home in New Orleans, James and John would ride their horses to the Woodlands, her estate bordering Ashland, where they would often spend the day. Anne expressed her pleasure to Henry in James's intelligence. In Henry's letters to Henry Jr. urging him to achievement, he frequently mentioned that his hopes rested on James and John too. In 1832 Henry sent James, at the age of fifteen, to work in the Boston counting house of Grant and Seaver as a continuation of his education. John was the baby of the family, and both Henry and Lucretia treated him as such. Always looking for ways to involve his sons in meaningful labor, Henry encouraged his youngest son to work with his stable of horses.[54]

James and John were clearly sons of Henry Clay. Like their brothers, they found it difficult to stay focused on a project. Both had fiery tempers that frequently could get them into trouble. James did not drink or gamble, but a diary John later kept indicates frequent nights of drunkenness, fighting, and carousing. James suffered from occasional depression, but John would be committed to the Lexington Lunatic Asylum with virtually the same symptoms as Theodore.[55]

James did not like the Boston counting house where his father placed him, but Henry did not chastise him as he had Theodore and Thomas. He first brought him home, then, reluctantly yielding to James's request, purchased a 563-acre farm in Missouri so James could be a farmer. As at Clay's Prairie, he bought equipment and seed, purchased cattle, and sent purebred stock from Lexington. Advice and encouragement made their way to James just as they had to Henry Jr.: "Above all, avoid dissipation. I hope you will never play a game. After much observation and some experience I can say, with perfect truth, that he who is addicted to play loses money, time, sleep, health and character."[56] And letters to James echoed those sent to Henry Jr. much earlier. "I am the more concerned about you," Henry wrote, "because John has lately given me great pain, and I almost despair of him."[57]

It was not long, however, until James complained that he felt isolated and unhappy. He did not have the means to go into society, and thus he had no friends. Like many exasperated parents, Clay yielded to the temptation to say "I told you so." He reminded James that he had agreed to the Missouri venture with reluctance, fully expecting his son to become lonely, but that said, he immediately offered James money to improve his social life. All James had to do was ask, he said: "The slightest intimation of your wishes to me, on that subject would have commanded them [the means]." He protested that he had refused his son nothing, and while he wanted James to avoid dissipation, he did not oppose, indeed he encouraged, the enjoyment of society.[58] That was an entirely different approach than he had used with Theodore and Thomas. On the subject of marriage, his approach was also different. Whereas he had reservations about Henry Jr.'s getting married and accepted Thomas's marriage rather matter-of-factly, he offered in an almost collegial way to help James find a wife. He quickly added that he suspected James would prefer to make his own choice.[59]

Clay worried continuously about John. Eccentric even as a young man, John Morrison Clay could be quite abrupt, and he was definitely opinionated. Unacceptable behavior at Enoch Wines's school was followed by rule violations that got him expelled from Princeton. Back home, he studied law, but like Theodore, he never practiced. Then, like each of his brothers, he tried farming. In 1845 John began to experience the same mental difficulties that Theodore had exhibited. After an infatuation with a young woman, he became irrational and a danger to himself and others, following his brother into the asylum.[60] According to Henry, his symptoms were worse than those exhibited by Theodore, but John benefited from ten years of reform in psychological methods. Although he would be committed several times during his life, he was able to function and even prosper outside the mental facility, whereas his brother Theodore could not. Henry worried about him, and he continued to live at home with his parents until their deaths.[61]

Henry Clay, then, did not spare money or energy in his efforts to educate his sons. He was not a perfect father by any means. His tendency to impatience often got the better of him, and he tended to be controlling.[62] Yet, blessed with five "prodigal" sons, he never gave up. Rather, he sought to understand their strengths and to help them find roles to play. To Henry's credit and to that of his sons, they fought their demons. Theodore was lost, but Thomas, Henry Jr., James, and John had opportunities available to them, largely thanks to their father. In the year of his death, Clay wrote, "As the world recedes from me, I feel my affections more than ever concentrated on my children and theirs."[63] He would help his sons until his dying day.

Chapter 3

BUILDING LEGACIES

Henry Clay rose quickly in the political life of the nation. John Quincy Adams recognized something special in him when he entered the U.S. Senate. The Kentucky Assembly saw something of talent, because they named him to fill that Senate seat before he had reached the legal age to do so. His charisma carried him literally on the shoulders of his constituents and to political office as a very young man. After filling two unexpired terms in the Senate, Clay returned to Washington, where members of the House of Representatives named him the Speaker. In that position he led an effort to create a war, then as a diplomat contributed to making a peace. As Speaker of the House, Henry Clay exercised more power than many of the antebellum presidents. He crafted a compromise in 1820–1821 over Missouri that reduced for a time the sectional tensions regarding slavery; and he fashioned a vision, the American System, that he hoped would unite the regions of the country and create political unity and economic prosperity. In 1825 he secured the position of secretary of state, a traditional stepping-stone to the presidency. The self-made man was a man with a mission. He believed he could be president.

The young politician had another dream. It was the same dream that brought him to Kentucky in 1797. He believed he could be the patriarch of a vast and impressive empire. That goal drove his continuing, indeed unending, efforts to establish his sons. His role as a parent did not end with the formal education of his sons. Henry Clay created what might be called the Clay Corporation, a "systematic and multifaceted" conglomerate involving agriculture, manufacturing, transportation, and banking for himself, his sons, and his sons-in-law. It was his private American System. Writing to John M. Clayton in 1842, Clay said, "I am executing here [Ashland], in

Henry Clay. Courtesy of
the Elizabeth Clay Blanford
Collection.

epitome, all my principles of internal improvements, the American System,
&c."[1] He then involved his sons and his sons-in-law in the operations. They
were the partners in an integrated, and sometimes confusing, system of
business relationships. Of one thing, however, there is no doubt: Henry
Clay served as chairman of the board.

When Clay moved to Kentucky, Robert Remini contends, he lost some
of his Virginia refinement in order to fit in with the other young lawyers
traveling the circuits. Typical young southern and western males, they
seemed always in competition. Whether at shooting, riding, playing cards,
or drinking, the standards of manhood required that they boast of their
prowess and prove it.[2] Henry Clay wanted to fit in, so he quickly gained a
reputation for riotous behavior.

It was, in reality, more than fitting in. Taking risks suited his personality. Intellectually quick, spontaneous, and energetic, he enjoyed the
adrenaline rush that comes with risks. According to family members, it
was never the money that drew him to gambling at cards but the ability to

gauge an opponent, to know when one was bluffing and when he should bluff. Like most upper-class Kentuckians of his day, he raced horses because it revealed the best of the breed, and the breeding shed was as much a challenge as the racecourse itself.

Clay gained quite a reputation as a gambler in his youth. Ben Hardin, a fellow Kentuckian, claimed Clay "set a bad example in Washington for gambling, drinking, and carousing." William Plumer, a senator from New Hampshire, called him a man of pleasure who was fond of amusements and gambled a great deal. Clay's bitter enemy Andrew Jackson called him "the typical western gambler," obviously forgetting that he too fit the description.[3] There were other charges as the years passed. His enemies, and sometimes his friends, called him intemperate, impetuous, and immoral. No less a judge of other men's morals than John Quincy Adams claimed, "In politics, as in private life, Clay is essentially a gamester."[4]

If his political ambitions were to succeed, Clay realized, he had to control his passions. Harriet Martineau observed in 1835, "Mr. Clay is a man of an irritable and impetuous nature, over which he has obtained a truly noble mastery. His moderation is now his most striking characteristic; obtained, no doubt, at the cost of prodigious self-denial on his own part."[5] Margaret Bayard Smith noticed the same effort to control his emotions. Robert Remini, Glyndon Van Deusen, Clement Eaton, and Daniel Walker Howe all note the same changes in Clay, though they may differ as to when he achieved that mastery.[6]

There are, however, other explanations for the change in Clay's behavior. Henry Clay did not learn control over his passions as much as he found ways to channel them. He found an outlet for his risk taking in the world of business. The breeding of livestock was a gamble, one he enjoyed immensely. Trading horses and other livestock called for special skills, not to mention a little luck. Kentucky horse trading has long drawn gamblers to its charms. It remains to this day as big a gamble as racing a horse. Competing in the southern trade to get high prices for his hemp, speculating on land in Kentucky, Missouri, and Illinois, or investing in a new invention fed his love of adventure or satisfied the gambler within him. Henry Clay never saw a business opportunity he did not like. Literally on his deathbed, he begged James to write him because he liked to hear "all the details of your business and operations."[7]

The channeling of his penchant for risk taking had another cause as well. He had played cards and paid homage, as he liked to say, to the "fickle

Julia Prather Clay. Courtesy of Ashland, the Henry Clay Estate.

goddess" enough to know the odds of long-term success. He also recognized in his sons and perhaps his sons-in-law the same tendencies toward risk taking. If he could steer them toward business, he might accomplish several goals. He could save them from the purposeless life they seemed intent on following, fulfill his duty as a father, and build the dynasty he craved. Parenting in Clay's definition clearly did not end when his sons reached adulthood.

Henry Clay found allies in the task of involving his sons in "meaningful work," and it appears to have resulted without his involvement. Henry Clay's sons did one thing extremely well. They married strong, stable partners, women who accomplished what Henry had been unable to do: give the second generation a sense of direction. Despite his father's concerns, Henry Clay Jr. married Julia Prather, the daughter of a wealthy Louisville businessman, on October 10, 1832. She came from sufficient wealth and station to be a very eligible young woman. Henry attended the wedding in Louisville and always expressed respect for Julia.[8] He also appreciated the economic advantages marriage brought to his son. Matilda Prather, Julia's mother, divided some property among her children, and that provided about $10,000 for each. With this wealth and borrowed money, often with his father as security, Henry Jr. invested individually and in partnership with his new relatives in commercial and residential property in the heart of Louisville and in farmland. A center of the new market economy, Louisville experienced significant increases in property values in the antebellum era. Henry Jr. became a wealthy man at a very young age.

Additionally, he found purpose to his life. He practiced law when his business interests allowed. At Maplewood, his farm just north of Lexington, he instituted progressive farming in partnership with his father and brothers. He also began to dabble in politics. Henry Jr. enjoyed his family and was devoted to Julia. Most important, he gained some control over the melancholy that had plagued him as a young man.

A few years later, the prodigal son, Thomas, also married. Writing to James, Henry said, "I suppose that you have heard that your brother Thom was to have been married, and I presume was married, last Thursday was a week. . . . We shall see if that event will make him steady. I sincerely hope it may."[9] Indeed, on October 5, 1837, Thomas married Marie Mentelle, the daughter of longtime Clay friends.

The daughter of Waldemar and Charlotte Victoire Mentelle, Marie, or Mary as the family called her, had known Thomas all her life. Her parents came from France during the French Revolution. They settled first in Gallipolis, Ohio, but moved to Lexington early in the city's history. Still a frontier town, Lexington had a gentry that dreamed of establishing a Virginia-style aristocracy both socially and politically, so they readily welcomed the émigré French. In fact, when one lacked money, being French was about the only way to gain access to Lexington's better citizens. The Mentelles had little money when they arrived, but being well read, musical, and dignified, they served well the purposes of the "Athens of the West." A gentry family—local historians disagree as to which—provided them with a house just across the Richmond Road from Henry Clay's Ashland, and Clay secured a position for Mentelle at Transylvania University.[10] On several occasions in the 1820s and 1830s, the Clays left their sons with the Mentelles when Lucretia accompanied Henry to Washington.

Nothing is known of the courtship, and given Henry's comments, he seems to have known little about it. Nevertheless, the couple married and quickly settled down to farming and raising a family. Thomas continued to have bouts of depression throughout his life, but at least alcohol no longer clouded his judgment or led to embarrassing actions. From comments in

Susan Jacob Clay.
Courtesy of Ned Boyajian.

his diary, there is little doubt that Mary provided the anchor for a family that soon included five children.[11]

Apparently rejecting his father's offer, James found his own wife. Suzannah (Susan) Maria Jacob was the daughter of one of Louisville's richest men, John Jacob, a merchant and real-estate speculator who had partnered with William Prather, Henry Clay Jr.'s father-in-law. Educated in the East, Susan was cultured, charming, and attractive. She also had enough ambition for herself and the rather complacent James. She delighted in being the daughter-in-law of a famous statesman, and she urged her husband to follow in his father's footsteps. Henry was delighted with Susan, and their correspondence quickly assumed the comfortable quality that characterized his letters to other intelligent women. He also appreciated her, perhaps, because she pushed James toward financial and political activity. Although Susan never said as much, her actions suggest that she expected her husband to equal and perhaps exceed the success of his father. More Clay than many blood relatives, Susan became a bulwark of the family after Henry's death.[12]

The sons married women who played far more than an ornamental role in their lives. In Paul C. Nagel's book *The Adams Women,* he describes

Abigail and Louisa Adams as "independent, strong persons, [who] bore no resemblances to the gentle, retiring females portrayed in journals."[13] With allowances for southern propriety, the same thing could be said of the women who married the second generation of Clay men. They provided unwavering support for their husbands and their children, but within the family they shared in decision making and occasionally dominated. Though not members of the family corporation, they played roles that made Henry's task a lot easier.

Clay appreciated the strengths of his daughters-in-law. He spoke warmly of Julia Prather and rarely failed in correspondence with Henry Jr. to ask about her health or invite her for long visits at Ashland. The James B. Clay branch of the family took great pleasure in the relationship that developed between Susan and Henry Clay. The family claimed she served for a time as his secretary. Such service would have been of short duration, but their correspondence did suggest a closeness or familiarity that developed from mutual respect. Susan wrote long, chatty letters to Henry, mentioning the purchase of clothes, home furnishings, and parties she had attended, subjects one might not expect to be interesting to a man in that era. She also felt comfortable enough to criticize her husband's lack of direction.[14]

Clay's greatest appreciation had to be reserved for Marie Mentelle Clay. Thomas settled peacefully into married life, accepting the responsibilities of husband and father, and farming the land Henry purchased for him. Thomas and his family ate dinner with Henry and Lucretia at least once a week, and when Henry was away from Ashland, Mary kept him informed about conditions on the Clay farms, the community, and the extended Clay family. He appreciated her letters, noting favorably the detail included in them as opposed to the abbreviated comments sent by Thomas and his other sons. On several occasions, Henry let Mary know that he appreciated the stability she contributed to Thomas.[15]

The Clay Corporation was also facilitated by the fact that the Clay children established farms close to Ashland. That, of course, occurred largely because of Henry's encouragement and financial support. In 1831 Henry helped James and Anne Clay Erwin purchase the Woodlands estate, which bordered Ashland.[16] The Erwins maintained a home in New Orleans, but Anne spent summers in Lexington. James Erwin conducted business in Lexington and in New Orleans with Henry Clay and on his own account. On a personal level, Henry and Lucretia were delighted.

Anne talked with her mother, and James and John, still boys at the time, visited frequently at the Woodlands. Henry discussed with Anne her attempts to beautify the estate, and they all enjoyed the varieties of plants she brought from Louisiana. Most of these, such as the pecan tree, died as a result of the harsher winters, but experimentation was a part of the agricultural experience all the Clays enjoyed.[17]

Henry Clay Jr. maintained a residence in Louisville near his wife's relatives, but he, too, purchased an estate on the outskirts of Lexington. Maplewood was close enough to Ashland to exchange livestock and laborers. Because Henry Jr. spent most of his time in Louisville, Maplewood became an extension of Ashland. His father or brother Thomas supervised the work at the farm if he was in Louisville, and when Henry was away, Henry Jr. often helped out at Ashland.[18]

Despite his misgivings about Thomas, Henry purchased a farm adjacent to Ashland's western boundary for him. In 1846 Henry commissioned Thomas Lewinski, a Lexington architect, to design and construct substantial residences in Lexington for Thomas and James. Mansfield became the home of Thomas and his family, and James took title to the Clay Villa, an imposing structure located between Lexington and Henry's estate. Clay was better at forgiving than forgetting: Thomas never owned his farm. It remained in Henry's name, and at his death it was placed in trust for Thomas's children.[19]

Clay delighted in the proximity of his children and also in their farms. Henry, as usual, had grand plans. His family enterprise, if he could manage it, would have national scope. It was ideally located for that purpose. In its reckless dependence on a one-crop economy—that of cotton—the South forsook the production of other products. Kentucky was ideally suited to ship to the South the things southerners needed most. Kentuckians provided pork to feed the slaves and produced denim for work clothes. They raised and sold mules. The need for bagging and rope to secure cotton bales fueled the Kentucky hemp industry. The Clays became involved in all aspects of that production. Central Kentucky could also look north across the Ohio River into Ohio and the industrializing regions of the country. Henry and his sons sought financial reward in commerce, manufacturing, and land. They owned stock in farm equipment companies and sought out new inventions that might make production easier and provide a handsome return on investment. They produced brick, lumber, and agricultural products such as thoroughbred horses, purebred cattle, and

European donkeys that they traded in northern states as well as southern ones. They also owned stock in banks. Clay had been an early investor in the Kentucky Insurance Company, more bank than insurer, and he was closely affiliated with the Bank of the United States until Andrew Jackson destroyed it. The Clay Corporation likewise invested in transportation, owning stock in turnpikes and canal companies. Anyone visiting Henry Clay from Lexington had to pay a fee to use the turnpike running by his home. The corporation also quickly saw the importance of railroads as that mode of transportation came online.

As Henry stated in his letter to John Clayton, he was executing not just at Ashland but at all the Clay properties the best principles of the American System, the Whig Party plan for the development of the nation's economy to which he contributed so much. It is difficult to tell whether he developed first a plan for his family's economic success or one for the nation's success. He was interested in both and optimistic about both. As a young married man he bought prime land and was involved in the commercial and manufacturing interests of his father-in-law and other enterprising citizens of Lexington. His economic interests at times competed with his political responsibilities. On several occasions he noted the conflict between his love of farming and his sense of duty to his constituents and to the nation. Nevertheless, he followed consistently the same principles of economic development for his family interest and those of his nation.

Clay gained a great deal of intellectual maturity, particularly relating to economic policies, while serving as an emissary in Europe in 1814–1815. At the conclusion of the peace negotiations, he went to England to discuss trade relations, and as he "played brag" with British leaders, he sensed their belief that they could continue to dominate their former colonies. They would do it economically if they could not do it militarily. Clay realized that if the United States did not compete commercially, its struggle for independence could prove to be for naught.[20]

He also recognized that the United States was a large country, larger than any state that had heretofore successfully established a representative government. Political thinkers had long believed that representative governments worked best in small city states; larger states were too geographically diverse and too divided by distance. Clay was no great scholar, but his own experience traveling by horse or coach from Richmond, Virginia, to Lexington, Kentucky, or from Lexington to Washington, D.C., taught him valuable lessons about distances and transportation. The nation would have to be unified economically and bound together in many other ways if its independence was to survive.

To a man who once believed Canada could be conquered by a few Kentucky militia units, a sweeping development plan to save the nation was no great task. The American System was his answer to the problem. Daniel Walker Howe claims, "Of all major figures in American political history, Clay had the most systematic and multifaceted economic program. If he had been able to implement it . . . he would have changed the course of United States history in the nineteenth century."[21] Through the creation of national manufacturing, agricultural production, domestic markets, and a national transportation system to link the country together, Clay hoped to create a prosperous and powerful nation, unified by mutual interests. As Howe suggests, Clay was not totally successful, but Abraham Lincoln, speaking shortly after Clay's death, said, "Our country is prosperous and powerful, but could it have been quite all it has been, and is, and is to be, without Henry Clay?" Clay added a series of tariffs to protect fledgling industries, a national banking system to provide sound currency, and internal improvements—highways and canals—to link the regions of the country. Charles Sellers, author of *The Market Revolution,* states emphatically that Clay preached and practiced the politics of market expansion more consistently and more unambiguously than any other politician in the country.[22]

With characteristically unbounded enthusiasm, Clay believed the nation would be unified through such means. He even believed the economy would grow so grandly that free labor would cause the demise of that greatest obstacle to national unity, slavery. Much of his dream would become reality in the twentieth century, but as Howe notes, Clay was a better ideologist than a politician. In his own day, the nation could not fathom the potential of his dream.[23]

Clay proved more successful in his local version of the American System. The Clay Corporation functioned primarily as an agricultural enterprise. Henry enjoyed the planning for cultivation of his fields, the breeding of his stock, and involvement in the production of the land. He wrote to Francis Brooke in 1830, "My attachment to rural occupation every day acquires more strength, and if it continues to increase another year as it has the last, I shall be fully prepared to renounce forever the strifes of public life. My farm is in fine order, and my preparations for the crop of the present year, are in advance of all my neighbors. I shall make a better farmer than statesman. And I find in the business of cultivation, gardening, grazing, and the rearing of the various descriptions of domestic animals, the most agreeable resources."[24] On another occasion he wrote, "I am constantly and agreeably occupied at Ashland."[25]

Even when in Washington, he knew what was needed for his farms to prosper. Whether working on the tariff compromise in 1832 or fighting for the national bank, Clay maintained contact with home. He constantly sent a stream of instructions to overseers and to sons regarding planting, harvesting, and the breeding of his purebred stock. In 1833, for example, he sent detailed instructions to his overseer, William Martin, on the operation of Ashland for the year. He named the slaves he wanted hired out and detailed the lease arrangements. He noted which timber to be cut, fields to be cleared, and animals to be weaned.[26] At Ashland, Clay practiced sound principles of farming. The progressive thinking required by the American System was equally important to the Clay Corporation. His crops were rotated according to the prevailing scientific advice. He used fertilizers and planted legumes. In a letter to a friend, he detailed his efforts to build "an enormous canal" to enable him to water-rot his hemp crop. If Kentucky hemp was to be competitive, a new method of breaking down the stems had to be developed. "I am going to rig the Navy with Cordage made of American Hemp—Kentucky hemp—Ashland Hemp," he wrote. A friend of several leaders in progressive farming, he sought advice regularly on how to operate his farm efficiently.[27]

Whether in Washington or Lexington, Clay seemed to be occupied full time not only as a politician but also as the head of his corporation. A constant stream of letters were posted to Ashland, demanding information and containing orders for the operation of the farm. Both Henry and his sons knew their livestock by name. He wanted to know when Blossom had her calf or whether favorite mares had fillies or colts. In December 1836, for example, in a letter to Henry Clay Jr., he noted that "the Shepherd Cow" had produced a dead calf and his hope that "the Hector calf" had recovered from lameness. Particularly interested in purebred stock, he became an expert in judging them and won prizes for his own animals. After attending a livestock show in London, England, following the negotiations at Ghent, Clay imported four Hereford cattle in 1817, the first in the United States. He also introduced Holderness and Durham shorthorn and longhorn to his farm. Orozimbo, his prize Durham bull, was not only one of the most important breeding bulls in the nation but also the only one to receive a eulogy on the floor of the U.S. Senate.[28] Clay imported a large number of cattle and produced even more, and he consistently shared breeding rights with his sons and son-in-law James Erwin.[29]

Clay recognized the importance of mules to southern cultivation, and that interest led him to import full-blooded jacks and jennies from Europe. The first imported stock came in 1827, but in the early 1830s, on a vacation in Europe, Henry Clay Jr. became involved. Amazed at the size of purebred Maltese and Poitou asses, he sent several back to Kentucky.[30] He and his father began breeding them not only to produce mules but also to produce breeding stock. They were quite successful. Thomas, James, and John were soon involved in the business. In 1836 Henry wrote to Thomas to sell two jacks he had just acquired from New Orleans if he could get $2,000 apiece for them. In 1845 Ashland sold fifty-two mules for $6,185.[31]

Clay also raised purebred sheep, pigs, and even chickens at Ashland. In 1829 Clay bought fifty merino ewes and rams from Pennsylvania, and in 1837 he imported Saxon sheep. Henry Jr. and James became involved, and the corporation was soon selling purebred stock, wool, and mutton. When marauding dogs threatened profits, however, the corporation quickly abandoned the sheep business.[32]

Of course, Ashland would not have been a Kentucky plantation without thoroughbred horses. Clay came to Kentucky with only the horse he was riding. By 1804 he had five. Clay's first stallion purchase came in 1806, when he helped create a syndicate, believed to be the first in the nation, to buy Buzzard, an English horse, and from that point he exhibited the enthusiasm that usually accompanied his business ventures. By 1809 he was raising horses, participating in the Lexington Jockey Club, and establishing his own racing track at Ashland. In 1830 Clay officially established the Ashland Thoroughbred Stock Farm. Taking advantage of his Washington connections, he learned that four Arabian horses, given as a gift to an American diplomat, would be sold. Horsemen had long been interested in the characteristics Arabian horses might bring to racing. Clay put interest into action. He purchased a half interest in Stamboul in 1831, and the next year invested in another of the Arabians, Kocklani. In 1835 he purchased the thoroughbred Allegrante from James Barbour, the governor of Virginia. When it came to business, the Clays never believed in half measures.

Ironically, the success of Ashland Stud, as his thoroughbred operation came to be called, rested on three horses that Clay received as gifts. In 1845

John Morrison Clay.
Josephine Clay Collection.
Courtesy of University
of Kentucky Special
Collections.

Dr. W. C. Mercer of New Orleans gave Clay a mare named Magnolia. It became one of the greatest broodmares in thoroughbred history. Wade Hampton offered him Margaret Wood after Clay visited Hampton's South Carolina farm. Finally, Commodore Charles Morgan presented Clay a gift of an imported stallion, Yorkshire. Those three horses would have a major impact on thoroughbred racing.[33]

Clay shared his largesse with his sons, all of whom became involved in breeding horses. Ashland stallions serviced mares owned by Henry Jr., Thomas, and James, but John received the largest share. He became the manager of Ashland Stud. His brothers resented his special treatment by their parents, and a good deal of arguing among them resulted. On one occasion, Henry wrote to John, "You cannot imagine how much I was gratified at hearing of your visiting at Thomas's and talking kindly together as brothers." Brother James implied that John got on better with animals than people, but whatever the brothers thought, John was successful. Under Henry's general oversight, John raced and sold horses across the eastern United States, and the corporation had another success in a very risky business.[34]

Clay believed in active management of economic matters, whether of national or family scope. He used the knowledge he gained in Washington to suggest business ventures for the corporation, and even decisions reached for other purposes could lead to commercial ventures. For example, a matter of months after placing his son James in the Boston counting house of Grant and Seaver, he began selling hams and wool across the northeast through the company.[35] In 1830 the idea of buying a sugar plantation in Louisiana in partnership with his son-in-law James Erwin was rejected because of reports Henry received in Washington that the production of sugar was outpacing the demand.[36] Nevertheless, he continued to advise Erwin on the sugar market. He also kept Erwin informed about bank fraud in Pennsylvania and Kentucky that could affect their business interests.[37] It seemed Clay wanted to unite the diverse regions of the nation with his own business interests.

Much of the business activity of the Clay Corporation originated in the family's agricultural interests, but all family members were too intrigued with the possibility of making money to pass up an opportunity of any kind. They speculated in land. Henry Jr. and James speculated in Louisville business property and residential development. James Erwin bought western lands, often calling on his father-in-law for financial support. Henry was probably involved in some of the efforts as well. He owned tracts of land in Illinois and Missouri throughout most of his life. When James was still in his teens, Henry used him as his agent in the sale of Missouri lands.[38]

Members of the family helped each other with business matters. When Henry was in Washington, he generally asked Henry Jr. to handle matters involving banking.[39] James or Henry attended board meetings for banks, turnpike companies, and railroads in place of their father, and Thomas handled routine business matters such as note collection and bill payment in the Lexington area. James Erwin also collected money, paid debts, and borrowed from Henry. Even Lucretia's brother-in-law James Brown became involved at times, and both he and James Erwin worked to save Henry's son-in-law Martin Duralde Jr., whose commercial interests in New Orleans suffered financial collapse in 1834.[40] At various times, James or Thomas held power of attorney to handle financial affairs for Henry Jr., and the brothers frequently cooperated in buying, raising, and selling purebred livestock.[41]

Clay acted as the family banker, lending money for his sons' independent projects or allowing his name to be used to acquire loans. He believed in keeping such obligations within the family. He wrote to Henry Clay Jr., "You are right in not placing yourself under obligations to others by getting them to endorse for you. I shall always perform that office for you with pleasure, whilst I live." He loaned Henry Jr. nearly $3,000 in 1834 to meet a personal debt and to pay a loan he had taken to purchase land.[42] James Erwin borrowed money repeatedly to cover debts on his varied business interests. On occasion this put Henry in a financial bind, because Erwin could not repay according to his promises.[43] As John Morrison Clay became involved in raising and training thoroughbred horses, he frequently asked his father for loans too. In 1847 Henry offered strong encouragement and security for loans so James could purchase nearly one hundred tons of hemp, but in March 1852 Henry had to refuse a request from James for $1,000. John and Thomas had made "some unexpected calls" on him. He also anticipated having to lend John another $500 for the completion of his stables. On April 28, 1852, however, just months before his death, Henry borrowed $4,500 for James from William B. Astor.[44]

The best illustration of how the Clay Corporation worked can be seen in the celebrated financial collapse of Thomas Clay's hemp business. Throughout the late 1830s and the 1840s, Henry kept abreast of the national hemp market from Washington. His legislative efforts to protect the Kentucky hemp industry are well known. In Kentucky, his son Thomas ostensibly controlled a hemp company, producing hemp, processing it, and manufacturing rope sold throughout the nation and bagging sent south to cotton producers. Of course, Henry's hemp and that raised by Henry Jr. at Maplewood also found its way through Thomas's manufacturing company. Additionally, Thomas bought hemp at Henry's suggestion with money loaned to him by his father. Clay informed Thomas and Henry Jr. on every aspect of the market: the width of the cloth preferred by Georgia cotton farmers; prices offered in New Orleans, Savannah, and Charleston; and the hiring of slaves (and at what price) to work the looms.[45]

In late 1842 the company failed, and historians have traditionally placed blame on the wayward son, Thomas. Remini calls it the failure of a bagging and rope venture Thomas had established with his brother-in-law. Henry went into debt, mortgaging Ashland to avoid disaster. Van Deusen notes that Henry was involved in "large-scale" hemp production, but he calls it Thomas's failure. Eaton claims that Clay's debt was incurred at least partially through "aiding his sons, particularly Thomas Hart Clay, who had failed in the hemp business." Only Joseph Rogers admits Henry's role in the business, and he does so reluctantly, citing Thomas Hart Clay Jr.'s biography of Clay.[46]

A close reading of the correspondence indicates that Henry, not Thomas, controlled the company. Indeed, Clay closely supervised all of Thomas's business actions. In the 1830s Thomas served as his father's agent, but he acted only under instructions from his father. He bred the prized stock and collected notes and rents as ordered. On at least one occasion, Clay sent him a letter authorizing him to attend a board meeting of a railroad company in which he owned stock. He also conferred to him his power of attorney so that he could act in a land sale that had gone to court.[47] It may be too much to say that Henry's trust in Thomas was fully restored. His letters to Thomas appear more reserved than those to Henry Jr. or James, and he continued to chide Thomas for unwise purchases and extravagant spending. As late as 1846, he could not resist a pointed bit of advice to his prodigal son: "Economy and industry ought to be your watchwords, without which you cannot succeed."[48]

Quietly, if not enthusiastically, Thomas paid penance for his youthful indiscretions. He raised mules for the southern market, perhaps in partnership with James and his father, and Henry tried to help him sell them through his contacts with southern planters.[49] At virtually the same time, he began the hemp company with his brother-in-law, Waldemar Mentelle. However, Henry, James, and James Erwin were partners in the operation at various times.[50] The business prospered until a major economic depression in 1841 affected commerce across the nation. Thomas worked diligently to save the business, collecting debts owed the company in order to pay what he owed others. His efforts proved unsuccessful, and the hemp company folded in late summer or fall 1842.

According to the traditional interpretation, Henry, the loving father, rushed in to cover the losses. There is certainly some truth to that account. In November 1842 Henry conveyed Ashland to Madison C. Johnson, in trust, to support a $20,000 loan because of the failure of the business. Henry Clay Jr., John Brand, H. T. Duncan, and Clay signed $5,000 notes, Clay endorsing all but his own. Henry Clay Jr. endorsed Clay's note. According to the editors of the Clay papers, Clay spent nearly $30,000 trying to keep the business afloat and settling the debts. After the auction of equipment, Thomas still owed him about $20,000, which, presumably, he never paid. In 1843 Henry asked his benefactor, John Jacob Astor, for another loan.[51]

As in so many of the family businesses, determining one member's responsibility from another's is difficult. James had an interest in the company until his father advised him to withdraw in late 1841.[52] Henry used Thomas's company for the processing and sale of his own hemp crop. He also made contracts, then expected Thomas to meet them. One of the reasons H. T. Duncan signed a note for $5,000 is that he had arranged a contract with one of his relatives, Dr. Stephen Duncan of New Orleans, for the purchase of Clay's hemp rope and bagging.[53] Clay encouraged Thomas to take out loans in order to purchase additional hemp to meet the contract. He also loaned Thomas money for hemp purchases he suggested and charged him interest. At the same time, he was encouraging his son to "practise all the economy you can, manufacture the articles well & purchase hemp as low as you can get it."[54]

Too late, Henry wrote Lucretia, "I have found the depression in every department of business, and the reduction of prices of every thing greater than I anticipated."[55] Thomas was forced to sell the rope and bagging below his costs. He then sold the land, buildings, and equipment in an effort to pay his creditors. All debtors except his father were paid. Although Henry Clay never admitted any personal responsibility for the failure of the hemp business, his reaction to Thomas and his comments about the failure differed significantly from his traditional approach to his son. Always quick to point out Thomas's shortcomings, this time he neither criticized nor offered advice. He was almost consoling in a letter written on December 12, 1842: "I see no alternative, I lament my dear Son to say, but the sale which you contemplated of your property." A few years later, claiming to have lost $25,000 in the venture, Clay said that Thomas's business failure had been caused more by bad times than by any fault of Thomas's.[56]

The Clay appetite for risk taking recovered quickly. In 1845 another hemp business was under way. Additionally, Thomas and James began a brick-making business at Mansfield in late 1846, and in 1849 Thomas opened a sawmill. Henry greeted each venture with enthusiasm. Indeed, he could not contain his excitement. He wrote to Henry Clay Jr. in 1845 that he was thinking about buying more slaves to work the hemp looms; noted additional plans for Mansfield, allegedly Thomas's estate; and discussed other business opportunities. Thomas's sawmill made a modest profit, but Henry learned of a circular saw that would cut ten times as much lumber. He urged Thomas to go see it in operation, then to buy it, and he loaned him the money for the purchase.[57]

Clay's motives were obviously mixed. With a strike-it-rich mentality, he loved the challenge and the risk of business. Enthusiasm and expectations frequently exceeded reality. In those values, Clay and his sons were alike. The costs of the sawmill proved higher than expected, but Thomas was happy, and, more important, he was involved in "productive efforts." Clay would gladly loan money, and did so repeatedly, to see his sons engaged in constructive work.[58] Meaningful labor should be, Clay believed, a family and national value.

Henry Clay proved enthusiastic about each of his sons. Unlike many nineteenth-century fathers, he acquiesced easily to their wishes as long as they involved business or a profession. He certainly was excited when the Clay Corporation proved the means to have four of his sons employed in meaningful enterprises and establishing their fortunes. He had successfully channeled a legacy of risk into productive activity.

Sons with significant estates allowed Henry to entertain another legacy—a legacy of service. With their father's encouragement, Henry Jr. and James made cautious attempts at public service. They knew the pitfalls. Their father was criticized for using Theodore even in an unimportant position. They heard the attacks of political enemies, and sometimes political friends, on their father. They saw his pain when he returned to Ashland beaten and worn by the charges against him and by the betrayals of men he thought were his friends. However, they also knew what virtually every politician, friend or foe, understood. Few men could question Clay's love of the Union. Service to the nation was not a choice; it was a duty.

Henry Clay viewed the efforts of his sons in the political world with caution as well. He offered his support, but he was far less aggressive than he had been in other aspects of his parenting. He allowed his sons to move at their own pace, generally staying in the background until his help was requested. Henry Jr. seemed initially to be content with discussing political issues with his father, but business interests in Louisville and Lexington led to more involvement. It was also clear that observers of politics fully expected the son of Henry Clay to play a political role. In 1833 Henry Jr. delivered a speech at the commencement service of Transylvania University. The local newspaper reported on it twice, and the *New York Observer* compared him to his father, even speculating as to whether Henry Sr. could have been such an accomplished speaker at the same age. In 1834 the young Clay served as a delegate to the Whig state convention and then ran successfully to represent Fayette County in the Kentucky General

Assembly, serving from 1835 to 1837. Like his father, he spoke most eloquently in defense of lost causes, but he made no serious enemies and was reelected from his district.[59]

Henry Sr. did use his political influence to help his son secure a diplomatic post. President William Henry Harrison promised Henry Clay Jr. an appointment to Belgium, but John Tyler later refused to authorize it. Daniel Webster then offered him the post of secretary of legation to Russia, but the Clays decided to decline because they did not trust Tyler's motives. Henry Clay held a grudge over the incident for many years.[60]

In 1845 Henry Clay Jr. considered running for the House of Representatives from the Louisville district. His father quickly gave his blessing and expressed his pleasure in his son's desire to serve. Jokingly, Clay questioned whether the connection to him would be of any benefit but hoped it would at least not cause harm to Henry Jr.'s candidacy.[61] The younger Clay chose not to run, instead supporting another Whig candidate, but he clearly had politics in mind. When the Mexican War broke out, Clay volunteered for service of another kind. Named a lieutenant colonel of Kentucky volunteers, he sought to add military glory to a prominent name. In the antebellum era, such a combination had obvious political advantages.

Henry also used his political clout to obtain a diplomatic appointment for his son James. On May 12, 1849, he wrote to President Zachary Taylor seeking an appointment for James. Noting the difficulties of a father describing the qualifications of a son, he suggested that James was "free from all habits of dissipation whatever, and has great industry, with remarkable capacity for the transaction of business." He also praised his skills as a lawyer. Henry could comment on those skills because he had resumed the practice of law primarily to help establish for James some "permanent & agreeable employment."[62] On May 28 Taylor responded that he would be delighted to find a position for the son of Henry Clay. Within a week, James received an appointment as charge d'affaires to Portugal. Henry also encouraged his friend John M. Clayton, Taylor's new secretary of state, to help James learn the skills necessary to a diplomat.[63]

President Taylor nominated James on January 4, 1850, and the Senate confirmed his appointment on March 24.[64] The position was an important one because Taylor intended to vigorously pursue claims against Portugal that had existed since the War of 1812. The claims centered on Portugal's failure to provide protection against British aggression for American ships in its ports. The largest claim involved the *General Armstrong,* an American vessel the British had attempted to board. Portugal should have extended protection but did not. The Taylor administration intended to demand full compensation.[65]

Both father and son approached James's diplomatic duties with characteristic Clay energy. And in this instance, they were joined by a third party, James's wife, Susan. James presented the American demands of the Taylor administration to the Portuguese government. The American position was harsh, and so was James's presentation of it. James had a temper and a strong sense of honor. Both were characteristics of several generations of Clays. James justified his undiplomatic language to his father by claiming he found a number of unanswered communiqués to the Portuguese government upon his arrival. He also believed his reception by the Portuguese to be less than it should have been for the representative of the United States. Finally, he argued that the claims had been on the table since the War of 1812 and the Portuguese had done nothing.

Historians have generally assumed a lack of diplomacy on James's part, virtually a repetition of his father's conduct at Ghent, but the State Department appears to have been urging a strong stance as well.[66] Henry proved to be the more diplomatic of the two. He urged James to tone down his language, and he worked in Washington to achieve some compromise. In conversations with the Portuguese minister, J. C. de Figaniere e Morao, Henry soothed feelings ruffled by James's abruptness. He visited the State Department regularly to read James's communiqués and maintained a dialogue with the Portuguese minister, essentially working out an agreement in their private correspondence. The ambassador agreed to convince his government to pay the smaller claims if the United States agreed to arbitration with regard to the *General Armstrong.* Henry defended James's request for the documents between Portugal and Great Britain on the issue, but he admitted that James's language could have been more discreet. On another front, in conversations with Sir Henry Bulwer, Clay sought to influence Lord Palmerston of the British government to negotiate in good faith.[67] Throughout the affair, Henry advised his son to speak diplomatically instead of as a lawyer. The brash young diplomat at Ghent had obviously matured. James, on the other hand, was in an enviable position for a young diplomat: he was getting advice from an experienced statesman who had his personal interest wholly at heart.[68]

The death of Zachary Taylor and the accession of Millard Fillmore allowed both the United States and Portugal to seek a compromise. Daniel

Webster, the new secretary of state, and the Portuguese minister agreed to a settlement similar to that worked out earlier by Clay. The smaller claims would be paid, and the *General Armstrong* case could be negotiated by the French head of state, Louis Napoleon Bonaparte. Anxious that James receive credit for bringing the negotiations to a successful conclusion, Clay asked President Fillmore to allow James to complete the work. Both Fillmore and Webster agreed. James stated in communication with Webster that he would have preferred a position more in line with the final settlement but had been bound by his instructions. He suggested that a new emissary might be more acceptable to the Portuguese government.[69] Though twice noting in a letter of November 5 that it was James's decision whether to return to Lisbon, Webster clearly preferred that someone else be appointed. He eventually named his own nephew to the position.[70]

David and Jeanne Heidler describe James's diplomatic venture as a failure, but the evidence supports a different interpretation. James did not complete the mission, but claims that had stained U.S.-Portuguese relations for nearly forty years were settled shortly after his departure. It would not be the last time the United States would use a carrot-and-stick approach to diplomacy. Moreover, James returned to the United States with a reputation as a successful emissary of his government and as a man who would stand firmly for his country. President Fillmore mentioned the negotiations and noted favorably James's role in his first message to Congress.[71] Henry was pleased. At the age of thirty-three, James was a good lawyer, an astute businessman, and a successful diplomat.

Clay expended significant effort to help his sons become productive members of society. His efforts suggest a more positive assessment than Remini's "wretched father." He recognized the strengths and weaknesses of his sons. Perhaps he recognized his own "passions" in them. Clay never stopped trying with any of his sons. To their credit, the four youngest sons made an effort as well. The depression suffered by each of the five sons was both episodic and of varying degrees of intensity. Such conditions would be frightening today; they must have been terrifying to a father in an age with little knowledge of mood disorders.[72] The Clay sons inherited from their father a sense of risk taking, but he helped them channel it into business ventures. He also sought to teach them the importance of serving their country. Observing four successful sons, Henry Clay undoubtedly took considerable pride, and credit, in the accomplishment.

Chapter 4

A DEEP ACQUAINTANCE
WITH GRIEF

If the struggles of his sons frustrated the rising statesman and politician, other events within the family humbled him. Indeed, the tragedies suffered by the first generation of his descendants contributed to that control of his passions noted by Daniel Walker Howe and other biographers.

Illness and disease plagued the Clay household, and death was too frequently the family's companion. Lucretia and Henry seemed constantly to be fighting one illness for another. Lucretia's plight was all too common among nineteenth-century women. Frequent childbirth weakened her, making it difficult for her to fight the illnesses common to the era. Henry also suffered from susceptibility to colds, flu, and practically any other contagious malady. There are more than a thousand references to his bouts of illness in the collected correspondence spanning approximately fifty years. In midlife he fell victim to consumption, or tuberculosis, the disease that eventually took his life. The Clay children suffered a susceptibility to illness staggering even in a century characterized by high infant and child mortality rates.

Henry and Lucretia virtually began their marriage with loss. Married on April 11, 1799, they welcomed the first of six daughters, Henrietta, on June 25, 1800. She lived less than a year. Losing children in their first year was a fact of life in the early nineteenth century. But the Clays would mourn the loss of all six of their daughters.

The deaths of two daughters were clearly entangled with Henry's career. In 1816, as was customary in the early years, Lucretia and the youngest children accompanied him to Washington. It was the dead of winter, and even in the best of times the trip was a grueling coach ride over rough cart paths that barely qualified as roads. It is little wonder that Clay supported a network of highways uniting the country as part of his American System. The Cumberland Highway, a portion of his route to Washington, was one of the first on his agenda. In 1816 several of the Clay children developed whooping cough on that cold, damp journey. The youngest child, Laura, just a few months old, probably should not have been taken on such a difficult journey, but in his youth Henry's enthusiasm for his role in Washington overshadowed common sense.

The family reached Washington, but Laura died on January 5, 1817. Margaret Bayard Smith wrote about Henry's reaction and the issues that entwined his sense of public duty and responsibility to family. Henry Clay sat by the child's bedside, holding her in her final hours. At her death he cried gently and tenderly kissed the dead child, remaining with her for some time. The next morning, however, he prepared to leave for the Capitol. Smith quoted him as saying, "I have no right to allow private concerns to interfere with public duty." Smith convinced him that his primary responsibility was to his family.[1] Henry reserved a plot in the congressional cemetery for his infant daughter. Many years later he would sit at the bedside of his son John, who had a life-threatening illness. He did provide care for his children, but the conflict of responsibilities led to difficult choices.[2]

The 1820s proved especially tragic for Henry and Lucretia. On June 18, 1823, they lost a third daughter, fourteen-year-old Lucretia Hart Clay. Apparently bright and vivacious, Lucretia attended the Lexington Female Academy. Henry served on the board of visitors and praised the school. According to a Lexington newspaper, Lucretia was chosen to read a composition at a celebration for the academy.[3] On June 11, 1823, Henry noted in a letter to Nicholas Biddle, the president of the Bank of the United States, that he could not appear in a court hearing in Cincinnati because one of his children was "extremely ill" and he did not want to be so far away from her.[4] Young Lucretia died a week later. No further mention of her illness or death appears in the family correspondence.[5]

In 1825 Henry and Lucretia lost two more daughters. The Clays set out for Washington in July because Henry would assume the duties of secretary of state in the Adams administration. Stung, no doubt, by charges of a corrupt bargain with Adams, he was anxious to get to the capital, where he could show his strengths in office. He was always excited by new opportunities, and this one had traditionally led to the presidency, the office he coveted. Before they reached Cincinnati, however, twelve-year-old Eliza became ill. Clay consulted a physician, but from that point it is difficult to verify the sequence of events because the only account comes from Clay. According to Clay, the physician assured him that Eliza's condition was sufficiently improved that the family could continue its journey. However, they stopped again in Lebanon, Ohio, because Eliza had taken a turn for the worse. The family rented lodging and remained for two weeks. Obviously impatient, Henry heard the physicians say she was recovering and that it was safe for him to proceed alone to Washington. Lucretia and the other children would remain in Lebanon until Eliza could travel. The day before Clay reached the nation's capital, he read in the newspaper that Eliza had died on August 11.

This time, Henry's sense of loss may well have been compounded by guilt at having left his family. His responses to Lucretia reflect his tortured thought. He apologized to Lucretia for leaving her in Ohio, but abdicated personal responsibility because he acted only after the physicians said Eliza was recovering. For a brief moment, he realized how self-absorbed he could be. He could understand Lucretia's grief only because his own was so intense. "I cannot describe to you my own distressed feelings," he wrote, "which have been greatly aggravated by a knowledge of what your's [sic] must have been, in the midst of strangers, and all your friends so far away."[6]

More than the conflict between public duty and private concerns affected Clay's decision making in such crises. He struggled with his own nature. Did he, in fact, hear the physicians say Eliza was recovering? Or is that what he wanted to hear? Obsessive at times, Henry Clay could easily convince himself that what seemed most important to him at the moment was equally important to others. A man of intense passions by nature, he could feel grief intensely and recover as quickly. Margaret Bayard Smith claimed that occasional depression seemed to give new vigor to his "elastic" power. What she meant by elastic power is unclear, but her account of emotional extremes is. As noted in chapter 1, Susan M. Clay, Henry's daughter-in-law, claimed he was "delicately strung." "A word, a touch, a memory," and certainly an opportunity such as the position of secretary of state, could create extreme agitation.[7] The same traits that made Henry Clay the politician change position too quickly, to seem ambitious rather than principled, appeared in Henry Clay the husband and father.

Scarcely a month after the loss of Eliza, tragedy struck again. Susan Hart Clay Duralde died of yellow fever on September 18, 1825. In the space of just over two years, the Clays experienced the deaths of three of their daughters.

Henry Clay's relationship with his two oldest daughters presents a picture of contradictions. Both daughters married very young, and Henry seemed to be more interested in the business potential of their husbands than anything else.[8] Susan Hart Clay married Martin Duralde Jr. of New Orleans on April 22, 1822. John Clay, Henry's brother, had married Julie Duralde, and Clay knew Martin Duralde Sr. through business and political connections. Given the business connections of many Lexington families in New Orleans, Susan's marriage could have been another effort to solidify Clay's own business interests. The Clays were delighted, however, when Susan presented them with their first grandchild less than a year after her marriage. A year later, she had a second son, Henry Clay Duralde, the first namesake. The correspondence between Susan and her parents suggests a comfortable relationship, almost one of equals. Lucretia and her daughter had sons nearly the same age. Susan wrote to her mother as if to a friend, discussing the health of her children and other bits of information.[9]

On September 19, 1825, Etienne Mazureau, a friend of the Duraldes, wrote to inform Henry of Susan's death. Barely twenty years old, Susan left two sons, one not yet weaned.[10] Susan's death may well mark the first time Henry questioned his own invincibility. Although he was so successful in his youth, the tragedies in his life were beginning to mount up. He had polled far fewer votes in the election of 1824 than he expected, then suffered the harsh criticism surrounding the Jackson camp's "corrupt bargain" charge. But he had also lost five daughters. Clay sunk into one of his dark periods, and a more sober, pensive Henry Clay emerged. Margaret Bayard Smith noted that "the coldness and hauteur of his manner has vanished and a softness and tenderness and sadness characterize his manner." The change was most evident in his discussion of family matters. He began to speak of the "afflictions" visited upon his family. Momentarily, grief overcame any concern with politics. Responding to a letter of condolence addressed to Lucretia, Henry wrote to family friend Charlotte Mentelle:

> Our last affliction has almost overwhelmed us. We were beginning to be composed, by reflection, by occupations, and by time, as to that which preceded it [the death of Eliza]. But this new, unexpected, and severe blow has opened again all the sources of our grief. The calm self possession with which our poor Susan met her untimely fate. . . . Her last care seemed to be for us and for her children. She knew, by her own feelings as a mother, what must be ours. Ah! Madam, is it not cruel out of six daughters to be deprived of all but one![11]

This time Henry tried to share the grief of his wife. He admired Lucretia's stoic acceptance of their fate, but he also found reasons to explain her ability to cope with their tragedies when he could not. He suggested that "the character of her sex" gave her additional strength to face such sadness, and he noted her strong religious convictions. Henry Clay had felt no personal need for religion, and although he would not officially be baptized until 1847, Lucretia's strength in the face of continuing crisis was not lost on him. He spoke more frequently of the hand of "Providence" after Susan's death. That said, he could not console others for thinking of his own losses. Writing to Christopher Hughes, who was returning to the United States from a diplomatic post because of the death of both his parents, he compared the grief of losing aged parents with the "greater loss" of two daughters, "just risen or rising into majority, concentrating a large share of our hopes and affections."[12]

Robert Remini has noted that Henry Clay suffered ill health throughout his term as secretary of state. From Clay's own words, Remini concludes that it was the twelve- and fourteen-hour workdays that sapped his strength.[13] The problem seems larger. The deaths of Eliza and Susan were only the beginning of the "afflictions" that plagued the Clay family during those years. Surely the grief and stress caused by the mournful family history in those years were equally important contributors to Clay's own health problems. After Susan's death, Theodore and Thomas confronted him with the worst excesses of their own behavior. Frustration and a sense of helplessness frequently appeared in his correspondence.

Clay limped back to Kentucky in 1829, forced into retirement by Jackson's victory and in need of rest and recuperation. He would achieve neither. In 1829 his stepfather, a brother, and his mother died in rapid succession. Clay also had concerns about the son historians have called his favorite. During his years at West Point, Henry Jr. had exhibited periodic bouts of melancholy that Clay could easily see in his two older sons. Clay had carefully encouraged Henry Jr., creating an intimacy that gave his son some confidence. When the young Clay began to practice law, he exhibited the enthusiasm that the Clays generally brought to new projects, but it was short lived. He wanted the golden ring without the labor required. Henry understood the problem, and he worried about his son.

He soon had greater concerns. Theodore's problems went far deeper than gambling, an inability to settle on a profession, or living in the shadow of a famous father. At the age of twenty-eight, Theodore found himself an inmate at the Lexington Lunatic Asylum, sent there by order of a jury called by the county sheriff.[14] Henry had noted the deterioration of his son. Theodore suffered from mood swings, exhibiting "a horrible temper." But in 1830 he became infatuated with a young woman who did not return his affections. With regard to her, according to his father, Theodore became "quite deranged."[15] He pursued her with diligence far greater than he had ever applied to his labors and sufficient to make her very uncomfortable. He stalked her in Lexington, went without sleep, and acted irrationally. Family correspondence is generally discreet, but court records and the *New York Times* claimed he went to the young woman's home with a pistol and demanded that the father give him her hand in marriage.[16]

Befitting Victorian discretion, the young woman's name was never mentioned in print; however, court records indicate who she was. John Brand and his son William brought charges against Theodore for lunacy and being a threat to their safety. Ironically, the Brands were close friends of Henry, and in June Henry Jr. had visited with William Brand and his sister Eliza when they were in New York.[17]

The family, particularly Henry, held out some hope that Theodore might be cured. Unfortunately, there was little. The mental hospital in Lexington was a custodial facility housing primarily those who posed a threat to themselves or others. Characterized by what Ronald F. White called a "cult of incurability," the asylum buried a much higher number of its patients than it cured.[18] Theodore appears to have received better care than most, perhaps because he was the son of Henry Clay. His physician, Dr. J. C. Jordan, seemed ahead of his time in his treatment. He decided that Theodore might be helped through exercise. Henry sent a horse and Theodore's saddle to the asylum. He also dispatched a servant to care for him. He wrote letters to his son when away and encouraged family members to visit him.[19]

After a series of short visits, Theodore was allowed to return to Ashland in late 1832. Lucretia, however, was convinced that he remained "deranged." A year later, the family, or at least a part of it, decided he had to be committed again. Henry Clay Jr. let his father know he had not been a part of the decision. Henry Clay Jr.'s explanation of the events suggests a young man who could not make up his mind, or one who feared his father's reaction to the news. He wrote to Clay that Anne, Mr. Erwin, and the rest of the family, "with the exception of myself," decided that Theodore's malady was growing worse. When the commissioners asked for his consent, Henry Clay Jr. responded that he would have nothing to do with the matter. In the letter, Henry Jr. seemed to deny responsibility even as he assumed leadership of the family in his father's absence. Although he had nothing to do with the decision, he did not object to Theodore's hospitalization. The asylum asked him, as the brother and "nearest relative present," to pay expenses and give his bond for $500. In fact, Lucretia and his older brother Thomas were both at Ashland. Henry Jr. then laid the responsibility for putting Theodore in the hospital on Anne: "This is my part in the affair. I am not the mover in the business, nor, I may say, a participant, for Anne selected her course without consulting with me. She placed him where he is. But now let me say, my dear father, without I beseech your having my motives impugned, that Anne has done right."[20]

The letter adds credence to Harriet Martineau's description of Henry Jr. as jealous. He wanted to be his father's favorite son. In the same letter, he mentioned that Thomas was drinking heavily again. Both older brothers diminished in his father's affections, at least as he interpreted it; and, if Clay opposed Theodore's incarceration, Anne's place in the family hierarchy might be jeopardized as well. Clay, in fact, approved of his daughter's actions when he learned the details. Theodore's conduct had become potentially dangerous to himself and to other members of the family.[21]

The family increasingly lost hope, but Henry continued to believe his son would recover. According to Dr. Jordan, Theodore reacted very badly to Henry's correspondence, so he urged Clay to stop writing and sending magazines and speeches to him. The doctors claimed that Theodore was deranged on two subjects: love and ambition. Miss Brand's impending marriage would solve the first problem. His ambition would be moderated, they argued, by humiliation. Henry's letters suggested to Theodore that his father valued his political opinions. As Henry Jr. interpreted the physicians, family members had too long listened to Theodore's eccentric political views without properly challenging them. Consequently, he had too high an opinion of his own views.[22] Henry reluctantly agreed to follow the doctors' advice.

In late 1833, however, Henry Jr. again suggested to his father that he distance himself from Theodore: "Let me say with a full knowledge of what I owe to you and to my mother, that we should allow the best physicians to operate with this most subtle and distressing disorder. When he [Theodore] was in the Hospital before, his health was reestablished and his mind certainly improved. Let us then curb our feelings and not destroy our brother and our child by mistimed affection."[23] Henry curbed his feelings, but he continued to provide for Theodore's needs. In Henry's last will, written in 1851, he provided funds to ensure support for Theodore at the asylum. Additionally, he designated $10,000 for Theodore, "should it please God to restore him to reason."[24]

Henry Jr.'s faith in the doctors at the Lexington Lunatic Asylum was, in retrospect, ill placed. Efforts to obtain Theodore's medical records have been unsuccessful, but it seems likely that the treatment as much as his condition led to further deterioration. Ten years later, John Morrison Clay, the youngest of the Clay children, would be committed with the same symptoms—described as worse than those of Theodore—but a reform movement at the facility had created enough progress that John could function outside the institution. Theodore walked the wards of the asylum, tapping the bars like "a caged beast," according to John Joyce. Joyce, who spent time as a patient in the asylum, recalled Theodore as a "chattering lunatic."[25] Local legend claims he would introduce himself as George Washington incarcerated against his will.

The family began to make its own history to explain Theodore's madness. If the account follows a normal pattern of Clay family mythmaking, it is based in fact and the interpretation twisted to meet family needs. While watching a servant cut wood as a child, Theodore was hit in the head by an ax that slipped from the handle. Dr. Pindell (probably Richard Pindell, Lucretia's brother-in-law) used a procedure called trepanning, or drilling a hole in the skull, to relieve the pressure. According to the Clays, Pindell said Theodore would eventually be forced into an insane asylum because of the injury. There is far too much evidence to the contrary to accept that version in its entirety. Although Theodore may have been seriously injured in his youth, the actions of Henry Clay's sons suggest a pattern within the family. Many of the Clays were exceptionally bright, intellectually curious people, but their "passions" often led to impetuous, even reckless behavior. Theodore was clearly the extreme, but the family had to commit an uninjured John Morrison Clay to the same asylum ten years later, suffering from exactly the same symptoms.[26]

The Clays would endure another "affliction" before being visited by John's mental instability. The daughter who gave Henry so much pleasure, the daughter who could be counted on to make difficult decisions even when his sons vacillated, Anne Clay Erwin, a twenty-eight-year-old mother of six, died on December 10, 1835. Henry Clay learned of her death a week later. Talking with colleagues on December 18, Clay received two letters. The first one, from James Erwin, said Anne was recovering well after the birth of her son, Charles Edward. The second letter, from Bishop Benjamin Smith, rector of Christ Church in Lexington, informed him that Anne had died.[27] When he received the news, Clay fainted. According to Margaret Bayard Smith, when he regained consciousness he said that "every tie in life is broken," and he began to weep uncontrollably. He was nearly destroyed by this loss, the last of six daughters and the one in whom he found such joy.[28]

Robert Remini writes that Clay had probably never been so affected by death. Yet, since the death of Susan, he had lived with a sense of foreboding. He had grown rather dependent on Anne. He wrote to Henry Clay Jr. in 1830, "The sole survivor of all my daughters, I feel on that account as well as for her excellent qualities, the greatest interest and affection for her." Clay rarely commented on family matters in political correspondence, but in an 1828 letter to Daniel Webster he wrote enthusiastically about an impending visit from Anne. Again, she was his "only surviving daughter," but she was also "the best of girls." On another occasion, he described her as one of the "few sources which I have of real happiness."[29]

Clay's grief may also have been deepened by the fact that, once again, he left the bedside of a daughter with strong misgivings about her health. Anne gave birth to Charles Edward on November 2. She had returned to Lexington, where her mother and the family servants could help her, but the scourge of nineteenth-century women had taken a toll on her. Seven pregnancies in twelve years (one ending in miscarriage) drained her physical resources. Clay debated the best course of action. He needed to be in Washington to lead the diverse factions of the anti-Jackson coalition if they were ever to coalesce into a united effort; and there seems little doubt that he genuinely feared a danger to the Constitution and republican government if the Jacksonians continued to control the national government. Yet, he worried about Anne as well. On November 19 he wrote to Lucretia, "I feel very uneasy about our dear daughter Anne. I sincerely hope that she may get well, and that all my apprehensions may prove groundless."[30] After a favorable report in early December, he wrote again, "My anxiety about her I cannot describe. Our only daughter—and so good a daughter—there is no event that would so entirely overwhelm us as that of her loss."[31]

Anne's death brought a major change in the priorities of the Clay family. Henry faced, perhaps for the first time, his inability to control the elements of his universe. He could neither eat nor sleep. He repeatedly broke into tears at the thought of Anne's loss. He wrote Margaret Bayard Smith, "My daughter was so good, so dutiful, so affectionate: her tastes and sympathies and amusements were so identical with my own; she was so interwoven with every plan and prospect of passing the remnant of my days, that I feel I have sustained a loss which can never be repaired.[32] Nearly three weeks after her death, he tried to address the Senate but broke down at the podium.

His letters to Lucretia again reveal the many facets of the private Henry Clay. As usual, he spoke of his own grief:

> Alas! My dear wife, the great Destroyer has come, and taken from us our dear, dear, only daughter. . . . If the thunderbolt of heaven had fallen on me—unprepared as I fear I am—I would have submitted . . . to a thousand deaths to have saved this dear child. She was so good, so beloving, and so beloved, so happy, and so deserving to be happy. Then, she was the last of six dear daughters. . . . Ah! how inscrutable are the ways of providence? I feel that one of the strongest ties that bound me to earth is broken—forever broken. My heart will bleed as long as it palpitates. Never, never, can its wounds be healed.

Clay questioned his religious faith. He had prayed for the restoration of Anne's health, but his prayers went unanswered. He grieved for James Erwin and for Anne's orphaned children. He then realized he should console Lucretia, attempted to console her, but fell back on his own grief: "My dear, I ought to endeavor to comfort you, and I am shewing my weakness. I cannot help it. This dear child was so entwined around my heart I looked forward to so many days of comfort and happiness in her company, during the remnant of my life, that I shall never, never be able to forget her."[33] He never managed to comfort Lucretia, nor did he return home to be with her.

The conflict of private and public duties continued, but this time it led to inertia. Clay could not forsake his duties in Washington to give or receive comfort at home, but he was too distracted, disinterested, and morose to function effectively. He wrote to Thomas Speed that he was considering retirement from public life.[34]

He did not retire, but what the harsh accusations of politics could not do, the "afflictions" experienced by his family could. Henry Clay was humbled. Letters spanning a decade revealed that this time he did not escape grief so easily. Now he wrote more woefully, and his correspondence suggests that he was less certain of the power of Henry Clay and more dependent on a merciful God: "My poor wife has suffered beyond expression; but she has in affliction a resource—a great resource—which I have not." In 1847 he consented to baptism by the Episcopal bishop, but the internal process began with Anne's death.

Nor could Henry escape the memory of his daughters. In 1844 he wrote to his friend Octavia Walton LeVert urging her to care for her health, comparing his reaction should anything happen to her with that he experienced when Anne died.[35] Painfully, he wrote to George McClellan in 1846, "Ah! My dear friend, I hope you have had a less measure of affliction than has fallen to my lot. Death, ruthless death, has deprived me of Six affectionate daughters, all that I ever had, and has now commenced his work of destruction, with my descendants, in the second generation. I bow submissively to the dispensations of an All-wise and merciful Providence thankful that I have been myself so long spared, altho' spared to witness and to feel these great misfortunes, not to speak of others which I have painfully experienced."[36] As the letter implies, Henry and Lucretia had not yet experienced their full quota of tragedies. Tragedy would engulf the third generation, but it had not finished with the second either.

In 1845 John Morrison Clay followed the same path to insanity as Theodore. In March Henry said that John "exhibited decided symptoms of mental aberration." Then, on April 5, Henry wrote to Henry Clay Jr.:

> The night before last he was roaming about the woods until two o'clock in the morning. Altho' he offered violence to no one, he was wild and boisterous in his language, and it was often incoherent. The painful conviction was at length forced upon me that it was necessary, and a duty on my part to have him confined. It has greatly afflicted me. He threatened his own life, and declared to more than one that he intended to terminate it last night. His passion for Miss J____ revived, and yesterday he attempted to see her, but she, being advised of his situation, properly declined to receive him.[37]

Concerns for John were compounded by past realities. The Clays compared the situation with the experience of Theodore more than ten years earlier. John's symptoms seemed worse than those of Theodore: "I find it extremely hard to bear this last sad affliction. It has put in requisition the utmost fortitude I can command." The family also experienced the same uncertainty they had known with Theodore. After a short period of treatment, John begged to be released. Henry wanted to bring him home yet feared doing so. He wrote that while in the asylum, John continued to comprehend his situation and felt his confinement with the keenest pain. His brother Theodore felt no pain.[38] Better treatment allowed John to live outside the asylum, but his behavior was eccentric at best, and he had a volatile temper. It was one more affliction Henry and Lucretia had to bear; they watched for the slightest symptom that might indicate a return of his illness.[39]

One further tragedy, actually a combination of tragedies, befell Henry and Lucretia regarding their children. On February 13, 1840, two weeks after giving birth to her fifth child in seven years, Julia Prather Clay died. Her death sent Henry Jr. back into the depths of depression. He wandered aimlessly, essentially abandoning his children to relatives. Although Henry Clay never used the word, he clearly feared suicide. He wrote to Lucretia that he entertained "great apprehensions as to the effects upon him [Henry Jr.] of this severe visitation." He also expressed his concerns to Thomas and James. With Henry Jr. he used all the inducements in his arsenal. He emphasized family: Julia had left him "tender and responsible duties to perform." He emphasized children: he had a duty to them. And he reminded Henry Jr. of his duty to his father: "How one after another are the objects which fastened me to this life passing away and leaving me with scarcely any wish but that I may soon follow them. Whatever might be my desire that must be my fate. During the short remnant of my life, I too shall need your kindness and affectionate attention. I beg therefore, on my account, as well as that of my dear Grand children you will take care of yourself."[40] Henry Clay knew his son well. On February 20, one week after Julia's death, Henry Jr. wrote in his diary, "I cannot divest myself of the idea that my wife and sister are calling me to a more perfect place of rest."[41]

Henry Clay Jr. did not commit suicide, at least in the traditional sense. He wandered about the country. There were times Henry did not know where his son was. His children lived in Louisville with Nanette Price Smith, Lucretia Clay's niece, or at Ashland with Henry and Lucretia. Henry Jr.'s wealth allowed him to provide financially for his children, but it did not help him find the peace he needed. He read books about melancholy suggested by friends, and he expressed his maudlin thoughts in his diary. When the Mexican War broke out, Henry Clay Jr. volunteered, despite the fact that his father opposed the war. There, too, depression seemed to overtake him. His enthusiasm for the war, if it can be called that, waned when he injured himself falling from a horse. It was rumored he had been drinking. He also found fault with his commanding officer, and he longed for the war to be over, convinced that he would find no honor in it. On February 23, 1847, wounded in the thigh in the Battle of Buena Vista, he ordered his men to leave him. At first they refused, but they finally did as he said, allegedly to save their own lives. Henry Jr. had time, however, to give the pistols his father had sent with him to Captain George Cutter, requesting that they be returned to his father because he had no more use for them. He died from multiple stab wounds by Mexican lancers.[42]

The stories surrounding his death resemble the myths that often develop around casualties of war, particularly in family versions. His legacy joined that of his father for later generations. It was a story of gallantry and courage, of patriotism and service. A lithograph titled "Death of Lieut. Col. Henry Clay, Jr." is in the collection of the Library of Congress, and his body rests in the military cemetery in Frankfort, Kentucky, along with others who gave their lives in the nation's wars. The Clay family had added its blood to its gifts to the nation.[43]

For the now aging statesman, "death, ruthless death" had visited the family again. Some wounds, he lamented like a modern Job, were "so deep and agonizing that He only can heal them, by whose inscrutable dispensations they have been permitted to be inflicted." So confident, so assertive, so in command, Clay now wrote to a friend that he was striving to "bow and submit, in meekness and humility." He left his beloved Ashland; it reminded him too much of his son. He left Lucretia; to look at her increased his anguish. In time, Clay began to console himself with thoughts of service. It would have been his son's choice, and his choice for that son—to die "on the field of battle, in the service of his country."[44]

Henry Clay suffered his own melancholy with this new affliction. For a time, the memories at Ashland plagued him so badly he found it difficult to stay in the place that meant so much to him. Leaving Lucretia in Kentucky, he traveled alone, seeking solace. He also submitted to baptism. But he did again achieve mastery over his emotions. Henry had three remaining sons and a new generation, his grandchildren, who needed his guidance. Henry and Lucretia Clay essentially had a second family of children. The major reason Lucretia did not accompany Henry to Washington, D.C., after 1835 was that the Duralde and Erwin children were often at Ashland, and in 1847 the children of Henry Clay Jr. became an additional concern.

As in the case of their own children, Henry took responsibility for the education of his grandchildren, Lucretia for their nurturing. He sent four grandsons to Transylvania. Martin and Henry Clay Duralde joined John Morrison Clay at the Edgehill Academy, and several grandsons attended a school in Jamaica, New York. Henry later sent the Duraldes and Charles Edward Erwin to the Lafayette Academy, a school in Lexington operated by Beverly Hicks, and he regularly received bills and receipts related to their board and tuition.[45] In 1847 Clay paid tuition for Eugene and Charles Edward Erwin, and Henry Clay III, the son of Henry Clay Jr., at the Kentucky Military Institute. Later he secured an appointment for Henry Clay III at West Point.

Clay offered his grandsons the same advice he had given his own sons, and with about as much success. Intelligent, personable, and energetic, they displayed the same patterns of behavior as his sons: lack of direction, reckless conduct, living beyond their means, gambling, and drinking. There were a few exceptions, but far too few. There were also too many early, and frequently senseless, deaths. In his letter to George McClellan, in addition to noting the deaths of his six daughters, Clay stated that death had begun its work in the next generation. He was referring to the death of Martin Duralde III in 1846. Duralde died of tuberculosis, but his habits had been suspect as well. Henry had secured for Duralde a position in the U.S. Navy, but the young man began to complain about colds and a loss of energy. Henry at first wondered whether it was not the dreaded dissipation. Both the Duralde grandsons were spendthrifts and gamblers. When Martin began to hemorrhage from the lungs, Henry took it more seriously. Martin spent the winter of 1845–1846 in Cuba, probably at Henry's expense, and then joined his grandfather at Red Sulphur Spring seeking a cure. In September 1846 he died at a Philadelphia sanatorium at the age of twenty-three. Henry resolutely paid his funeral bills.[46]

Henry Clay Jr. died in 1847, and the next year grandson James Erwin committed suicide. He had been drinking and gambling the night before. Henry Clay called him "promising," but he was dead at the age of twenty.[47] The loss of the presidential election in 1844 had sent Henry Clay into a period of depression, but there was no relief for him. Two grandsons and a son had died in less than three years.

As Henry Clay struggled with his own health and the effort to fashion the Compromise of 1850, he lost another grandson. Henry Clay Duralde had been beyond control since childhood. In 1845 Lucretia banned him from Ashland because of his behavior the year before. He admitted that his conduct had been "disgraceful in the extreme." Like his Uncle Thomas, he promised to reform. He had "frequented no places of amusement, nor tasted a drop of liquor." He begged to be allowed to return to his "beloved Ashland."[48]

Lucretia did not relent. Duralde went to New Orleans, hardly a city that lent itself to reform of the type Duralde needed. When his grandfather visited the city in 1849, Duralde would not see him. Later he wrote, "I, at once gave myself up to the gratification of my passions, making pleasure and dissipation my idols . . . almost ruining my constitution." He did not see his grandfather, he said, because he did not want to lie to him. Instead, promising once again to reform and blaming his problems on the temptations of New Orleans, he went to California, but no reform followed. On September 5, 1850, he drowned in the Sacramento River. The letters of consolation that flowed back to Kentucky described him in terms used frequently with regard to Clay family members: charming and friendly, a young man of talent, promise, and moral worth. He made friends quickly, though perhaps not wisely, and he spent lavishly, securing money on his grandfather's name. Henry paid his grandson's debts, and the funeral expenses.[49]

Other grandchildren escaped death, but they were no less taxing on Clay's fragile constitution. Clay expended great effort to get Henry Clay III, a son of Henry Jr., into the military academy, but the young man had already exhibited the less attractive Clay traits. He started projects then lost interest. He challenged all disciplinary rules. He performed badly in school. Clay convinced James to take the young man to Portugal with him in 1849. He thought travel might inspire Henry III. James found a school for him there, but the boy refused to study. James wrote that Henry III was "inert, lazy, and excessively selfish." Henry made excuses for his grandson, expressing the hope that he might mature. He even suggested to James that Henry III's faults could be worse. But then Henry clashed with his Aunt Susan, and that got him sent home. James wrote him a long letter citing his rudeness, irresponsibility, and selfishness, predicting dire consequences if he did not change, and like his own father, suggesting the embarrassment to the family the boy might cause. Disappointed but undaunted, Henry enrolled him at Georgetown College in Washington, D.C., writing optimistically to James that he seemed content there.[50]

Witty, urbane, and at least outwardly self-confident, Henry III wrote letters that resemble those of his uncle, Theodore Clay. He wanted to appear knowledgeable, but he was often glib and intellectually shallow. Unable to focus on his studies, he crammed late to survive academically.

What he could not control was his conduct. His grandfather secured an appointment to West Point, but his record reveals his inability to sustain the necessary effort. In his first year he ranked twenty-seventh in his class, but he fell to thirty-eighth in 1852. He found the academy too confining, and he began to collect demerits at an unbelievably fast rate. Young Henry was consistently late, particularly for breakfast, and he rarely conformed to military discipline. He received demerits for marching incorrectly, talking in rank, refusing to shine his shoes, failing to get a haircut, throwing bread in the mess hall, spitting tobacco juice in the hall, and chewing tobacco in the ranks. In a French class, he was caught reading for another class, and on several occasions he left his rifle in the hall or cafeteria. Henry Clay III was undisciplined and, on occasion, insubordinate.[51]

Henry begged his grandson to try harder. He tried the same arguments and offered the same advice used with his sons. Invoking the Clay name, he warned of the disgrace that accompanied failure. He appealed to his grandson's pride "as a man and as a soldier." He even alluded to the fact that he received the appointment rather than his cousin: "How would poor Eugene Erwin rejoice if he had your situation!" Henry Clay's parenting skills still succumbed to exasperation. There was, however, already a sign of defeat that one rarely saw in the correspondence of the statesman: "I am sorry that you find your confinement disagreeable; but my dear child it is impossible that you should ever become distinguished and worthy of your lamented father and worthy of me, without study, close study, and some sacrifices of ease and comfort." When young Henry wanted to leave the academy, Clay asked him what he would do if he left. "You must be employed," he wrote, "or you would be in the greatest danger of idleness and dissipation." He urged his grandson to work to remove the demerits that sullied his name.[52] He was unsuccessful.

With the exception of Eugene, the Erwin children were additional disappointments to their grandparents. Later generations, blaming the Erwins rather than the Clays for the numerous embarrassments in the family history, refused to speak about James Erwin and his descendants.[53] Grandfather Henry was appalled when Charles Edward and Henry Clay Erwin wanted to rush off to Cuba with a band of adventurers intent on incorporating the island into the United States. He was equally concerned when Henry Clay Erwin challenged Seargent Prentiss, a New Orleans lawyer and political kingmaker, to a duel. Though justifiably upset by remarks Prentiss had made about his father, Henry Clay Erwin was only twenty years old, and Prentiss had significant experience as a duelist. Henry Clay did not interfere, but when Prentiss retracted his harsh words, thus avoiding the duel, he sent a note of thanks that clearly revealed his concern.[54]

Thomas Hart Clay frequently complained in his diary about the habits of his children. They were extravagant, easily distracted, and enjoyed nothing in moderation. In fact, though incapable of seeing anything positively, Thomas should have been pleased. Unlike himself and many other Clay grandchildren, they did not add abuse of alcohol to their other bad habits. Each of the five children would make solid contributions throughout their lives.

Both Henry Clay Erwin and Charles Edward Erwin had drinking problems. Margaret Johnson Erwin, their stepmother, wrote to Eugene that Henry Clay Erwin was a "noble young man" except for his drinking. He risked throwing his life away because of alcohol. Mrs. Erwin told Eugene that if she had one drop of Clay blood in her veins she would never drink alcohol. Henry Clay believed his namesake selfish as well. But Charles Edward proved just as bad. Margaret Erwin called him a "vagabond." He wandered away to Cuba then to New Orleans, succumbing to a life of dissipation. Even Henry Clay Erwin worried about his brother. He claimed Charles Edward drank continually, gambled heavily, and squandered great sums of money. When Charles Edward thought he had $10,000 coming to him from his father's estate, he set out to spend it. He limped back to his brother without any money.[55] Both would die of tuberculosis while still young men.

The tendency among Clay's descendants to behave erratically existed only in the males until the third generation. Lucretia Hart Erwin changed that. Anne Clay Erwin had mentioned her tendency to fight with Mammy Lottie, the servant Henry Clay sent to help with the Erwin brood, but her temperament apparently did not improve after her mother's death. Henry sent her to school in Lexington, but the headmistress wrote him to say Lucretia had "difficulty . . . fixing her attention upon her studies," an interesting choice of words given the lack of perseverance in the Clay males. She and her stepmother did not get along at all, and apparently she became estranged from her father, because when he died, she refused to wear black, as required of southern women. She attended a party two days after his death and danced all night. She also frequently fought with her brothers.[56]

Henry Clay became involved when Lucretia suddenly decided to become a nun. Clearly not surprised, he nevertheless handled the issue with both caution and skill:

> I received and read attentively your letter of the 10h. inst. The pursual [perusal] of it touched and affected me very greatly, as it did your grandma. It was full of feelings and sentiments so just, conceived in such a true Christian spirit, and marked by such affectionate attachment to us and to all your relations that we read it with the deepest emotions. Whilst we could not disapprove, we were seriously and sorrowfully concerned by your resolution to adopt the veil and dedicate the rest of your life to the service of God in a Convent. We could not disapprove it, because you are solemnly convinced that it will be conducive to your present and future happiness. But it is a grave and serious step, resembling, in the separation from your friends and relations, which it involves, so much the awful separation which death itself brings about, that we could not but feel intense distress.[57]

He continued to praise her motives. Recognizing, no doubt, her concern about anti-Catholic bias, he assured her that he thought good Catholics had as much chance for eternal life as pious Protestants. He urged her, however, to "examine your own heart and consult your best judgment before you consummate your intention."[58] Henry need not have worried. A year later, she was married and expecting a child.

Some of the "afflictions" suffered by the family became common knowledge, but few of Henry Clay's friends or enemies knew the extent of the family burden he carried. As he tried to lead the nation, he also attempted to overcome the tragedies and crises within his family. He was no perfect parent, or grandparent, but rather a man, like most, who struggled with his own weaknesses as well as those of his descendants. He clearly recognized that each of his children required a different approach, and he never stopped trying.

The role of father to prodigal sons and grandsons at first glance seems to fit his personality. He perhaps recognized traits in his children and grandchildren as those he, too, struggled to control. Clay sought mastery over his "passions" all his life. Dancing one's way down a formal dinner table is hardly the action of a man who wants to be president, and alcohol is hardly the only explanation. Later outbursts of temper made bitter enemies and offended friends, and a case can be made that many of the mistakes he made—accepting the position as secretary of state, rechartering the Bank of the United States early, his letters on slavery—were made at times of severe stress in his life. He knew the difficulty of controlling such impulses.

Clearly, mood disorders existed in the Clay family. Theodore and John were institutionalized because of severe manic episodes. Some members of the third generation might have benefited from medical help (if medical help at the time could have been beneficial). A pattern of conduct seemed to characterize some family members.

Robert Seager, an editor of the Henry Clay papers, once commented that the genes of Henry and Lucretia did not mix well. The comment was a generalization; Seager was a historian, not a geneticist or a psychologist. However, he recognized traits in the family that have often been noted but with no serious effort at analysis. Modern studies suggest a genetic risk for both mania and depression. Children of parents with depression are more likely to experience the onset of depression in adolescence or early adulthood.[59] Although there was certainly enough tragedy in the family to indicate environmental causes, the frequent incidents of manic behavior, depression, successful or attempted suicide, fatal accidents, and alcoholism in the Clay family suggest a genetic contribution as well.

Because of her reclusiveness, suspicion falls immediately on Lucretia. Unfortunately, there is not enough evidence to draw a conclusion. The Harts were a prominent landowning family, but little has been recorded about their personal lives. Lucretia left virtually no record of her thoughts. Henry's comments suggest that she in fact exercised remarkable balance in the face of continuing tragedies. He first surmised that women were, by their very nature, more capable of coping with grief. A second explanation would receive more support from psychologists. He credited Lucretia's deep religious faith for her strength and lamented his inability to share it.

Perhaps the Harts did contribute, but the traits exhibited by later generations, both good and bad, more frequently recall Henry's personality. Bright, energetic, articulate, and with a few exceptions, gregarious, Clay's descendants could be equally eccentric, unpredictable, and prone to fiery tempers. And such characteristics apply not just to descendants of Henry Clay. Cassius Marcellus Clay, a descendant of General Green Clay and distant cousin of Henry, developed perhaps the most brilliant argument against slavery in Kentucky, but his conduct was often outrageous, violent, and, some would say, that of a mad man. Local lore is replete with stories of eccentric behavior from a variety of Clays who spent their lives in the Bluegrass of Kentucky.

Though aware of their weaknesses, Henry Clay chose to emphasize the potential for accomplishment in his children, and, within his means, to develop it. He had a right to be proud of their, and his, accomplishments. Susan and Anne had fulfilled the roles expected of them until their untimely deaths. Anne, particularly, had been all that he could have desired in a daughter and a confidante. She not only parented a major branch of the family, but she gained both the respect and appreciation of those who knew her. Henry Jr. and James showed remarkable business acumen, creating sizable estates despite their tendency to melancholy, and both Thomas and John had been "reclaimed" through the guidance of family and the work Henry found so important. The sons, like the father, and with the help of their wives, gained some control over their passions.

Tragedy may also have the effect of bringing a family together. Clay's sons, and their wives, saw the pain endured by Henry and Lucretia. They never stated as much, but their actions suggest they also recognized that over the span of Henry Clay's life, he found time for his family as well as for national and political affairs. Men who acquire fame often have tense relations with their children, but Henry's sons and daughters revered him. He was far from being a "wretched father" as Remini claims, and if he hovered over his sons at times as David and Jeanne Heidler contend, it was perhaps because he understood that their demons were his too.[60] Clay family life contained more than a fair share of tragedy, but there were successes as well. Henry Clay left a legacy through his actions that spoke to the importance of family.

Chapter 5

GOING IT ALONE

The nation paid little heed to the tragedies in the Clay family, but the death of the Great Compromiser was lost on few Americans. Henry Clay died in Washington, D.C., on June 29, 1852. The event was neither sudden nor unexpected. He looked like a ghost of his former self. Tuberculosis had taken a horrible toll. He had lost weight, and an incessant cough wracked his body. His family had urged him not to return to Washington, and once there, friends, and even old enemies, realizing his days were numbered, paid their final calls at his hotel. Early in May, Dr. Samuel Jackson, a specialist from Philadelphia, declared his condition hopeless.[1] Ever optimistic, Clay at first refused offers from James and Thomas to come to Washington to help him; then, accepting the inevitable, he relented. Thomas, the most prodigal of sons, made the journey to share his father's final days. At the news of his death, the nation mourned as it had done on few occasions in its short history. But the nation and the sons of Henry Clay mourned also for themselves. His passing meant both would have to go it alone. According to Daniel Walker Howe, Clay more than any other figure of the era had a vision of what America could be, but the country was not ready for it.[2] He was more successful in the vision he had for his sons.

At his death, Henry Clay had been a fixture in the nation's political life for nearly fifty years. Merrill Peterson in *The Great Triumvirate* called Clay, Daniel Webster, and John C. Calhoun the legitimate successors of Washington, Adams, and Jefferson. They were "a second race of giants," a part of the "furniture" of American history.[3] To this day, there are more paintings and sculptures of Henry Clay in the Capitol than of any other person. Scholars have emphasized Clay's overriding ambition, and he certainly had a full if not overflowing quotient of it, but by the end of his life he was also remembered for his patriotic service to the nation. A War Hawk in 1812, his nationalism helped get the young nation into a war it had no business fighting. He spoke rashly, without taking time to think about the ramifications. Appointed to the peace delegation sent to Ghent, Clay continued to press a strongly nationalistic agenda.[4]

The delegation is probably better known for its internal conflicts than for the negotiations. The rancorous relationship between Clay and Adams has been well documented. Historians have used Adams's diaries as the basis for their assessment, and consequently Clay has been seen as a hothead or a loose cannon, a charge that followed him throughout his life. Adams noted Clay's "excesses," although he certainly had his own. His diary clearly indicates his sense of superiority over everyone around him, which tended to isolate him from the other delegates. Unsurpassed intellectually, hardworking, and possessing a keen sense of his responsibilities, Adams had few skills in dealing with his colleagues. His memoirs contain criticism of virtually everyone. No one lived up to his expectations except his father, yet he was driven by the fear that he would not meet his father's dreams for him. Ambitious, he feared his own ambition. Longing to participate in parties and other social affairs, he feared dissipation, a word he used almost as frequently as Clay later used it.[5] At Ghent, Adams was demanding, condescending, and critical of any behavior that departed from his puritan sensitivities—behavior Clay most certainly exhibited. Adams criticized what he considered Clay's cavalier treatment of their responsibilities. Initially he chose to eat alone, grumbling that the others sat too long at dinner, wasting time when they, like him, should have been working. John Quincy Adams worked for the sake of it. The British delegation had to send virtually every issue back to London, so there was ample time to do more than work. Adams claimed that card games in Clay's rooms were breaking up as he went to breakfast.[6] In fact, Clay's most significant contribution to the negotiations may well have come from one of those characteristics Adams found most galling. As the family account suggests, Clay had learned at the card table to tell when an opponent was bluffing, and the British were bluffing. Clay was, as Adams later wrote, "playing brag with the British Plenipotentiaries."[7]

To be sure, both Adams and Clay were at times petty, even childish, yet each contributed to the creation of the treaty. Adams might well have given away too much to the British he admired; Clay compromised too little. During the negotiations, Adams remained diplomatic and reasoned, except when angered by Clay, while Clay was blunt, sometimes even threatening, demanding respect for the delegation and his nation. Even after the British capitulated on most American demands, Clay wished to try for more, but his colleagues outvoted him. The treaty was not a victory; instead it avoided losses. In the long run, however, it prepared the way for better Anglo-American relations. Both the head of the British delegation, Admiral James Gambier, and Adams formally expressed the hope that the peace treaty would be the last ever required between the nations. Henry Clay's demand that the United States be treated like a sovereign nation went a long way toward securing that hope.[8] He showed the British a side of the Americans some of the delegates seemed inclined to hide. In a touch of irony, Clay suggested at Ghent what his future enemy, Andrew Jackson, accomplished at New Orleans. There were Americans who would stand firmly for their sovereignty.[9]

Clay returned to the United States to the cheers of his countrymen, who saw in him a champion of its present and its future. Robert Remini criticizes him for not spending a "long vacation" with his family, yet just because Clay soon left Ashland for Washington, this should not suggest his presence at Ashland was any less pronounced.[10] Children at an impressionable age witnessed the gifts bearing the thanks of every section of the nation adorning the rooms and halls of Ashland. The lesson of service to one's nation rang loud and clear.

Shortly after Ghent, Clay began to piece together the outlines of his American System. Although its principles were founded in many of his experiences and supported his personal interests, the nationalistic aspect of the plan is readily apparent. Clay recognized lack of unity as the greatest threat to the nation. By region and by class, interests differed. Clay saw that on his long trip between Kentucky and Washington. He also saw it in his own community. The end of the Napoleonic Wars in Europe drastically reduced the demand for American goods. In Kentucky, many people had purchased land based on wartime prices and were quickly in default. Wildcat banks issued their own notes of wildly fluctuating value. It was said that debtors chased creditors down the streets with handfuls of worthless paper trying to pay their bills. A relief faction cried for government aid to such people.

Clay recognized the pain inflicted on people, but he also understood that the nation needed a stable currency. Earlier in his career he had opposed a national bank, but the economic depression changed his mind.

Personal interests were, no doubt, a part of the issue, yet it was also clear that businesses could not and would not function in the situation he saw in Kentucky in 1819 and thereafter. It cost him a good deal politically, but he believed a national bank would provide the kind of consistency needed to grow the economy in a unified way.

For Clay, the American System had less to do with government direction and more to do with binding the people of diverse regions, and even cultures, into a true nation. Evidencing Clay's usual enthusiasm, the American System would provide a cure-all for ills of the nation, at least as he perceived them. It would encourage national integration through commerce and transportation, create mutual economic dependency between regions, foster commerce and free labor, and eventually render slavery obsolete. Certainly far too optimistic, he was not alone. The American economist Henry Carey claimed as late as 1867 that if Clay had been elected in 1844, the economic changes of the American System would have precluded the Civil War.[11]

It was the institution of slavery that made Clay's aim to achieve national unity increasingly difficult. The slavery question dominated nineteenth-century life, hotly debated as a political, economic, social, and moral issue. For that issue, Carey to the contrary, Clay had no answers, although it was certainly not for lack of trying. Clay's enduring service to the nation is seen, at least in the public eye, in the compromises he fashioned to save the nation from itself. His efforts brought him great criticism and yet also admiration in a nation dangerously divided on the issue. His compromises were pragmatic; they sought to save the Union. Northerners and southerners claimed to stand on principle regarding the issue. For him, in a democracy, compromise had to be considered a principle. As historian Daniel Walker Howe puts it, for Clay, "saving the Union was a matter of continual adjustment of competing interests."[12] In 1820–1821 and 1850, he fashioned compromises that stitched a nation together, if only temporarily.

The nation was at odds over the issue of slavery, but so was Henry Clay. In fact, his perceived inconsistencies on the issue probably cost him the presidency as much as any other factor. A slave owner at the age of four thanks to his father's bequest, Clay nevertheless felt uncomfortable with the concept of slavery. He rejected the justification that blacks were less than human and stated emphatically that slavery was an evil. Writing under the name Scaevola in 1798, he condemned slavery in the local newspaper, the *Kentucky Gazette:*

> Can any humane man be happy and contented when he sees near thirty thousand of his fellow beings around him, deprived of all the rights which make life desirable, transferred like cattle from the possession of one to another; when he sees the trembling slave, under the hammer, surrounded by a number of eager purchasers, and feeling all the emotions which arise when one is uncertain into whose tyrannic hands he must next fall; when he beholds the anguish and hears the piercing cries of husbands separated from wives and children from parents; when in a word, all the tender and endearing ties of nature are broken asunder and disregarded?

He went further to proclaim slavery an evil not only depriving the slave of the "best gift of heaven" but also injuring the master.[13] Although Clay repeatedly argued the evils of slavery throughout his career, he, like many of his contemporaries, openly expressed attitudes toward blacks that today are clearly racist. He supported gradual emancipation linked to colonization. He acknowledged the intellectual potential of blacks, even their ability to reach equality with whites. But he did not believe white and black could live side by side without one dominating the other. Thus, there was no place for blacks as free men—and he believed they should be free—in American society. Although the Colonization Society initially attracted many abolitionists, it soon became the target of attack by many who believed it fostered racism against blacks. Clay's own inconsistencies regarding the issue—believing slavery morally wrong, yet owning slaves himself—reflected the inconsistencies of many, both in the North and in the South, and left him open to challenge.

Political enemies sought to weaken his popularity by questioning his relationship to his own slaves. On a number of occasions, they encouraged former slaves to accuse him of being an abusive master.[14] Lewis Richardson, a former slave, escaped and fled to Canada, where he claimed Clay was unusually cruel to his slaves. But Richardson's credibility is questionable, as records show that he was an alcoholic who had frequently acted violently toward other slaves on the estate. Apparently, Clay was glad to be rid of him, as evidenced by the fact that he did not pursue him when he escaped. Lewis Hayden, another former slave, claimed Clay had sold his wife and children to the South, but Clay emphatically denied that he had ever owned the man or his family. He stated further that he had never sold a woman and child down the river but instead tried to bring husband and wife together. Another slave was paid by abolitionists to leave Clay, but returned the money and came back to him. Not surprisingly, Clay claimed that his

Aaron Dupuy. Courtesy
of the Elizabeth Clay
Blanford Collection.

slaves received good treatment, and he often pointed to his manservant, Charles Dupuy, as a case in point.[15] He repeatedly took Aaron Dupuy, and later his son Charles, into many northern cities where they could easily have escaped. He also purchased Charlotte, Aaron's wife, so they could be together. Later, Henry freed Charlotte, her daughter Mary Ann, and her son Charles, but they remained at Ashland. The family supported Clay's claims of benevolence—again, not surprisingly—and his daughter-in-law, writing two decades after the Civil War, maintained he would never have left the freedmen without the financial means to support themselves.[16]

Charlotte Dupuy's efforts to emancipate herself, however, complicate the record and illustrate that no matter the treatment, most slaves—including those who belonged to Henry Clay—wanted to be free. Clay took Charlotte to Washington with the family, and while visiting her own family in Maryland, she went to court to seek her freedom. Clay immediately had her put in jail. Somehow the hostility was resolved, because

"Mammy Lottie" became a favorite within the Clay family. Clay sent her to New Orleans to help Anne Clay Erwin with her brood of young children and then to Portugal with James and Susan when James served as charge d'affaires in 1849–1850. Ultimately, Clay freed Charlotte, but she remained at Ashland. Her lawsuit demonstrates, however, not only the multiple ways slaves fought their enslavement but also the inconsistencies of Henry Clay's attitudes toward the institution. He may have vocalized the evils of slavery, but he remained a slaveholder until his death.[17] That, too, came with political costs.

Clay's internal struggle reflected the national struggle over the issue and resulted in the series of compromises he fashioned as a means of resolving, or delaying, the disagreements over slavery. In 1820 the question of statehood for Missouri raised the issue, leading to increasingly harsher rhetoric and talk of disunion. Desperate to resolve the worsening situation, Clay worked tirelessly to bring about a compromise acceptable to both antislavery and slaveholder factions. Remini remarks that the longer the debates continued, the more both sides realized that Clay, rather than politicking, was "intent solely on preserving the Union." When the final vote was taken, he could feel pride in having led the nation—temporarily, at least—beyond the narrow sectionalism that had dominated politics and focused attention on national unity. He received national accolades for his efforts, and, according to Glyndon Van Deusen, from that point on heard himself called "the Great Pacificator."[18]

For thirty years Clay sought to enshrine his principle of compromise. He would have other opportunities. The calm instilled by the Missouri Compromise proved short lived; Congress passed a protective tariff that significantly raised rates on imports in 1828, ensuring renewed sectional controversy. Southerners had long opposed such measures because they raised the prices of goods southerners needed and facilitated the development of a strong central government. John C. Calhoun claimed that tariffs bolstered the North's economy while weakening the South's. Four years later, another tariff measure brought the matter to a head. Under Calhoun's leadership, South Carolina's state government threatened to enact the states-rights policy of nullification. There was even talk of secession and raising a state army. Such words roused the righteous indignation of President Andrew Jackson. He presented to Congress the Force Bill, asking for authority to call out state militias to enforce the law. Civil War seemed imminent.

Henry Clay remained silent in the early period of the crisis. He had suffered a humiliating defeat in the presidential election of 1832. Then too, he had no reason to help Andrew Jackson out of a crisis at least partly of his own making. It is probably not overstatement to say that Jackson and Clay despised one another. Clay had first criticized Jackson when the latter exceeded his authority by invading Spanish Florida and executing two British subjects. Clay led the move to censure Jackson in Congress, and Jackson never forgave him.[19] In 1824 the Jackson camp created the corrupt bargain charge, an accusation that Clay had sold his support to John Quincy Adams in the presidential poll in return for the secretary of state position. It was, in fact, a "corrupt" charge; most scholars believe Clay, given the choices, would have supported Adams under any circumstances, but he faced the accusation for the rest of his career. Clay feared Jackson's military personality, and no doubt believed himself much better prepared to serve as president. Jackson later called Clay "the bases[t], meanest, scoundrel that ever disgraced the image of god." Even when out of office and approaching his own end, he claimed he should have shot Henry Clay and hanged John C. Calhoun, evidence, perhaps, that Clay was not totally mistaken in his impression regarding Jackson and tyranny.[20]

Foregoing any enjoyment of Jackson's situation, Clay introduced a compromise. His plan continued the rates set by the tariff of 1832 until 1842, but all rates exceeding 20 percent would be reduced by one tenth every two years. Thus, by 1842 the tariff would drop to a level near the tariff of 1816. Such a compromise would appease the manufacturing sector because it gave them nearly ten years of protection, and it assuaged southern sentiment because it promised an eventual end to the tariff.

Contemporaries and historians have questioned Clay's motivation. Some critics suggested the compromise was an attempt to regain his political leadership after the defeat of 1832. President Jackson had favored tariff reduction, and Clay sought to deny his attempt to be a peacemaker. Others suggested that he thought Jackson's policy the first salvo against protective tariffs, one of the foundation stones of the American System. Clay's aim was to save the principle by reducing the level of protection. It has also been suggested that he sought to balance his loss of votes in some northern states by creating alliances in the southern states. Then, too, being the champion of a successful compromise could only enhance future efforts to attain the presidency.[21]

The legacy to his family rested on a more laudable explanation of his motivations. They believed his love of country required him to rise above political and personal issues to avoid a civil war. Despite his dislike of Jackson, he fashioned a compromise that allowed the president and South Carolina to draw back from the horrible precipice. Though often written in hagiographic terms, the basic principles of the family interpretation do not lack support from professional historians. Robert Remini says Clay's concern for the welfare of the nation was no deception: "He did indeed act out of a deep commitment to the country and its people." Remini also acknowledges that Clay genuinely feared Jackson's inclination toward military force as a solution. Daniel Walker Howe gives Clay credit for "rising above his animosity toward Jackson by cooperating with the president in the interests of the Union." The people, too, generally praised Clay for the compromise. The Clay family took it all in; the praise both added to the mystique surrounding the patriarch and enhanced for its members the importance of service.[22]

The Great Pacificator had one more important compromise for the nation, though it is more important for what it says about his love of the Union than for his success as a compromiser. The territory received as a result of the Mexican War raised the question of slavery and its extension yet again. After much wrangling, a series of five laws, meeting the minimal demands of the slave and free states, became the Compromise of 1850. California was admitted as a free state; the territory of New Mexico was established; Texas gave up claim to land incorporated into the new territory; the slave trade was ended in the District of Columbia; and a new fugitive slave law required runaway slaves to be returned to their owners.

Clay designed the compromise in 1850, but the final version was not his. Clay's effort to link all five measures in an omnibus bill proved to be a political mistake, but failing health also limited his leadership. Clay was forced to sit to the side, occasionally attempting to speak, encouraging individual members of Congress, and donating his prestige—now enhanced because of his frailty. He could at times barely make it to the dais to speak, yet he refused to give up. Even bitter enemies admired his determination.[23]

From the beginning, Clay's concern for the nation was apparent. On January 21, 1850, despite his physical weakness, he made an appointment with Daniel Webster to seek his help in effecting a compromise. Clay's speeches and comments crisscrossed the nation in pamphlet form. Thousands gathered in New York and other cities to echo his love of the Union. On February 5 he began his speech in favor of the compromise he had molded. Glyndon Van Deusen claims it was "replete with love" for the Union, "a challenge, then and now, to all doubters of the grandeur of patriotism." Clay pleaded for compromise as a testament of respect for the Union, and he closed his speech by expressing his hope that he would not live to see a divided nation: "I know no South, no North, no East, no West to which I owe any allegiance. I owe allegiance to two sovereignties and only two; one is to the sovereignty of this Union, and the other is to the sovereignty of the state of Kentucky."[24] Repeatedly and consistently, Clay spoke for union. If Kentucky raised the flag of resistance, he would not fight under it. If South Carolina raised that flag, he would encourage Kentuckians by the thousands to stand against the state. Ironically, perhaps, when South Carolina did raise the flag of rebellion, the chances the South could win a civil war were substantially reduced. Time won by compromise worked in favor of the Union.

When the compromise measures passed, Clay received the appreciation of the people. Throughout the nation, a frail old man, now far beyond the presidency of which he had dreamed, was revered as the man who kept the country from splitting apart. All that could be done, however, was watch him wither away. No one, certainly not his sons, could fail to see his service to the nation.[25]

At Clay's death, President Millard Fillmore closed all federal offices and appointed a committee of six senators to attend his body.[26] In Lexington, church bells tolled, and the citizenry knew its favorite son was no more. The body lay in state in the Capitol building until July 1, the first time the rotunda was used for that purpose. Then the long procession back to Kentucky began. In an irony befitting a nation with such complex problems, the body of a Kentucky slaveholder was carried through northern cities and countryside and thousands lined the route to mourn. The train stopped the first night in Baltimore then went to Philadelphia, where thousands more observed his coffin. The scene was repeated in New York on July 3–4.

Clay's body was carried up the Hudson River to Albany on the steamboat *Santa Claus,* and the cadets at the military academy stood at attention when it passed West Point. Perhaps Henry Hart Clay was in the ranks. His grandfather did not live to see him expelled from the military academy for excessive demerits.[27] Thomas Clay did not record his thoughts as he accompanied his father's body that day. Now the father of sons prone to youthful excess, perhaps he could finally sense a father's disappointment when he, the son, had been expelled from the academy.

From Albany to Buffalo, the train stopped at every major city. In Buffalo the body was placed on another steamer to cross Lake Erie to Cleveland. From there, it traveled by train to Columbus and Cincinnati. From Cincinnati, Henry Clay's remains returned to his home state, drifting down the Ohio River to Louisville and, finally, completing the last segment of the journey by train to Lexington.[28]

The burial took place on July 10. Nearly thirty thousand people lined the route from Ashland, down Lexington's Main Street and west to the cemetery on the outskirts of the community. All businesses were closed, the town draped in mourning. The honor guard of troops reached the cemetery long before the last elements of the procession had begun their trek. Masons, Odd Fellows, Sons of Temperance, school teachers, government officials of all levels and branches, family members, and strangers participated. It was apparent that Henry Clay belonged to the nation.

In death as in life, Henry Clay cast a great shadow. Clay's sons knew— by what he said and what he did—that their father believed it one's duty to serve the nation. And in case there was any confusion, Henry Clay consistently encouraged them to live up to the family name by serving their country and their state. In a letter addressed to a "Dear Little Namesake," Clay emphasized the family's responsibility toward service and ruminated on the values he encouraged in his descendants. Writing to one of five namesakes among his grandchildren, he began, "Your parents have done me the honor to give my name to you." At their request, Clay penned the letter for the child to read when he became old enough "to comprehend and appreciate its friendly purport." Clearly, family members recognized the influence he might have on his descendants. Clay gave moral advice he had given before: shun bad company; avoid dissipation; study diligently; cultivate honor, truth, virtue, and religion. Near the end of the letter, he spoke about a subject especially close to his heart—duty to country: "Recognize at all times the paramount right of your Country to your most devoted services, whether she treats you ill or well, and never let selfish views or interests predominate over the duties of patriotism."[29] Although addressed to the grandson, the letter was read by most family members. They knew he had written it just months after the nation had seemed to turn its back on him in the heart-wrenching election of 1844. Service was not a choice but an obligation.

The central question for the family remained: Which of his sons would fill his place? Who would become the leader of the family? Who would

James B. Clay. Courtesy of
the Elizabeth Clay Blanford
Collection.

represent the family to the nation? Theodore was, of course, out of the
question. Each of the other three, Thomas, James, and John, were now
significant landowners with financial means equal to many American
politicians of the day. To some extent each wanted to don the mantle; yet
each showed a reluctance to step into his father's shoes. Each questioned
his own ability and feared the inevitable criticism and comparison. Yet,
each felt not only the duty to nation taught by their father, but a duty to
him. To avoid service seemed a repudiation of their father. James stated it
best: "Nothing would so much have added to my happiness as to have been
able to take my father's place at Ashland, and to have done all in my power
to have perpetuated his great name: not by any emulation of his fame, for
I am well aware I possess neither the qualities or abilities for this, but by
endeavoring to resemble him in his upright and virtuous life, to have continued to his descendants the respect of the world and the love of friends."[30]

Reluctantly, then, yet with a sense of obligation, Thomas, James, and
John Clay stepped into a world without their father. Henry Clay's death in
1852 and the Civil War less than a decade later tested the very fiber of the
patriarch's legacy. Fulfilling that legacy saw the brothers in competition

with one another. The period would also see them test the legacy of service under conditions as difficult as any their father ever faced.

Henry Clay had sensed some jealousy among his sons near the end of his life. Like so many painful topics in the Clay family, if discussed in correspondence, the offending letters have been removed from the collection. Only an occasional comment implies the problem. Henry, for example, expressed his delight when he learned that John and Thomas were talking "like brothers."[31] He also occasionally mediated differences between James and Thomas over business, and he gently chided James when the latter expressed a concern that Lucretia favored John over her other sons.[32] Then, in his last days, he cautioned both John and Lucretia to keep the papers that itemized his gifts and bequests lest they be challenged. In addition to land, John received Henry's stable of horses and most of his slaves.[33] Although he never stated it directly, Clay suspected James or Thomas might challenge the numerous gifts made to John near the end of his life.[34]

He was correct about the friction between his sons. The first battle among siblings occurred over the purchase of Ashland. Henry had made an effort to solve that problem too. His last will left Mansfield, consisting of the house built by Lewinski and 515 acres, to Thomas's heirs. In addition to horses and slaves, John received 200 acres from the southern end of Ashland. According to the will, Ashland, consisting of approximately 375 acres and the home after the bequest to John, was left for Lucretia during her life. She could live there or sell it as she chose. For a number of years, however, there had been discussions about James buying it. Henry had begun to talk about selling the estate to James as early as 1850, when James was in Portugal. In October 1850 Henry wrote James that he would like to sell Ashland to him, taking James's Lexington home, called the Clay Villa, as partial payment. Some months later he sold the Clay Villa for $9,000, but he teasingly wrote to Susan that he would have allowed James $10,000 for it toward the purchase of Ashland if he had been at home.[35]

James could not make up his mind. Not only in a state of disrepair, the house also suffered from structural damage. James worried about the safety of his family there. He eventually settled in Missouri as a farmer. With growing concerns about the health of his parents, he even expressed a desire to sell Ashland and move Henry and Lucretia to Missouri to live with him. Yet, later, he worried about the isolation of his family in Missouri, and the dangers to them should something happen to him.[36] Apparently, Henry Clay squashed any talk of moving to Missouri, because as his health deteriorated, James expressed a desire to relieve his mother of the responsibilities of such a large estate and the "care and trouble of so many negroes." A letter from Mary Mentelle Clay, Thomas's wife, to Susan M. Clay in 1850 suggested that Lucretia wanted Henry to sell Ashland to James for the same reason.[37]

Despite the inconsistent positions of both Henry and James, an understanding had been reached that James would have the opportunity to purchase Ashland at Lucretia's death or when she decided to sell it. James said he promised his father he would purchase the estate. Lucretia said as much in messages sent to James through J. O. Harrison, the executor of her husband's estate. According to Harrison, she wanted the estate settled during her lifetime, and she wished to honor her husband's desire that James be the proprietor of it. She expressed a willingness to live in the rooms of the wing or in the overseer's apartment. In February 1853 Harrison stated, "She says come on as soon as you please; there is plenty of room—plenty to eat and a hearty welcome."[38]

John raised only minimum resistance to James's ownership of Ashland. A shrewd businessman when in control of his faculties, he understood what a significant part of the estate he had inherited. A challenge to James could bring the entire will into question. Indicating that he would not mount a serious challenge, John began to build his own house, which he called Ashland-on-Tates-Creek, shortly after his father's death.[39]

Thomas raised the greatest obstacles to James. He gave evidence of the ensuing struggle early on. His telegraph to James about Henry Clay's death was short and cryptic: "Our Father is no more. He died this morning at fifteen minutes after eleven o'clock. Thomas Clay."[40] Thomas wanted Ashland for what it symbolized more than for its financial benefits. With John's 200 acres removed, the Ashland estate was smaller than Mansfield, but Ashland was the base for his father's fame. Moreover, since Theodore remained incapacitated, Thomas felt that the privileges and responsibilities of the oldest son had fallen to him. J. O. Harrison believed Thomas had acquired both confidence and ambition from attending his father in his dying moments. He reacted like a spoiled child, complaining that James had not been present at the time of their father's death, and telling anyone who would listen that he deserved the position of leadership vacated by his father.[41]

In fact, the legacy of their father was already being exploited by forces outside the family. Thomas was being encouraged to assume the favorite son role even before Henry's death. George W. Anderson wrote as early as 1851 to Thomas, "I want to see your name, as often as possible, before the publick. I want you to step into *your father's shoes*. I want to see . . . his oldest son, because if he would, he ought, representing his old District." Thomas Stevenson, later a political ally of James, urged him to purchase Ashland, and somewhat later Millard Fillmore encouraged Thomas to pursue elective office.[42]

If J. O. Harrison was correct in his assessment, such encouragement would appeal to a vulnerable Thomas. Harrison believed Thomas to be jealous of James because their father had sought a diplomatic post for him and because James had built a more substantial fortune. Thomas's anger should have been aimed at his own father, and perhaps at himself. Henry may have forgiven Thomas's youthful problems, but he did not recommend him for government service as he did James. Even in the family corporation, Thomas had less freedom of action than the other sons. Only in those last days did Henry place his needs and his trust in Thomas.

James Clay recognized his brother's jealousy and sought to assuage his fears. At one point, he agreed to step aside if Thomas wished to buy the estate, acknowledging Thomas's natural right as the oldest son. Harrison argued that Thomas did not have the means, and James expressed the importance of keeping the estate in the family. He wrote emphatically to Harrison, "This I promised my father. I think it gave him happiness, and it is my intention faithfully to perform my promise." Thomas may have been more concerned with what people would think if he did not assume family leadership than with accepting that responsibility.[43]

Family pride eventually proved stronger than personal feelings. Thomas realized he did not have the means to purchase Ashland and feared that someone outside the family might gain control of it. Harrison wrote that Thomas therefore "consents—or rather, acquiesces—in the purchase of it by you."[44] Thomas then expressed the concern that no one would bid against James and he would get the estate too cheaply. In March 1853 James suggested an idea that he hoped would relieve Thomas's fears. Again showing deference to Thomas, he noted that he wanted to share the idea with the executors but thought it proper to speak with Thomas first. The will did not preclude a private sale, and he feared giving people outside the family even a remote chance of purchasing the estate. Therefore, he suggested that two of their father's friends and associates be named to work with the executors to determine a fair price for the property. James would name one of the persons and Thomas the other. Thomas agreed to James's suggestion at the time, but he later changed his mind.[45] James bought the property on the courthouse steps for $140 per acre. Indicative of the power of the Clay name in the community, no one placed a bid against him.[46]

Whatever Thomas may have thought, he had in fact forfeited family leadership. In the public mind, that leadership went with the estate linked so closely with the Great Compromiser. James quickly moved to put his stamp on it both as a family dwelling and as a working farm. Tearing the house down, he began its reconstruction. Many were surprised, but some were angry. Some claimed he had a "mania for building." Others saw it as an insult to his father.[47] Too much of that criticism had its origins in political mudslinging and family jealousy. On several occasions, Henry Clay had allowed the condition of the house to deteriorate, but it also had serious structural problems. The New Madrid earthquake may have damaged the foundation, but water seeping through the limestone had certainly created problems. James and Susan wanted to make the house safe for their family and a suitable base for the social and political life they envisioned. As if to ensure the legacy of his father, however, James Clay rebuilt the house on the same foundations and according to the original blueprints.[48]

The rebuilding of the house suggested the beginning of a new era in the family's history. Henry Clay was dead, and his widow moved to John's home; Ashland would now serve the needs of the second generation. Susan and James spared no expense in decorating the interior of the house. Invoice after invoice from H. Belter and Co., furniture dealers, arrived at Ashland.[49] The purchases listed on one invoice containing shell-pattern sofa, armchairs, parlor chairs, a sideboard, and a few other items amounted to nearly $2,000. Under Susan's direction, Ashland became again a major part of Kentucky's social and political life.

The brothers learned best their father's love of business. In fact, they may have been more successful than he was. Henry Jr.'s fortune, administered after his death by the Prathers of Louisville, left his three surviving children, according to Henry Clay, in "very comfortable circumstances."[50] Henry also praised James for developing "ample means of support" for his family. James followed in his father's footsteps as a progressive farmer. He brought to Ashland significant breeding stock. In 1856 he paid more than $1,600 for a yearling shorthorn bull named Royal Duke. On his father's advice, James had sold his sheep when he lived in Missouri, but back at Ashland he paid $400 for a Southdown ram and several ewes. He was obviously able to protect them against the dogs and coyotes that Henry had said made the raising of sheep unprofitable. By 1857 he had printed brochures advertising shorthorn cattle and Southdown sheep for sale, and the prices were not cheap.[51]

Ashland remained a horse farm as well, but James decided on a different approach. While visiting the New York farm of his friend Edwin Thorne intending to buy cattle, he saw trotting horses and decided to introduce them to Kentucky. James's major stud horses included Mambrino Chief and Mambrino Jr., two horses that figure in the breeding history of many successful horses well into the twentieth century. Leaning on the Clay name to offset opposition from thoroughbred breeders, James introduced a new market for Kentucky farmers.[52] The successful breeding of trotting stallions to thoroughbred mares earned him a reputation as a pioneering scientific breeder and helped establish the trotter as a distinct breed, the standardbred.[53] In that sale of 1857 he listed mares, colts, and fillies as well as cattle and sheep. He sold Mambrino Chief that year for $5,020.[54] The prices he asked and received place him among the nation's most important producers of horses.

Again like his father, James Clay did not limit his business activities to agriculture. He owned stock in the Northern Bank of Kentucky and served as a director and stockholder in the Kentucky River Navigation Company, a corporation with a state contract to build and operate locks and dams on Kentucky's rivers. Looking into the future, the company also had the right to exploit coal and timber resources on lands near the rivers of Eastern Kentucky.[55]

Historians, relying on James Clay's contemporary critics, suggest that his financial activity was made possible by the use of his wife's money. Although marriage into the Jacob family certainly provided financial opportunities and a sizable inheritance, Henry Clay praised his son's business acumen on several occasions, and J. O. Harrison noted that James had made significant money before his father's death. James Clay did enter a number of real-estate purchases with Susan's favorite brother, Thomas P. Jacob. After the death of John I. Jacob, James Clay and Thomas P. Jacob bought Louisville property owned by the family and subdivided it for housing and businesses. Called the Jacob Enlargement, the plot ran from Arthur Street to Fifth, and at its greatest width, from Breckenridge to Broadway, a large section of the nineteenth-century city. Newspaper advertisements and the auction plot listed lots owned in partnership and others belonging to James alone. Susan, with Thomas P. Jacob as trustee, owned property on Jacob Street between First and Brook, near the center of Louisville, and she took an active interest in a store she owned on Market Street. Clay also occasionally served as a lawyer, mostly for the collection of debts owed him, and he still received funds from the sale of land in Missouri.[56]

James reveled in the risk involved in business. He participated in highly speculative ventures, and like his father, his brother-in-law James Erwin, and many others, he sometimes had trouble collecting what was owed him in time to pay his creditors. However, he clearly had sufficient assets to meet his obligations, a fact that his contemporaries and modern historians have ignored. In the mid-1850s his bank balances ranged from $2,500 to $6,000 each month, with money coming and going from and to a variety of sources. By 1858 those balances were between $13,000 and $16,000 a month, significant sums for the era.[57]

In 1858 Clay began to speculate in slaves. Between August 1858 and July 1859, he purchased eight slaves. All but one were still in their teens, and two had young children. Ironically, in 1850 Henry Clay noted James's aversion to owning slaves when they were discussing what he would do when he returned from Portugal, and as late as 1852 James said he would farm Ashland with "white laborers" if he purchased the estate. It would appear that he owned slaves as investments rather than to secure a permanent workforce. At the same time that he was buying slaves, he hired temporary labor for his fields.[58] *perhaps white*

James B. Clay was certainly not dependent on his father for business success. He had used his father's name as a means of acquiring loans as long as Henry lived, but that was not uncommon. Moreover, he proved quite capable on his own terms after Henry Clay's death. He had an economic base sufficient to support a political career if he wanted it. His father had trained him well.

Thomas and John seemed satisfied with simpler lives. Thomas raised livestock, hemp, and various grains at Mansfield. He owned enough slaves to work his land but complained frequently about their conduct. His business interests were far smaller than those of Henry Jr. or James, but they provided a comfortable living and allowed him to send his two sons to the University of Wisconsin. His diary indicates that he continued to suffer from episodes of depression, although, unlike John, he avoided commitment to the lunatic asylum. No doubt his wife Mary helped him through the darkest times.[59]

John seemed content to live with his mother at his new farm, Ashland-on-Tates-Creek. Irascible in temperament, he made numerous references in his diary to drinking too much and to fighting. He also argued with his brothers, but he lived within his capabilities. He kept Ashland Stud small, allowing him to provide care and attention to his horses. Consequently, he produced quality horses, then sold or trained them for the track. Magnolia produced Kentucky, one of the most important racehorses of its day. Although he had little of the ambition that had characterized his father, he gained a reputation for his knowledge of good horses and of the breeding of horses. He was also a good businessman. His nephew, Harry Boyle Clay, complained that John would not lend a dollar unless he received two in collateral. J. O. Harrison also noted his business ability in a letter to James: "John is very economical—has the best stock in the county—understands its management and may, by prudence and a little good luck, derive large revenues from it." During the discussions over the purchase of Ashland, J. O. Harrison warned James Clay not to take John lightly. He was a "first-rate" businessman.[60]

The three sons also sought to continue their father's work in politics. They did not always agree on what Henry would have done, but they could not forget his legacy. James could not escape those who saw him as the successor to his father, and Thomas could not let James make a move without him. John tagged along for a time, but to little effect.

The first effort was an attempt to save the Whig Party. In fact, the party barely outlived Henry Clay, producing a political vacuum nowhere more profound than in Kentucky. James Clay, largely in honor of his father, attempted to revive the Whigs, and John joined him in the effort. A group of Whig sympathizers gathered in Lexington, then Louisville, creating a document titled "Platform of Whig Principles and Measures." W. N. Haldeman, a Louisville newspaperman, and James's brother-in-law Thomas P. Jacob were among the signers of the document. It was a timid effort to heal the breach between northern and southern supporters of the old party. James communicated cautiously with the Massachusetts Whig Edward Everett, suggesting an effort to reunite southern and northern Whigs. He invited Everett to Kentucky to attend a proposed meeting on July 4, 1856. Despite a reputation for maintaining ties with southern Whigs, Everett declined. Although he congratulated the Kentuckians for trying to re-create the old-line Whig party, he cited the Kansas-Nebraska issue as too great a stumbling block. Too many southern Whigs had supported it. The extremists of North and South held the balance of power: "To be acceptable on either side of Mason and Dixon's line is to be odious to the other." He stated his desire to stay out of politics because he could find no ground to be claimed by a man of national principles.[61]

With the failure of the Whig party, Clay's sons had a choice to make. Both Thomas and James sought to follow the will of their father, but their interpretations of that will differed. Thomas, standing alone among family members again, joined the American Party. Based on nationalism, the party sought to maintain the values it considered central to American life, but it was infamous for its anti-Catholic and anti-immigrant stance. Despite the opposition of his family, Thomas declared it his duty to support "sound American principles," the principles, he wrote in his diary, that his father supported. He noted, however, that his mother, Clay's widow, vehemently disagreed and told him so. In his diary, he sought heavenly aid in honoring her, but he expressed the need to honor his father as well. Thomas served on the party's County Committee for Fayette County and, in the harried days of 1860, successfully ran for the state legislature.[62]

James Clay could not in good conscience join the American Party. He, too, sought to follow what he believed would be his father's position, and in his reasoning there is clearly the influence of Henry Clay. There is also a willingness to act independently. James attended one meeting of the American Party, but he reacted against the secrecy and the oaths to follow party leadership blindly. He specifically rejected the party's anti-Catholicism and its narrow interpretation of who should be allowed to hold political office. He argued that many of the principles of the Whig Party for which Henry Clay had stood, such as the national bank, were no longer issues in national politics. James's major reason for moving toward the Democratic Party echoed Edward Everett's phrase "man of national principles" and his father's desire to see the Union remain intact. James claimed he remained a Whig, but he supported James Buchanan because the Democratic Party was "the only party this day in existence worthy by its nationality and its principles to wield the destinies of a great and free people." Although he called for a continuation of the Union from a decidedly southern perspective, he nevertheless stated, as he believed his father had before him, the importance of preserving it.[63]

The old Whigs denounced him bitterly, but James stuck to his decision. His father's statement that he would rather be right than president justified his resolution. That phrase would become a base for many family positions or decisions, right or wrong. James Clay campaigned for Buchanan throughout Kentucky, Ohio, and Pennsylvania, and he withstood the criticism of former friends.

The criticism, however, very nearly led James into several duels. Daniel Walker Howe argues that southern Whigs were torn by a clash of values in the 1850s. One set of values emphasized self-discipline, as Whigs had traditionally done. Another standard required the defense of honor, leading to the resurgence of dueling throughout the South. Henry Clay had freed himself of the need to defend his honor, but like so much of the South, the Clay family stepped backward in the 1850s. Several of Clay's grandsons sought to prove their manhood through duels.[64] James, though brash at times, had been content to live quietly, tending to his business interests and his family. However, that changed in the 1850s. The weight of his father's legacy rested heavily on his shoulders, and when he felt challenged, he became decidedly uncomfortable. He believed he had to defend his honor, and that of his father.

James Clay made his first political speech in 1855 and contemplated his first duel shortly thereafter. George Prentice, the editor of the *Louisville Journal* and a founder of the American Party, made harsh charges against him, including several that implied a lack of respect for his father's memory. His newspaper criticized James for tearing down the home of Henry Clay. According to Prentice, James used the timbers of Ashland to make canes to sell as souvenirs. He was even accused of calling his father a liar. In a letter to John Cabell Breckinridge, James Buchanan's vice president, E. M. Bruce said he fully expected James to "dig up the bones of his father and sell them to the button makers." One article called him the "degenerate son of Henry Clay," and others accused him of caring so little about his father that he refused to attend the funeral.[65]

The abuse became so bad that even Lucretia entered the fray. A letter obviously meant for publication was sent to Judge Thomas Marshall and J. O. Harrison, who forwarded it to the *Louisville Courier*. The typescript signature at the end of the letter was that of Lucretia Clay. The letter obliquely criticized the *Louisville Journal* for the attacks on her son and more directly criticized those of her husband's friends who knew the attacks to be false yet did not defend James. She wrote, the letter claimed, out of a sense of duty to her husband. The charges against James were "utterly and unqualifiedly false"; he possessed the love, respect, and confidence of his father, and was to both parents a loyal son. His father, the letter read, had sought his advice when making his will, but he had not asked James to join him in Washington during his last illness because of a young family "in a distant State"; James "*was* present at his father's funeral, directing the mournful preparations, and offering words of consolation and of comfort to his widowed mother." Finally, the letter stated firmly that it had been the will of her husband that James should be the "possessor" of Ashland, and because of its "ruinous condition" she had begged him to purchase it before her death.[66] Of course, Lucretia Clay did not write letters. If this was her work, the widow of Henry Clay was remarkably astute politically. More likely, she had a great deal of help from her old friend and adviser J. O. Harrison, who also happened to be a close political adviser to James Clay. However, it would not have been wise to use her name without permission. Lucretia spoke her mind within the family, as Thomas's diary entries attest, and she did only what Lucretia wanted to do. James challenged Prentice to a duel, but the dispute was settled peacefully.[67]

Despite the criticism, James Clay's political star continued to rise. Many old-line Whigs tolerated his aberrant political actions despite their discomfort with them. James spoke regularly to groups of his father's admirers who looked to him for leadership. He consistently identified himself with the Whig tradition, invoked the name of his father, and stressed the need for leadership like that of his father that could unite the nation rather than divide it. That Buchanan had been involved in the corrupt bargain charge of 1824 made James's support for him repugnant to the old-line Whigs. James responded that there had been more recent enemies of his father, the traitors of 1848, and implied that they were members of the American Party.[68] The old-line Whigs also feared James was being used by Buchanan and the Democrats. Although there certainly was truth in the accusation, no pressure was placed on Clay to tone down his Whig comments while he campaigned for Buchanan. He argued that he remained a Whig at heart, but he had no Whig candidate to support in 1856.[69]

James learned to accept the criticism of his father's former allies, charges that followed him to the grave and may be primarily responsible for the reputation that survived him. President Buchanan sought to repay him with an offer of the ministry to Prussia, but James declined. He had stated repeatedly during the campaign that he would accept no position in a Democratic administration, and he kept his word. Given the situation, he certainly understood that acceptance of a post would lead to charges of a second corrupt bargain involving Buchanan and another Clay.[70]

Political advice from friends, containing promises of other opportunities, also allowed James to decline a post in Berlin. Thomas Stevenson, a political ally, wrote on March 13 urging Clay to decline the diplomatic post. He had news, he told Clay, that was too sensitive to put on paper but which he would be excited to hear. Clay's political activities had attracted the attention of a lot of people. James received hundreds of letters from people who thought his influence sufficient to gain them positions in the Buchanan administration, and Thomas Stevenson wrote in May 1857 to tell him that some in the Democratic Party wanted to run him for governor.[71]

While James's political star rose on one side of the political spectrum, Thomas's rose on the other. Thomas justified his support of the American Party by claiming that his father would have been one of its most prominent members had he been alive. Supporting the candidacy of Millard Fillmore in 1856, Thomas served on the council considering the party platform, and he attended the American Party convention in Philadelphia in February 1856. Torn between a sense that he might fulfill his father's legacy and a sense of humility resulting from a recent religious conversion, Thomas was a mass of contradictions. He wrote to George W. Anderson that his friends thought his influence at the convention would be "as great if not greater than that of any other Delegate." So impressed with his role, he claimed in his diary that he had been suggested as a presidential candidate, though such a suggestion does not appear to have been made publicly. Yet, he added later, "I am a humble agent; whatever influence I may have, is from my father's name and character."[72] Like many of his religious persuasion, Thomas's assessments carried the fervor of a crusade and a sense of persecution. Government had to be rescued from the "imbeciles and demagogues." Upset by the direction of politics, he allowed a letter to be published in which he criticized James for rejecting sound principles. James took exception, writing his brother, "Throughout this whole Presidential contest, your name has never in any instance public or private passed my lips in terms other than respectful to my father's son." He warned Thomas to respect his position as he had respected that of Thomas.[73]

Thomas sulked after Buchanan's victory. He thought the administration hopelessly corrupt. He did not blame James directly, but his repeated diatribes and his complaints about his mother's criticism of his politics suggest he felt very isolated. That isolation would be short lived. As James moved toward alliance with the Democrats, Thomas began to transfer his allegiance to the young Republican Party.[74]

Thomas did not offer a great deal of support when James, at the suggestion of his political supporters, sought the congressional seat from his father's old Ashland district in 1857. Running against Roger Hanson, a seasoned campaigner, James began weakly; but showing a determination uncharacteristic of his generation of Clays, he became a better speaker and a more astute politician as the election neared. He pushed Hanson to the limits in an aggressive campaign. Hanson thought about challenging him to a duel, but he knew such an action against the son of Henry Clay would not be tolerated by the electorate. In August 1857 James Clay was elected from Kentucky's Eighth District, Henry Clay's Ashland District, to the United States House of Representatives.

Had Henry Clay lived, he could have taken some pride in the lives of his three sons. He would have continued to worry about John's stability, but the youngest son had proved successful as a breeder of thoroughbreds, the direction in which Henry had encouraged him. He drank too much and gambled, but he had built a home for himself and his mother. Thomas, too, was settled at Mansfield, a successful farmer and increasingly involved in political issues. Henry might have taken some pride in his election to the state legislature. And James, forty-three years old at the end of the decade, had created a significant fortune, served as a diplomat, played a highly visible role in the election of 1856, and been elected to the House of Representatives. In addition, he had become the proprietor of Ashland, once more an impressive estate perpetuating the memory of the Great Compromiser. No son had filled the shoes of the father, but Thomas, James, and John were settled in meaningful work, their father's goal, and they were making contributions locally, nationally, and in business.

Chapter 6

CIVIL WAR, FAMILY STRUGGLES

As the 1850s ended, the nation and the Clay family felt the absence of Henry Clay greater than at any time since his death. Each crisis seemed to make the rhetoric of North and South a little shriller, and the election of Abraham Lincoln gave the fire-eaters of the South the rationalization for secession they had sought for years. They refused to listen to Lincoln. Though elected from Illinois, he had deep Kentucky roots. His wife's relatives owned slaves, and he had declared Henry Clay his "beau ideal" of a statesman. He stated clearly that the president did not have constitutional authority to alter slavery where it existed. It made no difference. There were firebrands on both sides who seemed too intent on creating a hailstorm of fury.

Despite the harsh rhetoric, the Civil War took many Americans, North and South, by surprise. Throughout the months between Lincoln's election and his inauguration, the nation seemed to expect some American leader to forge another compromise in the spirit of Henry Clay. Last-minute compromises had saved the Union so many times in the past. J. J. Crittenden from Kentucky sought to lead a compromise movement, although it was almost too southern to be called a compromise. James B. Clay was named a delegate to a peace conference chaired by former president John Tyler. Virginia, the cradle of so many American presidents, sought a settlement through that body. Distinguished leaders representing twenty-one states attended the conference, but there was no Henry Clay this time. The nation faced fears Henry Clay had predicted in 1850; the Clay family faced the greatest tests of the legacies of their patriarch.

Even after attending the peace conference, James Clay hoped that rebellion would be avoided. Predicting there would be no war, he encouraged his brother-in-law Thomas P. Jacob to continue their business efforts as usual. Other members of the family shared his views. Eugene Erwin, the most promising of Henry Clay's Erwin grandsons, assured his wary wife that the business he was struggling to build took precedent over the "present political difficulties."[1] But war came, and it engulfed the family. The Clays personified in many ways the fate of their home state, a border state. In *The Little Shepherd of Kingdom Come,* John Fox Jr., a Kentucky author who knew the Clay family well, described the division in the state caused by the Civil War: "As the nation was rent apart, so was the commonwealth; as the State, so was the county; as the county, the neighborhood; as the neighborhood, the family, and as the family, so brother and brother, father and son."[2]

For Kentucky, the name Brothers' War proved an apt one. Kentucky families of all social classes were torn apart by conflicting choices. William Sullivan, little more than a scrub farmer, claimed after the war to have looked in every battle for his Union brother. His intent was to kill him. George Prentice, the editor of the *Louisville Journal,* was a Unionist, but both sons supported the Confederacy. The Crittendens and Breckinridges, powerful and popular political families, saw members fight and support opposite sides. J. J. Crittenden remained with the Union; son Thomas became a Union general and son George held the same rank in the Confederate army. Robert J. Breckinridge was pro-Union; two sons wore blue, two wore gray.

The descendants of Henry Clay experienced similar divisions. Thomas Clay remained loyal to the Union, but James sympathized with the Confederacy. The eccentric John Morrison cheered first from the sidelines for the Union then condemned both sides. Six grandsons and the husband of a granddaughter served during the war. Four served the Confederacy: James Clay Jr., Henry Clay Jr.'s son Thomas Julian, Eugene Erwin, and Thomas's son Harry. Henry Clay III joined the Union army, and Anne Clay, the surviving daughter of Henry Clay Jr., was married to Major Henry Clay McDowell, USA. Thomas Hart Clay Jr. served in the state militia, but when Simon Bolivar Buckner chose the Confederacy, Thomas resigned and worked with his father for the Union.[3]

Energized by the effort to replace the "corrupt" Democrats, Thomas Hart Clay wholeheartedly supported the new Republican government. Though not officially a member of the party, he won a seat in the state legislature and helped keep Kentucky in the Union. Active among Kentucky Unionists, he used his status as Henry Clay's son to recommend

Harry Boyle Clay. Courtesy of
Dr. William D. Kenner.

Thomas Hart Clay Jr. Courtesy of
Ashland, the Henry Clay Estate.

James B. Clay Jr. Courtesy of the Elizabeth Clay Blanford Collection.

Kentuckians for patronage positions, and he developed business interests in the Union army, orchestrating efforts to provide horses, forage, and grain for the cavalry.[4]

As war became reality in 1861, the relations between Thomas and James deteriorated. Thomas voted against James as a representative to the peace commission only to seek reconciliation with his brother a few months later. Then, when James was arrested while attempting to join Felix Zollicoffer's Confederate army, Thomas at first supported James. Working with Thomas P. Jacob, he raised bail for James's release. However, two months later in Washington, D.C., Thomas accused James of having attempted to leave the state to further the cause of the rebellion, loose words that reached the office of the secretary of state.[5]

On October 21, 1862, perhaps courting border-state support, Abraham Lincoln appointed Thomas minister resident to Nicaragua. Clay later represented the United States in Honduras as well. Upon making the appointment, Lincoln allegedly called Thomas the "true son of Henry Clay."[6] The compliment to Thomas quite likely was also a reference to the treason of that other son of Henry Clay, James. Thomas successfully con-

Henry Hart Clay III. Henry Clay Memorial Foundation Collection. Courtesy of University of Kentucky Special Collections.

cluded treaties covering issues of trade and navigation with both countries, but otherwise his term was quite uneventful.[7] Thomas had believed the Democrats used his brother in the election of 1856; it would appear that the Republicans returned the favor when Thomas was essentially forgotten in a lonely Central American post.

There was also division within Thomas's family. Despite Thomas's Union sympathies and the fact that both sons had attended the University of Wisconsin, one son—Harry Boyle Clay—joined the Confederate army. Extravagant, adventurous, and energetic (another Clay male), Harry Clay volunteered when General Kirby Smith invaded Kentucky in 1862. Promoted to captain, he served in a number of commands before becoming a prisoner of war. By the end of the war, he was serving on the staff of fellow Kentuckian Basil Duke.

John Morrison Clay tried to remain in his home, raising horses as he had always done. He sent Abraham Lincoln a snuffbox used by his father and a letter in which he based his own pro-Union sentiments on the views of Henry Clay. His father, he said, had stated that he owed a higher allegiance to the constitution and government of the United States than to the constitution and government of any state. Like father, like son; John could not help but lecture the president slightly. He noted that another noble sentiment of Henry Clay's was that he would rather be right than president, and he hoped it would be Lincoln's feeling as well. Lincoln thanked him for the snuffbox and for remaining true to his father's principles.[8] Not long into the war, however, John began to show those eccentricities that had grown to characterize him within the family. When his sixteen-year-old nephew, James Clay Jr., came to say goodbye as he left for Confederate service, John gruffly characterized him as a "damned little monkey buckled to a sword." Whether he was angry that his nephew intended to support the South or covering his concern for the boy's well-being remains unknown. As his property became affected, John Morrison soured on the war in general. Slaves used the presence of the Union army as a means to get away from their frequently unbalanced master. He also suffered losses to the Confederates. John Hunt Morgan's men stole approximately $25,000 worth of horses on one of their invasions, including Skedaddle, an extremely valuable mare.[9] With little sympathy for a Union sympathizer, Morgan allowed him to buy the horses from the men who had taken them. Skedaddle, however, had been permanently injured. By this time John Morrison had seen enough of the war, complaining, "The Yankees steal my slaves, the Rebels steal my horses, and I don't give a damn for either side."[10] Whatever his sympathies, his loyalty to family was much clearer than that of his brothers. John helped Thomas's wife with the farming at Mansfield and James's wife at Ashland. He traveled to Montreal, Canada, in late 1863 to see his Confederate brother James, ill with tuberculosis, and he and his mother offered their home to the widow and children of his nephew Captain Eugene Erwin, CSA, who died at Vicksburg.[11]

James Brown Clay offered his sympathies to the Confederacy, but he could give little else. He tried to go south in disguise, but his party was betrayed. Union forces did not know his identity at first, but when they discovered it, they delighted in his capture. Frantic correspondence between the commanding generals, Secretary of State William Seward, and the president's office suggest that they thought they had accomplished a major coup. William Seward suggested that the writ of habeas corpus be ignored in order to hold him. The *New York Times* suggested that Ashland should be confiscated and made a shrine to the loyalty of Henry Clay and the treason of James Clay.[12] The family believed the harsh treatment James Clay received while a prisoner contributed to the rapid onset of his tuberculosis.

At Camp Dick Robinson, the Union army officers left him in the night air and deprived him of food and sleep.[13]

Marched back to Lexington in chains, he was mocked by pro-Union citizens who had once been his friends. James and Susan felt their honor somewhat restored when a Louisville jury released him claiming the Union army presented insufficient evidence that he was traveling for the purpose of joining the Confederate army. The humiliation suffered at the hands of the citizens of Lexington would become a part of the Clay family story.[14]

That was only the beginning of James's troubles. If the Union sympathizers mocked him, the Rebels tried to use him. When Braxton Bragg marched on Kentucky in 1862, he tried to persuade Clay to form a regiment of Kentuckians. In fact, he announced publicly that Clay had agreed to lead a regiment of volunteers. In a memoir written several months later, James Clay disputed that account. Clay wrote that he had told Bragg it would be impossible for him to play a military role because of his health and his lack of training. Of course, when the Union advance forced Bragg out of Kentucky, Clay, already arrested once, had to leave or face arrest again. He journeyed south, accompanied by his son Harry. He called himself a refugee.[15]

Clay sensed in a partial way the chaos that was to descend on his family. Fearing confiscation of his property, he established a trust for his wife and children with Thomas P. Jacob as its director. Clay had always exhibited a strong business sense, and this time he left nothing to chance. He listed all property and the debts remaining on the land, including that owed for Ashland.[16]

James Clay followed Bragg's army south, residing for several months at a plantation owned by Charles McGhee about thirty miles south of Knoxville. Leaving for Havana, Cuba, he passed through Charleston, where he met briefly with General P. G. T. Beauregard. It seemed everyone was aware of the value of the Clay name. Beauregard wrote to C. J. Villere, a Confederate official in Richmond, suggesting that the Confederacy send Clay to either Spain or Brazil, the South's natural allies. His rationale: "on account of his name."[17] The suggestion apparently went no further, because Clay continued his journey to Cuba.

In the years before the Civil War, a number of Clays, including Henry, had gone or considered going to Cuba, believing the climate good for those with tuberculosis.[18] But James Clay did not stay long. In summer 1863, having received a passport from the Cuban government, he went first to

Halifax, Nova Scotia, then to Montreal. The Union press quickly labeled him a traitor, claiming that he was a leader of Confederate elements in Canada working with such dissidents as Clement Vallandigham to create acts of sabotage and invasion. Considerable circumstantial evidence supports the suspicion of anti-Union activity. Surrounded by Confederate sympathizers, he received his mail, according to his daughter, addressed to the alias Robert Campbell Esq., Niagara, Canada.[19] He also provided money and assistance to J. O. Harrison Jr., the son of his lawyer, who had made his way to Canada after escaping from the Union prison at Camp Douglas. A letter to Harrison implies that he helped others as well.[20] Arousing further suspicion, when the war was over his daughter Lucretia copied portions of letters that Clay had written to Thomas P. Jacob, Richard Pindell, and others, then destroyed the originals.[21]

After the war, as the family's version of its history took shape, James Clay's wife and descendants argued that he was too ill to be plotting subversion. They also claimed that his attention was drawn, knowing death was imminent, to the state of his own soul. He became very religious, spending much of his time reading, thinking, and writing about religion and what it meant for him in his last year of life. Certainly, Union sympathizers had as strong a motive to declare him a traitor as the family did later to argue that he was not, and hard evidence is limited to the fact that he provided aid to an escaped prisoner. It also seems clear that his weakened condition limited any involvement.

With James in flight, Susan took charge at Ashland. Susan had suffered little hardship in her life. Accustomed to being surrounded by successful businessmen and politicians, she had reveled in her close association with Henry Clay. She bore ten children, helped plan the rebuilding and furnishing of Ashland, and encouraged James to pursue a political career. James was a good husband, although she wished at times he could be more focused. He was also a good father. James and Susan enjoyed their roles as parents and recognized their responsibility to instill solid values in their children. James gave advice like his father, and Susan's letters to her children offered encouragement and expressed confidence in them, although in one letter to the boys who were away at school she referred to the use of "Dr. Cherry's persuasive switch." The correspondence of both parents spoke repeatedly of the importance of family, honor, and virtue, Susan's more subtly than that of James.[22]

Life at Ashland had been everything Susan sought. A letter written to her sister Lucy Jacob about Christmas at Ashland reveals clearly the pre–Civil War Susan Clay. Santa Claus appeared

> under a beautiful Christmas tree covered with light, candies, oranges, apples, grapes, misseltoe [*sic*] and holly. All of us went forward and all bowed with much politeness to old Santa Clause [*sic*], who returned our salutation and handed me a folded sheet of paper. We then bowed ourselves out of the room and shut the door so as to give the old fellow an opportunity to make his exit up the chimney and then all crowded round me to see what it was that he had given to me. I found that it was a letter which Santa Clause had written to the children and I read it aloud to them. . . . After I got through with the letter the parlor door was again opened and there was a general rush to the tree and then such a scene, such noise, and such confusion and none would rest until the presents were distributed and then after they had time to admire their own and every body else's they returned to the dining room and passed the evening dancing and playing and every now and then rushing into the parlor to admire the tree and presents and where the boys took the liberty of kissing the girls under the miseltoe [*sic*].
>
> I love to see children happy particularly at Christmas and I enter very cordially into their happiness. I wish particularly that my own children when they are grown and perhaps scattered over the face of the earth, may look back with pleasure to the days when they were all united under their Father's roof and felt that they had much happiness there.[23]

Little did Susan know how drastically that picture of domestic tranquility she painted would change over the next ten years.

The troubles brought by the war left Susan alone and worried. Her husband was away and her teenage son had joined the Confederate army. Her optimism seriously dampened by the humiliation of her husband in Lexington, she believed Lexington's citizens enjoyed seeing the Clays experience difficulty. The jealousy of lesser men for those who had achieved some fame was a lesson she would repeat regularly to her younger children. Although little evidence supports her claim, it is known that the relatives of other Confederates, such as Henrietta Morgan, suffered some abuse. When Union soldiers foraged for wood and provisions on the Ashland estate, Susan clearly felt vulnerable and abused. In a letter to General Gordon Granger, commander of Union forces in Lexington, she expressed in a haughty manner her astonishment that the Union army would treat the property of Henry Clay, a man who had served the nation so long and so faithfully, with such disrespect. Granger stopped the foraging, but his response clearly suggested that Susan no longer had the authority she enjoyed before the war: "I have too much veneration for the memory of that patriot and statesman Henry Clay, to allow any member of his family to be unnecessarily annoyed, no matter how disloyal they may be. The mantle of his goodness and greatness must and can cover many and great imperfections."[24]

Susan's burden was a heavy one, particularly for one who had enjoyed the kind of sheltered life that she had. For nearly six months after James left, Susan did not know where he was. Newspaper accounts placed him in Cuba, Canada, and even Liverpool, England. Other difficulties occurred in Lexington. The conflicting armies fought on the grounds of Ashland and disease invaded the home. The skirmish of Ashland occurred in fall 1862. It was a minor affair as Civil War encounters are measured, but not to a woman with small children in the house. Charles Donald Clay later regaled his children with stories of how, much to his mother's consternation, he peeked over the window sills to watch the battle beyond. Numerous stories developed around the encounter and became a part of the Clay legacy. The cousin of the Confederate commander John Hunt Morgan, a young man named Washington Morgan, was mortally wounded in the skirmish. Mrs. Clay ordered her carriage prepared to take the boy to the home of Mrs. Morgan out of respect for the family. Moving her family to the second floor, Susan also allowed the Union to care for the wounded soldiers in the house at Ashland, and when a Union soldier asked permission to play the piano for his compatriots, she consented. Many years later, that soldier approached her in a northern city to thank her for her kindness.[25] That story may be part of the family mythmaking, given her harsh letter to General Granger, but it became a part of the way the Clays interpreted the Civil War and their role in it. It was part of that noble spirit with which descendants of Henry Clay were supposed to meet difficult situations.

Susan's struggle with disease did not end so favorably. An outbreak of diphtheria affected five of the Clay children. Susan buried three of them in a period of fifteen months. The youngest, Nathaniel, barely a year old, died on May 17, 1862. Two daughters, Susie and Lucy Jacob, fell to the disease in 1863. Sons Harry and Tom suffered heart ailments, according to Susan, brought on by the diphtheria.[26]

Susan Clay bore her losses alone. The first letter James received revealed clearly the heartache war can cause in a family. Susan first mentioned rumors she had heard as to where he might be and offered a prayer that her letter would find him. Then she delivered the horrible news of Lucy's death:

> Dear husband may God give you strength to bear a great affliction I am about to pierce your poor heart and it adds fresh anguish to my own. Nine months ago God took our youngest darling to himself, now he has taken our oldest. On the 7th of this month last Saturday Lucy's pure spirit passed from earth to Heaven. We have not to weep or mourn for her to die was to gain. . . . She lies by the side of little Nat, whom she loved so much. She sleeps with Jesus and will rise again, she and her little brother.[27]

James's reply to the letter is equally poignant: "I have received your letter of the 12th instant communicating the death of our poor Lucy. It was the first letter I have had from you, for now, six months, and you cannot imagine the joy with which I recognized your handwriting, only to be turned into grief when the contents were known." He wrote of living among strangers, miserable and lonely, gaining strength only in the hope that all might be well at home.[28]

With communication reestablished, they shared their grief in a series of letters, emphasizing a growing dependency on religious faith. A world that had seemed so full of promise in the 1850s had slipped from their grasp. Susan complained about the deterioration of affairs in Kentucky. In a letter to her son Thomas Jacob Clay, she wrote, "Every thing seems to be in a state of anarchy in our poor State. I can not send Teetee and Susie to School and Johnny and Harry go so irregularly that they can accomplish very little in the way of study. . . . I wish I could sell Ashland and get to Europe with you all."[29] It was not to be. Eight-year-old Susie died in September 1863.

In her correspondence, Susan also noted the insubordination of the slaves. As a result, she further divided her family. She sent Teetee, Tom, and Harry to stay with her sister Kate Jones in New Jersey. She also began to sell off the slaves and to consider the sale of Ashland. James agreed on a price of $60,000 exclusive of the furniture and stock. But nothing came of it. James was at the point of death himself.[30]

James Clay's health deteriorated rapidly from the ravages of consumption, or tuberculosis. Facing certain death, he spent his days in religious thought and contemplation. By late 1863 the family, knowing the signs of imminent death from the last days of other family members who had died of the disease, began to journey to Montreal. John Morrison Clay traveled from Lexington to see his brother for the last time. Susan rented Ashland to her sister-in-law and gathered her children for the trip north. Susan and Mary had maintained close family ties despite the political differences of their husbands. Mary and her family provided support for Susan through the harsh losses of 1862–1863. That support continued as Susan made her plans to go to Montreal. James Jr. sought leave from General Breckinridge and ran the Union blockade to be with his father. James died on January 26, 1864, barely forty-six years old. If the family is to be believed, he achieved a serenity that had rarely characterized him before his end.[31]

James B. Clay left a family that would be seriously challenged by the magnitude of war and defeat. James Clay Jr. had already felt the impact of war. Not yet eighteen at his father's death, he experienced war too young. Susan had relented to his request to join the army when John Cabell Breckinridge agreed to take him as an aide. Breckinridge's son Clifton was about the same age as James, and Breckinridge promised to keep them out of trouble. Their earliest duties consisted of serving as messengers far behind the lines, but those lines and the boys' roles blurred quickly. James missed the battle at Murfreesboro because of an attack of typhoid fever but rejoined his unit at Tullahoma, Tennessee, in January 1863. When the First Kentucky was ordered to Mississippi to reinforce the army of General Joseph E. Johnston, James took part in the campaign. Breckinridge recommended him for promotion as a result of his actions. After accompanying captured battle flags to Richmond, James rejoined Breckinridge in time to participate in the Battle of Chickamauga. No messenger boy in that battle, Clay experienced combat under heavy fire. Breckinridge's division took heavy casualties, among them men who had helped James Clay Jr. grow from a boy into a man.

When Breckinridge became Confederate secretary of war in 1865, Clay joined the staff of General John B. Echols until the war neared its end. He rejoined Breckinridge, however, in the effort to help Confederate president Jefferson Davis escape. Released from service near the Florida border, he and Clifton Breckinridge turned north for home. Captured near Macon, Georgia, he was sent to Nashville, where he took the oath of allegiance to the United States. The family claimed proudly that he was the last Confederate officer decommissioned at the end of the war.[32]

James Clay Jr. carried the scars of the Civil War to his death. A veteran of a losing army at the age of twenty, he had experienced not only a war

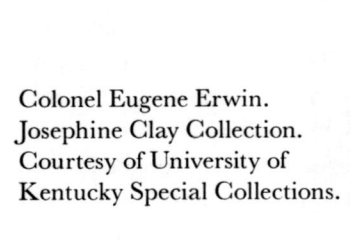

Colonel Eugene Erwin.
Josephine Clay Collection.
Courtesy of University of
Kentucky Special Collections.

but the deterioration of his army. After the Battle of Saltville in 1864, he wrote to his mother about the killing of wounded black troops who lay helpless on the field. He proclaimed his pleasure at seeing so many faces from Lexington among the victims. As late as 1877 he claimed his brother did not deserve to be called a Clay because he agreed to command buffalo soldiers in the West. He came home embittered and addicted to alcohol.[33]

Four other grandsons participated in the war. Eugene Erwin had married by the time war came. Erwin first met Josephine Russell, the daughter of Colonel William Russell, when she visited Ashland at the age of seven. She was probably more impressed at the time with the fact that Henry Clay signed her memory book.[34] She took Eugene more seriously when they met again in California, and they were married shortly after. Settling in Independence, Missouri, Eugene established a business outfitting wagon trains heading west. With a successful business and a happy marriage, he seemed content with his prospects. Erwin wrote to Josephine on May 14, 1861, "You may set your mind at rest about my engaging in the present political difficulties. Although my feelings could prompt me to rally to the standard of the Confederate States, my duty to my family restrains me. I

Josephine Russell Erwin
Clay. Josephine Clay
Collection. Courtesy of
University of Kentucky
Special Collections.

am not willing to risk my life in the present unsettled condition of business. My family and their happiness is all that I have to live for, and so long as my wife continues to be what she is I shall esteem it my first duty to consult her wishes and happiness." On May 25 he again assured her that "your fears are groundless in regard to my joining the army." Like a number of Clay men, he changed his mind quickly. In August 1861 he joined the Missouri militia.[35] Although Josephine supported her husband, his decision must have created difficulty within her family. Her father campaigned for Abraham Lincoln in the presidential election of 1860 and was appointed U.S. consul in Cuba, and she shared his political sympathies.[36]

Eugene Erwin quickly proved himself the most successful of Clay soldiers. By all accounts brave to the point of being foolhardy, Erwin won the respect of the men around him. The Missourians were rough men who skirted the boundaries of acceptable military conduct and followed only those who could prove personal valor as they defined it. On one occasion, his regiment charged with depredations against civilians, Erwin defiantly defended them, then offered to pay the costs out of his own pocket.[37] Erwin rose rapidly in rank, receiving the rank of lieutenant colonel in the Sixth

Missouri Infantry on May 15, 1862, and that of colonel after the Battle of Corinth.[38] At Corinth, he led his men in an almost suicidal assault. As his men exchanged fire at near point-blank range, Erwin sat on his horse calmly encouraging them. Wounded in the foot, he was carried to the rear.[39]

With time on his hands as he recovered, Eugene turned to another battle, the winning of his wife. He wrote to Josephine that he believed he had built a reputation in which his "angel wife and darling children" could take pride. He assured her that he was being economical so they would have money at the end of the war. Again it is difficult to tell whether he wanted to convince Josephine or himself, but he declared his belief that the war would be over by June 1, 1863, and that the Confederacy would win. He was not the first member of the Clay family to allow his logic to be overwhelmed by his enthusiasm. Why did he believe the war nearly over? "The dissensions in the North, the demoralization in the Federal Army, the state of their finances all indicate it."[40]

Erwin was rarely in command of his unit between October 1862 and March 1863. Recovered from the wound to his foot, he suffered from illness. Kent Masterson Brown suggests that Eugene probably suffered from tuberculosis or one of many other diseases sweeping through the Confederate army. Given the Clay susceptibility to tuberculosis, that diagnosis is not surprising.[41]

Leaving two daughters behind, Josephine and her oldest daughter, Lucretia Clay, or Lula, began an arduous journey to join him. In addition to having great distances to travel, Josephine had to first acquire a pass through Union lines and then, that achieved, sift through the poor communications of the Confederates to find her husband. They were finally united south of Vicksburg, where the Sixth Missouri was defending approaches to the city, and Josephine assumed the role of nurse. On May 1 Erwin left his sickbed to lead his troops toward Port Gibson to meet the attack of Union forces led by General John A. McClernand. There he suffered a second wound. Josephine remained with her husband; in fact, she became pregnant again. Eugene, however, would not live to experience the birth of his youngest daughter. On June 25 he fell before a volley of musket fire.

With the fall of Vicksburg, Josephine sought a way to return to her home. In a war fought between brothers and fellow countrymen, unusual relationships developed. Two of these came to Josephine's aid. She met Lieutenant Edwin H. Hickman, a member of the Sixth Missouri and a friend of the Erwins before the war, who agreed to try to help. Though a prisoner of war, he had earlier befriended a Union prisoner of war from Missouri, Colonel Thomas Fletcher. The tables now turned, Fletcher agreed to approach General Grant on behalf of Josephine. In a meeting with Grant, she told him that her husband was Henry Clay's grandson. Grant gave her two passes and allowed Lieutenant Hickman to accompany her back to Missouri. When Grant offered his hand, however, Josephine refused it. It was an action she later regretted, but at the time she could not acknowledge the kindness of one involved in the death of her husband.[42]

Josephine's story, like that of Susan Clay, shows the price women paid for the wars men fought. Like many others, she experienced the horrible siege of Vicksburg, suffering from limited food, living almost underground in unhealthy conditions. Returning to Missouri a penniless widow, she gave birth on January 26, 1864, to a daughter that she named Eugenia. The child lived only a few days, certainly another victim of the trauma caused by war.[43]

The Henry Clay Jr. branch also suffered tragedy as a result of the war. Henry III, Anne, and Thomas Julian, orphaned at a young age, spent much of their time in Louisville under the care of Nanette Price Smith, but they also lived with Henry and Lucretia at Ashland on occasion. Both Henry III and Thomas Julian were intelligent and witty yet rash and hotheaded. Anne clearly was the most levelheaded of Henry Clay Jr.'s three children. Educated primarily in Louisville and Lexington, she learned the social skills so important in that time. Calm and dignified like her aunt of the same name, she grew to maturity with the gentility Henry Clay would have loved to see exhibited by his sons and grandsons. On May 21, 1857, Anne married Henry Clay McDowell, a member of a Kentucky family as distinguished as the Clays. McDowell was no stranger to the children of Henry Clay Jr. The McDowells were prominent citizens of Louisville, and he and Thomas Julian Clay were classmates at the University of Virginia. Named assistant adjutant general of volunteers for the Union army, McDowell achieved the rank of captain on November 19, 1861, and Anne supported his Union sympathies. Henry Clay III also volunteered for service with the Union army. Thomas, however, defiantly supported the Confederacy.[44]

Henry Clay McDowell and Henry Clay III spent the first year of the war together. Henry Clay III wrote his sister Anne from Camp Nevin with characteristic excitement. Despite his dismal record at West Point, he had made many friends there and delighted in renewing acquaintances with

Thomas Julian Clay. Henry
Clay Memorial Foundation
Collection. Courtesy of
University of Kentucky
Special Collections.

them. He wrote humorously about camp life, complaining good-naturedly about cold feet at night and the loneliness. He also begged his sister to write.[45]

Henry Clay III and H. C. McDowell shared a dilemma undoubt-edly faced by many citizen-soldiers of the border states. In letters to his wife, McDowell noted their fear that they might suddenly recognize their brother, Thomas Julian, through the smoke and dust of battle. Thomas, on the other hand, seemed less concerned. Assigned to the staff of General Simon Buckner, he reached the rank of major and served as adjutant and inspector general.[46] He enjoyed fighting. He did not like the Yankees and did not hide it in his letters to his pro-Union sister. In one of those cruel twists of the Civil War, everyone was elated when they learned that he had been captured in the fighting around Fort Donelson. Everyone, that is, except Thomas Julian. He became a prisoner of war at a camp in Columbus, Ohio. A letter to his sister expressed his shock that they were happy he had been captured. He also shared his disdain for the North and its supporters, and the mental gymnastics the family had to exercise to separate political loyalty from family loyalty:

> If my letter struck you with delight you certainly struck me with surprise, that you would be rejoiced that yr brother was to be the subject of the humiliation, insult and privation necessarily attendant upon being a prisoner in the hands of a people so devoid of all generosity and even humanity as those of the North. Exceptionally we have met officers who endeavoured to alleviate our condition, but so hampered are they by orders from "the best government the world ever saw," that their efforts are almost entirely unavailing. . . . I did not like the north very much when I left Ky; Do you imagine that I like it any better now? I certainly do not and the intensity of my hatred for its people seems even to myself almost criminal.[47]

He seemed oblivious to the fact that his brother, brother-in-law, and the sister to whom he wrote supported the cause he criticized so sharply. Indeed, in the same letter, he spoke forcefully to the attitude regarding family that characterized the Clays: "I was surprised to hear that you attributed my not writing to you as a supposition on my part that you had lost yr affection for me. I assure you that, loving and esteeming you as I do, I could not have so low an opinion of you as to suppose that you would cease to love a brother who, however much he might differ from you, you knew to have acted upon what he believed was right."

The brothers would not meet across battle lines. Henry Hart Clay died of typhoid fever on June 5, 1862. And Thomas's death soon followed. Henry Clay McDowell tried to obtain a parole for his brother-in-law. His greatest obstacle, however, was Thomas Julian. He wrote in frustration to his wife that Thomas made it more difficult because he would not keep his mouth shut. To tweak the phrase of Henry Clay's that became the family motto, Thomas Julian would rather shout his principles than be paroled. In fact, he expressed his anger that McDowell would expect him to accept a parole if one were offered.[48]

Neither Thomas nor the McDowells recognized the dangers of Civil War prisoner-of-war camps. Like so many others, he fell ill with a fever that slowly sapped his strength. Nanette Price Smith, Anne Clay McDowell, and other relatives—Union sympathizers—rushed to Columbus to care for their Confederate kinsman. In April 1862 the Union placed him in the care of his guardian, Thomas Smith, and six months later they exchanged him for a captured Union officer.[49] Thomas recovered, or at least got better, because he returned to the Confederate army intent on fighting again. However, on October 13, 1863, Lieutenant James B. Clay Jr., CSA, wrote his pro-Union cousin that her brother was dead. James was unusually sensitive. Thomas had not seemed very ill when the cousins had met two days earlier, but he died on October 12 of "congestive fever." James went to Atlanta to have him buried and look after his property. His efforts to console Anne were typical of a growing sentiment perceptible in Clay correspondence: family might just be more important than politics.[50]

The Civil War took a terrible toll on the Clay family. James died during the war, and Thomas did not survive it for long, his health destroyed by conditions in Central America. Nearly a year after the war, he returned to the United States. There the Ku Klux Klan hounded him because of his service. Thomas Clay died a broken man in 1871. Of the six grandsons that served in the war, three died, either from wounds or from disease. James Clay Jr. returned from the war impaired by alcoholism and his sense of defeat. Three children of James and Susan died as a result of disease, and in the fourth generation the infant daughter of Eugene and Josephine was surely a victim of war. Political principles hardly seemed worth the price. The family loyalty demonstrated in the life of Henry Clay took on new meaning to his descendants.

Chapter 7

A NEW IMAGE

The Confederacy suffered a devastating defeat at the hands of the Union. The men who had fought as rebels knew it. The women of the South knew it as the men came stumbling home with an arm missing, or a leg, or with spirits broken. Far too many men did not come home at all. The Civil War took more than six hundred thousand lives. The South would later take a morbid pride in the fact that more Union soldiers died than Confederate, but as a percentage of the total population, the losses of the South were significantly larger. Scarcely a family had not lost a father, brother, uncle, or nephew. The empty sleeve and the peg leg provided more realistic symbols of southern manhood than cavalry sword or the honorary title of colonel in the years after the war. Henry Clay's grandson Harry Boyle Clay may have spoken for many Confederate veterans when he told his Union cousin H. C. McDowell, "In regard to my future political disposition you may very safely say that no future efforts of mine will be directed against the security of the Govt which could put a million and a half men in the field and the most magnificent navy afloat in the world and that my only desire is to be permitted to cultivate my farms and to support my family."[1]

Southerners found their defeat hardest to accept on a psychological level. Proud people who had talked so much about honor and the nobility of their cause, southerners had emphasized social order, manliness, ideal womanhood, and the certain blessing by God of a region superior to others in all respects. Although the world created in myth had never existed for many southern people, it remained the idealized view of the South. The "late great unpleasantness," however, left the South in shambles. Southerners faced real poverty. Currency was worthless, livestock and farming equipment destroyed, and the infrastructure, severely limited before the war, now virtually nonexistent. They believed themselves despised by northerners, and that was not entirely untrue. In addition, there was cultural change. Three and a half million black slaves had been freed. It constituted a psychological revolution for people who believed strongly in white supremacy.[2] Southerners also faced the reality of what they had done. Treason, horrific sacrifices, and tragic conclusion were bitter pills to swallow.

To escape the burden and the shame, the South resorted to a traditional method for alleviating problems and justifying actions. Mythmaking had long been a standard of southern life. According to Paul M. Gaston, myths "are combinations of images and symbols that reflect people's way of perceiving the truth."[3] One might also say they are the means by which people create a truth they are able to perceive. History and memory blend to smooth the rough edges of painful images. The South looked to its past, and out of the ashes it created the Lost Cause, a collective memory of honor and duty, of courage, of brave and noble soldiers like Robert E. Lee, of well-bred ladies and gentlemanly men—all part truth but highly exaggerated—that helped southerners withstand the psychological trauma of their defeat.[4]

Never has the South been more successful than when it etched the Lost Cause mentality into its collective consciousness, and to a large degree, that of the North as well. As the Lost Cause goes, Confederate soldiers and officers were honorable men fighting for a cause in which they believed. Thomas Julian Clay expected the understanding of his pro-Union sister because he believed in his cause. They called it the War between the States, a much more genteel term than "civil war" or "rebellion." The South had not fought a war to extend or protect slavery; the issue leading to rebellion had been states rights, guaranteed, as the most complex arguments claimed, by the American Constitution. What the proponents of the Lost Cause chose to exclude was the fact that the right the states most wanted was to protect and extend slavery, or at least white supremacy. Southern culture was agrarian by choice; plantation owners were almost Jeffersonian yeoman farmers who absorbed positive values from working the land, or having others work it for them. Southern culture was also a bastion of Christian principles; or, if it better served the purpose, the American South was the heir of Greece and Rome. In the aftermath of the war, southerners wondered aloud how God could have abandoned their cause, finally deciding that he intended to teach far nobler lessons in the experience of defeat. The rural, agrarian, and Christian South was far superior to the greedy and aggressive industrial society of the North. Slave masters had been kindly folk, even accepting certain slaves as family members, and had provided slaves both Christianity and the discipline those of African descent needed. Aspects of the myth can still be heard from local barbershops to college classrooms across the South. Southerners with pedigrees still claim their ancestors were kindly masters who treated their slaves well. Ignoring the thousands who fled as Union armies approached, they proclaim the few who stayed on the kindly southerner's plantation.

The personification of the Lost Cause was Robert Edward Lee of old Virginia, lately the commander of the forces of rebellion but soon the remarkable gentleman without character flaw. All southern males were to follow his example, and the ladies delighted when they found one who even hinted at his nobility. The myth grew quickly. The Daughters of the Confederacy and Protestant ministers preached it. Veterans groups adopted it. College fraternities taught its standards as ideals, if less frequently practices. Blending easily with late-Victorian ideals of masculinity, it caused even northerners in time to look at Lee as a shining example of the Christian gentleman. Defeated, certainly, but quick to construct justifications and hardly reconstructed.[5] The Lost Cause had many intertwined tenets and principles. It explained everything, always to the advantage of the South and its people, its white people. It was above questioning. It became very much the South's identity.

Whether Union or Confederate in sympathies, Kentuckians also suffered serious physical and psychological damage from the war. Kentuckians as a whole lamented the outbreak of civil war. They hoped for compromise reminiscent of their favorite son, Henry Clay, but his protégé, J. J. Crittenden, was not up to the task. Governor Beriah Magoffin attempted to create a policy of neutrality, but that was wishful thinking. Too strategic geographically and as a source of supplies for neutrality to be honored by either side, Kentucky was also divided ideologically. The state remained in the Union, but its people divided. Approximately ninety thousand men joined the Union army, but forty thousand, including a large number of Central Kentucky's elite, became Confederates.

Kentuckians loved the concept of Union, perhaps another part of Henry Clay's legacy, but they adamantly opposed emancipation. Lincoln's Emancipation Proclamation of 1863 did not directly affect slavery in Kentucky, but the state reacted violently to it. Richard T. Jacob, Susan Clay's brother and a Union army officer, was charged with sedition and banished to the Confederacy when he spoke against it. The recruiting of black soldiers, more than twenty thousand of whom came from Kentucky, completed the alienation of the state. Belatedly, Kentucky became a southern state.

There were other problems. The state experienced a significant amount of violence. During the war, Confederate and Union armies seized virtually any property or supplies they wanted. Neither showed much respect for the guarantees of the Constitution; they arrested people at will, interfered with elections, and held prisoners without trial. Near the end of the war, guerillas and deserters created mayhem across the state. The breakdown of police and courts allowed local and family feuds to erupt in violence on city and village streets across the state. And the Ku Klux Klan and other vigilante groups harassed blacks and Republicans after the war. Murder and mayhem characterized Kentucky until the beginning of the twentieth century.

The descendants of Henry Clay also experienced devastation in the wake of the war. David Goldfield notes in his book *Still Fighting the Civil War* that tragedy is a central element to establishing and fostering tradition.[6] Divided loyalties, tragic deaths, loss of property, and loss of influence—the Clays, like the South, experienced a psychological trauma too painful to embrace. They too needed a myth on which to rebuild. That myth was a family version of Robert E. Lee, a "marble man," a new image of Henry Clay.[7] As the South did with Lee, the Clays used Henry's personality and contributions as a base to build an image useful to the present, and, they believed, the future. Because the Lost Cause became so strong in the postwar era, its tenets became intertwined with the new image of Henry Clay, creating a "collective memory" that impacted the values and actions of day-to-day life.[8]

Robert E. Lee had loved his state. Henry Clay loved his nation. His loyalty became the path for the "southern" Clays back into the Union. He quickly became in the Clay memory the foremost statesman of the antebellum era, the one American who could have solved the race issue and avoided the Civil War. Henry Clay had the answers for the nation before 1852, if the nation had just chosen to heed him. He also had the traits a true gentleman of any age needed to ensure success and adoration. And, in a period of difficult transitions, Clay's ultimate stance—I would rather be right than president—became a source of strength and justification.

By 1865 the descendants of Henry Clay were divided into five major branches. They did not all need the family memory in the same proportions because the war had impacted them differently. Of Henry Jr.'s children, only Anne remained. Her husband, Major Henry Clay McDowell, was not related to Henry Clay but, like so many other Americans, had received his name because of the respect in which the statesman was held. He had remained loyal to the Union, and with his own fortune and that of his wife, he was poised to take advantage of the economic opportunities created by another postwar southern myth, the New South Creed. Nevertheless, living in Kentucky, the family was forced to pay homage to the Lost Cause. Although the major remained Republican, he adopted southern dress and manners and used the image of Henry Clay to help ingratiate him with the southern, and northern, businessmen and politicians he needed to cultivate.

Mansfield remained the home of the Thomas Clay branch. Thomas died in 1871, but Mary and her daughter Minnie lived there until the 1890s. The two sons settled elsewhere. Thomas Hart Clay Jr. took his pro-Union sentiments to New Jersey, where he served as an editor of *Youth's Companion,* a moralistic publication that, somewhat ironically, affected the development of the Clay myth some years later. In a biography of Henry Clay, he would publish much of the new image the family created. After retiring, he returned to Lexington, but he left two daughters in the North.

His brother Captain Harry Boyle Clay, CSA, married a wealthy widow from Rogersville, Tennessee, and settled there after the war. His family constituted another branch that responded to the myths in a much different way, although Harry was quite a storyteller, adding to and perpetuating the new image of "Grandfather." In a generation, that branch looked to another family, the Kenners, who were more closely associated with the region where they lived.

The descendants of Anne Clay Erwin, the fourth branch, suffered horrid losses. Tuberculosis took Henry and Charles Edward Erwin as the Civil War began. Lucretia Hart Erwin Cowles disappeared, her family emerging only in the late twentieth century. The major group consisted of Josephine, the widow of Colonel Eugene Erwin, CSA, and her three surviving daughters. Left destitute, she brought her daughters to Kentucky in 1866.

Mrs. James B. Clay and her children remained scattered immediately after the war. The economic climate forced Susan to sell Ashland to Kentucky University, and the family wandered from relative to rented house until she purchased a farm four miles west of Lexington in 1883.

They called it Balgowan, and Susan lived there with an unmarried daughter, called Teetee to distinguish her from all the other Lucretias, and a bachelor son, George. After a career in the military, son Thomas lived with them as well. James Jr. lived at Iroquois Farm, a thoroughbred operation adjacent to Balgowan, and at the turn of the century, Charles bought a nearby farm.

Susan Clay became the principal architect of the myth of Henry Clay. She had lost so much as a result of the war that she perhaps needed the myth more. The war cast deep shadows over Susan's antebellum dreams. The military occupation of Ashland, the contempt of neighbors and friends, and unruly slaves damaged her self-assurance. Her husband and three of her children died during the war, then she lost the beloved Ashland. She wandered for nearly twenty years before settling at Balgowan. Her sons restored the home, creating a pleasant Tudor cottage surrounded by native trees, flower gardens, and pastures. The name Balgowan was suggested by Dr. James K. Patterson, first president of the present-day University of Kentucky. It meant "land of flowers." However, Susan called her home "the Shanty," a description true only in relation to Ashland. Although the house would be razed in the 1920s, the land became the centerpiece of Calumet Farm, a major twentieth-century thoroughbred business. A diary entry found among her papers suggests the depths of her despair. She wrote, "Passed Ashland—there, the shadow was upon my heart—the misty vale of sorrow over my eyes. . . . I looked upon the sloping lawns and familiar walks but oh my heart cried out—where are my loved ones?"[9] Thomas L. Connelly claims that ex-Confederates used Lee as a balm to soothe their defeat; Henry Clay became Susan's remedy for lost prominence and lost hope. Too many losses haunted her present. Her world was in shambles.[10]

Alone and uncertain herself, Susan Clay had to help seven children find their roles in a world in disarray. She owned property, but she suffered from the same cash-flow problems that affected people throughout the South. Consequently, she sold Ashland and its furnishings. Adding to her misery, even some of the family heirlooms she wished to save were auctioned by mistake.[11] The family told stories claiming Susan at times had a mere five dollars a month in cash.[12] Recalling their hostility during the war, she expected her neighbors to try to take advantage of her sex. She was also convinced her brother managed her estate badly while he prospered, and she faced a challenge from her oldest son. As oldest sons traditionally did in the South, James undoubtedly expected to assume his father's role as leader of the family. Besieged from all directions, Susan Clay created a new image of the patriarch to buttress her matriarchal control of the family. The picture of Lost Cause feminine dignity, charm, even submissiveness in public, she ruled the family with an iron hand.[13]

Susan sought to instill in her children that same iron will. The family was nearly destitute, at least as she told the story. Not only had they lost their fortune but no family member now enjoyed a place of national prominence as they had in the past. "The Clay star," she wrote to one son, "is not in the ascendancy just now." But she also taught them that there was a Clay star. They were blessed with the name of Clay. The Victorian era placed great emphasis on bloodlines; Susan believed, and taught her children, that the genius of Henry Clay flowed in their veins.[14]

Using an ancestor to teach values and pride is not uncommon. Elizabeth Stone in *Black Sheep and Kissing Cousins* argues that families of all social classes use a grandparent or an uncle as a symbol of the kinds of values a new generation should develop. The Clays transmitted the family names through each generation; there are so many Henrys they called several of them Harry so they could tell them apart. As practiced in the South, family naming practices and family duty made it extremely difficult to escape the demands of the past.[15] The Clays were like any other family in instilling their values; there was just so much ammunition. The Clay homes—Ashland, Mansfield, Balgowan—were perfect for the storytelling used to instill an image of family. Sitting around the table or in the parlor after dinner, families traditionally talked about the past—their own and that of the nation. In the Clay homes, the walls were adorned with imposing portraits of distinguished people. Gifts to Henry Clay from the silversmiths of Boston and New York and furnishings purchased by Henry and Lucretia adorned the rooms. A story accompanied each artifact. The papers of Henry Clay had also been preserved. Susan, Aunt Teetee, Anne McDowell, and others, pulled from trunks letters signed by George Washington, James Madison, Daniel Webster, Zachary Taylor—in fact, most of the leaders of the country in its first seventy-five years. The children learned what Bertram Wyatt-Brown calls their "place." They understood that their family had mattered in the nation's history. In addition to "Grandfather," Henry Clay Jr. had died heroically at the Battle of Buena Vista, James Clay had served as diplomat and congressman, and Thomas had been called the "true son" of Henry Clay by a president of the United States. Even the Confederate sympathizers embraced Lincoln's words.

They also learned about collateral families; Harts, McDowells, Jacobs, Browns, and Peppers had contributed their abilities to community, government, and various professions. Elizabeth Stone claims children learned the "shared sensibilities" of the family through such means.[16] Clays learned the importance of service, honor, and integrity. Susan and other family members polished the stories in just the right way to provide the values they wished to convey to the next generation. They did not change the facts, but the stories were told in the most pleasant light.

The success of Susan Clay's efforts can be seen in the actions and characteristics of following generations. It can also be seen in the vast collections of correspondence and papers preserved by the family. The preservation of the family papers is in itself evidence of the importance placed on the family in the Clay homes. The papers were essential to telling the true story of Henry Clay. Additionally, should someone equal Henry Clay's contribution, the papers would be necessary to tell that story as well.[17] Each branch treasured the record of the past. Family members also published biographical accounts that reveal aspects of the myth. In the 1880s Susan Clay began her own biography of Henry Clay, providing a written record of the information that she had shared with her own children. The extended family also adopted most of the details of her family epic. Like the tenets of the Lost Cause, it seemed to be absorbed by some process of osmosis. The same anecdotes, and interpretations, can be seen in a biography written by Thomas Hart Clay Jr. in 1906 and published posthumously in 1910. Madeline McDowell Breckinridge, a great-granddaughter, wrote several articles about Henry Clay for *Century Magazine* and talked about him in numerous speeches. Because the Clay descendants remained prominent in Lexington, Josephine Clay, Madge Breckinridge, Louisiana Simpson, and Henrietta Clay gave speeches and published short stories about Clay. Those speeches wrapped him in the fabric of the Lost Cause. Madge Breckinridge epitomized the strength of Clay myths. Her family had supported the Union, and she believed in a strong and active national government. In speeches throughout the country she urged the South to forget the Lost Cause and embrace a philosophy that led to progress, a position not unlike that of her father. However, she accepted most of the family image of Henry Clay, including its Lost Cause traits. Pervasive to an extreme, the Lost Cause affected virtually all southerners in one way or another. The various branches of the Clay family saved newspaper clippings, and family members frequently wrote to newspapers to correct mistakes about Henry or other family members published in books, magazines, and papers.[18]

The new Henry Clay was the marble man—a picture of perfection. After the Civil War, masculinity became increasingly important, not just in the South but throughout America. Henry Clay was tall for his time, but his build was slender and his health was always tenuous. He regularly mentioned illnesses and the need to gain weight. All but one of Susan's six sons were small boned and slight like their grandfather. In Susan Clay's version, Henry Clay became the epitome of manhood. At about six feet one inch in height, Susan declared, Henry was well proportioned. He became something of a Roman patrician: "His head was well shaped, his forehead high, his nose straight and clear cut, his mouth broad rather than large. His upper lip was long and both lips were thin and firm, but flexible and changing with every emotion." He walked "with a slow, soft, measured and slightly springing step, like that of a panther, full of dignity and grace. The poise of his head was grand, and his bearing was lofty and commanding." Susan portrayed Henry as aggressive, manly, and athletic.

The physical description was measured, however, when compared to his personal characteristics and skills. The characteristics attributed to him applied more to the postwar era than to Clay's own. She created a Victorian and southern gentleman. The depiction of Clay read like it originated in Samuel Smiles's *Self Help*, or another Victorian success manual. Clay was exact and punctual, frugal and punctilious. System and method always constituted a part of his morals. Something about his manner and presence impressed those around him, and beneath the manner lay a power, a force of character to be respected, feared, followed, and honored. He possessed a clear sense of honor, never forgetting a friend or departing from honesty with friend or foe alike. Applying late-Victorian values, Susan emphasized, in one long list, "his manliness, his truthfulness, his boldness, his direct honesty, his scorn of petty intrigue, and of all that was sordid, selfish and deceitful; his sublime patriotism, his self-respect, his chivalry, his undaunted courage, his pure moral perceptions."[19] It was a description worthy of Robert E. Lee. So effusive it probably would have made even the excitable Henry Clay blanch in modesty.

In family accounts, Clay had the best grasp of the issues facing the nation during his lifetime. He had studied at the feet of the founders, great men like Wythe, Jefferson, and Madison. She pointed to all his triumphs and to failures when he was right. She told one son, "He mixed well with his fellow man, even while greatly the superior of most men and while he never stooped to a petty, mean, low action to gain any thing (he would have died first) yet—he fought the fight of life manfully, improving talents God had given him and raising himself with God's help to be first in the nation."[20] The patriarch had consistently understood the problems of the nation and just as often created solutions to them. The U.S. commissioners at Ghent were well selected, "but among them Henry Clay, Primus Inter Pares, if not Facile Princeps, exerted a commanding influence." He had been the champion of democracy for the peoples of Greece, South America, and the United States. She adamantly rejected the idea of the corrupt bargain with Adams, as did Thomas Hart Clay Jr. in his biography. Clay had merely made the best, and most obvious, choice for the nation. David and Jeanne Heidler, the latest biographers of Clay, essentially repeat the argument of Susan and Thomas Clay Jr. Given William Crawford's physical condition and Andrew Jackson's military personality, Clay had contemplated the outcome very early in the process.[21]

Thomas's and Susan's chapters on Clay as a member of the House of Representatives, as Speaker, and as a defender of South American independence proclaimed a reasonable account of his role. Since Thomas's biography was published posthumously, it is difficult to tell how much editing occurred. His accounts follow the same tendencies as Susan's but in more subdued language. Both believed Henry Clay deserved the title Great Compromiser. Susan wrote, "Thrice he saved the Union from civil war, and had he been alive in 1860–61, every heart and every eye would have turned to him to take the helm again. But alas! He had gone and taken his mantle with him."[22] Madeline McDowell, in an article published in *Century Magazine,* claimed that a former judge and admirer of Abraham Lincoln stated he believed there would have been no place in history for Lincoln if Henry Clay had been spared a little longer.[23]

No detail was too small for the family's attention. They rejected, for example, the idea of Henry Clay as some poor "mill boy of the slashes." That was not uncommon in the late nineteenth century. Both southern gentry and new industrial families sought noble origins even to the point of marrying their daughters into European nobility. At the very least, they downplayed the recent origins of their wealth. Robert Lincoln, for example, tried to erase the record of his father's log-cabin origins.[24] Henry Clay's father was a simple, "godly" preacher, Susan claimed, but he stemmed from "an old and prominent family in Virginia, tracing their ancestry through many generations to Sir John Clay, of Wales." Susan cited Reuben Durrett, an early Kentucky historian who said Clay had claimed humble origins as a means to acquire votes. In fact, no one of noble status named Sir John Clay existed in Wales, although an early Clay in Virginia may have been legally named Sir John Clay.[25] The Clay Family Society supports an ongoing DNA study in the United States and England in an effort to determine the family's origins.[26]

One chapter in Susan's collection is titled "Henry Clay, the Christian Statesman." Clearly uncomfortable with the fact that he did not receive baptism until 1847, Susan sought to emphasize his Christian spirit. Both Susan and Thomas claimed that he frequently walked the mile and a half from Ashland to the Episcopal Church and had kept a pew there for years. So intensely devoted to the good of others, he had little opportunity to think on religious matters; but his family had been Christian for generations, and she pointed to statements made throughout his career that indicated his religious nature. He had always been a kind and sensitive man, devoted to his family and to the less fortunate. For evidence of his innate spirituality, she turned to the eulogies written at the time of his death. Thomas Hart Clay Jr. said he had always been interested in religious subjects.[27] As has been shown, Henry Clay saw little personal need for religion until late in his life. He acknowledged the church as a civic responsibility, but the emphasis on religion belonged to Susan. She had turned to religion in the trauma of war and wanted those around her, most notably her children, to share it.[28] A religious spirit also characterized the new southern gentleman.

The Clays could not escape the charges of drinking, dueling, gambling, and womanizing that plagued Henry's political career. There were too many sons in the family clearly as prone to excess as Henry Clay had been in his youth. In explaining the patriarch, however, they tended to put as positive a spin on the charges as possible. Henrietta Clay admitted that Henry had a temper that occasionally got him into trouble, but she quickly noted that he had not killed anyone in a duel. The story about purchasing John Randolph a new coat after Clay's bullet damaged his original one was a favorite throughout the family. It showed such gallantry. Even before the Civil War, James B. Clay had written to several people present at the duel because he believed an erroneous account was gaining credence. Clay's gambling also had to be explained. Thomas Hart Clay Jr. noted that it was characteristic of the Kentucky frontier. His grandfather's gambling was a social activity and no more or less than was socially acceptable at the time. He said the same thing about his drinking.[29] The Clays were particularly sensitive to John Quincy Adams's charges about Clay's activities at Ghent. They rejected accusations that his behavior had affected his role there. Instead, they claimed he recognized the British diplomats were bluffing because he had sat so many times at the card table that he could read his opponents masterfully. His gambling, then, became an opportunity to serve his nation.

The charges of being too fond of the ladies proved particularly sensitive in the Victorian age but relatively easy to explain. The Old South had placed its pure women on a pedestal, and the Lost Cause kept them there. From the pedestal they were to be admired, respected, and protected. Again, a number of scholars have challenged the myth. That pedestal was often so high it served as a prison. No Clay woman would admit that, at least in public.[30] But Henry Clay had truly enjoyed the company of women, and he practiced gallantry as well as any southerner. Family members noted the affection he felt for Lucretia, particularly in their declining years. They might also have mentioned his relationship with Susan and Anne, his daughters. Madge Breckinridge suggested both humorous and sad reasons for his flirtations. In *Century Magazine,* she related the story of an elderly woman who recalled that as a little girl she had received a kiss, and a dime for it, from Henry Clay. It was not the only girl, she noted, young or otherwise, that he had kissed. She suggested that his fondness for women might have resulted from the loss of all six of his daughters. She also emphasized his great sensitivity.[31]

As the nineteenth century progressed, the Clays increasingly portrayed the patriarch as a warm, generous, and caring elder statesman. They emphasized his love of family and his gentlemanly nature. Though certainly not untrue, the facts chosen to support the image indicate a very selective memory. Contemporaries and historians noted how easily he expressed friendship. The family attributed the trait to a sensitivity that others had overlooked. Both Susan and Thomas Hart Clay Jr. called attention to the peculiar nature of his emotions. Clay's nervous system, they wrote, was "so delicately strung, a word, a touch, a memory would set it in motion." Thomas Hart Clay Jr. credited J. O. Harrison with the description; Susan Clay claimed it as her own. Thomas Hart Clay Jr.'s biography focused primarily on his grandfather's political role, but he mentioned Clay's love of family, particularly his relationship with a favorite granddaughter.

Lucy Clay. Courtesy of the Elizabeth Clay Blanford Collection.

Although he did not mention her name, it was surely Lucy Jacob Clay, the daughter of James and Susan. Lucy suffered from a spinal injury that left her deformed and subject to constant pain. Biographers have traditionally thought she suffered the condition from birth, but in a cruel twist of Lost Cause mentality, Elizabeth Clay Blanford suggested that as an infant Lucy was dropped, perhaps intentionally, by a slave.[32] Lucy's maturity and courage won the love and respect of seemingly everyone in the extended family. Henry's attachment to her was more than family mythmaking, but it certainly enhanced the image they wished to portray. Susan Clay had known Henry, but Josephine, Madge, Henrietta, and Louisiana Simpson told stories they had heard within the family. In *Century Magazine,* Madge noted that few remained alive who knew him, but they remembered him fondly; she also mention the special affection for "an invalid granddaughter," again certainly Lucy Jacob Clay. Ironically, Susan Clay, the child's mother, did not mention the relationship of her daughter with Clay. Perhaps it remained too painful.

The impact of the Lost Cause on Clay mythmaking was particularly pronounced in the attitude toward African Americans. North and South shared a racism that has shaped much of American social history. The New South Creed, another southern myth, encouraged southerners to look beyond slavery and the Civil War, but its proponents did not mean to create a world of racial equality in the bosom of the old Confederacy. Edward L. Ayers notes in *The Promise of the New South* that the New South Creed allowed southerners to have it both ways: they could reconstruct a proud South and partake of "northern" industrial prosperity. In fact, it allowed southerners to claim they had moved past slavery, yet maintain white supremacy.[33] Although blacks must be considered of equal importance in any definition of the region, southern whites have spent perhaps their best energies trying to keep them unequal. They desperately needed blacks as a source of labor, yet whites feared, loathed, and mocked them even as they tried to entice or force them to work the land. James B. Clay Jr.'s delight at seeing Lexington blacks shot to death as they lay wounded on the battlefield at Saltville may or may not be an extreme. Blacks who dared express feelings of equality to white southerners were found in earthen dams as late as the 1960s. The thought that a former slave could look a white in the eye, testify against a white in a trial, or even successfully farm a privately owned plot of ground often riled white southerners angry over defeat and humiliation, or, as Paul Gaston suggests, frustrated by the high degree of failure experienced in southern life.

How would a free black population be controlled? The infamous Black Codes excluded blacks from jury service and from testifying against whites, and placed restrictions on their employment, ownership of land, and right to make contracts. New laws limited their social mobility and their economic opportunity. Much to the surprise of southerners, the North responded with contempt for their arrogance. The South had, after all, lost the war. The codes were repudiated, but they did not disappear. Local sheriffs essentially enforced them for nearly a century. The law does not protect if local officials choose not to enforce it.

An immediate need in the South was to get the labor force back to work. Southerners tried many avenues to accomplish the task. Again, force was always a handy tool, but northern authorities voiced disapproval when such efforts became too blatant. The Freedman's Bureau sought to limit the method, though northern racial prejudices were revealed even as its officials sought to aid the freed slaves. In order to have labor, some landowners gave or sold land to their former slaves; free blacks congregated in small hamlets near the plantation, living in their own homes, working their own land and that of their benefactor. Others were far less charitable. James F. Robinson, Union governor of Kentucky during the war, produced a plan for the state legislature that would have made freedmen indentured servants for seven years. Benevolent whites would teach them the ways of freedom and give them fifty dollars when the term was concluded. The most successful measure in ensuring labor was the crop lien system, or sharecropping. It had the added advantage of controlling poor whites as well as free blacks. Men, often aided by their wives and children, worked the land for a portion of the crop. The method provided the means to turn back the clock. Southern agriculture remained essentially the same, and the southern states continued to be overwhelmingly agricultural.

In the Lost Cause myth, "faithful black slaves" became "faithful black servants," at least in the minds of whites. The Lost Cause mentality changed the causes of the war. The Civil War had not been fought to maintain slavery—though slavery, southerners claimed, had not been as bad as northerners maintained. The plight of northern immigrant workers provided a welcome foil for the myth. Blacks had actually benefited from slavery, the myth suggested, by receiving the advantages of Christianity when they were brought to this country. Most southerners treated their slaves kindly; twenty-first-century southerners have numerous anecdotes to prove it. Slave owners had, of course, exercised discipline, a trait much needed by the African, and the myth admitted to some excesses, though they were rare and not a fit subject for conversation.

From acts of the Klan to legal lynchings, the South seemed to decide that if they did not talk about the incidents, such "unpleasantries" did not occur, and if someone did talk about them, he or she really disliked the region and wanted to impugn the reputations of the good people of the South. The genteel southerner considered the faithful black servants members of the family, and children were taught to call them uncle or aunt as they aged—though as late as the 1970s in the deep South, "Aunt" Mary rode in the back seat of the car when she was driven home at the end of the day. Southern white children, even those of moderate social status, remember a kindly black servant or nanny who taught them good manners and chastised them if they misbehaved. Blacks and whites settled into a relationship that blacks accepted for fear of retaliation and whites accepted because it existed. If black children went to a separate school, it was merely the way things were. At its most mythical, it could be explained as the way blacks preferred their education. As late as the civil rights movement in the 1960s, it was not the good southern black who was causing trouble but northern agitators, even Communists, who wished to disrupt the idyllic life enjoyed by the southern people.

Clay descendants adopted most aspects of the myth because they were part of a society that practiced it. Their status as the descendants of Henry Clay and as members of an elite family gave them a natural feeling of superiority over most whites. Blacks had never figured in that equation. That very sense of noblesse oblige, however, softened actions, if not beliefs. The old adage that southerners loved the individual but despised the race was as applicable to the Clays as any such generalization could be. First, they would not agree that they despised any group; they merely felt superior and were frustrated when inconvenienced. They also used black labor, and, as the myth suggested, servants often held a special place in the Clay households. Nevertheless, they felt a need to use the patriarch to justify the racial attitudes of a new age.

They began their new image with the best of the Lost Cause myth. Henry Clay had been, of course, a kind master. Mrs. Minor Simpson, a great-granddaughter in the Erwin branch, recounted that Clay, learning that a female slave he had just purchased had a child, bought the child to keep the family together. Actually, Clay did purchase Charlotte, or Lottie, because she was married to his manservant, Aaron Dupuy. The Clays also told stories about individual slaves. Uncle Aaron and Mammy Lottie were favorite subjects of Clay stories for generations, and descendants quickly noted that the Dupuys had stayed with the Clay family even after Henry freed them.[34] An account written by Teetee Clay clearly reflects the Lost Cause mentality. Her mother, she recalled, said that Uncle Aaron "was the finest specimen, physically, of the Negro race that she had ever seen." She wrote of his naive acceptance of Clay's political views, never understanding completely but repeating what he had heard. Aaron and Charlotte had accompanied James Clay to Portugal, and the Portuguese people were enthralled by Uncle Aaron, again according to Teetee. The implication was that he had taught the Portuguese the benefits of American life. Nearly a century later, Elizabeth Clay Blanford delighted in telling the same stories. Teetee concluded a four-page tribute to Aaron with a statement that reflected the nostalgia of the Lost Cause mentality: "Mammy Lotty and Uncle Aaron belonged to the old regime, they lived with a family that respected them and they were self respecting—and happy."[35]

The McDowell "family." Henry Clay Memorial Foundation Collection. Courtesy of University of Kentucky Special Collections.

Mrs. Simpson told a number of stories about a favorite slave named Uncle Harv. In the James Clay branch, the stories were about Uncle Daniel. Most of them had a decidedly Jim Crow flavor to them. A photograph in the McDowell papers also illustrates attitudes about race in the family and in the South. A "family photograph" includes black servants as well as the McDowells, a kindly gesture not uncommon in the era. However, the family is posed by race, African Americans on the left, McDowells on the right.[36] Madge Breckinridge included in her speeches humorous stories about kindly old black men and women, but generally with a clear implication of superiority.

The harsher attitudes of the Lost Cause were more apparent in what the family wrote. In the 1870s Harry Clay, a grandson, wrote a highly critical essay about the Civil Rights Act of 1866. He declared it ill advised and a waste of effort.[37] Even as Aunt Matt and Millie Lawson worked in her kitchen, Susan Clay wrote an essay titled "Slavery in Politics: A Plea for the Negro." Painful to read because of its blatant racism, it used Henry Clay's views on slavery as justification for her attitudes on the racial question. She began by emphasizing his lifelong opposition to slavery. He had said that if he lived in a state that did not have slavery, he would oppose its introduction. She then began to warm to her cause. Henry Clay had been "a consistent emancipationist with colonization." She did not mention his belief that blacks were capable of achieving intellectual equality with whites, but she emphasized his statements that passions and even normal competition would make it difficult for the two races to live together unless one dominated the other. At that point, she began to add her own views: "Social, moral and political depradation [sic] would be the inevitable lot of the colored race." Like other advocates of the Lost Cause, Susan did not blame the South for this, but implied that in its haste, the North had done a poor job of emancipation. The former slaves had "asked for bread and been given a stone. They were released to freedom without moral strength, without any sense of personal obligation or responsibility, without preparation for liberty, and wholly unfitted for the duties and responsibilities of life." Led to believe the Fourteenth and Fifteenth Amendments and a school education would bring equality, they had been sorely misled and thus disappointed. The "Afro-American citizens" had become social pariahs and would remain as such. Their Christianity was a thin veneer of bad teaching, "crude and mixed with superstition." In a touching sense of noblesse oblige, she noted "some exceptions," but she lamented the vast sums of money wasted in an attempt to educate blacks. Henry Clay would never have allowed such a thing. Indeed, had Abraham Lincoln lived, "reason would have held the helm" because he modeled his views on those of "that other great statesman," "his beloved chieftain."[38]

Susan Clay aligned herself with the harshest Lost Cause critics of the African American. She concluded her essay by suggesting that perhaps "some day Henry Clay's hope in colonization might be realized." In an obvious contradiction, she expressed the hope that a colony of former slaves might become "the germ of a great Christian empire on the dark continent." Apparently, their Christianity was good enough for Africa, though not for the American South.

The Clays successfully converted Henry Clay's views, selective views, to their own purpose. But that is what myths are about. They did not make up facts about Henry Clay, but they certainly omitted some, and, as myths tend to do, they painted a portrait without flaw. Ironically, if the terms of endearment are stripped away, the image of Henry Clay presented by the family is not significantly different from that presented by historians and biographers, past and present. Most scholars agree with Thomas Hart Clay Jr. that Henry Clay's drinking and gambling must be put in the context of early Kentucky history. Most also agree with Susan that it did not negatively affect his contribution, although there are differences regarding how it affected his chances of becoming president. Madge Breckinridge said Abraham Lincoln may have been unnecessary had Henry Clay lived, and the economist Henry Carey claimed a Clay presidency might have avoided the Civil War.[39] The historians at the University of Kentucky also shared much of the Clay view. A collection of "blue books," containing test essays written by Susan Jacob Clay, a great-granddaughter, while a student at the University of Kentucky, told the family story of Henry Clay. She received A grades and compliments from her professors.[40] Moreover, the family attitudes about race were probably no worse than the pseudoscientific explanations of Negro inferiority trumpeted by the Dunning School of Columbia University. America was a racist society, and the Clays were members of it. As Laura F. Edwards argues, the South was a part of the nation, and their central themes were frequently the same.[41]

The new image of Henry Clay was meant primarily, though not exclusively, for the Clay family. Like the image of Robert E. Lee, it set a standard for new generations. The image reflected what his descendants needed as they faced an unfamiliar world. Stripped of fortune and prominence, the James Clay branch gained a sense of importance and perhaps entitlement from the myth. It helped all the descendants, whether Union or Confederate in sympathies, fit into a new image of the South that quickly encompassed Kentucky and, to some degree, the nation. Pro-Union family members practiced their Republican Party politics quietly but conformed to the social requirements of the Lost Cause. Confederate sympathizers looked back to Henry Clay's patriotism in a time when the nation was united. Clay's contribution provided, in their minds at least, the credentials that would allow them to rejoin the Union as equal members. For all the descendants, it provided a sense of place and a bedrock confidence born of family contributions. Family difficulties, even eccentricities, paled in the shade of the mighty patriarch.

Chapter 8

LEGACY OF FAMILY

The Clay descendants who survived the Civil War needed no new image to embrace Henry Clay's legacy of loyalty to family. War taught them that family was far more dependable than political parties or principles. Susan, Thomas, Mary, and John had experienced the family loyalty of the patriarch. They had seen the pain Henry and Lucretia suffered from the afflictions that plagued their family. Thomas and John lived on farms Henry Clay had provided. Their collective definition of family would evolve over the years, but it continued to be based on his example and on their memories of him. Henry Clay's legacy became the basis for establishing the concept of family as one of the most important aspects of being a Clay. It was an honor and a privilege to be a descendant of Henry Clay.

Kentucky author John Fox Jr.'s writing notes the discords created in Kentucky families by the war. Another Kentucky author, Annie Fellows Johnson, based her popular "Little Colonel" series of books on the conflict between an ex-Confederate and his daughter who married a Union officer after the war. The rifts were not just fiction: the war deeply divided many Kentucky families. Not so the Clays. The emphasis Henry Clay placed on family helped his descendants recover from the divisions of war with astonishing ease. The Clays harked back to the days before the war, when Thomas provided pasturage if John needed it for his horses, and James collected debts for his father and brothers. The family had acted as one when necessity, convenience, or the chance for profit dictated it.

Henry Clay helped ensure that the branches of the family would continue to work together through the provisions of his will. He had deeded his best horses to John Morrison Clay, but breeding rights to his stallions were to be shared with his other descendants. James Clay Jr. proved to be the most unreconstructed of the family rebels, at least among the males, but "General" Clay, of the Confederate Veterans, left his rebel sympathies at home when he conducted business with his pro-Union kinsmen, John Morrison Clay and Henry Clay McDowell, because he valued the breeding rights to their horses. The descendants of Henry Clay chose to avoid past politics. They talked to one another to establish breeding schedules, discussed the ebb and flow of markets for their product, and traded horses. They provided hay or grain as one or the other needed it, and they paid social calls on one another as family members do.[1]

McDowell's relationship with kinsman Harry Boyle Clay proved even closer. Harry Clay had served under John Hunt Morgan and Basil Duke, and raided Kentucky along with them. If by chance he had not participated in the "liberation" of Kentucky horses, he certainly could not have escaped the reputation, since Morgan was as much horse thief as cavalry leader. Yet, as early as August 1865, he brazenly asked Major Henry Clay McDowell, USA, to use his Union connections to help him regain his citizenship and his property. Harry Clay married Nancy Bynum of Rogersville, Tennessee, near the end of the war, and the marriage brought him approximately eight thousand acres of farmland in Hawkins County and some city property in Rogersville. Overzealous Union officials, however, encouraged freedmen to take possession of one of his farms, and they confiscated much of the furniture, including family portraits and other artifacts. McDowell agreed to help, and the relationship remained strong for the remainder of the two men's lives.[2] Harry Clay traded information about progressive farming practices and stock development with H. C. McDowell and later his sons. The two men were occasionally business partners, and Clay frequently asked McDowell for advice on investments. Clay's daughter Elsie lived with the McDowells while she attended school in Lexington, then in 1893 she married Henry Clay McDowell Jr., cementing the family relationship. McDowell also used his Republican connections to help other Confederate kin. He frequently wrote letters of recommendation for both Thomas and Charles Clay, James's sons.[3]

In a similar fashion, Thomas H. Clay laid political differences aside. Despite the contentious relationship with his brother James, Thomas, only recently back from Honduras, gave James's widow Susan and her family a place to stay at Mansfield after she was forced to sell Ashland. Even when the Ku Klux Klan harassed Thomas and his family, political sympathies did not divide the family. Similarly, learning that Josephine Erwin had been left virtually penniless with three young children, Henry's widow and son John invited her to live with them in Lexington. Josephine refused at first. After the war, however, she visited Kentucky, perhaps to take possession of her children's inheritance from Henry Clay's will.[4] She did not leave. She stayed at first with Susan at Ashland, but when the estate was sold, she moved her family to John Morrison Clay's estate. John was a curmudgeonly old man known around Lexington for his eccentricities, sometimes funny, sometimes not. Josephine was a bright and charming young widow. When they were married on July 7, 1866, it became the talk of the town. The town wags gleefully talked of incest, but though she had been married to John's nephew, there was no blood relationship.[5]

That marriage may have been a family response to postwar needs. It certainly did not begin as a romantic affair. John matter-of-factly wrote in his diary, "Married Jo today," and Josephine maintained a sense of independence uncharacteristic of women of that era. Josephine, however, needed financial help for herself and her three daughters. In the nineteenth century, women of the upper classes did not go to work when widowed; family cared for them. And John certainly needed someone to help him. He drank excessively and still suffered periodic bouts of mental instability. The marriage remained a subject of gossip for years, but in fact, John and Josephine became a good team. She provided stability for him. Learning about raising thoroughbreds, she helped him immensely with his stock. He became a parent to her daughters. One of them later gave her son his name. He adopted her faith, converting to Catholicism, and curtailed his drinking significantly. His letters to her reflect his shifting moods. He would respond angrily on occasion, then with moving affection in another letter. It was an unusual union, perhaps, but the times and the needs called for unusual solutions.

The Clay women made the greatest effort to unite the family. That, too, was a woman's role in the South.[6] At the end of the war, Henry Clay McDowell was the only adult male capable of leadership, but in matters related to the family, he yielded responsibility to the women. Anne Clay McDowell kept the increasingly far-flung family in contact. Always paying respect to rank, she referred to Susan and Mary Mentelle Clay as Aunt, and recognized Susan's role as family historian. Both she and her husband often referred questions about Henry Clay to Susan. Any family business also had to be approved by all, but the older generation carried more weight than younger ones. On a more social level, however, Anne

Anne Clay McDowell. Henry Clay Memorial Foundation
Collection. Courtesy of University of Kentucky Special
Collections.

functioned as the family head. Kentucky University purchased Ashland
from Susan Clay, but in 1883 Henry Clay McDowell made it the home of a
third Clay family.[7] Ownership of the family home gave Anne status virtually equal to that of Susan and Mary. She began the practice of inviting
the ladies of the family to lunch at Ashland, where they could catch up on
family matters. Susan, Teetee, and Eliza, James Jr.'s wife, came from their
farms four miles outside Lexington. Aunt Mary and her daughter Minnie
made the brief trip from Mansfield. As Victorian manners demanded, the
invitations were always reciprocated.[8]

The women also cared for family members in times of sickness. Mary Mentelle Clay had been at the bedside when Lucretia Clay died. John C. J. Clay, Susan's son, died of typhoid fever in 1872 at Mansfield, and Anne Clay McDowell helped Susan, Mary, and Josephine on the frequent occasions when they or members of their families were sick. Josephine was as proud to be a member of the Clay family as Susan and Mary. Though a member of the family only by marriage, she arranged to have the body of Eliza Clay exhumed in Lebanon, Ohio, and reinterred in the family plot at the Lexington Cemetery, and the novels she wrote reflect both the values of the family and her attachment to it.[9]

The Clays came together for marriages and funerals. Susan and Teetee made the trip to Rogersville, Tennessee, to help with the wedding of Henry Clay McDowell Jr. and Elsie Clay, and they were at Ashland when Nettie McDowell married. Clay males, former Confederate and former Union officers, walked side by side as the century drew to a close, carrying family members to the grave. The Clays had learned a hard lesson. Henry Clay would have been delighted to see his descendants act "like brothers," and he would have appreciated the efforts and attitudes of the women who had married his sons and grandsons. The memories of the patriarch united the family as never before.[10]

The Clays still faced the difficulties and uncertainties of a new era. While the image of the patriarch comforted the older generation, they realized that their children needed it as an anchor. Using the papers and artifacts and the art of storytelling, they inculcated the values they wanted the youth of the family to carry into a new age. There was time for storytelling then. Modern technology did not yet compete with older family members for time with children. They sat in the parlor in winter months, or on the lawns in summer, listening to stories of American history, of family heroes and heroines. Veterans of the Civil War visited frequently at Ashland and Balgowan, living memories of a heroic past.[11] The family stories rarely changed, from the telling in different branches or in the accounts told to different generations. Elizabeth Clay Blanford repeated the stories many times as she aged. There was a rhythm to each story. She laughed or grew somber at the same point in the story. The highly descriptive adjectives and adverbs remained always the same. Clay children learned about their family and its values. They absorbed values and mental images of the past through the seductive instruction of the previous generation.

No child could escape the importance attached to being a Clay. They were the descendants of a great American. The family expected their sons to accomplish great things, but also that the nation would recognize and facilitate their contributions. James Clay Sr. wrote his son Jimmie in 1858 that he expected the latter to occupy the "large, white House in Washington" some day. Susan Clay was so certain of Henry's contribution to the nation that she expected government officials to help her establish her sons in acceptable positions. She wrote to congressmen and to Presidents Ulysses S. Grant and Rutherford B. Hayes seeking positions for her sons as the grandsons of Henry Clay. She described her sons as "polished," comfortable in society, and manly boys. She also stated that the nation owed favors for the service Henry Clay had performed.[12] At Yale University, Henry Clay McDowell Jr., even in his first year, found doors open to him because professors, New Haven businessmen, and even the president of the university learned that he was the great-grandson of Henry Clay. The family expected him to be a success, perhaps equal to the patriarch for whom he was named, and he seemed to have shared the high expectations. Joining his first law firm, McDowell expressed his intent to conquer Saint Paul, Minnesota, in a week. His brother shared his confidence. William Adair McDowell planned to be president of the bank where he worked or to seek his fortune elsewhere, where people appreciated his abilities. Meant to be humorous, such comments nevertheless reflect high expectations. Establishing a law office in Denver, Harry Clay enthusiastically entered politics. Although the city was dominated by Republicans, he hoped that through a rising Democratic party, "my political ambitions will be gratified."[13] He was already practicing his signature—H. Clay—just as his grandfather had signed it.[14]

Foremost among the lessons Clay children learned was that of confidence. Sometimes this led to brashness, but most frequently it was the foundation for a quiet belief in the potential for success. It was a given that Clay sons had the potential to contribute. They also learned that they were to conduct themselves according to the standards for upper-class young men of that era. Young men at their level of society learned about virtue, honor, and social position. The Lost Cause spoke a lot about these manly virtues. The Victorian age, regardless of region, also emphasized them. The South had Robert E. Lee. In the nation as a whole, President Teddy Roosevelt has prevailed in historical accounts as the example of rough-and-ready manhood in the period. At the time, a group of military men were just as pronounced. Confident to the point of cockiness, dedicated to physi-

Thomas Jacob Clay. Courtesy
of the Elizabeth Clay Blanford
Collection.

cal fitness and sports, they set a standard of masculinity. Donald Mrozek,
writing about the impact of the military on late nineteenth-century manliness, suggests General Leonard Wood as the prime example of the type. A
Harvard graduate and medical doctor, he served in the West then became
chief of staff under President William Howard Taft. Mrozek claims his
prominence came from his service under General Nelson Miles, another
rugged, masculine soldier, during the campaign against the Apaches.
Wood served with Colonel Henry Ware Lawton, who commanded a group
of men known as Lawton's athletes. One of the athletes was Lieutenant
Thomas Jacob Clay, a grandson of Henry Clay's.[15] Thomas Clay learned
about the obligations of manhood from stories about his grandfather.

Thomas J. Clay was a strapping six feet two inches tall, a champion
marksman, and confident enough of his ability riding horses that he did

not have to brag about it. That was not true of all the Clays. Henry Clay's physical traits were transmitted to his descendants as powerfully as his wit and passion. With the exception of Thomas Jacob Clay and Thomas Clay McDowell, the descendants inherited Clay's long, thin stature. They also inherited a susceptibility to illness that weakened their constitutions. Henry Jr., William, and Thomas Clay McDowell suffered from typhoid fever and, at various times in their lives, tuberculosis. Harry Boyle Clay's son also suffered from tuberculosis. In the James Clay branch, typhoid, diphtheria, and heart problems plagued family members. H. C. McDowell encouraged his sons to learn boxing, a popular, manly venture of the era. He proudly wrote to his wife when the instructor at Yale praised Henry Clay McDowell Jr.'s abilities. No doubt the coach referred to his zeal or aggressiveness because the young man was as thin as his great-grandfather. The elder McDowell promised to send the instructor two more sons "of better physiques than Henry." While at West Point, much to the consternation of his overly protective mother, Robert Clay tried to join the boxing team as well.[16]

Clay males seemed continually aware of the need to appear manly. The tendency of some family males to speak quickly and bluntly may have been compensation for what they lacked physically, but it often got them into scrapes they could have avoided. Photographs of Charles Clay in his military uniform suggest a young man trying desperately to appear masculine despite a very boyish face. He, in turn, emphasized manliness so strongly that Charley Jr. found himself involved in fights, often with larger opponents, over his honor or that of someone he felt called upon to protect. Both H. C. McDowell and Susan Clay told a son on more than one occasion to "bear his problems like a man."[17] In a Louisville political campaign, Susan's son Harry Independence Clay threatened to show a heckler his mettle with his fist. A local paper admired his "pluck," but his pluck and insistence on honor were largely responsible for his death. A perceived slight, and too much to drink, led Clay into an altercation with Andrew Wepler, a city councilman and saloon keeper in Louisville, who shot Clay dead in 1884. The *Louisville Commercial* recalled Clay's "noble, manly character," but he pitted himself against a brawler and a bully. It was a story painfully familiar to the Clay family.[18]

Closely associated with manliness was the trait of honor. In the Clay family it was both personal and family honor that was to be exhibited and protected. Their ancestor had declared that he would rather be right than president; they were expected to uphold the principle. Each generation added to the examples for the next. James Clay had purchased Ashland out of a sense of duty to his father. Thomas declared himself a "humble agent," his accomplishments in honor of his father. During the Geronimo campaign, Captain Thomas Clay, along with Leonard Wood, thwarted an effort by fellow officers to kill Geronimo while under a flag of truce. Such an act would have been dishonorable. Clay developed a respect for the Indian chieftain, and according to the family, Geronimo reciprocated. In the Clay papers, a letter signed by Geronimo and Naichez (Natchez) asked Clay for his help. The army had not met its promises to the Native Americans at the time of their surrender. According to Elizabeth Clay Blanford, Clay testified on behalf of the Indians. Apparently, he preferred to be right than to be promoted. He retired after many years as a captain.[19]

Over the mantle in the parlor at Balgowan, an Indian bridle and a pair of binoculars hung as symbols of Clay masculinity and honor. The bridle allegedly was a gift from Geronimo. The binoculars recalled Harry I. Clay's participation in an expedition to the Arctic. The harshness of the region required masculine traits; Clay cut short his participation over a matter of honor. There were other stories. William Adair McDowell operated a bank that failed during the economic depression of 1892. The family took pride in the fact that he repaid every penny, the act of an honorable man. Thomas Clay McDowell had a reputation as a southern gentleman of the racing track. The assessment was based on both his manliness and his sense of honor and fair play. Finally, wounded in the Philippine Insurrection in 1899, Charles Clay personified the Clay character. Quoting a fellow officer, the *Lexington Leader* stated, "The Captain never forgot for a second that he was a Clay." A bullet lodged dangerously close to his spinal cord, but because his wife was pregnant with their second child, he refused to have it removed, fearing his death might cause them harm. It was the responsibility of an officer and an honorable man; the duty of a descendant of Henry Clay. He kept his bloodied uniform to show his sons the evidence of family masculinity, duty, and honor.[20]

Other traits in the family had to be addressed. No Clay could avoid the problems caused in the first three generations by gambling, drinking, and dissipation. Like any family, they urged their sons to avoid what Henry had called "the fickle goddesses," but in this family there was added concern. The Clay family history clearly revealed a legacy of risk, a topic that is treated in more detail in chapter 9. Like Henry, later generations

Lieutenant Charles D. Clay.
Courtesy of the Elizabeth
Clay Blanford Collection.

sought to transfer a love of risk to the business community, but gambling continued to stimulate excitement among a number of Clays. In constructing the myth of Henry Clay, the family sought to give gambling a kinder, more gentlemanly face. They made it a source of humor. Confronted by a woman who questioned Henry's gambling, Mrs. Clay had replied that she did not mind because he nearly always won. It became a sign of his social class. He played poker regularly with John Bradford, the editor of the *Kentucky Gazette*. Although they owed huge sums to one another, like true gentlemen they always allowed the other to recoup losses or forgave them. It also became a way to show his chivalry. Gambling along the route to Washington, Clay won from its owner the hotel where he stayed. Elizabeth Blanford loved to complete the story. The next morning, he left the deed under the plate of the owner's wife. While cautioning against gambling in the present, the family historians justified Henry's card playing because it was common in his day and he played with style. It hurt no one and actually helped the nation.[21]

Thomas Clay McDowell, a great-grandson, gambled large amounts on his horses, but that was not clearly a Clay trait because his father also wagered heavily at the racetrack. George H. Clay also liked to gamble on his horses. His sister Teetee was aroused to the heights of her Victorian indignation when he used the winnings from a wager on one of his fillies to buy every lady in the grandstand a glass of champagne. Impulsiveness, or spontaneity, was also a Clay trait. It won them many friends, but it could also lead to recklessness and danger. Mary Webster Clay Anderson, Josephine's daughter, placed her two sons in military school after the death of her husband, and followed the racing circuit throughout the country. According to a descendant, she carried a purse full of gold coins to cover her wagers.[22] Try as they might, the keepers of the family code failed miserably at limiting gambling. The story of James Erwin Jr.'s death after a night of gambling and drinking served as a lesson to gamble in moderation if at all, but Henry Clay McDowell Jr. worried about his brother's wagering, and Susan Clay warned her sons Harry and Charles not to gamble away their resources.

Concerns about alcohol consumption produced even more poignant lessons. It had been one of the most damaging accusations in the career of the patriarch, and it had continued to be a problem in the family. On more than one occasion, members of the family noted that alcohol did not mix well with Clay blood. In the second generation, Theodore, Thomas, and John had drinking problems. Family stories about the drinking habits of James Clay Jr. masked sadness and shame with attempts to be humorous. James asked for the hand of a beautiful and talented young woman, Maggie Beck, but her father, Kentucky senator James B. Beck, refused because of James's reputation as a heavy drinker. Mrs. Blanford recounted that James proved quite successful as a breeder of horses, but about once a month he would ride into Lexington to drink with his friends. Inevitably, he drank too much. His friends would put him on his horse and point it down the Versailles Road. "Uncle Jimmy," she said, "was too intoxicated to find his way home, but the horse always turned at the right gate."[23]

Those close to the Clay family did not find the matter humorous at all. Margaret Johnson Erwin, the second wife of James Erwin, wrote her stepson Eugene that if she had one drop of Clay blood in her veins, she would never touch alcohol. Susan used James Clay Jr.'s problems to warn her other sons against drinking. She wondered, she said in one letter, what he might have accomplished if not for drinking. Too many Clays, she said,

Thomas Clay McDowell. Henry Clay Memorial Foundation Collection. Courtesy of University of Kentucky Special Collections.

had suffered from excessive use of alcohol. She warned them that "love of drink and extravagance is the Scylls and Charybdis of the Clay family and I have seen many fair young lives wrecked upon them." She cautioned one son, "Drink no alcohol, not even beer."[24] Her son Charles and his son Charles Jr. suffered periodic problems with drinking. Mrs. Charles Clay claimed that Charley Jr. had been perfect "but for the mistake of ever touching whiskey," and she exacted a promise from her second son never to touch it. She wrote, "It is a curse to be avoided by a Clay." The Erwins and the McDowell sons were also inclined to overindulgence. One of the McDowells was driving an automobile involved in a fatal accident, probably the result of drinking.[25] The lessons did not go completely unheeded. Some Clays avoided alcohol or limited their consumption, perhaps because of the stories and the examples they saw personally. Like the patriarch, they turned their energies to more productive outlets.

A more serious problem also reflected a concern that had worried Henry about his sons and grandsons. The Clay sons could not seem to find a sense of direction in their lives. Bright and curious, they could and often did excel in diverse areas, but it was hard for them to become, and remain, focused. That made them more susceptible to the dissipation the family had feared. Thomas Hart Clay complained that his two sons enjoyed "nothing in moderation." Thomas Jacob Clay trained to be a doctor and established a practice in Saint Louis, only to leave it to join the army. His brothers Harry and John moved to California, where they speculated in land around San Francisco. However, John, seeing instant fortune, sought to sell too soon. Harry left a promising law practice in San Francisco to establish one in Denver, then Provo, Utah, before returning to Louisville. Elected to political office, he resigned to go on an Arctic expedition. Henry Clay McDowell Jr. stayed very briefly in Minnesota before moving to Big Stone Gap, Virginia, a community his father was trying to build into a transportation and industrial center. William Adair McDowell bounced from job to job before his father established him as a banker. Thomas Clay McDowell suffered from a problem similar to dyslexia, so he moved from one school to another, eventually dropping out of the University of Virginia to work with his father's horses. In Tennessee, Harry Boyle Clay's son also moved from job to job, usually returning to something arranged by his father.[26]

Susan Clay condemned the trait as a lack of perseverance. In a letter to her son Harry written in the 1870s, Susan described the characteristic in strong terminology:

> Recollect that it is a characteristic of your father's family to be in the beginning too sanguine, then too despondant [sic]. You do not set out in the beginning expecting to meet difficulties and determining to conquer them, (for there is nothing in the world worth having that does not give us pain and trouble to get) but you start out viewing every thing through rose colored glasses and when the glare and the heat and the dust of the journey face you

to put on green goggles. You begin to see everything in a sickly green melancholy light and think you have been cheated and mistaken and look upon yourselves as martyrs and doomed men upon whom Heaven frowns and with whom every thing goes wrong. When the truth of the matter is the fault lies all within yourselves and energy and determination and courage and endurance, last the not least is all that was necessary but was also wanting.[27]

She wrote equally blunt letters to sons Thomas and Charles. In another missive to Harry, she wrote, "Your fault my son is I fear a want of stability and perseverance. You must acquire both or you will never succeed. Don't lose courage. Be a man and a Christian and persevere in well doing." Charles Clay, who experienced frequent criticisms on the subject from his mother and should have known better, consistently demanded focus and discipline from his two sons as a responsibility owed to the family. As Bertram Wyatt-Brown has suggested regarding southern families, it became nearly impossible for sons to escape the legacy of the past.[28]

A number of Clay sons eventually became successful. James, Thomas, and George Clay and Thomas Clay McDowell gained tremendous respect from their peers as breeders of thoroughbred horses. Thomas Clay was highly regarded as an authority on the rules of racing. Henry Clay McDowell Jr. became a federal judge. His wife complained that he did not know how to stop working. Other family members became successful bankers, lawyers, and businessmen. Once engaged, Clay sons embraced the more positive aspects of their legacy, but their early years caused no small amount of concern for the older generations.

Perhaps Harry Independence Clay represents most clearly the promise and the tragedy that characterized the family. A graduate of Washington (and Lee) College, Harry thrived on the comparisons to his grandfather. He practiced his oratory and the writing of his signature, H. Clay, until both resembled those of the patriarch. He was also an excellent political campaigner, winning office in Louisville at a young age. Harry had the intelligence, personality, and ambition to succeed. In a hurry for success, he did at times lack perseverance, or patience. Having won political office, he resigned abruptly to participate in an expedition to the Arctic. In his preparation for the journey he did not lack perseverance. He studied geography, climate, and the histories of earlier expeditions, keeping detailed notes. Arriving in Greenland, he studied Greenland's history, writing long letters to his mother and sister explaining the Danish settlement, early conflicts with the native people, and their eventual conversion to Christianity. He

Henry Independence Clay. Courtesy of the Elizabeth Clay Blanford Collection.

studied native languages and compiled elaborate lists comparing the words to English and Latin. He visited frequently in the homes of the European settlers and the native people. Even the climate appealed to him. He wrote that he was gaining weight and had never been happier.[29]

An incident with the expedition's physician, Dr. Octave Pavy, cut short his travels. The child of a native family that had befriended them fell ill, but Pavy refused to treat him. Clay offered to get medicine although it would have required a dangerous trek on his part. Pavy still refused. To Clay, Pavy's actions were disgustingly dishonorable, and he feared an "incident" if he remained in the man's company. Recognizing that the physician was more valuable to the expedition than himself, he submitted his resignation to Adolphus Greely, the commander of the party.[30]

Harry went back to Kentucky, but his association with Greely was not over. Weather conditions made it impossible to extract the party, and a great debate arose over how to save them. Having studied the region, Harry recognized the path the expedition would take and urged that supplies be left in several key locations. Only one of his suggestions was followed. Ironically, some fruit was left for the Greely party wrapped in copies of a newspaper detailing Harry's plan. Facing the tremendous cold without food, the expedition set up a camp where they would await death or rescue. Adolphus Greely named it Camp Clay after Harry.[31] By the time the party was rescued, most of the members had died and there was suspicion of cannibalism.

Greely, David Brainard, and several other survivors wrote to Harry Clay thanking him for his efforts. His plan would have avoided some of the deaths, but army politics thwarted his labors. He would have joined an expedition to save the party, and his brother Thomas volunteered as well, but their services were rejected.[32] The Louisville press delighted in Harry's stories of the Arctic. He clearly hoped to use his fame for political purposes. However, tragedy intervened. Losing a close election in which he challenged the Louisville political machine of Boss John Whallen, Clay drank too much and became involved in the altercation with Andrew Wepler that took his life. He had been compared favorably to his grandfather as an orator. Energetic, outgoing, a gifted lawyer, Harry Clay appeared to have the qualities that could lead to a successful political career. A newspaper account spoke to a problem too common in the family: it noted that Harry was friendly and charming until he drank too much, but "one drink of liquor to him meant a dethronement of reason." The article also noted that he had been the great hope of his family to restore the prominence of his grandfather.[33]

The daughters shared the education of their brothers in some important aspects. Namely, they heard the stories of Clay success and contribution. They learned that they too were part of a great family, and that the genius of Henry Clay ran in their blood. Most of the family stories centered on the men of the family, but a few included women. Henry Clay's mother had faced the dastardly British general Banastre Tarleton when he invaded the Clays' Virginia farm during the Revolutionary War. She had stood silently and strongly as the British drove bayonets into her husband's fresh grave seeking silver the family might have hidden. They heard stories of their grandmother, Susan Clay, and how she had faced the Union soldiers in the "Battle" of Ashland. Yet, southern lady that she was, she had allowed the Union army to use the ground floor of Ashland as a hospital for their wounded. The stories often told of sorrow and sacrifice, but they ended with displays of honor and virtue as surely as did the stories of the men.

Clay women, however, faced limitations on the contributions they were allowed to make. The Lost Cause placed women on a pedestal where they were to be admired, respected, and observed but do very little. Most modern scholars challenge the myth of the southern lady, but like many myths, it included a grain of truth. Boys were supposed to grow up to be gentlemen, but it was acceptable to be boys along the way. Women were to be ladies all their lives. The myth became the standard by which women were judged. As Margaret Ripley Wolfe notes in *The Daughters of Canaan,* if women were imprisoned, they often served as the wardens of their own prisons.[34] Mothers taught young women the principles of ladylike behavior, and fathers, brothers, the extended family, and the community helped to enforce the standard. Although Barbara Welter's "Cult of True Womanhood" has been thoroughly critiqued, and dismissed by some, it contains some truth for women well into the twentieth century. Women as a whole exercised great piety. They were supposed to be submissive, demure, and genteel, and they mastered the arts of domesticity. That remained the public persona. Even in the North, though challenged more forcefully, the Victorian codes yielded slowly. Strong mothers like the Clays were no exception: they taught their daughters the requirements of a lady and cringed when a forward question or action threatened a daughter's status in society. The house of cards fell easily; to question one tenet endangered the collapse of the entire edifice. Moreover, beneath the genteel and hospitable exterior, southerners could be unmerciful in the treatment of a woman who violated or questioned the codes. Strong southern women trembled at the thought.

The Clays became advocates of society's traditional view of women. Contribution, from the daughters' perspectives, meant becoming a lady and ultimately making a "good" marriage. They would then support the careers of their husbands and teach their children the same values that they had been taught. In the Clay family, however, it proved difficult to teach intelligent young women that they had the genius of Henry Clay in their veins but were also to be submissive, demure, and genteel. Nevertheless, they tried.

Each generation of Clay daughters received an education in schools that emphasized the place of women common at the time. Susan and Elizabeth Clay of the James Clay branch attended the Miss Ella Williams School in Lexington, and the Rogersville Clays sent their daughters to a boarding school in Staunton, Virginia. Elsie Clay of the Rogersville Clays attended school in Lexington, living with the McDowells at Ashland. Madeline

McDowell sisters Julia, Nettie, and Madge. Henry Clay Memorial
Foundation Collection. Courtesy of University of Kentucky
Special Collections.

McDowell attended Miss Porter's School in Connecticut. The emphasis
was on female education. Even Madge, later such a force for women's
rights, spent more time on social preparation and literary subjects than a
full curriculum including math and science. Susan Clay, the daughter of
Charles D. Clay, became distraught when she could not learn math as easily as she learned everything else. In a hastily called conference, her father
and Miss Williams decided she did not have to study it. Colonel Charles D.
Clay, preparing his two sons for the entrance exams to West Point, would
not have allowed them to avoid mathematics. Some years later in a sworn
deposition, Mrs. Clay stated that the education of the two sons took priority
over that of the daughters. If something happened to Colonel Clay, the care

of Mrs. Clay, Susan, and Elizabeth would be the sons' responsibility.[35] Like many southern women, the Clay daughters were exposed to what Mark Twain called the "Sir Walter disease," a devotion to the romantic novels of Sir Walter Scott. Many years later, great-granddaughter Susan Clay's husband would call it training in "King Arthur and rainbows."[36]

Lexington gave the Clay daughters ample opportunity to show their social skills. In the 1880s the Clay family experienced a renaissance of sorts when Ashland, a Clay home for the third time, became again a center of Lexington's social life. Cabinet officers, railroad magnates, representatives of the emperor of Japan, and even Adolphus Busch, brewer of Budweiser beer, visited to see the horses Major McDowell sold.[37] A Lexington newspaper called Ashland a center of southern charm. Family members attended the receptions, dinners, and other events for such dignitaries, so the daughters learned how to conduct themselves in the presence of important people. When Nanette, Madeline, and Julia, the three McDowell daughters, became young adults, they invited their own set to Ashland. Ashland became a gathering place for young writers. Robert Burns Wilson visited regularly. He patterned the characters in his novel *As the Dawn Breaks* on members of the Bluegrass elite. John Fox Jr. was also a frequent visitor, and Thomas Nelson Page, a literary contributor to the myth of the Lost Cause, wrote glowing accounts of his visits to Ashland and of the McDowell daughters. The local newspapers described teas, dinners, and dances in elaborate detail. The local country club provided a place for the McDowells to meet others of their own class, and the Once a Week Dancing Club seemed composed primarily for members of the Clay family. The young people, male and female, of several branches attended, and the parents, even the soldierly Colonel Charles D. Clay, acted as sponsors and chaperones. In the James Clay branch, many social opportunities centered on reunions of Confederate veterans, while the McDowells traveled to the homes of well-placed business associates of the major or of friends Madge made at Miss Porter's School. As young adults, Clay women played the role of southern lady effortlessly.[38]

Historians and biographers generally choose strong, successful women for their subjects. They prefer to chronicle the opportunities for women, emphasizing progress, particularly when created by women themselves. However, the vast majority of women, including the successful ones, felt the strong hold of traditional values. Instilled over a lifetime, the myth of what a woman should be, even when refuted intellectually, did not quietly disappear but attacked in moments of despair or tragedy. Linda Kerber argues that the old order continued to be "patched up" and "reconstructed." Margaret Ripley Wolfe has noted that many women have been "haunted by the specter of 'the southern lady.'" Wolfe writes, "For every woman in Kentucky, the South, or America who has actively challenged the status quo there are thousands who have supported it, and passively opposed change; still others, whatever the reason, have been too helpless to be involved."[39] The Clay women fit neither category easily. They wrestled, one suspects like the vast majority of American women, with the contradictions. They felt keenly the impact of the community and family traditions holding them to place, but they struggled to be Clays—to make the contribution they knew their heritage made possible, and required.

The oldest McDowell daughter, Nettie, became the stereotype of a southern belle. Even the *Atlanta Constitution* sent a reporter to Kentucky to write a biographical sketch of her, including it in an article about prominent young southern women. Educated in Lexington, she knew how to perform the responsibilities of a young woman of the upper class. A bit flirtatious, perhaps, she could converse without creating conflict, and her letters were multipage ramblings saying virtually nothing. One correspondent noted that Nettie seemed to enjoy the social life of Ashland so well he wondered if she would ever marry.[40] But traditional values did require marriage, so Nettie married. Major McDowell provided a lavish wedding. More than three hundred guests were shuttled back and forth from Lexington throughout the evening. Though he grumbled a bit, the major acquiesced when Nettie wanted him to buy an expensive home in Louisville for her; from there, she entertained regularly and planned an intricate social calendar. She would later show her leadership ability, but it took a bad marriage and a son with physical and mental ailments to force the transition.

Lucretia, or Teetee, was even more a mixture of Clay energy and cultural confinement. A small sprig of a woman, she was the epitome of the southern lady—at least publicly, most of the time. She was engaged shortly after the Civil War, but she broke it off because of political differences. Her fiancé was from Wisconsin. She never married, claiming that all the good men had died in the war.[41] It seems likely, however, that it was her sense of Victorian propriety that caused her to remain unmarried. Yet, she could not be completely satisfied with her prescribed role. Her mother claimed to wish Teetee had been born a man because society robbed her of the ability to demonstrate her intelligence. She remained at home, keeping

Lucretia "Teetee" Clay.
Courtesy of the Elizabeth
Clay Blanford Collection.

her brothers "on the straight and narrow road of good behavior." In her spare time, she wrote a long novel typical of those written by women of the late nineteenth century. Exhibiting perfection in Victorian morality, her characters overcame poverty caused, for the most part, by the baseness of lesser men—the lesson her mother had taught—to recoup a lost fortune and find true love at the end of 350 pages. She even included a suffrage advocate in the novel, but then claimed that women's most powerful rights existed outside the ballot box. Teetee could not avoid a criticism of men: they were responsible for the prevailing debasement of society. That was a theme she shared with Josephine Clay, another family novelist. Many of Teetee's characters clearly resembled members of the Clay family, always exhibiting gentility, virtue, and honor. She also wrote biographies of family members and treatises on religion, corresponding with theologians on a variety of topics.

Teetee was active in the Daughters of the Confederacy—a must for southern ladies of the postbellum era—as well as the Daughters of the American Revolution and the Woman's Club of Central Kentucky. Karen J. Blair suggests that women's organizations often prepared women for more active political leadership, and some progressive leadership did develop within the Woman's Club, but not from Teetee Clay. She was neither progressive nor an advocate of suffrage. She replaced her mother as the enforcer of Clay standards, further molding the image of Henry. Quick to pronounce a violation of the Clay code, she remained convinced that her brothers broke the rules far too often. Although most of the Clays practiced their religion merely as civic responsibility rather than deep spiritual conviction, Teetee enforced the family religion. The Clays had been, were, and would always be Episcopalian. When Maria Pepper Clay, Teetee's sister-in-law, joined the Christian Science congregation, Teetee became so outspoken that a rift developed within the family. Ria Clay did not visit Balgowan for years thereafter. Steeped in Victorian morality, when breast cancer became obvious, Teetee refused to see a male physician until a servant informed her brothers of her condition. By the time she saw the physician, the disease had spread too far. Nevertheless, Miss Lucretia Hart Clay claimed she had been betrayed.[42]

Teetee's niece Susan Jacob Clay Sawitzky illustrates the "double bind" of the Clay women better than any member of the family. A poet, she published two small books of poetry as a young woman and single poems in journals and magazines, the most prestigious of which was *Poetry: A Magazine of Verse.*[43] Like Emily Dickinson, she left hundreds of unpublished poems.

Susan's life is a portrait of extremes. Intelligent, energetic, and beautiful, she enjoyed from childhood the encouragement of parents who saw her as the personification of Clay genius. When she was just five years old, the local newspaper began to compare her to Henry Clay. The oldest grandchild on both sides of her family, she was smothered in attention. As noted in chapter 2, an uncle told her mother, "Give the little filly her head, so she'll have spirit." Susan had spirit, and she responded badly when, at puberty, uncles, aunts, parents and teachers began to attempt to channel it. When she wrote a poem about autumn as a kind of death, the trees losing their leaves, colors fading into dull, drab winter hues, her father scribbled a note in the margin urging her to write happier verses. Her mother worried constantly about her "melancholy" verse and the ideas that she expressed so spontaneously. When she wrote a paper at the Miss Ella Williams School questioning the relationship between Romeo and Juliet, both parents and

Susan Clay Sawitzky.
Courtesy of the Elizabeth
Clay Blanford Collection.

Miss Williams became concerned lest her reputation be damaged. Susan was full of questions and comments. As she matured, her poetry reflected what Susan Gubar and Sandra Gilbert have called the conflict between confinement and freedom in women's poetry.[44] Henry Clay Jr. wrote in his diary of being in the shade of an aged oak; Susan Clay's poem "Portraits" noted the confinement by the traditional ideas of the family's "aged mandarins." Like Sinclair Lewis's character Carol Kennicott, she longed to experience a world beyond her small hometown, and she escaped it through poetry. When she graduated from high school in 1914, she had no options. Her mother suggested that if she took a job, Lexington would think her father impoverished.[45] She could only wait until some Lexington lawyer, farmer, or horseman swept her away from her father's house to his own.

Susan Clay believed she had a contribution to make. In fact, it was an obligation of her heritage. But she felt thwarted at every turn. As a young woman she threatened and attempted suicide. She expressed her independence, however, when in 1927 she eloped with William Sawitzky, a Russian émigré. It was her attempt to achieve freedom. He promised literally to show her the world. Sawitzky, seventeen years older than Susan, became almost as protective as her father, and Susan proudly proclaimed to her mother on her eleventh wedding anniversary that she loved and respected him so much it was easy to obey him, just as her mother had taught her.[46]

Susan continued to write, amassing a body of work that clearly expresses the southern woman's desire for freedom and the right to make decisions for herself. Yet, when she suffered a miscarriage in 1928, she wondered aloud whether it was God's punishment for her defiance of her parents. She wrote poetry that would really have worried her mother had Susan shown it to her. She challenged the image of the southern belle and questioned the authority of the patriarch and other family males she saw in portraits at Clay homes. She lashed out at her husband for being too protective, and she challenged God to end her life. In the pain experienced over her miscarriage, she did not care to live. In her poetry she laid bare the hypocrisy of the myths that dominated southern life, but in her daily life she doted on her husband, helped him in his groundbreaking work on early American painters, and after his death in 1947, continued his work in art history, forsaking her own work to publish a number of articles in his field. Never free from the traditional values that bound a woman to place, she refused to quietly occupy the pedestal. She consistently believed her heritage made her special. All documents and manuscripts were signed Susan Clay Sawitzky or SCS. She remained a Clay, and a print of Ashland adorned the wall of every home in which she lived.

Two scraps found among her papers illustrate the forces in conflict within her. Visiting Balgowan as a young woman, she stopped at a locust tree where years earlier her Uncle Tom had attached a doll's face beneath a wedge-shaped fungus common to such trees. The children named the face Matilda, and it had been the subject of countless stories created on lazy summer afternoons. A symbol of childhood joy, with the passage of time the face was nearly covered by the fungus, giving it new meaning: "When I found her canopy had completely overgrown her face and she was imprisoned forever . . . I whispered against the spot where she had gone under, 'Matilda, the same thing has happened to me.'"

On another piece of paper, after the loss of her child, she wrote:

I will listen to saints and prophets,
I will sit at the feet of wisdom,
But I will reserve O God
The right to wonder. [47]

Tradition and modernity collided. Susan yearned for freedom, physical and intellectual, but she could not escape the traditions of family and community. She died in 1981 in a small apartment in New Haven, Connecticut. She had barred the windows, covered the walls with extra insulating material to keep out the noise, and added a door over the original one for increased security. [48] She had created her own prison.

The family member who came closest to reestablishing the political prominence of the Clay family appeared in the fourth generation, and that member was female. Madeline McDowell Breckinridge may well have been the most successful politician in Progressive Era Kentucky despite the fact that she could neither vote nor hold office. Beginning in Lexington, she helped create the Civic League, an organization that raised funds, encouraged reform, and labored at improving conditions in the region. Compared frequently to her great-grandfather, she certainly inherited his energy. Madge persuaded, cajoled, and maneuvered men to redevelop blighted areas of Lexington, improve the education system, and fight the epidemic of tuberculosis in the state. She is perhaps best known for her role in the women's suffrage movement. In that cause she enlisted her sisters, her mother, Aunt Josephine, and a sister-in-law in addition to friends she had made when she attended Miss Porter's School. The men of the family said nothing. One suspects they preferred being silent to being "right." Even in the most traditional branch of the family, the James Clays, the large body of correspondence is tellingly silent on Madge and women's suffrage.

Madge Breckinridge stepped beyond the confinement of southern womanhood in her reforming activities. She traveled broadly to learn the latest theories in social work, tuberculosis treatment, and education reform. She was highly critical of men and southern values that undervalued women. Having rejected suffrage reform with significant contempt for the measure and for those who sought it, Kentucky politicians urged women to participate in the preparedness campaign as the United States entered World War I. Madge fired back, "Kentucky women are not idiots—even though they are closely related to Kentucky men. You can't ignore them

Madeline McDowell Breckinridge. Courtesy of Ashland, the
Henry Clay Estate.

and treat them as though they were kindergarten children, and then when
work is needed expect them to do a man's share."[49]

Yet, Madge Breckinridge remained the genteel lady Anne Firor Scott
notes in her work *The Southern Lady: From Pedestal to Politics.* She and her
kinswomen went to suffrage rallies in fashionable hats and long gloves.
Madge consistently used her legacy as the great-granddaughter of Henry
Clay and her social standing in the cause of suffrage. Her father had sent
her to Miss Porter's School in Connecticut, but he brought her back after
one year because he did not want her to lose the values she shared with the

community in which she would live. Major McDowell was proud of his daughter's intellect, but he saw her role from the perspective of tradition. Melba Hay, Breckinridge's biographer, argues that she learned her sense of noblesse oblige from her father. She later adhered to the concepts of scientific philanthropy, but there remained within her thinking the sense of class superiority and social obligation learned in her youth. Many of the traditional moral values expected of women remained with her as well. She wrote from Europe that having experienced the American stage, she thought herself beyond shock until she attended a French play. Years later, suffering from her husband Desha's infidelity, she met the contempt of Lexington with the dignity expected of a southern lady. Hay suggests that at one point Madge may have even blamed herself to some degree for Desha's unfaithfulness.[50]

The traditional views of the Clay family reflect not only adherence to regional values but a growing defensiveness about the family name. Increasingly, family members thought Lexington and the nation sought to demean the character of the family and the contribution of Henry Clay. Each branch of the family reserved a folder or a box for newspaper and magazine stories about Henry Clay and other family members. Annie Green Clay, the daughter of Thomas H. Clay Jr., created a huge scrapbook with newspaper articles about Clay from throughout the country. Noticeably missing were the numerous negative stories about her ancestor.[51]

Family members became increasingly sensitive about inaccurate and unfavorable accounts. Given the harsh, politically motivated attacks on Henry and later James Clay, that branch of the family was particularly sensitive, but there was enough sensitivity to supply the entire family. Lexington had always enjoyed a good story at the expense of the Clays. Lexington's fame had grown with Henry Clay's political success. Monuments to his fame were everywhere. Sculptures and portraits adorned city hall, libraries, and universities. In more modern times, even a local McDonald's decorated its walls with pictures of Clay and Ashland. Like the family itself, the town seemed ready to proclaim each new family member the successor to the patriarch. His legacy to Lexington should have insulated the Clays from attack, but if anything, it made gossip worse. Despite the existence of two universities, Lexington remained intellectually a small town. Quite class conscious since frontier days, Lexington's gentry were extremely competitive. Elizabeth Murphey Simpson claimed in *The Enchanted Bluegrass* that the gentry were preoccupied with bloodlines. She attributed it to their fascination with the horse, but in reality it predated the introduction of the thoroughbred. The town early on proclaimed itself the Athens of the West, presumably a cultural center, and welcomed cultured visitors and settlers, particularly the French, to its community. Mary Austin Holley, who came from Boston when her husband accepted the presidency of Transylvania University in 1818, wrote to friends about the pretentiousness of Lexington's elite citizens. Margaret Preston Johnson complained about Lexington's gossip, and Harriet Martineau claimed that "Lexington people bicker so much that Mrs. [Anne Clay] Erwin, who quarrels with nobody, hardly knows how to get on among them." Mary Todd Lincoln, a native, found the city's social airs stifling. Many a newcomer to the town found entry to its highest levels of society barred to them.[52] Nothing could remove the Clays from the town's elite society, but that invincibility merely made them more vulnerable.

The town's citizens clearly enjoyed a good story at the expense of the Clays, and even family members admitted that Clay eccentricities provided incidents to talk about. But the word "incest" flew about when John Morrison Clay married Josephine Erwin, and again when Henry Clay McDowell Jr. and Elsie Clay wed. The charge was also leveled when a member of Henry Clay's family married a descendant of the Clays of Paris, Kentucky. As late as the 1980s, a local volunteered, "They marry their cousins, you know." Moreover, not only the sons but occasionally the daughters gave Lexington something to talk about. Clay spontaneity produced great stories. When prominent national leaders such as Theodore Roosevelt suggested that H. C. McDowell run for a seat in Congress in the late 1890s, McDowell received a letter intimating there were too many instances involving himself and his children that could be publicized if he chose to run. Small-town gossips took far too much pleasure in Desha Breckinridge's infidelity. Surprised by his lover's husband, he descended the fire escape at the Phoenix Hotel, allegedly with trousers in hand. The story became something of an urban legend. Despite the fact that it occurred in the early hours of the morning, most of Lexington, including the entire membership of a college fraternity, claimed to have witnessed it. Desha quickly became "Dash-away" among some in the community.

Lexington's elite delighted again when Susan Jacob Clay, greatgranddaughter in the James Clay branch, eloped with a twice-divorced Russian émigré nearly her mother's age, gossiping that he was actually a "Polish Jew," and when Henry Clay Anderson started living with Tessie

Williams, a working girl at Belle Brezing's house of ill repute, the town had a reason to once more forget its boredom. It was rumored his mother paid him to get out of town.[53] The antics of Henry McDowell Bullock, the last family resident at Ashland, also delighted Lexington. He occasionally fired a shotgun from the second-floor balcony to frighten neighborhood children away, and according to legend, he greeted one group of distinguished ladies at the front door of Ashland in the buff. Shortly thereafter, he was discreetly moved away from the estate.[54]

The Clays certainly brought some of the criticism on themselves. Increasingly enamored with the importance of Henry Clay and the Clay family, some members seemed to live too much in the past and to rely on the past in their assessment of their own importance. Even those who married into the family, particularly males, grew tired of hearing the Clay saga.[55] Increasingly defensive about the slightest criticism of Henry or other family members, they occasionally lashed out rather harshly. From the time James Clay was paraded through the streets in 1861, Susan, his wife, had believed Lexington enjoyed the Clays' discomfort. She taught her children that jealous men watched the families of great men in order to pull them down to their own level. The Clays themselves laughed at George Clay's antics, Charles Clay's military bearing, and Henry Clay Anderson's social missteps. Learning that Bob Clay intended to write a family history "with all its idiosyncrasies," Susan Clay Sawitzky wrote that she expected to be a major subject of the book.[56]

Local enjoyment of those eccentricities was another matter. As late as 1951, Susan Clay Sawitzky, visiting from Connecticut, wrote of "the old hostility of Lexington," and her sister, forty years after that, lamented in tears, "Why does Lexington hate us so?" Lexington did not hate the Clays, but its leading citizens did not realize how painful the gossip was to them. The last Clay descendant from the James Clay branch left Lexington in 1939. Three members of that branch made a decision not to move back to the region because of the scrutiny and hostility they perceived as real. Other branches warned their children that their actions reflected on the family name, and at least implied that Clays received more scrutiny than others.[57]

It was not just Lexington, however, that attacked Henry Clay or his family. As late as 1991, Clara Rising, writing a popular biography of Zachary Taylor, succeeded in getting authorities to exhume the general's body because she claimed Henry Clay had poisoned him. Wood Simpson, a great-great-great-grandson of Clay, rose to the defense. Henry Clay was a man of honor who settled his differences in the open, Simpson claimed. "It makes me angry," the local newspaper quoted him as saying; "I'd like to take her out and horsewhip her." Although Wood's proposed solution was more akin to Andrew Jackson than Henry Clay, the incident reflected both the ridiculous charges made against Clay and the frustration family members often felt.[58]

Letters exchanged a century earlier between Major Henry Clay McDowell and his friend Benjamin Helm Bristow, secretary of the treasury under Ulysses S. Grant, indicate that the concept was not new: "I have seen the dirty, lying newspaper story about Mr. Clay. Of course, it is the creation of some penny-a-liner, but as you say a great many will believe it. And the worst of it is that the friends and admirers of Mr. Clay can do nothing about it. A denial would undoubtedly cause the story to be repeated with great positiveness and it would be more generally read."[59]

Attacks on Henry Clay increased in the 1880s and 1890s. Henry Wise, a Virginia Whig and Confederate general, published attacks on Clay in 1872. In 1887 Lucius P. Little's biography of Kentuckian Ben Hardin made unnecessarily harsh and perhaps unsubstantiated criticisms of Clay. Attacks by moralists led Susan M. Clay and Thomas Hart Clay Jr. to start biographies of the patriarch. Attempting to preserve American values in an era of rapid change, Victorian writers renewed the old charges about Henry Clay's drinking and gambling. James Parton began the attack in an article published in *Youth's Companion,* the same journal that employed Thomas Hart Clay Jr. as an editor. The article asked a question that has been at the base of much historical writing, though few historians admit it: What personal faults had kept Henry Clay from becoming president of the United States? Parton claimed Clay never became president because of the evils of drinking, smoking, and chewing tobacco.[60] The first charge was an old one. The dangers of smoking and chewing tobacco had not been included in the long list of Clay's moral transgressions during his lifetime, but as Victorianism became more committed to the conversion of everyone to their ideas, the list of unacceptable habits grew longer. The Dawes Severalty Act of 1887 sought to destroy American Indian culture, and other movements—some considered efforts of reform (e.g., prohibition, antiprostitution) and some seeking to maintain tradition (e.g., Anthony Comstock's war on contraception)—took on a militant character.[61]

Heeding Bristow's advice, McDowell chose not to respond to negative articles about Clay. Instead, the McDowells cooperated with those who sought to publish more-favorable or more-professional accounts of Clay. He and his wife continued a tradition of loaning artifacts from the family collection and corresponding with serious scholars. James B. Clay had originally intended to publish some of his father's correspondence, but he acquiesced when his brother Thomas wanted Calvin Colton to work on it. Both Thomas and James sent parts of the collection for Colton to use.[62] Thomas Hart Clay Jr. also gave assistance to Carl Schurz in the 1880s.[63] George Poage and Glyndon Van Deusen spoke to the McDowells and with Susan Clay before publishing books.[64] Teetee Clay also helped Judge Charles Kerr and other writers. When *Century Magazine* asked that a family member write an article on Clay, the task was assigned to great-granddaughter Madge.

Family members, however, rarely found works on Henry Clay to their liking. Susan M. Clay was the harshest in her criticism. She became to Henry Clay what Jubal Early was to Robert E. Lee. She had helped make the myth, and she would seek to destroy anyone who challenged it.[65] When Parton's article appeared, she wrote the editor of *Youth's Companion* correcting the errors and demanding a retraction. The editor agreed to make some corrections at a future date, but Susan remained dissatisfied. She enlisted the aid of J. O. Harrison, the executor of Henry Clay's estate and a close friend, to write a long rebuttal, but the editors refused to publish it.[66] Increasingly suspicious, Susan poured over national newspapers looking for the slightest criticism of Clay. Adopting the nom de plume Paul, she responded to spurious attack or reasonable analysis if it appeared at all critical of Clay.[67] She argued that most criticisms were "almost too absurd to notice," but she noticed them anyway, fearing that despite their "silliness," if "constantly reiterated and seldom answered," they would be believed. She called the authors "foul birds" too ready to "soil their nest" by attempting to dwarf and disparage the memories of great men. In the *New York Daily Tribune* she attacked Parton and Edward Everett Hale, who published a similar article in *Cosmopolitan Magazine* in October 1891. Extremely harsh for one who, at least in public, sought to appear so Victorian, she undoubtedly believed by identifying herself as male she could use stronger language. When the *New York Daily Tribune* picked up a story first published in the *Louisville Courier-Journal,* she wrote, "Sir: A most disgusting article was recently published in 'The Courier Journal,' a vile slander against the memory of a great and good man—Henry Clay." She praised Clay's role at Ghent, pronounced his nobility of spirit in all things political, and denied that he drank too much or was addicted to gambling. Such attacks should be censured by everyone who felt pride in their country. Susan Clay wrote as Paul, but it was a family concern.[68] The McDowells collected the attacks and Susan's responses, preserving them in their own papers.[69]

Thomas Hart Clay Jr. also reacted to the Parton and Hale articles, but with more tact. Lizzie Lee, a member of the Preston Blair family, wrote Thomas that she shared his "distrust of Parton." Thomas wrote to Parton asking for clarification of the charges about Clay's drinking and gambling. Parton agreed to reconsider the criticism in print but never did. Thomas also wrote to Hale, who claimed he got his information about Clay's gambling from the diaries of John Quincy Adams. Additionally, Thomas sent a long list of corrections to Joseph Rogers after the publication of his biography. Rogers responded that Clay was being vilified in the East, and it was better to admit minor faults so the true importance of the Great Compromiser could be realized.[70]

Susan M. Clay began to organize Henry Clay's papers, intending to write a biography. Unfortunately, she started to destroy letters and papers as a means of protecting the family name. Scholars have long believed the papers to have been purged. There is, for example, virtually no indication of Henry's drinking or gambling except an occasional warning to sons or grandsons about the dangers of such activities. Remini noted that there are in the collection no letters from son John Morrison Clay. The harsh letter Clay wrote after J. J. Crittenden led the Kentucky delegation to abandon him in 1848 is also missing. According to George Poage, author of *Henry Clay and the Whig Party*, George Clay read the letter to him in 1920, but it is not in the collection presented to the Library of Congress three years later.[71]

Other members of the family consistently noted reasons to withhold letters from publication, edit them, or destroy them altogether. Working with Calvin Colton in the 1850s, James Clay suggested the removal of some letters lest his brother John be embarrassed. Susan Clay also remarked that a number of letters were suppressed because the writers were still living and might be hurt by the disclosure.[72] After Susan M. Clay died in 1905, Teetee, sitting by the fire, continued to organize the Clay papers long after her brothers had gone to bed. The portraits of family members she wished the public to see are evident in the biographies she wrote for Judge Kerr that appeared in William Connelley and E. Merton Coulter's five-volume *History of Kentucky*. Teetee altered numerous letters and admitted destroying others. She wrote to her brother Charles in 1916 that she had been through most of the papers and urged him to go through the rest: "Occasionally you may find a passage which should be omitted, one for instance about Randolph in a letter from Kit Hughes, an intimate friend of Grandpa." In the same letter, she said her mother's letters should be published, "such passages left out as you may think necessary."[73]

Reading the letters, Teetee decided what to save and what to destroy. She copied some letters, omitting the offensive sections. There are also letters that abruptly end at what appears to the reader to be a critical point. Either a page is missing or a section has been torn away. Fortunately, she often failed to destroy the original letter or to delete sections of others mentioning the issue more discretely. She also added notes that allow the reader, having read other correspondence, to fill in the blanks. Frequently, she even noted the missing section with a row of x's. Many of her deletions are unimportant; they merely reflect her Victorian sensitivity. Susan Clay had written to her sister that several of the children had been sick. Teetee inserted her x's in a line: "quite ill xxxxxxxx, and dear little Susie . . ." The actual letter read "quite ill with flux," but that was one of those unmentionable subjects to Teetee. In another letter she notes that she copied only parts of a letter: "The account of my sister's death, and my mother's overwhelming grief seems too sacred for the eyes of any except members of her own family." More seriously, in a fragment of a letter she identifies as one to Henry Clay, she quotes, "I again say, that I am most thoroughly convinced that you were most untruthfully, and therefore unjustly treated; for I have never seen any evidence to substantiate at all the charge xxxxxxxxxxxxx." It has been impossible to reconstruct that letter. Finally, in the margin of a letter is a note in Teetee's hand: "Copy and burn."[74]

The practice was not uncommon in the late nineteenth century. Families kept personal matters within the family as much as possible, and sensitivity about certain subjects kept them out of public discussion. Elizabeth Clay Blanford, refined, genteel, and quite proper in her conduct, would probably have been more comfortable in the nineteenth century. Echoing the sentiments of her grandmother and her aunt, she wanted to destroy letters or portions of letters that could be "misunderstood" or that could be used by the unscrupulous intent on disparaging a family member. There were also letters that were on delicate subjects or that might embarrass people. Her father, for example, created a charade to avoid discussion of the breeding of horses. He did not keep stallions on the farm, shipping his mares away "to visit with their friends." Elizabeth and Susan knew better, but they maintained the charade. Papa was a gentleman, and after all, Elizabeth Blanford said, there was no need to announce to the neighborhood that the family cat had birthed kittens under the back stairs. She also wanted to destroy a letter from her father to George Clay, her uncle, chastising him for trying to sell the family papers. Although it was a family joke that George would sell anything he could get his hands on, she feared that the letter might give an unfair impression of him. He was, she said, really a delightful man and did not deserve to be considered greedy or disloyal to his family. Similarly, a poem her sister had written, titled "To Elizabeth," appeared to criticize a young woman from Lexington. (Actually, it both criticized and cautioned the southern belle.) Although the woman had died years ago, Elizabeth Blanford feared the unflattering portrait would embarrass the woman's family. Finally, although no member of her branch lived in Lexington after 1939, she did not want to make things difficult for members of the McDowell or Erwin branches still living there. The papers, she said, were unimportant anyway and should be destroyed.[75] Fortunately, a love of history overcame Victorian sensitivity; she chose not to destroy the papers.

The emphasis placed on family can also be seen in the Clays' attitudes about marriage. Henry Clay had taken a rather cavalier attitude toward the marriages of his children. That legacy abruptly stopped. Particularly in Lexington, marriage still very much represented a union between families. In the Tennessee branch, Mary Clay Kenner apparently had the final voice in most matters, whether to ensure social goals or just because she was so dominant. Just as in the case of the McDowells, her children represented two prominent families. Harry Boyle Clay told stories about the Clays, but his daughter Mary increasingly emphasized the name of her husband's family, because it was better known in East Tennessee. There, the significance of family became a case of entitlement. The Kenners were important people, and Mary Clay Kenner intended to keep it that way. She forced one daughter back to Tennessee when she disapproved of a relationship. Dr. William Kenner, a Clay descendant and a practicing psychiatrist, characterized his family as cold, distant, and unable to express love. He tied it to being related to a great man and knowing the fame could not be achieved again. According to Kenner, the family was extremely dysfunctional, leading to a number of unhappy marriages. Kenner's father was shot and killed by a woman who most likely had been his mistress. Chasing him down the street with a pistol in each hand, she shot him eleven times before he fell. The defense attorney declared him a man who would "rule or ruin." The jury acquitted the woman.[76]

The McDowells expected their children to make good marriages, and they had better luck than their Tennessee cousins. They made no great objection to Nettie's marriage to Dr. Thomas Bullock, although perhaps they should have. They were less excited about the marriages of the other two daughters. Madge eventually married Desha Breckinridge, a member of another old Kentucky family, but the couple postponed the event for several years because of family opposition. The Clays had long felt some animosity toward the Breckinridges. The first marriage of W. C. P. Breckinridge, Desha's father, had been to Thomas Hart Clay's daughter Lucretia, although Clay opposed it. He wrote in his diary, "There is an odor about R.J. Breckinridge I do not admire. The sons are just commencing the practice of law with I think a poor prospect of success. . . . They are a coarse family." Lucretia died in childbirth less than a year later. Breckinridge, a veteran of the Civil War and a U.S. congressman, married again but was involved in a scandal. He promised a young woman to marry her when his wife died but quickly married a third woman. The scandal became public, and Major McDowell considered challenging him for the legislative seat. Unlike Nettie's wedding, that of Madge and Desha was a quiet affair with only family members present. Some years later, Mrs. McDowell opposed the marriage of Julia to William Brock. She did not like his family and generally believed the Brocks beneath them.[77] Ironically, that may have been the happiest marriage of the three. The McDowells seemed less concerned about the marriages of their sons. Henry Clay McDowell Jr. married his cousin several times removed, the daughter of Harry Boyle Clay of Tennessee. William and Thomas married into prominent Kentucky families.

In the James Clay branch, Teetee never married, and Susan Clay insisted so strongly that her sons postpone marriage until the family fortune had been recovered that the James Clay branch nearly ended. The emphasis on proper marriages for the sons and the ever-present tragedies explain in part the fact that no living descendants of Henry Clay have his last name. All family members now descend through females. James, the oldest son, married against his mother's wishes, and Charles, one of the youngest, did not marry until nearly forty years old. Pedigrees were always an issue, but so was money. George Clay wrote on one occasion that he had lost his heart to a young women and expressed the hope that his mother and sister would approve "this time."[78] When Charles exhibited an interest in a young woman in 1882, Susan M. Clay wrote ordering him to break it off and to quit "being silly" about the young woman: "If a man has no means of his own, he should marry a woman who has, or not at all." Remember, she counseled, "when poverty comes in the door love flies out the window."[79] Susan noted in the letter that she had given her son Tom the same advice. In another letter to Charles nearly a year later she wrote, "You have no right to expect that wealth will come to you in jumps, unless like Wick Preston, you marry rich." Again, she had given the same advice to Tom. Susan finally agreed to Charles's marriage when he was thirty-nine years old and the only one likely to continue the family line.

The pressure became stronger in later generations, particularly in some branches. Josephine Clay apparently expressed some concern when her daughter Lucretia, or Lula, wanted to marry Minor Simpson, a hard-working but socially inferior man from a nearby county. The McDowells, who knew him through farming connections, interceded on his behalf. Bill LaBach noted discontent from his grandmother with several marriage choices in the family and a tendency to question any choice. No potential partner seemed to have the pedigree worthy of union with Clay descendants. Again, the James Clay branch exceeded the others. Although merely fourteen years old, Charley Clay, a great-grandson, provoked a family crisis when he started horseback riding with a neighborhood girl about his age. The bachelor uncles and aunt expressed their concern to his parents that there had been some mental problems in the girl's family. The friendship had to be curtailed. Similarly, when his brother Bob was at West Point, his parents tried to interfere in his relationship with a young woman in Lexington. Several members of her family had suffered nervous breakdowns. Incensed, Robert wrote that if a God could be so cruel as to pass such burdens from one generation to the next he would refuse to believe in him. Clearly, part of his own family history had been kept from him.[80]

Robert learned to use the family's sensibilities to his own advantage. When he decided to marry, he first became engaged, then told his parents he wanted to bring her to meet them. The Clays were not happy, but propriety demanded that they accept his fait accompli. Ironically, however, Robert would order his own son, Robert Pepper Clay Jr., to break off a relationship he believed unacceptable by family standards.[81]

Robert's sisters, Susan and Elizabeth, expressed their delight with his show of independence, for both young women felt suffocated by their parents' protectiveness. Colonel and Mrs. Clay greeted any prospective beau with a coldness that could not be missed. Susan was convinced her father had broken up one of her relationships in her teens, although her fears may be more important as a reflection of their relationship than fact. Mrs. Clay's sister, Lizzie Pepper, even spoke to a Christian Science practitioner, seeking help for Elizabeth. The Clays, she believed, were ruining their daughter's life. They interfered in one relationship, fearing the young man did not have enough money. Elizabeth did not marry until after the death of both parents. Susan, at the age of twenty-seven, eloped with William Sawitzky because Colonel Clay had threatened to shoot him if he attempted to see her.[82]

The concern about mental difficulties in the families of prospective marriage partners suggests an unspoken fear that permeated Clay homes regarding issues of health. Henry Clay left a legacy to his descendants of severe susceptibility to disease. Henry and Lucretia lost all six daughters to disease, a son to war, and a son to insanity during their lifetimes. They also began the process of burying their grandchildren. Nineteen of twenty-nine grandchildren died before their thirty-fifth birthdays. Contemporaries and historians have written disparagingly of James B. Clay because he did not seem capable of filling his father's shoes. But Clay had amassed a large estate, served as a diplomat and in the U.S. House of Representatives, and helped elect a president before dying of tuberculosis at the age of forty-six. Madeline McDowell Breckinridge was a successful Progressive Era reformer but died at forty-seven, a victim of tuberculosis and heart disease. Tuberculosis, typhoid, diphtheria, and heart disease stifled many promising members of the family. One young Clay descendant died suddenly after participating in a University of Kentucky track meet. Plagued by tuberculosis until after World War II, family members frequently had to disrupt their careers to "take the cure."[83] Untimely death also continued to plague the family. Robert Pepper Clay Jr., the last male capable of continuing the family name, died while scuba diving in 1973 at the age of thirty-one. So many tragedies in the family understandably led to an element of fatalism. Young members of the family were urged to make their contributions early because death seemed so frequently the family's companion. So many bright young men and women were taken too soon.

When Harry Independence Clay died in 1884, the *Louisville Courier-*

Journal noted that he had been the hope of the family to restore the prominence of his grandfather. Another local paper noted, however, that he had a "presentiment" that he would die young. He stated it in a humorous, perhaps falsely brash way: he would "die with his boots on."[84] The Lexington papers lamented the untimely death of Madeline McDowell Breckinridge, a descendant who showed the promise of her distinguished ancestor. And William Stucky, a McDowell descendant who reached the rank of commander in the navy during World War II and became a prominent journalist and playwright, died suddenly at age forty-five. It seemed to be the burden of their gift. At least two branches of the family saved a clipping from an unidentified newspaper that articulated what the family knew too well. Titled "Brilliant—but Short-Lived," it talked about the bright young members of the family who died too soon. One Lexington resident called the legacy the "Clay disease." For some members of the family, it remained an unspoken burden.[85]

The legacy of family proved to be both a blessing and a curse. Ironically, the women of the family seemed to gain most from family memory. Susan M. Clay, Josephine Clay, and Mary Clay Kenner dominated their branches of the family, and Teetee, Madge, and Mary Webster Clay Anderson were strong forces. Members of the James Clay branch found the name most suffocating. Too much was expected of each young man or woman even as the past limited the opportunity. For the McDowells, it was more a matter of confidence. Madge Breckinridge used her great-grandfather's fame to help the cause of women's suffrage. Waiting to address the all-male legislature of North Carolina, she gained courage from his portrait.[86] The Kenners were removed from the pressures of Lexington, but Dr. William Kenner, a respected psychiatrist, has suggested that at least some of the dysfunction in his family came from the shadow of a great man in family memory.[87]

For all members, the name opened doors in Lexington and throughout the nation. It transmitted a keen intelligence and a sense of duty. No Clay filled the shoes of the patriarch, but leadership is required at state and local level, in the professions, and in many other ways. The "afflictions" suffered by the family appear almost overwhelming, but they were not shared by all; and even those who suffered, like Madge Breckinridge, her brother Henry Clay McDowell Jr., Susan M. Clay, Josephine, and a host of others, overcame serious illness, depression, or the loss of someone close to them to make solid contributions.

Others found the name a burden even as they cherished it. Susan Clay

Ashland-on-Tates-Creek. Josephine Clay Collection. Courtesy of University of Kentucky Special Collections.

Sawitzky loved her family but found it stifling. Yet, Clay remained a part of her signature. The last member of the James Clay branch left Lexington in 1939. James Clay descendants sometimes visited, but they chose not to live in the community because of the burden public scrutiny carried for them. Robert Pepper Clay, after a successful career in the army, chose to settle elsewhere, deciding he did not want his children to experience the pressure he had known as a child. However, he proudly gave family artifacts he inherited to the Henry Clay Memorial Foundation after 1950 when the estate became a house museum. Henry Clay Simpson Sr., when asked his relationship to the statesman, would claim he could not remember. Yet, he, along with other family members, developed one of the most beautiful sections of Lexington out of John and Josephine's Ashland-on-Tates-Creek farm. He also served on the board of the Henry Clay

Memorial Foundation, and his wife, like so many women who married into the family, took pride in the name and supported Ashland throughout her life. Clearly, confidence and a sense of duty from the family heritage overcame adversity in many instances.

Chapter 9

LEGACY OF RISK

Bill LaBach, a descendant of Henry Clay with four greats to his name, has a PhD in mathematics and a law degree. After age sixty-five, he enrolled at the University of Kentucky as a Donovan scholar and became a published historian. Normally a very reserved man, he has a twinkle to his eye that betrays his heritage. A photographic portrait hangs in his home showing LaBach dressed as a Mississippi riverboat gambler accompanied by his appropriately attired wife. No gambler at cards or horses, he is not slow to wager on his own abilities. "Always a gamester," John Quincy Adams said of Henry Clay; but it was the challenge, or the risk, that excited him. Henry Clay found it in card games, politics, and business ventures. His descendants inherited the legacy but expanded its application.

That legacy fit the profile of the post–Civil War South. Economic recovery in the American South required risk and courage. Paul Gaston says of that era, no amount of nostalgia could alter the fact that the South was desperately poor, despised or pitied, and saddled with unwelcome burdens. That was almost an understatement. Confederate currency was, of course, useless. Banking capital dropped from $61 million in 1860 to $17 million ten years later. Much of the region's wealth had been in the form of human property, now freed, and land, the value of which had been based on the productivity of slave labor. Moreover, the land had been crisscrossed by marauding armies. John Morrison Clay did not stand alone when he complained that the Yankees took his slaves and the Rebels stole his horses. Armies destroyed supplies to keep their enemies from using them. They took horses because that was the major means for moving war materiel and for cavalry. Soldiers had to be fed; an army of sixty thousand men moved like a horde of locusts across the land. In the case of Sherman's armies, the destruction was calculated, and as the war neared its end, deserters and stragglers added to the misery. According to Stanley Engerman in *The Cambridge Economic History of the United States,* southern production in 1870 was only about two-thirds what it had been in 1860. Property levels dropped significantly, and southern per-capita incomes fell to nearly one-half the national level.[1]

The losses were even more telling in terms of livestock. John Hervey, an authority on thoroughbred racing, claims the use of horses prolonged the war significantly and in the process decimated the horse population, most particularly the blooded stock. Nearly five hundred thousand horses and two hundred thousand mules were destroyed during the war. Farmers lost more than a million cattle and a like number of sheep. Six million hogs served to feed Yankees, Rebels, and guerillas. The prewar value of southern livestock would not be recovered until the turn of the century, and the losses led to endemic poverty, malnutrition, and even starvation. As Gaston notes, the South needed a "harmonizing rationale" that could restore faith and provide a path out of the postwar despair.[2] Given the obstacles, it would take some gambler's luck.

The myth of the Lost Cause provided part of the answer, or at least the delusion of one, but there was also a second myth. In 1886, speaking before the New England Society of New York, Henry W. Grady, the editor of the *Atlanta Constitution,* captured the imagination of the North and many in the South with his declaration of a New South. He decreed the Old South of slavery and secession gone, replaced by a new South of union and freedom. The public pronouncement of the end of slavery by a southerner was meant for his northern audience. The real purpose of the New South Creed was to bring the region out of poverty and to reestablish its national influence. The founders of the creed walked a thin line between the old and the new. For northern consumption, at least, they argued that the war was in the past and that if the South was to compete, it would have to adopt some northern business practices. B. H. Hill, a former Confederate general, argued that slavery had kept the South bound to an outmoded, stultifying economic system that saw the region fall behind other areas of the nation. A southern renaissance depended on exploiting the natural resources of the South through diversified industry and progressive agriculture. Farmers could grow cotton, but southerners should also produce textiles. The region would need northern capital and a more sympathetic view from northern entrepreneurs, hence Grady's talk of an end to slavery and the beginning of freedom. The old prejudices would not produce sympathy among northern entrepreneurs or consumers. The New South Creed allowed southerners to believe in the region's ability to compete successfully with the rest of the country economically. By combining the two myths, they could believe the South's quality of life remained superior to that of other regions.

Though more progressive than the masses in the South, the advocates of the New South Creed continued to believe in white supremacy. Like the Lost Cause, the New South Creed was fraught with self-delusion and outright deception. Its creators paid homage to new freedom to appease northerners and looked the other way when the Klan sought to keep blacks "in their place" and when politicians limited educational opportunities for blacks. Although they claimed to look to the future, they also sought to restore southern faith in the region's distinctiveness. Consequently, as the New South Creed developed, it served to buttress the house of cards erected to preserve the southern image. Seventy years after the Civil War, Franklin D. Roosevelt, much to the consternation of many southerners, called the South the nation's number one economic problem.

Just as with the Lost Cause, the image of Henry Clay helped guide the Clay family to acceptance of the New South Creed. Residents of a border state, they had always been willing to make money in manufacturing as well as agriculture. Henry Clay's American System had encouraged economic connections to all regions of the country, and the Clay Corporation knew no regional boundaries when money could be made. The second generation continued those interests. James Clay held commercial and residential property in Louisville, where he competed to a degree with the husband of his niece Anne Clay McDowell, and Thomas Hart Clay seemed most excited about his life when securing contracts to supply the Union army early in the war. Later generations continued the enjoyment of business.

Gambling, the "fickle goddess," did not lose its attraction for some family members, as noted earlier, but the gambling spirit revealed itself most prominently in other ways. Henry Clay complained that Charles Edward Erwin and his brothers, Clay's grandsons, wanted to rush off to Cuba with a band of adventurers intent on incorporating the island into the United States, and Henry Clay Duralde, worn out by drinking and gambling, decided to find focus and fortune in the California gold rush. Lucretia Clay Erwin wrote to her grandfather declaring her intention to enter a Catholic convent, but a year later she was married and expecting a child. Henry's assessment of the marriage suggested her decision was a somewhat spontaneous one.[3]

From instruction or experience, many Clay sons learned the dangers of the "fickle goddess." Like alcohol, it cost too many Clays too much. The risk of business was a different matter. Many Clays experienced success; some found it difficult to avoid any speculative venture. The message of the New South Creed was an optimistic one: there were fortunes to be made. Since this was an acceptable outlet for their gambling spirit, family members sought every opportunity a new economy offered them. Each new business venture promised the fortune that had been lost. But like the creed, the Clays would blend the old with the new. The legacy left by the patriarch had many facets.

Agriculture remained the financial base for many members of the family throughout the remainder of the nineteenth century. John Morrison Clay held on to the land inherited from his father, and Thomas's wife and unmarried daughter continued to live at Mansfield, sharecropping the land with tenants. Harry Boyle Clay farmed the land his wife inherited in Tennessee. Susan M. Clay bought a small farm for her son James Jr. and, in 1883, the larger one that became a home for her, her daughter, and eventually two sons. Finally, the McDowells lived on a large farm in Franklin County called Woodlake until Henry Clay McDowell purchased Ashland from the University of Kentucky in 1883.

Even in agriculture, with one exception, the family practiced the riskiest form of production. Although Harry Boyle Clay grew corn and cattle on his Tennessee farms, the Kentucky Clays bred and raced thoroughbred horses. Modern scientific efforts to determine the important traits of a racehorse, the best mare to breed to the best stallion, and how to keep horses healthy have not produced significantly greater results than the hippocket approach of yesteryear. A horse purchased for millions of dollars can be a dud at the racetrack, and a cheap one, $75,000 or so, can win the Kentucky Derby. A very few foals out of those produced make it to the racetrack, where any bettor knows the odds of success. Finally, a horse that is successful on the track may prove useless as a sire of future winners. The great sire Lexington, for example, while leading the sires list twelve times between 1861 and 1874 and twice posthumously, sired 533 foals from 963 mares bred to him.[4] At 55 percent, he had an astounding record. The thoroughbred is a fragile animal made more so by years of inbreeding. Recent years have seen "sure winners" felled by broken bones, infections, and a host of other maladies. With the exception of H. C. McDowell's Ashland Stud, the Clays did not have the advantage of playing the numbers—that is, the more horses one foals the greater the chance of producing a winner. They operated small farms and produced a few horses each year. Although there were times when financial collapse threatened, they proved themselves very good at producing quality horses and making both a living and a contribution to the industry.

John Morrison Clay survived the Civil War with his Ashland Stud intact. John Clay had difficulty in his personal relationships, but with horses, he showed both skill and sensitivity. Later his wife claimed he had inherited the magic voice of Henry Clay, and the animals responded to it.[5] They would lift up their heads at the sound of his voice. Of the foundation horses in Henry's stable—Yorkshire, Magnolia, and Margaret Wood— John received Margaret Wood and her Herold filly and Rally as a behest and Yorkshire for one dollar.[6]

Yorkshire, Magnolia, and Margaret Wood became the basis for the significant contribution to the thoroughbred industry made by the Clay family. Twelve Kentucky Derby winners shared the bloodlines of the three foundation horses in the Clay stables. There were also winners of the Preakness, the Belmont, the English Derby, and other important national and international races.[7] John Morrison Clay's success can be attributed largely to three factors. Most important, he inherited three extremely good horses, but he was also able to breed the two mares, Magnolia and Margaret Wood, to Glencoe and Lexington, two of the most important sires in the history of racing. John also provided greater care for his horses, training them himself, and taking them to tracks throughout the country. They had his undivided attention. And finally, his marriage to Josephine added stability to his life and a partner who became a respected horsewoman in her own right.[8]

Charles E. Trevathan, author of *The American Thoroughbred,* rates John Morrison Clay as one of the most successful breeders of American thoroughbreds. In the smaller operations of the postwar era there is truth in the statement. Sending Margaret Wood to Glencoe, Clay produced Star Davis, later one of his premier studs. Star Davis would sire Day Star, a Kentucky Derby winner. Magnolia produced a colt by Lexington named Kentucky, at one time considered the greatest racehorse foaled in America.[9]

In the years after the Civil War, the contests of Kentucky, Norfolk, and Asteroid helped revive racing in America. The rivalry brought northern and southern horsemen back to the racetrack, healing old political wounds in the process. Northerners with capital, an essential element to southern recovery according to the New South Creed, invested again in horses, and crowds returned to the tracks at Patterson, Secaucus, and Saratoga.[10] That helped the Kentucky economy.

Magnolia, known as the "Empress of the Stud Book," produced many great horses. According to John Hervey, more stakes winners descend from her than from any other mare foaled as late as 1867.[11] In addition to Kentucky, she produced Victory, a winner at racetracks across the country. His fate, however, was nearly as star-crossed as that of John Clay. Purchased in 1873 by General George Armstrong Custer, who shortened the name to Vic, he was ridden at the Battle of the Little Big Horn. Custer, of course, died there; the fate of Victory is unknown.[12] Magnolia was also the second dam of a horse named Maggie B.B., as well as the dam of the first American-bred horse to win the English Derby and the first horse ever to win the English Derby, the St. Leger, and the Prince of Wales Stakes.

Maggie B.B. illustrates other characteristics of the Kentucky thoroughbred industry in the late nineteenth century. The breeders of race horses composed a small, intimate group. They shared breeding information and valued the knowledge learned through experience. They named horses for people or events significant to the region. Horses named Daniel Boone, Henry Clay, and even Minnie Clay raced the tracks of North and South. Bred to the stallion Australian, Madeline produced a foal that John Clay called Magpie. Because Clay's brothers had been given breeding rights by Henry, John Clay sold his share of the horse to his nephew James B. Clay Jr. in 1869. James Clay renamed the horse Maggie B.B. in honor of Maggie Beck, the woman he had wanted to marry. In 1870 Maggie married a much wealthier man, James K. Corcoran of Washington, D.C., but she died soon after. Maggie B.B. became one of Clay's most successful horses.[13]

John Clay exhibited another of the risk factors in thoroughbred breeding. It is difficult to know when a horse will mature as a racer. The famous John Henry lost money for several owners before he decided to run. John Clay's horses often blossomed after he sold them. He sold Kentucky and a second horse in 1864 for a mere $6,000, but Kentucky then won twenty-one of twenty-two starts for other owners. He also sold Survivor, the winner of the first Preakness, and Maggie B.B.'s success came after he gave up his interest in the horse.[14] He thus contributed to the industry, but saw small profit from it.

When John died in 1887, Josephine continued Ashland Stud. Proclaimed the "pioneer horsewoman of the Bluegrass," she was actually the only woman actively involved in the sport for a long time. Well into the twentieth century, many horsemen considered it bad luck for a woman to enter the breeding barn. Some even believed it would cause a mare to miscarry. But Josephine Russell Erwin Clay was no ordinary woman. Unable to join the Jockey Club of New York, the Lexington Racing Association, and other clubs because she was a woman, she talked horses with farm managers at the Phoenix Hotel. She closed John's racing stable but bred the mares and sold their colts. She increased her stable from the twelve mares she inherited from John to fifty. Like the men in the family, she became a successful thoroughbred breeder. She bred Semper Ego, Semper Lex, Loki, and other horses that won significant acclaim on the track. When she died in 1920, the *Lexington Herald* proclaimed her "the world's most noted and successful woman owner and breeder of fine thoroughbred horses." Obituaries rarely contain unflattering remarks, but the *Herald* only echoed what other accounts had been saying for more than twenty years. Josephine entered the business with more knowledge than she admitted, but less than anyone, certainly a woman in a man's world, needed to succeed. Through hard work and study, she added to the Clay contribution to the thoroughbred industry.[15]

James Clay Jr. operated Iroquois Farm on the outskirts of Lexington. He too was known for his knowledge of horses and his skill in matching them to produce good racers. Though never a major breeder, he raised sound horses and enjoyed a reputation for unquestioned integrity.[16] Adjacent to Iroquois Farm, James Clay's brother George raised horses on land purchased by his mother. The farm consisted of approximately two hundred acres, land that eventually became a part of Calumet, one of the most important Kentucky thoroughbred farms. Like John Morrison Clay, George probably got on better with horses than with people. He studied law with General Basil Duke, but he never practiced. He was uncomfortable around women and never married. Known within the family as "poor George," he once wrote one of his brothers that unlike them, he was not subject to great disappointment because he had not harbored great ambitions. George, too, suffered frequently from depression, but on such occasions he seemed to find peace of mind among his horses.[17]

George Clay knew well the risks of raising thoroughbreds. After the economic panic of 1893, he consistently used his horses as collateral to acquire loans to keep the farm running. In early 1893 he mortgaged two of his finest horses, Ballet and Thundercloud, to save the farm, and the next year he forfeited ten colts to secure an additional loan. Finances became so bad that his brother Charles considered postponing his marriage in 1896 to help alleviate the family debts. Even earlier, George, as comic relief, wrote a short poem about the risks he faced:

> I tried to raise thoroughbreds fast
> At first all the future looked bright
> But destruction and death came at last,
> And now all's as black as the night.
>
> Bad luck has o'ertaken me now,
> I am both very sad and forlorn,
> My hands I must put to the plow,
> And work like the devil in corn.[18]

Perhaps less than good poetry, his effort could be a lesson for any who enter the industry. There is no evidence that George Clay had to plow corn. In fact, he continued to breed successful horses. George owned Ballet, a mare bred by John Clay, which was successful both on the track and as a broodmare. He also bred Modesty, the first filly to win the American Derby, and Peg Woffington, a mare he sold to kinsman Thomas Clay McDowell.[19] Nevertheless, he seemed constantly to be visiting the bank, securing loans to keep Balgowan solvent.[20]

Thomas J. Clay joined his brother after his retirement from the U.S. Army in 1894. Although he had some success as a breeder, he made a more important contribution as a racing official, serving as president of the Kentucky Association and as a track judge. Thomas J. Clay took tremendous pride in upholding the family's reputation for honesty and integrity. A *Lexington Herald* article of 1917 said, "Both the Clay brothers [are] sportsmen of the highest type, breeders with rare knowledge of blood lines, practical horsemen and inbred with the highest ideals of fair dealing and great sports-

Captain Tom and Mr. George. Courtesy of the Elizabeth Clay Blanford Collection.

manship."[21] Such a reputation was an extension of the principle of Clay honor inherited from Henry Clay and taught by the second generation.

Captain Tom and Mr. George, as they were called in Lexington, became legendary as the best of the traditional horsemen of the Bluegrass, but they were to see that era come to an end. New money, earned in northern businesses, bought Kentucky land and raised horses on a grander scale. George, in particular, resented the intrusion. He scoffed at the palatial stables built by Warren Wright, the developer of Calumet Farm, who purchased land adjacent to Balgowan. When Wright whitewashed his fences, however, George just got mad. He believed whitewash damaged the vision of his horses, and he threatened to take Wright to court. The invasion of new money was something even a Clay could not stop. After the death of their sister Teetee in 1923, Captain Tom and Mr. George sold Balgowan to Wright and moved to the Phoenix Hotel in Lexington.[22]

The most successful family operation was that of Henry Clay McDowell and his son Thomas, but they too experienced periodic losses. In 1883 McDowell moved his stables from Woodlake, a farm outside Frankfort, to the McDowells' new home at Ashland. He adopted the name Ashland Stud despite the fact that John Morrison Clay also operated under that name. McDowell, however, took a different approach to racing. Like James B. Clay Sr., he raised trotting horses rather than thoroughbred racers. He minimized the risk inherent to the business of racing by diversifying his operation. He trained both riding and carriage horses. Benjamin Helm Bristow, a close friend and secretary of the treasury under Grant, wrote to McDowell about his team, purchased from Ashland Stud, using terms evocative of much later young men's descriptions of the power and beauty of their automobiles. Others saw teams from Ashland and wrote to McDowell describing the qualities they wanted in their carriage horses. Ashland Stud also provided horses to the French, Belgian, and Japanese governments for military mounts, and it sent blooded horses to the stables of the emperor of Japan.[23]

Though not a Clay by blood, Henry Clay McDowell shared the family love for risk. One of a new breed of southern businessmen, he blended the soft gentlemanly image of the southern aristocracy with the harsher methods of the new industrialism. He has been called "a Kentucky robber baron" with some justification. Another description seems to have some merit as well. Operating in an area with great affinity for the South, he practiced in business the admonition of his friend Teddy Roosevelt: Walk softly but carry a big stick. McDowell recognized the value of the Clay name and the importance of the Lost Cause mentality. In a masterful stroke of advertising, he included in his sales catalogues a nostalgic history of Ashland and its association with Henry Clay. He noted particularly Clay's devotion to scientific farming and breeding. Mindful of the interest in the antebellum statesman, he often referred his customers to Susan Clay for additional information about Henry and the Clay family.[24] McDowell cultivated the image of the southern gentleman. He used his military rank of major, but emphasized its origins in the Union army only where it helped his business plans. He wore a beard in a style fashionable in both North and South, and dressed like a southern plantation owner. As noted previously, Ashland became a center for entertainment for the McDowell Corporation, a family business not unlike that Henry Clay had created. The McDowells opened their home to the Mexican War Veterans, to the

Major McDowell. Henry Clay Memorial Foundation Collection. Courtesy of University of Kentucky Special Collections.

Masons, and to delegations from Venezuela and other South American countries wishing to pay homage to Henry Clay.[25] Of course, those visitors saw his horses as well.

McDowell worked diligently to reestablish Kentucky in the breeding of standardbreds. Beginning his effort as a hobby (he sold only three horses in 1875), by 1882, just before the move to Ashland, he sold more than eighty horses. He encouraged Kentucky breeders to join the National Association of Trotting Horse Breeders, and he became a vice president of the organization in 1876. Almost immediately, he became involved in a sectional, but decidedly uncivil, war. This time, however, he was on the side of the southerners. In the 1870s, if a horse was being used for breeding or racing, it was registered in *Wallace's Trotting Register,* a publication edited by John H. Wallace. Wallace wielded dictatorial control over the trotting horse industry. According to John Hervey, an authority on American racing, Wallace believed in his own infallibility and resented the expression of opinion by others if contrary to his own. Hervey described him as sarcastic, heavy handed, and vindictive. McDowell soon experienced his wrath. A group of Kentucky breeders formulated a new trotting standard to bring order to the field. Wallace published the standards but then attacked them in the March 1879 issue of *Wallace's Monthly*. He submitted his own standards, which were subsequently adopted by the National Association of Trotting Horse Breeders, and charged the Kentuckians with attempting to gain a local advantage. His contempt for "southerners" was painfully apparent. Wallace used his power as the editor of the *Register* in an unethical manner to defeat the Kentuckians. According to Hervey, he "assailed the Kentuckians individually and as a body, their stock farms, their breeding stock, and their breeding theories, their institutions and their integrity."[26] He delayed the registration of their horses, and used his journal to attack McDowell and other Kentucky breeders.[27]

Wallace underestimated the man he chose to vilify. McDowell signaled his intention to be a major force in the industry when he teamed with David and A. A. Bonner to buy a horse named Dictator, a brother to Dexter, the first member of the Hamiltonian family to set a world trotting record. The three men paid $25,000 for the horse, a figure equal to $500,000 in 2003 according to Jeff Meyer, the former curator at the Henry Clay Estate. Wallace attacked immediately. He claimed that there was no man a big enough fool to spend such a sum on the horse. When that failed to curb the excitement, he used his resources to spread rumors that the horse was spavined and that his get were notoriously unsound. McDowell threatened to sue, and Wallace apologized. However, his apology, written to avoid the suit, continued to foster doubts about Dictator.[28]

By 1890 Wallace's arrogance had alienated a large number of breeders from both North and South. A meeting of breeders formed the American Trotting Register Association and bought Wallace's interests. Over the next eight years, McDowell helped to standardize the rules for racing and for the registration of horses. He also encouraged what was called kindergarten racing, the running of horses at a younger age in an effort to discover natural speed.[29]

Despite the victory over Wallace, McDowell's stables were about to experience a more dangerous enemy. The economic panic of 1893 affected all of McDowell's business interests, but it was particularly hard on his stables. The breeding and sale of trotting horses had become a fad; one breeder belatedly called it a "bubble." Everybody was raising a trotting horse. Even the wife of the president of Georgetown College, a Baptist school, wrote to McDowell thanking him for helping her husband own one. However, the bubble had collapsed by 1893. John Dupee, a friend in the business, wrote

McDowell, "You notice, perhaps, that good carriage horses at auction are outselling trotters."[30] McDowell began to sell his horses.

In his 1889 catalogue, McDowell announced that he had brought his son into the business. Thomas C. McDowell had been interested in horses since childhood. Unlike his two brothers, he was not much of a student. Suffering from dyslexia, he preferred the stables to the classroom. He failed to gain admission to Yale and attended the University of Virginia only briefly, despite the efforts of his older brother Henry to keep him focused on his studies. Enthusiastically, he joined his father, managing the trotting stable and experimenting with thoroughbreds on his own. Thomas McDowell preferred the speed of the thoroughbred.[31]

The younger McDowell quickly made a name for himself in the thoroughbred business. He turned to his relatives, Josephine and James Clay, to purchase mares that traced their lineage to Magnolia or Margaret Wood. He purchased Peg Woffington from George Clay. Then, he foaled, trained, and raced horses such as King's Daughter, Lady Anne, Maid Marian, and Ashland. He foaled stakes-winner Batten and the winner of the 1902 Kentucky Derby, Alan-a-Dale. Another horse trained by McDowell, Rival, ran third in the 1902 Kentucky Derby.

McDowell partnered with the Vanderbilts and trained horses for them. He exhibited the family ability to judge the potential derived from the mating of bloodlines, and he placed a similar emphasis on honesty and integrity. A *New York Telegraph* article saved in the family papers said he emphasized kindness and good treatment for his horses. Another article said he contributed to the sport through his character, sportsmanship, and skill. Governor James McCreary appointed him to the state racing commission at a time when such characteristics were truly needed.[32]

Ashland Stud closed with Thomas McDowell's sudden death in 1935. His son Goodloe McDowell sold the horses. Family members continued to use horses at the Iroquois Hunt Club and for polo, but the thoroughbred industry had changed with the introduction of so much industrial money. Although they continued to visit the racetrack, the Clays could no longer afford the risk involved in the breeding and racing of thoroughbreds.[33] However, breeding and racing had provided an acceptable outlet for their love of risk, and the family had given critical leadership to both the thoroughbred and the trotting industries. They also helped Kentucky capture the premier rank in those industries in the years after the Civil War.

The element of risk revealed itself in other family business ventures. Captain Harry Boyle Clay proved true to his word in the aftermath of war. In addition to farming his wife's land in Hawkins County, Tennessee, Clay became involved in businesses that exploited the raw materials of the region. If the Clay family is any example of southern thought, Henry W. Grady and others were merely recognizing what many southerners were already thinking when they articulated the New South Creed. The South had vast deposits of coal and iron, and virgin timber grew throughout the Appalachian region. Many southerners apparently saw that the exploitation of raw materials provided a way to regain their fortunes and to invigorate the southern economy. Immediately after the war, Harry Clay partnered with his brother Thomas Hart Clay Jr. and his cousin Harry of the James Clay branch to form a tanning company. It did not last long, but it suggests the optimism with which the Clays looked to investment. Harry later created the Wolfe and Clay Company, a timber firm dealing in furniture and flooring woods such as oak, ash, and walnut, and he invested in coal, railroads, and other businesses. On several occasions, he purchased the rights to coal on large sections of land and sought the help of Henry Clay McDowell in selling it. He clearly recognized the business acumen of his cousin, seeking his advice throughout the late nineteenth century and partnering with him more than once.[34] He also became involved in the business boom created by McDowell in Big Stone Gap, Virginia. He created a second lumber business there, delegating the daily management to his son Harry Jr.

The James Clay branch preferred the more traditional approach of farming, but a promising business or speculative venture quickly caught their attention. On at least one occasion, they invested in an oil well, believing their fortunes about to be restored.[35] Susan M. Clay worried incessantly about recovering the fortune the family had lost. Her concerns were characterized by near hysteria. When she chastised her sons, it appears often to have been precipitated by the issue of money. Whether it was marriage, gambling, or their opportunities, the overriding issue was the recovery of the family's financial position. Fearful that her brother was misusing her portion of her father's trust fund, she demanded that Harry look into the matter. Susan also gave unsolicited advice, or orders, to her sons long after they had become adults. Her concern was also apparent in her efforts to obtain positions for her sons. Unfortunately, her emphasis on family included a belief that the world at large owed the family op-portunities because of Henry Clay's service to the nation. Kentucky senator J. W. Stevenson must have become extremely tired of the stream of letters that came from Susan seeking his influence on behalf of her sons. She also wrote to David Davis, a U.S. senator and friend of Abraham Lincoln's. Davis's response indicates that Susan invoked the name of Henry Clay: "It would give me pleasure to serve you and assist in advancing the grandson of Henry Clay—if in my power." Taking a cue from his mother, Charles Clay wrote to John M. Harlan, a Kentucky Republican, asking for his help in securing a position: "I have no political influence, for since the deaths of my grandfather and father none of my family have been in public life. I can simply ask the position in the name of him who was in the public service half a century. It is not much that I ask—it is simply to serve my country, and since my grandfather devoted fifty-five years of his life, . . . certainly if there is any patriotism left in the land, or any appreciation of patriotic service I ought to be entitled to some consideration."[36]

Susan wrote a blistering letter to President Rutherford B. Hayes in 1877 when she thought the Clay family had been wronged by an act of Congress. Thomas Jacob Clay had received an appointment in the U.S. Army in April 1877. After eight months of service with the Tenth Infantry at Fort McKavett, Texas, he learned that the Senate had refused to confirm several appointments, including his. Susan unleashed all her sense of class, entitlement, and frustration in her letter:

I learned a few days ago that the Senate of the United States has refused to confirm the appointment of my son, Thomas J. Clay as 2nd Lieut. in the army. This news overwhelmed me with grief and anxiety. . . . He is compe-tent to fill the position or he could not have passed his examination and he is a gentleman in every sense of the word—refined, chivalrous, high-spirited, honorable—Why then is this young life full of freshness and hope to be blasted? Surely the august fathers of the Republic have drunk of the waters of Lethe or they could not immolate the grandson upon the very spot on which his grandfather served so well and to the last, his country—a fruitless sacrifice, for Republics are forever ungrateful, and in proof, today the U.S. Senate gives a death blow to his grandson. . . . A sad commentary is this, Mr. President, on human greatness—not a great many years ago I went with Mr. Clay from his home of Ashland thro' the northern states to Boston. From beginning to end it was a grand oration. Wherever he went the whole populace turned out to greet and welcome him, almost to worship him.

A few years later and his dead body was borne from Washington to New York and from thence to Kentucky cities and towns and villages draped in mourning. The nation was plunged into grief, the whole country mourned the loss of a great and good man—the Senate and Congress adjourned and when they met again, senators and congressmen could scarce find words eloquent enough to express their sorrow and admiration. Today the senate meets to crush his grandson. Henry Clay is forgotten. I know not whether my son's appointment can be brought again before the senate for confirmation. But I pray God that it can be, and that some influence may be brought to bear upon it in his behalf.[37]

Perhaps the strongest letter Susan wrote, it was by no means the only one intended to provide opportunities for her sons. Clearly one of her major goals was to find positions for them that would allow them to recover fame and fortune. Her advice to them was at times equally demanding. In her advice on delaying marriage, the primary criterion was the need to acquire enough wealth to sustain a lifestyle worthy of their class, at least until she realized her sons were nearly too old to continue the family. That was not an unusual family demand in the Victorian era. Nor was Susan's demand for frugality. She frequently criticized her sons for borrowing money and for spending too much.

That was another characteristic seen often within the family. Henry had repeatedly borrowed money from John Jacob Astor, and his friends magnanimously paid his debts on several occasions. His descendants continued to exercise little discipline when it came to finances. There was one exception. For all his faults, John Morrison Clay was almost miserly. Harry Boyle Clay, who was not, complained that his uncle refused to lend money unless he received two dollars in collateral for every dollar he loaned. Thomas Hart Clay had complained about the spending habits of both his sons. The McDowells shared similar characteristics. H. C. McDowell sent large sums of money to his sons when they were at Yale University and the University of Virginia. Nettie received an allowance for years after she was married. All the children loved spending money. Major McDowell grumbled occasionally about the costs, but he continued to support them.[38] It was not always an issue of purchasing things for themselves, although they all expected to live well. They could also be quite generous. They seemed to expect the funds to always be available and thus paid little attention to the details.[39]

Though not a Clay by birth, Susan could be equally extravagant. In the aftermath of the war, she felt it essential to maintain the lifestyle her family had always enjoyed. Undoubtedly, that was a part of her effort to hold her head high in the face of the criticism and enjoyment she felt the community took in her losses. In 1872 she speculated in California lands, buying hundreds of acres near San Francisco for each of her children. She also borrowed $5,000 for her son Harry at 10 percent interest. With a depression looming, she was inviting financial trouble, but Susan Clay was in a hurry to recoup the family fortune. Harry Boyle Clay noted that she worried incessantly about money, "understanding it as little as she does." When she wanted to purchase a farm for son James, then decided that she wanted one for herself in the early 1880s, Thomas P. Jacob, her brother, urged her to reconsider. She would have to mortgage or sell what he called "two choice pieces of city property." They were indeed choice, sitting at the very heart of the city. Today the properties would be worth millions of dollars. At the time, the early 1880s, Jacob said her income from them would provide "such luxuries as you would like to indulge in." Susan had valued her estate at more than $200,000 near the end of the war; in 1882 she estimated it as worth $32,000.[40]

Nevertheless, Susan frequently chastised her sons for their lack of frugality and a tendency to make hasty decisions. She blamed it on the Clay family: "Recollect that it is a characteristic of your father's family to be in the beginning too sanguine, then too despondant [sic]."[41] Chastising Charles for overspending, she reminded him of earlier failures in the family. In another letter to Harry, she described his fault as being "a want of stability and perseverance" and advised that he would need both to succeed. She told him to "make haste and make a fortune saving every dime until you do and having made a name for yourself too, come further east to St. Louis or Louisville."[42]

The most astute businessman in the family was Henry Clay McDowell. He managed the assets of his wife, Anne, as well as his own, and as mentioned, he built a family corporation not unlike that Henry Clay had developed for his sons. Anne inherited business and investment property in Louisville from her father, Henry Clay Jr., and from her two brothers who had died in the war. McDowell also controlled significant business property in the center of Louisville's business district. By the late 1880s the property was bringing the family $2,700 per month in rents.[43]

McDowell proved to be capable of the harsh business mentality of the late nineteenth century. He unashamedly referred to his own busi-

scheming

ness practices as Darwinian, and he certainly conducted his affairs with a "survival of the fittest" mentality. In Big Stone Gap, where the family developed entrepreneurial interests, his associates, including his sons, called him "the capitalist." When his property manager in Louisville sought to make repairs on some of his rental property, McDowell retorted that "demands for repairs increased in proportion to the ease in which they are complied with." He chastised his agent when rents were late. Tenants were like children; they would pick up bad habits if allowed to be late paying their rent. And he was concerned about the business of his tenants only if problems developed. His tenants operated clothing stores, pharmacies, and dry goods stores and sold general merchandise, but one of his tenants operated a gambling room until he was raided, and another established a somewhat seedy saloon in one of McDowell's Main Street properties.[44]

Income from the rental property provided a base for McDowell's riskier ventures. Recognizing that great opportunities existed immediately after the war, he acquired much land at very cheap prices. McDowell bought lots in Chicago, additional commercial property in Louisville, and land in Tennessee, Kentucky, Nebraska, and Missouri.[45] In 1883 he purchased Ashland. He said it was because he thought his wife would like to live in her grandfather's home, but given his later use of Henry Clay's name, it seems likely he also saw its commercial value.

McDowell's efforts clearly followed the model of the New South Creed. In fact, he blended the Old South with the New. While raising carriage horses and pure-blooded cattle, he invested in railroads and other industrial opportunities. As a Union veteran, it was not difficult for him to lay the Civil War aside, as Grady and McDowell's friend Henry Watterson, editor of the *Louisville Courier-Journal,* suggested to the South. He saw the advantage of working with northern investors to make profits from southern raw materials. McDowell saw the scheme in grand fashion. The Appalachian mountain chain was a barrier to western trade with the populous East. In frontier days, Kentucky had flirted with leaving the nation and joining Spain, partially because of that barrier. McDowell sought to develop the small Virginian mountain town of Big Stone Gap, resting at a pass through those mountains, into a transportation and industrial center joining the Eastern Seaboard with the midwestern states. In the process, he also intended to exploit the vast coal, iron, and timber deposits of the region. It was not an entirely new idea. Alexander Arthur, a relative of President Chester A. Arthur, attempted to develop Middlesboro, Kentucky, for the same reasons. McDowell's plan called for building a railroad from Lexington, Kentucky, through Clay City and Jackson, eventually reaching Big Stone Gap, where it would join other roads coming from the East. His group of investors intended to build a city called Three Forks City at the junction of the Middle and North Forks of the Kentucky River as a secondary hub for the railroad. The minerals and timber of the region would flow to both cities to be sold and distributed to other regions of the country. In Big Stone Gap, the plan called for the construction of two large blast furnaces, a street railway, electric generators to produce lighting, a waterworks, a hotel of three hundred rooms costing approximately $150,000, and a bank. They also developed intricate plans for an interstate tunnel through the mountains. Their goal was to "fix the destiny of Big Stone Gap as one of the mightiest manufacturing cities and railroad centers on the continent."[46]

The group left no opportunity unrealized, creating a series of bewilderingly interlocked companies to mine every dollar of profit they could. The key corporations were the Big Stone Gap Improvement Company, the Kentucky Union Land Company (KULC), and the Kentucky Union Railroad Company (KURC). The KULC purchased the land and created traffic for the railway in the form of lumber, coal, brick, and steel. State governments in Virginia and Kentucky proved extremely generous. Virginia allowed the Big Stone Gap Improvement Company to own up to 10,000 acres within ten miles of the small town. Kentucky and the city of Lexington allowed the KULC to purchase (condemning it if owners refused to sell) wide swaths of land from Lexington through Clay City and Jackson. By 1890 the KURC owned in fee simple 550,000 acres in Kentucky and Virginia. Additionally, they often sold sections of the land at a significant profit to obtain operating funds.[47]

As the railroad progressed toward Big Stone Gap, new corporations were created. The South Appalachian Land Company and the Goff Land Company purchased promising lands adjacent to the route of the railroad. The Dictator Coal and Haddix Cannel Coal companies mined coal along the railroad right-of-way. The Kentucky River Iron Manufacturing Company and the Appalachian Steel and Iron Company mined the iron ore; and the Red River Lumber Company took the timber, until it combined with the Central Kentucky Lumber, Mining, Manufacturing and Transportation Company in October 1888 to function as the Central Kentucky Lumber Company.

To say that the various corporations were interlocking is to understate the matter. One company cut timber to sell to the railroad for cross ties; the railroad carried coal mined by a corporation that owned a portion of the railroad and the timber company; and all these companies were controlled by the Kentucky Coal and Iron Company. The KULC owned all the stock of the Dictator and Haddix Cannel Coal companies. The Main Quiksand Lumber Company, the Kentucky River Iron Manufacturing Company, Kentucky Industrial Consolidation Company, Kentucky Improvement Company, and the Goff Land Company owned or were owned, wholly or in part, by the KULC or KURC. On one occasion, L. T. Rosengarten, the secretary-treasurer of the Kentucky Coal and Iron Company, wrote a letter to its directors on KURC letterhead announcing a meeting at the offices of the KULC.[48]

Not only were the companies hand-in-glove but so were the people. The same names appear as directors and officers in most of the companies. Partners Ballard Thruston and J. Stoddard Johnston were leading citizens of Louisville; the Stolls and General Rufus Ayers had influence in Lexington. St. John Boyle, Arthur Cary, and others also had considerable influence throughout the state. (In fact, they often were asked to join the group because of their influence.) McDowell also found positions for his sons in the companies. Henry Clay McDowell Jr. went to Big Stone Gap in 1887 and began to purchase land for his father and the corporations. He was one of the bright young men John Fox Jr. wrote of in his novels about the region. William Adair McDowell became the president of the bank created by the Big Stone Gap Improvement Company, and H. C. McDowell Jr. served as legal counsel for several of the corporations. Both sons served as treasurer, secretary, or director in a number of the companies. McDowell also bought stock in the name of his sons and his daughter Nettie.[49]

For any effort so massive in scope, political influence was essential. That story cannot be completely told. Neither businessmen nor politicians usually keep records of the transactions that become part of such partnerships. Of course, railroad executives of the era were known for their efforts to influence politicians. McDowell did business and socialized with Milton Smith, who controlled the L&N Railroad and, perhaps, a state government or two. He was also a close friend of Benjamin Helm Bristow's. Bristow's biographer, Ross A. Webb, damned Bristow with faint praise by comparing him to other railroad executives: "Although often accused of shady dealings, Bristow was never convicted—not even by the press. This does not establish beyond doubt his unswerving honesty, but it does mean that his integrity was above that of most of his associates."[50]

Information gleaned from correspondence in McDowell's papers suggests that he and his associates exercised considerable political influence to have their way. McDowell was given the responsibility of swaying the Lexington politicians. In 1889, for example, he negotiated with the mayor for a strip of land through the city farm that would be used as railroad right-of-way. He also sought from the county court the right to extend the Fayette County subscription, a means of raising more funds, and he signed many of the agreements with the city. One of the partners, Arthur Cary, urged McDowell on one occasion to use his influence with Joseph Simrall, "the one man who could cause trouble for the efforts of the Kentucky Union Railroad." St. John Boyle wrote that he was delighted matters were working "to our view" in Fayette County. He was courting the officials of Clark County. Prominent Lexingtonian C. H. Stoll wrote that he believed their interests would be safe "as long as Judge Scott remains on the bench." In 1890 the KULC sold a farm to Judge P. P. Johnston, who also heard cases relative to many of the companies.[51]

Building railroads through mountainous regions and constructing complete towns required significant capital. The Big Stone Gap group followed the tenets of the New South Creed in acquiring it. Corporate officials bought shares, of course, and they distributed other shares at reduced prices to gain influence. They also encouraged friends and business acquaintances to buy bonds and stocks, most often at full price. McDowell encouraged a number of people who purchased his horses to buy shares in his other businesses. The corporations also sought northern and international investors. Southerners did not take a back seat to anyone when it came to promotion. Carefully crafted brochures and a bit of southern hospitality brought significant investments of cash in the early years of the venture. Along the railroad route, the group set aside sections of land as hunting preserves. The largest one, the Mountain Park Association, consisted of three thousand acres near Big Stone Gap that they fenced, then stocked with game. They intended it to be "one of the finest shooting parks in America." In an era when manliness was so much in fashion, the game park proved popular with potential investors. Of course, state and local politicians received invitations to hunt with corporate officials as well.[52]

McDowell, however, went further. The icing on the cake was frequently an invitation to Ashland, the estate of Henry Clay.

In the early years, the Big Stone Gap partners were quite successful at raising funds. J. Kennedy Tod and Company of New York invested heavily in the corporation. Just as in the case of Middlesboro, Kentucky, individuals and corporations in Scotland, England, and Holland, looking for places to invest the capital accumulated from late nineteenth-century industrial growth, became interested in the project. The Duke of Marlborough visited Big Stone Gap then traveled to Lexington, where he stayed at Ashland and bought several of the major's horses. Marlborough believed he could get money from the Rothschilds, the leading banking firm in Europe.[53]

Henry Clay McDowell and his sons undertook a level of risk that might have made even Henry Clay step away. Like generations of Clays before them, they would pay a price for it. The Panic of 1893, a national economic depression, can easily be seen as the high point of the McDowell crisis, but it was not the beginning of it. In the 1880s and 1890s McDowell let his Louisville rental properties deteriorate. Tenants complained of leaking roofs and structural problems in the buildings. His property managers noted that some real estate could not be rented until repairs were made. And the city of Louisville demanded repairs on other properties. The trotting-horse industry also began to collapse. The price of horses dropped precipitously. Even the Big Stone Gap project was having difficulties before the panic became an issue. Building a railroad through Eastern Kentucky proved to be more of a project than the corporate partners had suspected. In winter and spring, rivers and streams swelled far beyond their banks. Bridges had to be more intricately planned. Cutting through the mountains took longer than they expected. In April 1889 they offered the South Atlantic and Ohio Railway $500,000 in South Appalachian Land Company stock to complete the railway in one year. It did not happen. In June 1890 Levi Hege, the superintendent of construction, wrote to McDowell that they needed to construct nearly nine miles of track in ten days to meet their deadline, and he had asked the state for convict labor to accomplish it. As construction costs and delays mounted, L. T. Rosengarten used funds from the Three Forks City subscription, and probably others, to support the KULC and the KURC. In February 1891 the KURC went into receivership. Between 1891 and 1893, virtually every one of the companies went bankrupt.[54]

The family suffered substantial losses, but they weathered the crisis. J. Kennedy Tod and Company created a new railway company, purchasing the assets of the KURC at ten cents on the dollar. The company then asked H. C. McDowell to be the president of the new Lexington and Eastern Railroad. William Adair McDowell was forced to close the bank in Big Stone Gap, but he paid its indebtedness in the years that followed. He followed his father as president of the new railroad company and, after merger with the L&N, remained in charge of that branch. McDowell's losses were substantial, but he had invested early and taken some profits. Purchasing bonds and stocks at reduced prices, he then sold many of them at face value or drew a 5 percent interest payment on them. In 1896 conditions forced McDowell to borrow $30,000 from the Northwestern Life Insurance Company using the Louisville property as collateral. By that time he was consolidating his assets. In failing health, he resigned from several of the boards of the remaining companies and placed Thomas in charge of his stables. The stress of his business affairs in the 1890s undoubtedly aggravated his heart condition.[55] McDowell died on November 19, 1899.

The McDowell sons began a trend away from high-risk ventures. Thomas continued until his death to raise thoroughbred horses, race them, and gamble on them, but his son chose the quieter life of public official and manager of Lexington's Phoenix Hotel. William McDowell became a prominent banker in Lexington and operated a small farm. Henry Jr., largely through his father's influence, became a federal judge. He managed the family trust for his mother, brothers, and sisters. He invested in some riskier ventures—railroads and oil wells—but he was generally more conservative than his father, operating the trust to produce income rather than increase the family worth.[56]

George and Tom Clay sold Balgowan after Teetee's death and lived in the Phoenix Hotel. Tom did help the McDowells sell some of the lots when they began to subdivide Ashland in 1919. The Andersons and the Simpsons also subdivided Josephine's farm in the Tates Creek section of Lexington. Bill LaBach noted that his grandfather never had much of a head for business. He tried to subdivide his portion of the estate just as the Great Depression descended on Lexington.[57] Though it began slowly, the family developed a section of Lexington called Chevy Chase, one of the city's most attractive residential neighborhoods.

Although occasionally a Clay descendant would show the family characteristics of risk and speculation, by the fourth and fifth generations many chose to become college professors, lawyers, and more conservative businessmen, thus minimizing the risk earlier generations had enjoyed. The pride and some sense of obligation associated with the family name continued, but duty to family included honoring the name through another legacy—that of service to the nation, to community, and to those born to less fortunate circumstances than themselves.

Chapter 10

LEGACY OF SERVICE

"If any man wants the key to my heart," Henry Clay proclaimed, "let him take the key of the Union." Contemporaries and historians point to ambition as Clay's defining force, but no one questions his love of the Union. Clay's definition of service evolved throughout his career in politics. Going to Washington as a representative of Kentucky, he looked after the interests of the West, but he increasingly played the role of statesman as well as politician. In 1850, battered and bruised by political foes and friends and suffering from the tuberculosis that would take his life, his speeches on the compromise amounted to a plea to both North and South to love country enough to make sacrifices so it could remain whole.

A measure of a man's true beliefs is better made when the advice is to his family rather than to politicians. Henry Clay clearly hoped his descendants would follow him into service to the nation. His most profound statement of duty to country came in a letter he wrote one of his many namesakes in 1845. In addition to his normal advice to honor the family name and, of course, to avoid dissipation, he wrote, "Recognize at all times the paramount right of your Country to your most devoted services, whether she treats you ill or well, and never let selfish views or interests predominate over the duties of patriotism."[1]

Clay's descendants did not misunderstand his message. Copies of the letter were passed among family members, and they knew he had written it shortly after the nation had turned its back on him in the presidential election of 1844. Reluctantly, because they knew the pain politics caused him, they sought to serve the nation as an honor to him. Clay descendants sought careers in military service and in politics. As the legacy of the family grew, their definition of service expanded as well. They developed a sense of noblesse oblige, a duty to give back to society a portion of their time and money. Clay descendants saw themselves as rich in terms of a heritage irrevocably linked to the nation. Their patriarch had been an integral part of the construction of the nation. The death of Henry Clay Jr. in the Battle of Buena Vista added another dimension. It was as if the "self-made" family had arrived. The sense of duty continued to evolve. State and the community deserved the involvement of its leading families, but those families also had an obligation to protect the less fortunate. The Clays, despite accepting the tenets of the Lost Cause mentality, and even to some degree because of them, saw themselves as the protectors of the African American against the excesses of lower-class whites. As the Clays served nation, state, and community, they saw it as a part of the legacy handed down through the generations from the patriarch.

With parental caution, Clay had encouraged his sons to pursue public careers. Clay hoped to interest Theodore in diplomacy while he was secretary of state, and he volunteered support when Henry Clay Jr. considered a run for public office. He openly asked for a diplomatic position for James. Moreover, ironically for one who genuinely feared the role of the military hero in politics and suffered so frequently from defeat at the hands of just that type of candidate, Clay believed the military an honorable profession and an essential aspect of citizenship. Two sons and a grandson attended the military academy because Clay secured appointments for them. Clay also found a place for a second grandson in the navy.

The Clays have not been considered one of America's military families, but perhaps they should be. Descendants of Henry Clay have served in the armed forces of the United States from the Mexican War in 1848 through Vietnam. At least one descendant enlisted during the Iraq and Afghanistan operations, although he did not serve in a combat role.[2] Several female descendants married career army or navy officers who served as well.

Six descendants attended the military academy at West Point. Henry Clay sent sons and grandsons to military schools, perhaps hoping to instill some form of discipline, and that tradition continued for several generations. Five Clays died in uniform. Six grandsons and the husband of a granddaughter served in the Civil War. After the war, Thomas Jacob Clay joined the army and participated in the Indian wars of the Southwest. His brother Charles fought in the Spanish-American War and the Philippine Insurrection and at sixty-five years of age returned to the army in World War I, retiring as a colonel. All branches of the family

Henry Clay Simpson. Courtesy
of Clay Simpson.

responded to the nation's call during World War I. Goodloe McDowell, a great-great-grandson, dropped out of Yale University as a sophomore during World War I, serving as a commander of artillery and achieving the rank of captain. Henry Clay Simpson and Kenneth Kenner also entered the military during that war. William Stucky and Henry Clay Brock of the McDowell branch became commanders in the navy during World War II. McDowells, Kenners, and Andersons of several generations of descendants saw military service. Robert Pepper Clay, a great-grandson, was a decorated veteran of World War II and the Korean Conflict. He received medals from the United States, France, and Yugoslavia. Some Clays fought as career soldiers; others merely did their duty as countless Americans have done, but their consistent service in virtually all the nation's wars marks them as one of America's significant military families.

One of the ironies of this sense of duty through military service is that throughout the generations, the Clay "personality" hardly seemed suited to military discipline. Impulsive and "high spirited," they could be too blunt and too quick to defend honor when they believed themselves or their family slighted. Taught to lead, they disliked following orders, particularly when the directives seemed to lack imagination, a trait of many military commands. Unlike the patriarch, few learned to exercise strong control over their passionate and spontaneous natures.

The family members who attended West Point clearly reflected the family personality. Only two of the six graduated. Parker LaBach of the Erwin branch chose to leave the academy to pursue training in medicine, but three Clays were expelled.[3] Officially, Thomas was expelled because of deficiency in mathematics. His father feared it might have been because he participated in a student protest against army discipline. Even Henry Clay Jr. nearly had his career end before it began by a show of temper and defense of honor. His son Henry Clay III epitomized the lack of discipline and perseverance that characterized many in the family. Out of respect for his fallen son, Henry Clay worked diligently to acquire an appointment to West Point for Henry Clay III. The young man was intelligent enough, but he lacked discipline. He ranked twenty-seventh in his class the first year, but he broke new ground in collecting demerits. In his first year, he accumulated 188 demerits. Between June 16, 1852, and January 14, 1853, he received 289 demerits and was expelled.[4]

His grandfather tried to make him see the seriousness of the issue. Expulsion would carry a significant price in personal embarrassment as well as for his grandfather. He encouraged Henry III to work harder in honor of his father and the Clay family. In November 1850 Henry III had only 17 demerits, and his grandfather was elated. He continued to improve until late November 1852 when he had trouble with a professor in a philosophy class, and it appears he decided to get himself expelled. He collected 62 demerits in December and 184 in January, ensuring his dismissal.[5]

The next Clay to attend the academy entered in 1918. Colonel Charles D. Clay had struggled up the ranks but had left the army before World War I as a mere captain. He wanted to see his sons educated at West Point, and he taught them to be soldiers from their youth. His son Charley Clay, the "Charley of the future" as his father called him, was asked to leave the academy within a year because of excessive demerits.[6] The family softened the disappointment by claiming that Charley intentionally accumulated the demerits to get into the fighting. The story may have been inspired by the fact that his cousin Goodloe McDowell left Yale University to enlist in the army. The truth is probably more complicated. Charley Clay inherited the intelligence of his ancestors, but he took to heart the lessons of family values taught him in his youth. As a small boy, his father, an army officer, was often away from the family. His mother, Ria Clay, preferred to stay in Central Kentucky, where she had help with her children from her family in Frankfort and the Clays at Balgowan. Charley, at the age of six and seven, was expected to be the man of the house. His older sister Susan frequently failed to use good judgment when a creative idea excited her, so Ria placed responsibility on Charley to protect her. The young man was always older than his years, and he carried the honor of the family name upon rather thin shoulders. Reserved and cautious, he sought to be what his parents expected of him. At Balgowan he learned of the gallantry of his uncles and other members of the family. He became the protector of all who proved incapable of protecting themselves. Sent away to school to prepare for the entrance exams for West Point, he found himself getting into scrapes with bigger boys because they harassed the younger students. In a time far different than today, the headmaster wrote to the Clays that Charley needed to learn how to pick his fights. His sister called him Sir Galahad; his father called him the hope of the family. The hazing common at West Point did not play to his strengths. There is no record of how he earned enough demerits to be suspended, but a few years later, when his brother Bob entered the academy, the cadets still remembered Charley. Bob wrote home that he was being hazed because of his brother's reputation.[7] Bob Clay did graduate from West Point, but he too struggled at times with academy culture and his intense sense of honor.

Henry Clay III became a soldier despite his inglorious beginning. He joined the Union army to fight in the Civil War. His flippant letters about camp life, cold feet, and loneliness might be interpreted as a continuation of his immaturity, but there was more to it. His correspondence suggests a desire to prove himself to old West Point friends with whom he renewed acquaintance, and he was sobered by a fear he might meet his brother Thomas Julian across the battle lines.[8] As noted previously, six of Henry Clay's grandsons donned uniforms between 1861 and 1865. Three of them—Henry III, Thomas Julian, and Eugene Erwin—died during the war. Henry III did not meet his brother in battle. Henry Clay Jr.'s sons exhibited another characteristic of the family: Clays died of disease almost as quickly as they could die as a result of bullets. Henry III, however, brought honor to the name he had embarrassed as a West Point cadet. That gave him a place of respect in the family saga.

The Civil War added new stories of honor and valor to the family myth. Like the Lost Cause, the Clay myth considered all its combatants heroes. War had been so very costly to the family they needed a heroic interpretation to it. Each Clay honored his principles; he answered the call of duty. The Civil War contributed significantly to the belief that Clays served their country in times of crisis. Although Josephine married again, she never forgot the bravery of Eugene Erwin. She wrote a novel that retold his story for all to share. Colonel Erwin had shown loyalty to his men, and he acted bravely under fire. He had resumed his command at Vicksburg despite being wounded and ill, and he joined Henry Clay Jr. in dying a heroic death. Sewing his uniform and the flag of the Sixth Missouri into her skirts, Josephine brought the symbols of his valor to be shared by later generations of the family.[9] Henry and Thomas Julian also held a place in the family saga. Each had served and died as his conscience dictated. In a tragedy worthy of the ancient Greeks, Henry Clay Jr. and his sons had died honorably in service to their causes.

In the James Clay branch, James Clay Jr., despite his drinking problem, became an example of honor. Elizabeth Blanford noted with pride that General Breckinridge had been unable to keep "Uncle Jimmy" out of the fight despite his youth. She implied that he was, after all, a Clay. Because he was such a fine horseman, the family saga noted, when the war ended at Appomattox, James was ordered to ride south with the news so no more men would have to die. The Clays told their stories in the most favorable setting; that is the nature of mythmaking. They did not invent facts, but the emphasis was on the traits—duty, honor, and service—that they saw at the heart of the family.

Although the members of the family succumbed easily to the Lost Cause mentality, incorporating its concepts into their own myths, they also rejoined the Union with remarkable ease. Henry Clay's loyalty had been to the Union, and he was their patriarch. The war ended and they became citizens again, ready to serve their nation. For the James Clay branch, military service seemed an appropriate place to show their loyalty, and perhaps to restore family prominence. Henry Clay McDowell must have agreed, because he repeatedly recommended his kinsmen Thomas and Charles Clay for military positions. Thomas and Charles had been too young to fight in the Civil War, but they had been old enough to be caught up in the sense of adventure and excitement. The "Battle" of Ashland was little more than a skirmish, but to five-year-old Charles it was a battle, and nearly a century later it was still a battle when Elizabeth Blanford told the story. The lessons of gallantry and nobility of character clearly resonated in her account. The Confederates were victorious, of course. They gathered their wounded before leaving. The Union wounded, however, needed care, and honor trumped political loyalties. Susan Clay allowed the enemy to turn the first floor of Ashland into a hospital. Charles and Thomas heard the stories of their brother James's bravery and the sacrifice of Eugene Erwin as well as that of their own father, James, who had died an exile from his home.

Thomas trained to be a physician. Graduating from medical college in 1873, he established a practice in Saint Louis after interning in New York City. He claimed in a memoir written later in life that doctors had to struggle for years before establishing a lucrative practice. Charles sought his fortune in the wool business, traveling the West buying raw wool for textile firms in Saint Louis. Raised on the stories of Clay manliness and service, both young men grew restless and dissatisfied. Susan Clay wrote to President Grant in 1876, just three years after Thomas finished medical school. As usual, she invoked the name of Henry Clay, "bringing to your [Grant's] remembrance his greatness and goodness, his public services and pure patriotism, his underlying love for his country and his death which was as truly in his country's service as if he had died on the bloody battle-field. In *his name*, I ask of you this position for his grandson before you retire from your high office as chief ruler of this mighty nation."[10] There was no mention of the Confederate sympathies of James, of course. Grant had no civilian appointments, but Clay eventually received a commission as a lieutenant and began his career as a soldier. His younger brother followed him into the military a few years later.

Thomas and Charles brought most of the characteristics of the Clay legacy to military service. Despite childhood illnesses that nearly killed him, Thomas grew into a strapping, robust young man. Thin like his grandfather, he was approximately six feet two inches tall, wiry, and athletic. An excellent horseman, he also became an expert marksman, winning division competitions on several occasions. In 1884 Thomas placed second in army-wide matches after riding a train all night returning from the funeral of his brother Harry. In 1885 he volunteered for service with troops operating in Sonora, Mexico, against Geronimo. In a plan caught up in army politics, General Nelson Miles sought to take an aggressive stand against the Apaches, both to end their marauding and to embarrass General George Crook, his predecessor, who had believed surrender could be obtained through negotiation. Miles chose Henry Ware Lawton to command a group of men who would pursue the Apaches until the exhausted Indians surrendered. Lawton picked men who exemplified the late nineteenth-century principles of manliness in an effort to out-muscle Geronimo. The troops, dubbed "Lawton's Athletes," were strong, agile, competitive, and aggressive to the point of cockiness. Leonard Wood— later a famous general, and like Tom Clay, a physician turned soldier—was also in the command. Donald Mrozek describes Miles, Lawton, and Wood as national symbols of manliness in the late nineteenth century. Hermann Hagedorn, Wood's biographer, describes Lawton as six feet five inches tall and 230 pounds, "a gigantic Beowulf." Tom Clay was a "worthy third" to Lawton and Wood.[11]

Miles's plan shared characteristics with a later war of attrition that was supposed to force the Vietnamese into surrendering, most notably an underestimation of the enemy. Lawton pursued Geronimo over 2,500 miles in four months. The group marched a lot but saw the Apaches only when the latter wished to be seen. Tom Clay's manliness did not stop him from complaining about riding army "plugs" in desert and mountains. Lawton also criticized the lack of supplies. His men killed beef for food and made shoes out of the hide. The men of the U.S. Army were so tired they needed to surrender. Lawton wrote to his wife in 1886 that he had only fifteen men capable of fighting. The rugged terrain of Arizona and Mexico sapped the strength and destroyed the health of many of Lawton's men, including Tom Clay. They also faced problems with Mexicans who resented the U.S. Army crossing the border at will. Lawton finally decided that some negotiation could be tolerated. He called in Lieutenant Charles Gatewood, one of Crook's best negotiators, to convince Geronimo to talk. Gatewood succeeded in getting Geronimo to return to the United States and talk with General Miles. The result was the surrender, or capture, of the notorious Apache chief.[12]

Because of Clay's reputation as a marksman, Miles ordered him to guard the wagons carrying Geronimo and his lieutenants. Geronimo had escaped on an earlier occasion. Clay then commanded a unit of Native American and buffalo soldiers who took Geronimo and his band east. Clay later told a story worthy of Hollywood moviemakers. Stopping in an Arizona town, his men faced a group of drunken cowboys who did not like Indians or black soldiers. Clay said his men could have killed them if necessary, but instead he offered to buy them all a drink at the local saloon, diffusing a potentially lethal situation.[13]

The legacy instilled in Thomas Clay served him both well and ill in the campaign against Geronimo. He had the confidence worthy of a descendant of Henry Clay. He treated men with respect; but disrespect, even when it came from a superior officer, could not be tolerated. An incident with his commanding officer, Captain Lawton, almost ended his career. In late August 1886 Lawton and the Mexicans met at Fronteras to discuss the Apache problem. Leonard Wood claimed the Mexicans put something in the wine and Lawton became "not only drunk but stupid," calling the Mexican officers names and insulting them. Clay and Wood got Lawton away from the Mexicans and put him to bed. When Clay later tried to wake Lawton, the latter threw a coffee cup at him, then started toward him in an aggressive manner. According to Clay and Wood in separate accounts, Clay drew his revolver and threatened to kill Lawton if he attacked him. Slightly sobered, Lawton ordered Clay arrested. Wood and another officer encouraged Clay to file charges and pledged their support, but Clay refused. He claimed Lawton was drunk and did not know what he was doing. Wood claimed credit for convincing Lawton to release Tom Clay the next morning. Clay's career was perhaps saved, but he never thereafter advanced in rank. In his report on the capture of Geronimo, Lawton failed to mention Clay at all, even though Clay participated in important ways.[14]

On other occasions, Thomas Clay also took the high road. He recognized in the Native Americans honesty not always present in the American soldiers. When Geronimo entered the American camp, some of the officers wanted to kill him, Naichez (spelled Natchez by most historians), and other leaders despite the fact that the Native Americans came under a flag of truce. Clay, Gatewood, and Wood objected strenuously, even threatening violence themselves if the killing was carried out. A few days later, Clay, Gatewood, and Wood found themselves in roles that were reversed. Out of fear of the Mexican Army, Geronimo had demanded the right to keep his weapons on the march to meet General Miles. Lawton's troops guarded the rear and flank of the party. Clay, Gatewood, and Wood rode with the Apaches. Lawton and the main troop became separated and failed to join the party at dusk, so the three men remained in the Apache camp. They were clearly at the mercy of the Apaches. Perico, a brother-in-law of Geronimo, seeing that they had no food, asked the three Americans to join the Native Americans to eat. The nobility of the gesture was not lost on the grandson of Henry Clay.[15]

Clay continued to jeopardize his career as a result of the Geronimo campaign. Promises had been made to Geronimo that the United States did not keep. In the Thomas J. Clay papers, a letter signed by Geronimo and Naichez asked Clay to help them if he could. Elizabeth Blanford said that Clay did testify before a commission, although she could recall no specifics. It was an honorable act, though perhaps a foolish one in a peacetime army characterized by "good old boy" politics. Clay saved among his papers the letter from Geronimo and Naichez and a small, faded photograph of a group of White Mountain Apaches with names listed on the back.[16]

Clay also championed the cause of Lieutenant Gatewood. Miles and Lawton were as good at self-promotion as they were at emphasizing rugged masculinity. Their efforts created a controversy that lasted for many years. Tom Clay believed, like many historians, that Gatewood had been robbed of his importance in the bigger struggle between General Miles and General Crook. Writing to a Mr. A. Mazzanovich in Hollywood, California, and to Gatewood's son, who tried to redeem his father's reputation, Clay said Geronimo would not have surrendered had it not been for the actions of Lieutenant Gatewood. He credited Miles with organizing and directing the expedition, and Gatewood for negotiating the surrender.[17] Clay too had his role largely forgotten. In 1890 Miles recommended him for gallantry in the Geronimo campaign, but the authorities decided that his role was not sufficiently established.[18]

Retiring from military service in 1894 because of heart problems aggravated by the harsh conditions of the West, Clay returned to Lexington, where Captain Tom became something of a local institution. Within the family, he personified important values. Honor, duty, integrity, and service footnoted every story his sister and his brothers told about his career. A crude Indian bridle hung about the fireplace at Balgowan. It was interpreted as a gift from one honorable man, Geronimo, to another, Thomas Clay. A new generation learned their values from the tales. The stories may have been slightly embellished, but there was no escaping the fact that Thomas had served heroically.

Charles D. Clay, like his brother, entered the army after attempting to find success in another field. Family training rarely produces consistent results, and where others suffocated in military life, he thrived on it.

Charles Clay was military to the core. Educated to family responsibility by his mother, Susan, he spoke often of duty and honor. He carried himself with a military swagger and was fastidious in both dress and manner. The family papers contain a large number of photographs of Charles in uniform, looking as stern and soldierly as the small-boned, slight young man could muster. He grew the manly mustache of the era to hide a boyish face that remained prominent until well into his forties. Assigned as a lieutenant to the Seventeenth Infantry, he served in several dull outposts in the peacetime army of the late 1880s and 1890s. In 1896 he married Mariah Hensley Pepper of Frankfort, Kentucky. His mother approved of the marriage, probably because he was the last member of the family apt to continue it and he was approaching forty years of age. Mariah, called Ria, tried her best to take some of the stiffness out of Charles. Her efforts worked only during their courtship. Although he promised openness and sharing with her, his training as a Clay and as a soldier demanded that he be the dominant, protective husband.

The Spanish-American War accentuated that attitude. Off to do battle for his country, Charles wrote letters to his wife that contained a mixture of bravado, awe, and carefully concealed fear. Ria, a young bride and quickly a young mother, experienced the sudden realization of many soldiers' wives. The military may be uniforms, honor, and duty, but husbands also die. Her fears surfaced quickly, and Charles sought to protect her from the truth. She learned of the dangers he experienced only after his return. Stationed at Columbus, Ohio, she heard Charles and his friends recounting the events in which they had participated. By the time he sailed with the Seventeenth Infantry to participate in the Philippine Insurrection, she knew that he did not always tell her the truth.

That conflict gave Charles Clay more to conceal. As he was leading his men in a skirmish at a place called Ban Lac, a bullet pierced his neck narrowly missing the jugular vein, spiraled downward, and lodged in the shoulder muscles dangerously close to his spine. He remained on the battlefield for several hours, later claiming his men expected him to die. The army wanted to perform surgery immediately, but Clay refused. Having survived his own trauma, he sought to spare his wife from danger. Ria was pregnant, and he feared bad news might harm her or their unborn child. He wrote a misleading letter suggesting that the wound was not a serious one. The army shipped him back to Lexington, where he had surgery a month after Charles Donald Clay Jr. was born. Once again, Ria learned that he had misled her.[19]

The wound forced Clay to retire from the army. He held a series of civilian positions, including being commandant of Clemson College, but his military discipline led to unrest among the cadets, and he resigned. In 1918, at the age of sixty-five, Clay went back on active duty in the Quartermaster Corps. Retiring at the end of World War I, Clay returned to Kentucky with the rank of colonel. He was proud of his service and never lost his military bearing. When an acquaintance implied that his rank might be of the honorary Kentucky Colonel variety, he quickly informed her that it had been earned on the battlefields of the nation.[20]

Colonel Charles D. Clay looked back on a military career that was less distinguished than he would have liked. Perhaps for that reason, he planned from their births military careers for his two sons. A family photograph showed son Robert in a uniform with sword when he was three years old. Around the dinner table and in the parlor, Charley, Bob, Susan, and Elizabeth heard stories of Clay gallantry from Henry Clay Jr. to Uncle Tom. The children could see the price of their father's service. Particularly in cold weather, he complained about pain from his wound. They also saw the bloodied uniform that was always on display and the bullet that was saved for Charley Jr., the "Charley of the future." But the colonel was also magnanimous. He placed no blame on the man who shot him. A soldier, the man only did what he was supposed to do. Clay sent his sons to private schools known for preparing young men for the entrance exams at West Point. Colonel Clay later said he dreamed of walking down Lexington's Main Street with a soldier son on each side.[21]

Colonel Clay placed a great deal of pressure on his two sons. He spoke too much of duty and honor. Perhaps it was that pressure which robbed him of his dream. Expelled from West Point, Charley Clay returned to Lexington. He took classes at the University of Kentucky, but according to his sisters, he lived with a sense of failure; he had failed his duty to the family and he had sorely disappointed his father. In 1921 he took an examination that qualified him for a commission as a first lieutenant. By November 1922 he was stationed at Fort Snelling, Minnesota, and the Clays believed all was going well.

On November 23, 1922, a telephone call from Fort Snelling told them Charley Clay was dead. The army declared the death a suicide. Charley

Charley Clay. Courtesy of the Elizabeth Clay Blanford Collection.

had been drinking heavily, the army report noted, and he had been unhappy. Colonel Charles Clay had another war to fight, a war with the army he had served. The death of his son was hard enough to take; he refused to believe it was suicide. His son's honor, Clay honor, perhaps his own honor were at stake.[22]

The Clays, as families in such situations often do, collected the evidence to support their claim. Charley's letters to the family had been filled with enthusiasm. He enjoyed his unit and had expressed his pleasure with his sergeant, a veteran soldier, who, Charley said, knew how to handle men. He had also established a satisfying social life through the web of Lexington connections that meant so much at the time. The Foster family of Saint Paul and Lexington treated him like a son. Dunster Foster Pettit, many years later, recalled going places with him unchaperoned. Mrs. Foster answered criticism, obviously not limited to the South, by claiming that Charley Clay was as trustworthy as if he were a member of the family. Dunster Foster helped him pick out Christmas presents and said he looked forward to a trip home to see his family. Charles Clay also received a visit

Lieutenant Charles Clay Jr. and friends. Courtesy of the Elizabeth Clay Blanford Collection.

from a man who claimed Charley had been murdered and that the commanding officer sought to cover it up to protect his own reputation.[23]

Charles Clay called in favors from his years on active duty. General R. C. Davis ordered a new hearing, which reversed the verdict. On April 24, 1923, an investigating board declared that Lieutenant Charles Clay had died in the line of duty under undetermined circumstances and "not of his own willful misconduct." No one was ever charged in the matter of his death. One suspect, a hardened veteran of the war, deserted his unit and fled to Canada. Charley's friends thought he was the culprit, but the army never sought extradition. Still, the primary goal had been achieved. The Clay family never fully recovered from Charley's death, but they did learn to live with it once the verdict of suicide had been removed.[24]

Some correspondence suggested that the Clays suspected the causes of Charley's death even if they did not know for certain how he died. Susan, his sister, wrote later that the family never really knew whether he committed suicide, but the remark was made amid an explanation of the family's imprisonment in the past. The Clays also knew the pressure Charley had been under. The young man constantly struggled with the obligations of personal honor and the need to make compromises in a real world. Certainly, his struggle for perfection could have created conflict for a fresh lieutenant with a battle-hardened veteran, but it could have also led to the melancholy he shared with so many members of the Clay family. There was also the family susceptibility to alcohol. In admonishing Bob Clay about alcohol, Ria wrote that Charley's character had been "perfect but for the mistake of ever touching whiskey." Alcohol and the melancholy suffered by so many members of the Clay family did not mix well. Ria entreated her son, "Always remember your sacred promise to Marm [the children's name for Mrs. Clay], my precious, that you will never touch it. It is a curse to be avoided by a Clay."[25]

Robert Pepper Clay suffered from the same pressure felt by his brother. Entering West Point in 1920, he felt the weight of family responsibility, increased significantly because of his brother's death. Bob's letters to his parents reflect the misery of a young man confronting the difficulties of the plebe year at West Point and a deep sense of obligation to his family. He also struggled with the academic requirements of West Point. He found it nearly impossible to learn French, but he also found philosophy and mathematics very difficult. He worried incessantly about making the grades required of him, the grades that would allow him to visit home at the breaks. He begged at times to be allowed to resign. He tried to put a rational slant to it. His father was getting older; Bob thought he could help on the farm. He questioned military life: "I have been disappointed with everything about this place and I'm absolutely disgusted with it in every respect. In my estimation the whole system including the army after graduation is one endless line of foolish, unfair, red tape."[26]

The pressure from home was apparent in the correspondence. His mother reminded him that his father would be terribly disappointed if he resigned. His father, shaken by the death of one son, offered encouragement, but he also spoke of duty and family. On November 21, 1921, Bob Clay wrote to his mother, "I was very disappointed in the tone of Pop's telegram. I don't remember ever having done anything to make you lose confidence in me but you seem to have lost it. . . . I'm no baby, I'm a man now, neither am I a weak kneed effeminate cad. I have my full share of pluck and determination, but I'm not cut out for this life. . . . If you all are willing to ask me to stay against my will and judgment I will, but. . . . the very minute this first year course is over I hand in my resignation."[27]

Cadet Robert P. Clay.
Courtesy of the Elizabeth Clay
Blanford Collection.

Robert Pepper Clay remembered his duty. He did not resign. He was never a stellar student, but the West Point yearbook noted on his graduation, appropriately, that he was known at the academy for his horsemanship. Bob Clay showed the "pluck and determination" that often characterized the Clays when they set their minds to it. His sisters said he was a soldier through and through. He graduated from West Point and had a distinguished career. A decorated veteran, he exemplified the sense of duty to country required of a descendant of Henry Clay. He exemplified a second characteristic of the family as well. Taught from childhood the sense of honor required of a Clay, like his uncle Thomas J. Clay, he was often willing to stand on a principle to his own detriment. A story told within the family illustrates the trait and perhaps its consequences. Clay desperately wanted promotion to general. When a friend was promoted, he said to Colonel Robert Pepper Clay, "Pep, do you know how I got these stars? I never made an enemy." Clay allegedly replied, "I would be ashamed to admit it."[28] The response sounds a great deal like "I would rather be right than . . . general." Robert Pepper Clay retired with his honor but at the rank of colonel. The words of Henry Clay echoed through the generations of his family.

Robert Clay receiving service medal. Courtesy of the Elizabeth Clay Blanford Collection.

As noted previously, World Wars I and II saw numerous descendants serve and then return to civilian life at war's end. Kenners, Stuckys, Simpsons, Andersons, and Brocks entered the service like many Americans. Robert Pepper Clay fought through the Korean War. During the Vietnam War, Bill List, six generations removed from his illustrious ancestor, served four tours as a helicopter pilot. He died of cancer in 1998 at the age of fifty-three. Although the army denied it, some family members believed his death resulted from contact with Agent Orange. If so, another Clay descendant died fighting for his country.[29]

Despite the family's being unsuited for military service physically or by temperament, its record is outstanding. No descendant reached the rank of general, but Clays did their duty to the nation because it was an obligation, to family and to country. With the exception of the James Clay branch in the late nineteenth century, they did not think of themselves as a military family. They filled the ranks of subalterns and subordinates, positions that must be filled in any significant endeavor if it is to be successful. Taken in its entirety, however, the family fulfilled a legacy of responsibility bequeathed by its patriarch.

Service through political office would seem to be a more poignant requirement of the Clay legacy. However, Henry Clay's descendants generally avoided politics. It is difficult to determine a single reason for all generations. Undoubtedly, the political prominence of their patriarch cast such a shadow it would be difficult to step beyond its reach. That certainly seems to have influenced the second generation. Henry Clay Jr. served in the state legislature and thought about running for higher office, but his efforts were characterized by reluctance. James and Thomas became involved in the period before the Civil War but seemed to know they could not step into their father's shoes. They sensed an obligation and made feeble attempts to fulfill it, albeit reluctantly. Both sons claimed there were movements to make them governor of the state, and they each served a Civil War government. Clay's sons had seen the abuse their father suffered, and subsequent generations saw how James and Thomas had been used by the Confederate and Union governments. In later generations, family idiosyncrasies and the incidents inspired by them also served as a deterrent. When Henry Clay McDowell considered running for Congress against W. C. P. Breckinridge, he was threatened with the exposure of family scandal, although the nature of that scandal was not recorded. The family, notably Henry Clay McDowell Jr., encouraged him not to seek the position. Henry Jr. implied that family business interests could best be served behind the scenes and that the family's wealth and prominence placed its members above the rough-and-tumble world of politics. George Clay attributed his aloofness to a lack of ambition, but he too seemed alienated by the mudslinging and deal making. Reluctance to seek political office tended to characterize most members of the family. Political opportunities would occasionally pursue a Clay descendant, but Clays rarely thrust themselves into the arena.

Of course, exceptions occurred, perhaps the greatest of which was Henry Clay McDowell Jr. Moving to Big Stone Gap, Virginia, as a representative of his father, he quickly became an organizer of the rapidly growing community. The novelist John Fox Jr. called him one of a group of young men who took over the operation of the town, creating public

Judge McDowell. Henry Clay Memorial Foundation
Collection. Courtesy of University of Kentucky Special
Collections.

services such as fire and police protection and introducing cultural activities that would make the community attractive. He purchased town lots,
built houses, and helped develop the railroad and business property. His
father's friendship with Theodore Roosevelt catapulted young McDowell
into a federal judgeship. He served from 1901 to 1931 as a judge of the
U.S. District Court for the Western District of Virginia. He was extremely
pro-business in his rulings, and his record was distinguished by the sheer
number of cases he heard.[30] McDowell had also ingratiated himself with
Virginia political leaders such as J. S. Mosby and Campbell Slemp. He
quickly became a rising star within the Republican Party. Mosby, working

in the Justice Department, recommended him for a Supreme Court appointment. McDowell wrote to his mother that he and his wife had lunch with President and Mrs. Taft and the subject was discussed. McDowell thought the luncheon meeting went well, but no appointment resulted, despite the fact that Taft named five justices to the Supreme Court in his own brief tenure as president.[31] McDowell was also mentioned as a possible vice presidential candidate, but nothing came of it. He shared the Clay susceptibility to tuberculosis, but there seemed to be no danger of a lack of perseverance or dissipation. He worked continuously. Elsie, his wife, complained that he rarely remembered a holiday or celebrated one, and when he started playing golf in the 1920s, he worked at that as hard as he did at his profession.

McDowell's sister Madge can also be considered a successful politician, and she clearly recognized the legacy of her great-grandfather. Although she never held political office, her influence in the state capitol and in the country as a whole proved immense. A Progressive Era reformer, she cajoled, manipulated, and occasionally threatened male politicians on a variety of issues. She addressed state legislatures and lobbied governors, senators, and presidents. She organized the Clay family and countless others in support of women's suffrage. Like Henry Clay, Madge had a charismatic personality. Former classmates at Miss Porter's School remained lifelong friends and readily joined her reforming crusades, whether women's suffrage, education, treatment of tuberculosis, or philanthropy. Politicians must have dreaded seeing her arrive at state houses, but she refused to be ignored. A Clay and a McDowell, married to a Breckinridge, she could not be ignored by any Kentucky politician, and she used that heritage to force open the doors of more than one state house.

Harry Independence Clay, sufficiently practiced at writing his signature "H. Clay" like his grandfather, seemed always to have a political career in mind. A newspaper later claimed he was the great hope of his family for a return to political prominence.[32] After giving up on the West, Harry moved to Louisville, where he had enough connections to enter society at a level suitable to him. His uncle Charles Jacob served several terms as mayor, and the Clay family had connections with leading attorneys in the city. Harry had studied law with the Confederate hero General Basil Duke, who practiced in the city.

Louisville was a city in transition from "good old boy" politics to the political machine in the 1880s, and Harry immediately became a lightning rod. He won an election as prosecuting attorney but resigned to join the Arctic expedition. In that election, he was, of course, accused of running on his name rather than his ability, a typical charge leveled at family members who chose to run for office. His decision to resign clearly had political ramifications as well. He was too young to have a war record, but the popularity of Arctic exploration would add the manly quality necessary to a political career. Returning to Louisville, he became an advocate of reform, pointing out corruption, attacking the leadership, and demanding honest government. In 1883 he used the trial of a city official accused of complicity in the embezzlement of city funds as a forum to accuse and chastise leading aldermen Henry Murrell and George Griffiths. He also attacked his uncle Charles Jacob and former mayor John G. Baxter. Money had been embezzled, but not by Philip Hinkle, Harry's client. Clay won an acquittal. In a second case of public corruption, Clay won acquittal in the Kentucky Court of Appeals. Harry's oratory in the trials was compared with that of his grandfather, but he did not prove as successful at soothing ruffled feathers after the disagreements. The *Louisville Courier-Journal* prophetically wrote, "There, in the Board of Aldermen, in the holy sanctuary dedicated to his worship, in the presence of the high priests who officiated at his altars, to question the veracity of John G. Baxter was worse than treason—it was downright blasphemy." The article suggested that Clay was a marked man.[33]

Counting on his notoriety, Harry sought the seat as representative to the state legislature from the Louisville district in 1883. He apparently did not care that the city was rapidly falling under the control of a political boss named John Whallen. According to Clay, Whallen, Jacob, Baxter, and several alderman made an "unholy alliance" to defeat him. The campaign was one of the nastiest in Louisville's history. Jacob and Baxter were known for spending large sums of money to buy votes, and Whallen used a saloon network to garner support. On election day, Whallen's men stood outside polling sites offering money in return for votes. Harry personally secured a warrant against John Whallen's brother and several others. At one point, Whallen and Clay appeared simultaneously at the clerk's office and appeared ready to do battle with pistols until the police separated them.[34] Harry Clay lost in a very close vote. A few months later, in September 1884, he lost his life when Andrew Wepler, an ally of John Whallen, shot him.

Surely, the death of Harry Clay reinforced a family aversion to politics, but the trial proved even more prophetic to family members. Wepler, a known brawler and bully, was portrayed as a poor German immigrant who had risen by his own efforts to own a business and serve on the city council. Clay, on the other hand, was an aristocrat, a man with a long line of brilliant ancestors. "Who made it law," the defense attorney sneered, "that a saloon keeper must nurse a drunken lawyer?" Wepler received a two-year prison sentence, and Whallen's allies immediately sought his release. An attorney complained, "The great name of Clay had undue influence upon the trial."[35] Susan M. Clay's warnings about the treatment of great men by lesser men gained additional credence. Any Clay who ran for elected office in Kentucky heard charges of misusing the reputations of his or her distinguished ancestors—even Bill LaBach, who ran for a judicial office in Lexington more than one hundred years later.

Henry Clay List, six generations removed from the patriarch, had all the qualifications of a good politician. More outgoing than many of his kinsmen, he is, like the patriarch in his own time, strikingly tall and agile, friendly, and intelligent. He served one term in the Kentucky legislature then chose to pursue business interests. Locally and statewide, historians, journalists, and others shook their heads in dismay that the descendants had not lived up to their birthright even as they criticized them when they attempted to run for office. Little wonder, most members chose to avoid the publicity that accompanied politics.[36]

Yet, they did serve. Henry Clay List served in the state legislature. Thomas C. McDowell accepted a governor's appointment to the state racing commission, and numerous others served on state and community boards. Kenneth B. Kenner followed the lead of his grandfather Harry Boyle Clay by serving on the city council of Rogersville. He also performed duties in county government. Goodloe McDowell retired as a young man and moved to Naples, Florida, where he served for ten years on the city council. His cousin Henry Clay Anderson followed a similar path of retirement and service in local government roles.[37]

Certainly, no Clay descendant equaled the prominence of Henry Clay. However, at least two members of the family came close to attaining such prominence. What would historians and journalists have said if Henry Clay McDowell Jr. had been named a Supreme Court justice? And what might have been accomplished if Madeline McDowell Breckinridge had been allowed to vote and hold office? The Louisville press and politicians believed Harry Clay had a political future, but his spontaneity or lack of restraint, a family characteristic, proved his undoing. Others served at different levels. Leadership is required at the county or town level as well as in Washington. Volunteerism is as important as paid politicians in keeping small towns functioning. Seeing service as a family obligation, the Clays often met those needs.

The Clays could not deny the duty to service. Henry Clay had encouraged it. The legacy of family absorbed by each generation demanded it. Increasingly, in the last years of the nineteenth century the legacy of service evolved into a sense of noblesse oblige. A principle of ancient Greece and Rome, it finds antecedents in the Jewish tradition and in the Christian Bible. In Luke, the successful are admonished, "For unto whosoever much is given, of him shall be much required." The United States had no nobility, but some were more equal than others. Although Thomas Jefferson had talked about a nation of yeoman farmers, his was a system of deferential politics. The yeoman farmer would cast his vote and then let his betters lead the nation. The Clays saw service in the military as a function of noblesse oblige.[38]

A second form of noblesse oblige is closely associated with the United States of the late nineteenth century. Rapidly becoming the most industrialized nation in the world, it produced great wealth. Noblesse oblige suggested that the rich had duties to the society that had enriched them. The use of the term noblesse suggests a sense of superiority, but no one can deny the importance of Roosevelts, Rockefellers, Carnegies, and the like, to American charity.[39] The Clays made donations to charity as well, but their emphasis was on the riches that came with tradition. They were blessed—not, perhaps, with great amounts of money, but with reputation, intelligence, and a knowledge of community needs. Much of the pressure placed on each generation stemmed from the sense that the descendant families were among the elite of Kentucky and must conduct themselves accordingly.

To serve the community was a requirement. It also became a way of life. Teetee Clay donated five dollars in the name of her five-year-old niece Susan to the Spanish-American War Relief Fund in 1898 so that Susan's name would be on the list. It was intended as a lesson for the child and an announcement to the community about Clay philanthropy. The McDowell children were taught noblesse oblige as they were growing up by giving small gifts of money to the black servants at Christmas, birthdays, and other holidays.[40] Virtually no fundraiser in Lexington failed to solicit the McDowells or the Clays. It is possible that Major McDowell saw noblesse

oblige as a business obligation, but he gave his time and money nevertheless, and his children learned by example. McDowell essentially kept the
Lexington Lunatic Asylum in operation for years, fixing roofs, repairing
and eventually replacing the boilers, and seeing to other repairs.[41] After
the major's death, Anne Clay McDowell dispensed the charitable gifts.
Henry Clay McDowell Jr., administering the family trust after the death of
his father, told his mother on one occasion that she did not have to give to
every charity that asked. To his discredit, he urged her to stop contributing
to the racially integrated Berea College as the education of blacks became
a political issue at the turn of the century. Anne Clay McDowell, Josephine
Clay, the Simpsons, the Andersons, and the James Clays made significant
gifts to Madge's charities.[42]

At various times women of all the Clay family branches in Lexington
supported the charitable activities of the Woman's Club of Central
Kentucky, the Associated Charities, and the Civic League. It was often the
women who took the lead for the family. Since they practiced religion as a
civic responsibility, they also supported the charities of the local Episcopal
Church. Thomas Hart Clay Jr. and his wife, a descendant of Lexington's
Gratz family, became involved in literary and civic movements after their
return to Lexington in 1895. He served as president of the Lexington
Public Library when Andrew Carnegie's contribution helped build the
stately structure that housed it for many years. After Clay's death in 1907,
his wife served as president of the library for nearly twenty-five years. They
also supported the Lexington Orphans Society, among other charitable
groups.[43]

The foremost philanthropist in the Clay family was Madeline
McDowell Breckinridge. In fact, if her age had afforded women the opportunities it gave men and if she could have escaped the legacy of ill health
Henry Clay bequeathed to so many family members, she may well have
rivaled the Great Compromiser. Slender and athletic, Madge McDowell
did everything well. She loved horseback riding, tennis, and golf as a young
woman. She was attractive but not beautiful. Doe-like eyes were her most
outstanding feature, but her face suggested that there was much more to
know beneath her pose. She practiced the manners of the Victorian era
with ease. Optimistic, energetic, and charming, she, like her grandfather,
drew attention effortlessly.

She was also extremely intelligent. Teachers at Miss Porter's School
urged Julia, Madge's sister, to come for a visit, no doubt hoping she would

enroll and expecting her to be nearly as gifted as Madge. James Kennedy Patterson, a much-beloved professor and the first president of the state college in Lexington, praised her abilities and urged her to pursue a degree. She did not do so for a number of reasons. Although Major McDowell sent his sons to Yale University, he opposed sending Madge away to school. Her biographers argue that he feared for her health, but they also hint at a more traditional concern. Sophonisba Breckinridge wrote that McDowell did not want to send her away because he had "a clear understanding of the risk of separating her during four impressionable years from the community in which she expected to live out her life." Although McDowell appreciated Madge's ability, he was as tied to social attitudes of gender as were more traditional branches of the family. Daughters married local men and raised their children to fulfill the same roles.[44] Additionally, Madge suffered from an affliction common to both McDowells and Clays. In her late teens she began having problems with a foot. After she saw physicians across the country, the ailment was diagnosed as tuberculosis of the bone. In June 1896 doctors amputated her foot. Portions of her leg would later be removed, and she would deal with the debilitating effects of tuberculosis the rest of her life.

Madge's biographers agree that Major McDowell taught his daughter a sense of noblesse oblige by his own example and by training to her social class. Madge took the lesson far further than the major would have imagined or approved, making the transition from noblesse oblige to "scientific" charity. However, her efforts at reform remained primarily within the acceptable limits of noblesse oblige until after his death in 1899. In that year she led a group from Christ Church Episcopal in establishing a social settlement near Beattyville in the mountains of Eastern Kentucky. The major would have found that acceptable. She also led a crusade against a family of thugs led by a man named King McNamara. The movement might better be described as against an incompetent police force. Kentucky had suffered from feuds and general lawlessness since the Civil War, and the legal system proved unable or unwilling to do anything about it. Just as in the murder of Harry Clay in Louisville, the case against the McNamaras was handled in a cavalier fashion. Local citizens, however, were growing tired of criminals going unpunished. Madge and her husband Desha led the effort to bring the McNamaras to justice and to demand stiffer penalties for violent crimes. The major died in the midst of the struggle. He probably would have thought the effort hopeless, but he would not have disapproved. While the major lived, Madge remained the perfect daughter. She belonged to the Daughters of the American Revolution, the Golf Club, and the Young Ladies Fishing Club. She also tried her hand at writing in Desha's newspaper, generally book reviews, and for *Century Magazine.* She attended teas, parties, and club meetings. She was exactly the daughter Major Henry Clay McDowell expected her to be, except, perhaps, for the fact that she married Desha Breckinridge.

In 1900 Madge joined others to create the Associated Charities and the Civic League. Highly influenced by Sophonisba Breckinridge, Desha's sister, who was both a lawyer and a pioneer in modern social work, Madge began the transition from noblesse oblige to scientific charity. Both types of philanthropy carried an air of superiority and the hint of blame directed at the poor. Using the casework method, they attempted to determine the deserving poor, which included an estimation of ability to regain independence. Scientific charity also sought efficiency in charitable activities, eliminating overlapping efforts.[45]

Finding her calling, Breckinridge began a crusade with the enthusiasm of her great-grandfather. She traveled extensively to see model programs and sought to apply her knowledge in Lexington. With Sophonisba's help, she met the leaders in the field and considered attending the University of Chicago. Forced to balance her reforming activities with her own health needs, she had to give up the idea of further formal education; but on her trips to doctors and tuberculosis treatment centers around the country, she scheduled visits to facilities that helped her learn the new methods just as thoroughly. Everywhere she looked, there seemed to be a need for reform in Kentucky. Through the Civic League, she urged the building of parks and playgrounds in Lexington, compulsory education, the development of kindergartens, and the inclusion of manual training in the schools. She also sought child labor laws and the raising of the age of consent in the state.

Breckinridge worked the state of Kentucky the way Henry Clay worked Congress a half century earlier. She used Desha's newspaper to publicize her reform interests, the Woman's Club and the Civic League to garner support and exert influence, and the prestige of the Clay and McDowell names to twist the arms of politicians too often mired in the do-nothing mentality of Kentucky politics. She convinced Progressive Era reformers to visit Lexington to augment her authority on the issues. In 1903 Jane Addams, nationally recognized for her settlement house work, visited Lexington and, fittingly given Henry Clay's role, spoke at Morrison Hall on the campus at Transylvania University. Traveling to Colorado with her mother to seek treatment for tuberculosis, Madge met Judge Ben Lindsey and observed his juvenile court system at work. She devised such a system for Kentucky and invited Lindsey to visit in her efforts to gain support for it. The legislature adopted her program.[46]

Efforts to address the problem of tuberculosis went beyond the fact that the disease was virtually pandemic in the state of Kentucky. It was a family issue for Madge McDowell Breckinridge. Susceptibility to it was inherited from both the Clays and the McDowells, but the disease had been ruthless in its devastation of the Clay family. The discovery in 1882 by Robert Koch of the tubercle bacillus led to the use of the modern term "tuberculosis." However, the disease has been identified in bones dating to times before the existence of the written word. Evidence of tuberculosis has been found in Egyptian mummies and ancient Native Americans. Thomas M. Daniel, author of *Captain of Death: The Story of Tuberculosis,* claims the disease tends to ebb and flow, with centuries between episodes. It rose to new heights in the nineteenth century. Even in modern times, one-third of the world population is infected with the germ, and it causes the death of eight million people each year.[47]

The disease is generally transmitted by inhaling the bacteria when an infected individual coughs or sneezes, and in the late nineteenth century, by drinking unpasteurized milk. The bacteria may then remain dormant for years, attacking the individual later in life. Eleanor Roosevelt is perhaps the best known example of this.[48] In the nineteenth century, medical authorities and the public believed there could be a familial susceptibility to what they called consumption. Several studies have suggested a genetic basis for it, but no gene has been identified.[49] In the Clay family, familial susceptibility hardly mattered. The family immune systems were so weak that Clays fell victim to virtually every contagious disease, and in Kentucky it was impossible to escape contact with the tuberculosis bacteria. The first known victim in the Clay family was Henry Clay's daughter Lucretia. Then, Martin Duralde III. The disease took Henry in 1852, and three Erwin grandsons succumbed to tuberculosis within a decade. The disease took James B. Clay at the age of forty-six in 1864. Harry Boyle Clay Jr. died as a result of tuberculosis in 1917. Madge's mother and three brothers suffered from the disease, and several members of the Simpson family were also victims. Not until the late 1940s, when a cure became widely available, could the family escape its fears of the illness.

In 1905 the Civic League launched a campaign to fight tuberculosis. Louisville had initiated plans to build a sanatorium. In Lexington, Madge appears to have been the driving force behind the creation of the Fayette Tuberculosis Association. She studied the question in great detail and, according to her biographer Melba Porter Hay, was on the leading edge of reform thought. A measure to create a state sanatorium was defeated by the Kentucky legislature, but as usual, she continued to charm, flatter, pressure, and threaten Kentucky legislators and governors until her project was approved. Never one to ask from others what she was unwilling to do herself, she served on the state tuberculosis commission and raised approximately $50,000 for the Blue Grass Tuberculosis Sanatorium while the politicians tried to find the strength to keep up with her.[50]

Madeline McDowell Breckinridge is best known for her efforts on behalf of women. By 1905 she had become involved in the Kentucky Equal Rights Association. Founded in 1888 by Laura Clay, the daughter of abolitionist Cassius Marcellus Clay and a distant relative, it had laid some groundwork for the suffrage movement. It had secured the right of a woman to her wages, previously controlled by her husband. It also won for women the right to vote in school-board elections. The Victorian era had praised women as society's authority on morals, the keeper of the Christian home to which a man could retreat from the harsh world. Arguing that the schools required strong moral leadership to prepare a new generation, women gained some leverage through the education establishment. Madge became involved because she came to believe the vote was the only way women's efforts at reform would be heard by lawmakers. Increasingly, she became frustrated by the complacent attitude, if not ignorance, of men toward social problems. When the legislature repealed an 1892 law giving Lexington's women the right to vote in school-board elections, Madge could barely hide her frustration and contempt. In fact, she radicalized the female members of her family over the issue. As the legislative chair of the Federation of Women's Clubs, she lobbied to regain the right. Her sister Nanette, or Nettie, ran for superintendent of schools, and when the politicians tried to keep her off the ballot, she sued to have her name reinstated. Regaining the right to vote in school elections, Madge, her mother, her sisters Nettie and Julia, sister-in-law Elsie, and Aunt Josephine fought for full suffrage for women. Madge served as president of the Kentucky Equal Rights Association from 1912 to 1915 and from 1919 to 1920, and as vice president of the National American Woman Suffrage Association from 1913 to 1915. She campaigned for the Nineteenth Amendment and is credited with its ratification by the Kentucky legislature.[51]

When Clay descendants went public, the inevitable comparisons to the patriarch were made. Newspaper accounts of Madge's speeches noted her confidence and skill as traits inherited from her great-grandfather. They might also have mentioned her biting wit, her storytelling, her energy, and her demeanor, which could quickly turn from charm to anger. But she also had the perseverance that so many of the family, including the patriarch, sometimes lacked. Despite the painful and energy-sapping illness that plagued her, she sought to do more rather than less. And despite the infidelity of her husband, which had to have struck a proud woman at her core and embarrassed her in the community, Madge buried herself in her work. Madeline McDowell Breckinridge reaped another legacy of the Clay family. Brilliant, but short lived, on November 25, 1920—Thanksgiving Day—she died at the age of forty-eight. Madge McDowell Breckinridge suffered a stroke as she gathered items to give to the poor in the holiday season.[52]

Each branch of the Clay family felt an obligation to help the needy. Incidences of family members going to the aid of the weak and seemingly defenseless abound in the family records of all branches. There was, of course, a sense of superiority involved in such matters. Madge Breckinridge's letters and speeches are filled with examples of a paternalistic attitude. Her support of manual education rested on a belief that many whites and most blacks were incapable of higher functions. That was, of course, the attitude of most of the people who heard her speeches as well. Nevertheless, the aid was real. Madge Breckinridge helped poor blacks and whites alike in Lexington. She encouraged the building of playgrounds in several sections of the town, and she sought a safe means for children to cross a railroad track on their way to school. Whites, blacks, working-class children, victims of tuberculosis, and the laboring class as a whole needed someone or some group to speak for them in an age that had ignored their problems. Madge even contemplated the advantages of a socialist system, and she certainly believed government should temper capitalism with sensitivity.

Madge was merely the most obvious example of a principle held by the Clay family. Her brothers provided support for family employees long after they were unable to work. Harry Clay left his Arctic expedition because of his contempt for a physician who refused to treat the child of an Eskimo family. Tom Clay's defense of Geronimo and the other Apaches reflected a sense of noblesse oblige and honor. In the following generation, Charley Clay frequently went to the defense of those being picked on, and his brother Bob, who had many excuses for leaving West Point in his plebe year, claimed he could not remain associated with an institution that allowed upper classmen to harass defenseless plebes: "The plebe is a bashful, stupid sort of fellow and he is made the butt of all the jokes and insults these two upperclassmen can think up. Any system that allows this sort of thing to go on is unfair and unjust and I don't intend to stand it any longer."[53] Years later, after his retirement, Bob Clay worked diligently to help poor young men of Greenville, Mississippi.[54]

The goals of the Civic League also continued to motivate the family long after Madge had died. Nettie McDowell encouraged school reform but also visited schools in poorer neighborhoods seeking to inspire the students there. Mrs. Henry Clay Simpson Sr. helped at Ashland and with other charities, and the widow of Eugene Simpson provided funds to help establish the Donovan Scholars program, a plan that continues to allow retired Kentuckians to take classes at the University of Kentucky. In many smaller ways, family members contributed to their community through their churches and community charitable efforts.[55]

The sense of noblesse oblige also required the elite to provide for and protect the "good" blacks of their community. The attitude of the Clays toward their black servants and neighbors when compared to what they wrote about African Americans reveals the complexity of race relations in the South. Like most southerners, the Clays accepted the end of slavery, but they did not believe in the equality of blacks. That they attacked civil rights legislation and suggested a late nineteenth-century colonization of blacks indicates that they stood with the traditionalists of the South. Susan Clay's "A Plea for the Negro" constituted a demeaning and thoughtless statement that in a more modern era is painful to read. She left no doubt that she believed in the innate inferiority of African Americans. Later generations continued to reflect the racial views of the society in which they lived. James B. Clay Jr. told his brother Thomas he had no right to call himself a Clay when Thomas agreed to command black troops in the Tenth Cavalry, and Charles Clay complained bitterly about the conduct of black troops in the Spanish-American War. Although he sought a commission to lead Kentucky volunteers, he did not want to command black troops. The family also complained frequently about black servants and farm hands. Henry Clay McDowell hired a black laborer for $3.50 a week while he was sending his son at Yale University $200 nearly every six weeks. The family then wondered why they found blacks worked so slowly or chose to miss work frequently. Susan M. Clay complained that she was "as usual" without servants but also that the cook she did have was unsatisfactory. Nettie McDowell, like her Uncle John, apparently had difficulty working with servants. Announcing in a letter to her mother that another servant had left her employment, she wrote, "Tell father that he must not think there is something wrong with me. I do not believe Mary ever intended to stay longer than during the summer with me." She went on to say that Mary did not believe she was treated equally with another servant.[56]

The Clays clearly believed African Americans existed to serve them. Charles Clay took a servant from Lexington to Columbus, Ohio, when he served there with the Seventeenth Infantry because he did not believe he could find good servants in the North. Similarly, when Henry and Elsie McDowell needed a house boy in Big Stone Gap, her family sent them a young man from Rogersville to meet their needs. William C. McDowell proved somewhat more stoical. Managing the farm at Ashland in the early twentieth century, he frequently noted that work had been slower than he had hoped because his black laborers decided they did not want to work. During the Negro Fair, work essentially stopped for a week. He accepted the situation matter-of-factly, but he carefully explained it to Henry Clay McDowell Jr., to whom he reported.[57] Madge noted the inconsistency and the dilemma of the master class. Inconvenienced by a servant who needed time off, she was at first upset. Upon reflection, however, she realized that the servants had lives and needed time to attend to personal matters just as she did. Madge was clearly the most forward-thinking person in the family, but she too reflected many of the prejudices of her day. She used the fact that, at least legally, black men could vote in many states as an argument justifying the vote of women. She also emphasized manual training for both lower-class whites and blacks in the school systems of Kentucky. That Madge was revered by the black community clearly reflects the evolution of race relations. Implicit in her reforms is the sense that blacks were inferior. Yet, for her time, she was quite liberal. She recognized the need to improve the plight of the African American community and worked diligently to further that cause.

Fortunately, noblesse oblige trumped Lost Cause, at least in public. Noblesse oblige and Henry Clay's legacy required civility in the relationship to African Americans. Ironically, Susan M. Clay could be quite inti-

Uncle Daniel. Courtesy of the Elizabeth Clay Blanford Collection.

mate with her servants even as she damned the race as a whole. Reflecting the influence of the Lost Cause, the Clays told stories of faithful slaves and servants from the family's past. The patriarch had been a kind master, of course, and the entire family told stories about Uncle Aaron, Mammy Lottie, and other favorites. Mrs. Minor Simpson, a great-granddaughter in the Erwin branch, praised Henry's kindness to his slaves. The family added other faithful servants to their stories as the century progressed. Inevitably, they were stories about black women used in the homes or elderly black men who drove wagons or did odd jobs. The children were taught to call them uncle or aunt, and many adults continued the practice. Mrs. Simpson, as noted, related stories about a slave named Uncle Harv. In the papers of the James Clay branch, there is a newspaper obituary telling the story of Uncle Daniel. Born a slave, he worked hard and outlived his employers. He was declared intelligent but could not read or write. He "knew his Bible and had an abiding trust in God." This was the kind of black man whites liked. The family stories certainly had a Jim Crow flavor, but some also contained lessons for whites. Teetee told her nieces and nephews about Daniel, an old servant who worked at Balgowan. On a trip to Lexington, the horse was going too slow to suit her, so she told Daniel to hit him with the whip. Daniel replied in the slow drawl that was also a part of the Lost Cause portrait, "No, Miss Teetee, ain't gonna hit dat horse." In a story to children, it attributed a kind of wisdom to the old man and, by implication, the right of a black man or woman, when done properly, to teach whites a lesson.[58]

Black hands and servants stayed with branches of the family for a lifetime. Blacks helped Thomas McDowell with his horses, and servants in the house helped raise several generations of the family. Aunt Matt cooked for Susan, Teetee, and George at Balgowan. She was probably more trusted by Teetee than any white friend; she spent far more time with her. And it was Aunt Matt who went to George to express concern when Teetee would do nothing about the cancer that was killing her.[59] Millie Lawson worked first for Susan M. Clay, who then "gave" her to her son Charles's family. A tall, stoical woman, Millie brought her daughters with her, teaching them the skills they would need later in life. She also taught the Clay children. Elizabeth and Susan credited Millie with providing them a strong moral base, and that claim reflects more than nostalgia. Crowding into the kitchen on winter days, the children of Charles Clay, the last of the James Clay branch, sampled Millie's cooking and enjoyed the stories she told. Elizabeth Clay later wrote the stories down, in dialect, and asked Millie to correct them. Her carefully prepared copies remain in the Clay papers. Those stories contain strong moral lessons based on the Bible or life experiences that the children never forgot. She also taught them to behave in her kitchen. Reproof from Millie Lawson brought tears as readily as that from their mother or father. She did not scold or punish; "her quiet look of disapproval was enough to make any child, white or colored, 'mend his step.'"[60]

Millie Lawson proved to be highly important to the sanity of Elizabeth Clay. As Elizabeth became a woman, she was not happy in her father's house. Her parents suffocated her with their protectiveness and the emphasis on family duty. They disliked her friends at the University of Kentucky. Their coolness drove young men away, usually after one visit. Elizabeth remained at home, unmarried, into her early thirties. Millie listened to her expressions of loneliness. Elizabeth's father died in 1935, but she stayed with her mother. When her mother died in 1939, Elizabeth, the last member of the James Clay branch in Lexington, was free to leave. But she had been confined so long, freedom seemed frightening. Millie urged her to go.

Aunt Matt. Courtesy of the Elizabeth Clay Blanford Collection.

Years later, in an article submitted to the *Christian Science Monitor,* Elizabeth wrote, "So she sent me out into the world to find a new life, and I found it—a lovely new life, but the other day when I sent her a flowery Easter bonnet all the way back to Kentucky from California, I thought of how she had served every one of us—my family for three generations, her own family and all her friends and neighbors in Slickaway, and the words of one who was master of all came back to me, 'Whosoever will be chief among you, let him be your servant.'"[61]

Elizabeth Clay left Lexington in 1939, but she wrote regularly to Millie Lawson and saw her each time she visited Kentucky. Millie's daughter Susan Lawson Brown, named for Susan Clay, read the letters to her and wrote her responses. Susan and Elizabeth Clay, great-granddaughters of a statesman, sent letters and occasionally gifts to Millie and her daughter for the rest of their lives, and saved her letters to them.

The relationship of black and white in the South was far more complex than historians have dared calculate. Unquestionably, such incidents of intimacy or concern have been used to soften the rough edges of discrimi-

Millie Lawson. Courtesy of the Elizabeth Clay Blanford Collection.

nation. Clearly, even the patrician elite insisted on black subservience, but on a family level, life was often more integrated than historians relate. The picture in the McDowell collection showing the white McDowells with their black servants raises difficult questions for the historian. Should we place the emphasis on their inclusion in the picture, their segregation, or both? The McDowells never paid Theodore, a lifelong employee, a reasonable wage; they did, however, provide him a house and an allowance after he could no longer work. During the Great Depression, black servants took food they cooked in Clay homes back to their own families, and the Clays and McDowells often intervened when their employees, or the sons of their employees, had difficulties with local police officials. The communication between the Clay sisters and their former servants occurred long after there was anything but affection to account for it. Susan and Elizabeth continued to exhibit the teachings of their youth. Until her death, Elizabeth referred to "her colored family," and there were attitudes of superiority that must have proved difficult for Millie Lawson and Susan Brown. Yet, there was also a sense of responsibility. Returning to Kentucky in the 1950s, Elizabeth Clay Blanford learned that there was no headstone on Millie's grave. She purchased a stone and, at the dedication, citing the book of Proverbs, publicly declared herself one of Millie Lawson's children. In the 1990s, when the local airport threatened to take land for a runway that would disrupt the black community she called Slickaway, Elizabeth wrote from Gloucester, Massachusetts, urging the city to respect the historically black community. Years later, when Susan Brown lost her husband and his Social Security, Elizabeth tried to send money every month. Given her own financial situation, it was a sacrifice, but she firmly believed one shared with one's family, regardless of race.[62] Paternalistic, sometimes self-serving, often demeaning, the legacy of service nevertheless required that Henry Clay's descendants provide some aid to their African American neighbors. It is less than what should have been, but more than was given by many.

The legacy of service remained an integral part of the training of each new generation of the family. Proud of their heritage, descendants recognized they had a duty to give back to the society that had blessed them. There were exceptions, as there always are, but as a family they paid homage to the legacy left by their patriarch.

CONCLUSION

The legacies of Henry Clay, like so many family legacies, proved to be both blessing and curse to his descendants. Blessed with quick minds and boundless energy, they were taught, and most believed, that they inherited some small portion of his genius. Yet, as Henry Clay Jr. wrote in his diary, it can be difficult for a small tree "to grow in the shade of an aged oak." For some, a sense of being overshadowed competed with an effort to accomplish.[1] Because of the Civil War, the emphasis on family responsibility grew significantly. Some branches placed tremendous pressure on their young to restore the prominence enjoyed in the days of the patriarch. Others expected their children to understand their place in society and develop the manners associated with their class. In addition to the family, the community and the nation seemed to be waiting for success or watching for failure. Clays living today have noted an unspoken pressure, a sense that their actions were continually observed. Frequently, the pressures were stated openly. Great-granddaughter Susan Clay was declared the perfect representation of a noble family by the local newspaper at the age of five. Julia McDowell, the same paper decided, represented the intellectual and physical presence of her great-grandfather. Madge and Harry Clay regularly heard or read comparisons of themselves with Henry Clay. We note almost in passing the fact that an eighteen-year-old freshman was invited to dinner with the president of Yale University because he so admired the young man's great-grandfather, but how much anxiety does such an event produce at that age? Many members of the family tried to avoid mention of the connection. George Clay made jokes about the heritage. Henry Clay Simpson claimed to have forgotten how he was related to Henry Clay. Others sought to live their lives and do their part because they were descendants of Henry Clay, but to draw as little attention to themselves as possible.[2]

The pressures were the strongest on those who remained in Lexington. Bertram Wyatt-Brown has noted how difficult it could be in the South to escape the demands of one's ancestors.[3] That seems true in any region, in any family, where the emphasis is on living up to the principles of a myth. For the Clays, it was equally difficult when living in the shadow of Ashland. Family home and "place" have always been important concepts in the South. Place can be community; it is most frequently estate or home. It is linked to the ownership of land, but it has an implication of values. Great-granddaughter Susan Clay wrote of a place, of portraits on walls, of aged mandarins, and of values grown dry and acrid with age. The Clay descendants of Rogersville, Tennessee, escaped for the most part the ties of Ashland, but only to establish new ones to the Kenners and their "place." The Appalachian region is notorious for its sense of place. Thomas Hart Clay Jr.'s daughter Annie Clay Gibson enjoyed her status as a descendant of Henry Clay from the comfort of Pittsburgh, Pennsylvania. She could admire the few artifacts passed down from her father, remember the visits to historic Lexington where the Clay and Gratz families, her ancestors, were prominent, even admire the work of historians such as Glyndon Van Deusen, who had contacted her when writing his biography of her great-grandfather. Her sister Henrietta, who returned to Lexington with her parents, did not have the buffer of distance. Others such as Goodloe McDowell and Henry Clay Anderson moved to Florida, invoking ancestry only when they chose to do so. Susan, Elizabeth, and Robert Clay, the last of the James Clay branch, left Lexington and returned only to visit. Susan complained each time she visited about the incessant gossip that characterized the small town. Robert retired from the army but chose to live in Greenville, Mississippi, rather than subject his children to the pressures of Lexington. Although lessons about proper conduct in those of the refined social classes continued to be taught, as they were in most upper-middle-class families, less emphasis was placed on the connection to Henry Clay.

The Clays also sold the land that had served as the family base as they made the transition from agrarian to urban living. The homes Henry had built for his sons no longer remain in the family. The Clay Villa and Mansfield were sold, and the Woodlands, Anne Clay Erwin's home, became a city park and residential housing. In 1919 the McDowells began to subdivide the land at Ashland. Lexington grew toward the estate and needed additional space for housing. Soon, only the streets recalled the names associated with the family. The Wrights and Calumet Farm absorbed James Clay Jr.'s Iroquois Farm and acquired Balgowan from Tom and George Clay after Teetee's death in 1923. The Charles Clay farm was sold after his death in 1935. Despite the Great Depression, the Anderson and Simpson descendants began to subdivide John and Josephine Clay's estate in the 1930s. Ashland Park and Chevy Chase, the old McDowell and John Clay estates, provided necessary housing for the citizens of Lexington. Streets lined with ash, sycamore, and gingko trees remain today in some of the most beautiful residential sections of the city. The McDowell developments were laid out in a grid, but the Andersons did not like straight lines, so streets curved gently through Chevy Chase. The different patterns seem to fit the Clay heritage.

Nettie McDowell Bullock occupied the house at Ashland, but it was closed to visitors at her husband's insistence. Artifacts that had so long told the story of Clay contribution became increasingly scattered among family members. In times of financial need, some members sold pieces of their heritage. Others kept family silver, china, letters, and papers locked away, out of sight and often out of memory. Some members of the family continued to feel pressure from within the family or within themselves. The family names were still repeated through the generations. Henry Clay Simpson, Senior and Junior, Henry Clay Brock, Henry Clay Anderson, and Henry Clay List could not escape the name itself. Lucretia, Susan, Josephine, Lucy, and Thomas were also repeated regularly. Certainly, many were proud to carry the family names.

Henry Clay and the Clay family also receded to some degree from public memory. The faster American life moved, the less it concerned itself with the past. As people sped by on the stately four-lane boulevard that ran along the northern border of the estate, it might be recalled that Ashland had been the home of Henry Clay. The newspaper carried an obligatory article about Clay on the anniversary of significant events in which he had participated, and the obituaries of family members, although increasingly inaccurate, duly noted the connection to Henry. Occasionally, an example of Clay eccentricity would provoke discussion in the community, but there were no longer many of those.

That did not mean the importance of family disappeared. Nettie Bullock, once frivolous, the ultimate socialite, and typical Clay spendthrift, became the organizer of a movement to honor Henry Clay and his de-

Nettie McDowell Bullock. Henry Clay Memorial Foundation Collection.
Courtesy of University of Kentucky Special Collections.

scendants in perpetuity. Difficult times matured Nettie. Unsuccessful in
business and medicine, Thomas Bullock, Nettie's husband, suffered in later
life from illness and ennui. After failing in New Mexico, he accepted a
home for his family at Ashland where he did virtually nothing for twenty-
five years. Additionally, Nettie's son Henry Bullock, even as an adult,
required her constant care. In fact, he provided most examples of family
eccentricity after World War II. Nettie became by default the leader of her
immediate family, and she created an area of service for herself. In return
for living at Ashland, she helped run the McDowell Trust—that is, the
financial interests of her mother, brothers, and sisters. Early on, she cared
for her mother and worked with Madge in the suffrage movement, becoming involved in local reform efforts. After Madge's death, Nettie honored
her sister each year at the school Madge founded.[4] After the death of her
husband, she opened Ashland to visitors again. Included in the McDowell
papers are numerous articles about Monticello, Mount Vernon, the Red

Hill Mansion of Patrick Henry, the restoration of Colonial Williamsburg, and the creation of other house museums throughout the country. Nettie and Madge had talked about creating a memorial at Ashland, and Madge had bequeathed some money for that purpose. Ashland had been the home of three families of Clays. Nettie set about creating a lasting memorial.[5]

Once her decision had been made, Nettie resorted to the same methods her sister had used in her reform efforts. She sought help from Lexington's gentry leaders. The Woman's Club of Central Kentucky and other civic organizations supported the idea of a house museum. Judge Samuel Wilson, a respected lawyer and local historian, led a movement that involved leaders from the University of Kentucky. The Masons offered to make a contribution if the state would buy Ashland, because Henry Clay had been grandmaster of the Kentucky Masonic Order. The Sons of the Revolution wanted to make Ashland a shrine. Nettie also sought help from the press. The *New York Times Magazine* wrote in favor of making the estate a museum, and there were articles in the Louisville and Lexington papers.[6]

Efforts to sell the estate to the city and state governments became embroiled in politics. The purchase of the estate as a park failed to win support on the ballot because the cost was considered too high for park land and, some of the family believed, because of old jealousies. When the state attempted to buy it, the city of Louisville countered with a request for $100,000 to purchase a building for the Filson History Club. Nettie would not be deterred. In her will, she created a perpetual memorial to the family. Operated by the Henry Clay Memorial Foundation, the estate was dedicated on April 12, 1950.[7]

Nettie's effort provided a magnificent gift to both Lexington and the Clay family. For Lexington, the estate symbolized a history irrevocably attached to the career of Henry Clay. In a parklike atmosphere, the grand old estate attracts neighborhood residents to its walks and garden as well as visitors from across the nation and around the world. The Henry Clay Estate, for the fourth time, became a family estate; but this time it was different. It was no longer the property of the family. With the transfer of "place," family members seemed less in the shadow of their illustrious ancestors. They looked at the family heritage in a positive light, with much less of that foreboding sense of responsibility that characterized the earlier generations. Ashland provided a source of pride for family members. Slowly, they began to loan or give artifacts to the estate. The difficulty of such philanthropy should not be ignored. To part with the tangible evidence of one's heritage, even if it had primarily occupied boxes and closets, cannot be easy. As the family expanded, however, the artifacts became increasingly scattered. Family members realized that Ashland was a place where all members could share their heritage. Additionally, a new generation turned its talents to the study of the family. In the Erwin branch, Bill LaBach has studied both the genealogy and landownership in the family. Henry Clay Simpson Jr., after retiring from a career in banking, brought business efficiency to the study of the past. In a very short time, he researched and wrote a book about Josephine Clay, and he continues to add information about the extended family. Clay, his brother Wood, and their late mother have helped other historians and worked on an exhibit at the Kentucky Horse Park about the Clay contribution to the horse industries. Clay Simpson also gifted family papers to the University of Kentucky. The LaBachs and the Lists have also lent artifacts for a variety of exhibits. Two generations of the James Clay branch gave numerous artifacts to Ashland. They agreed to give the papers that were not sold to the Library of Congress to the University of Kentucky, and Ned Boyajian, five generations removed from the patriarch, has done detailed research on the James Clay descendants and worked with members of other branches. Dr. William Kenner of the Rogersville Clays and Julia Brock, a McDowell descendant, have been equally generous with family artifacts and papers. They now take pride in renewing family relationships and sharing the stories that have come down through the increasingly widening circle of families. Most important, they bring to the study of the family curious minds interested in understanding the family's past. Pride is not restricted by knowledge of the hardships or the idiosyncrasies. Elizabeth Clay Blanford wanted to destroy a letter her father had written to her Uncle George chastising him for wanting to sell the family artifacts. Even though family members laughed at the fact that he would sell anything he could get his hands on, he was, she said, a good man, and she did not want people to get the wrong impression of him. He was, indeed, a good man, who wanted to sell the family papers.

That may well be the best description of the family as a whole. Their heritage extends from the second generation of American leaders and traverses the history of the nation. Each generation faced a new time in the nation's history with strengths and weaknesses. The Clays met new challenges complicated by the baggage of the past. Southerners, particularly, have suffered from that dilemma. Confined by the values of community, even those inclined to be forward thinking are limited by the restrictions of place. The Clays carried additional baggage. The legacy of Henry Clay and family promised great opportunities. There may not have been genius in their veins, but there were few if any family members who lacked the ability to make a contribution at some level. And a broad spectrum of contributions has been made. Family members have given their time and their blood in service to their country. In a time when the elite of America send few of their sons and daughters to the military service of their country, the Clay heritage stands as testament to duty. They have provided leadership in business, in the professions, and in state and community government. They did so with the threat of bad health hanging over their heads. This was no phobia: there were too many bright, capable men and women who died young of tuberculosis, typhoid, diphtheria, and other maladies. And their idiosyncrasies provided moments of humor—to themselves and to a community too anxious to share a story of Clay eccentricity.

Family members who struggled with illness or other obstacles contributed despite the burdens. As Melba Porter Hay has noted, Madge, learning she suffered from tuberculosis, merely began to work harder. She managed her "blue periods," tuberculosis, and her husband's infidelity to serve her community.[8] Other Clays reacted similarly. Susan Clay Sawitzky struggled with the confinement of tradition, but she wrote gripping poetry that speaks to the Clay heritage and the history of women. Henry Clay McDowell Jr. suffered from tuberculosis, but he was highly respected for his work on the judicial bench. Others raised horses, taught at the university level, practiced law, and developed real estate. In short, they provided the leadership that is necessary to sustain a democratic society.

Historians, implying that his family limited Henry Clay's efforts to be president, have emphasized the problems they experienced without thorough analysis of them. The emphasis should be on their accomplishments in spite of problems. If we can argue back to Henry Clay, perhaps the same thing should be said of him. He struggled to control his passionate nature. He made career-shaping mistakes primarily as a result of stress, and his temper and biting remarks angered foe and friend alike. These surely were factors in his failure to become president. Yet, his energy helped build a great country and a significant family. The history of more than five generations speaks to the legacy of a father. It also speaks to the resiliency of an American family.

ACKNOWLEDGMENTS

A book is more than the work of one person. The debts to individuals and institutions increase as the process moves from research to publication. It starts with librarians and archivists, and I owe much to individuals at the Library of Congress, the National Archives, the Rhodes Library at Oxford University, the United States Military Academy, the Kentucky History Center, the Filson Historical Society, the University of Kentucky, the University of Louisville, Georgetown College, and Transylvania University. I am particularly appreciative of the support of Claire McCann, Terry Birdwhistell, and Bill Marshall at the University of Kentucky, B. J. Gooch of Transylvania University, and Suzanne Christoff at West Point. Their knowledge of their collections and their enthusiasm for history have helped me immensely.

I am also grateful to colleagues in my discipline as well as others. Owen Connelly of the University of South Carolina has provided inspiration through his meticulous research and dedication to scholarship. Steven May and Fred Hood encouraged my efforts through their determination to research and write despite heavy teaching loads and institutional responsibilities. May and Hood have also complimented, criticized, read, and edited as needed. Despite a heavy schedule of teaching, research, and speaking, James C. Klotter, the state historian of Kentucky, seems always available to help other historians. In addition to providing a careful and insightful reading of the manuscript, he has for many years offered the encouragement and support that keeps such a project going. Harold Tallant has shared his expertise on slavery and an unparalleled knowledge of historical literature. At a liberal arts college, one has the added benefit of close relations with members of other disciplines. Dr. Woodridge

Spears in the English Department introduced me to Mrs. Elizabeth Clay Blanford and the first collection of Clay papers. Professors Macy Wyatt and Regan Lookadoo in the Psychology Department provided advice when my research forced me to know more about their field. A friend since undergraduate days, Professor Bill Ellis read portions of the manuscript, and two former students, Eric Fruge and Sarah Hardin, now professional historians, offered valuable criticism at important stages of the writing.

The staff of the University Press of Kentucky has made the process of turning a manuscript into a book far more enjoyable than I would have thought possible. Steve Wrinn, the director, has shared his enthusiasm and optimism. Allison Webster and David Cobb have directed the publication process and me with clear, precise, and sensitive direction, and the production team has moved flawlessly toward the ultimate goal. The press also provided excellent readers, to whom I offer my thanks. There are few in my discipline whose work I respect as much as that of Bertram Wyatt-Brown. To have him read my work and offer his support and suggestions was an unexpected reward for my labor. Melba Porter Hay, an editor of the Henry Clay Papers and biographer of Madeline Breckinridge, has the knowledge to write this book, and she shared it graciously in her valuable reading. Finally, I am indebted to Liz Smith, whose watchful eye for detail has saved me from a number of embarrassing mistakes.

Special appreciation must be extended to the staff at the Henry Clay Estate. Jeff Meyer, a former curator, introduced me to members of the family and led me to important sources. Members of the current staff have not only accurately answered my queries but also offered warm enthusiasm for this research. The people at Ashland are extremely dedicated to the house museum and to the memory of Henry Clay. Mary Ellen Carmichael, Wendy Bright-Levy, and Ann Hagan-Michel asked poignant questions stemming from their enthusiasm and curiosity. Eric Brooks and Sue Andrew opened the curatorial files, shared their knowledge, and read the manuscript, correcting errors of detail that seem inevitably to evade the eye of the writer. Eric's help in the selection and preparation of the images has also added significantly to the book. But most importantly, the curator's office provided the opportunity to spend wonderful hours exploring ideas about the Clays with knowledgeable and sincerely interested people.

To no person or group do I owe more than to members of the Clay family. The book simply could not have been written without their input. Beginning nearly twenty-five years ago, Elizabeth Clay Blanford shared her collection of Clay papers and her unfailing memory for detail. Clay and Wood Simpson and their late mother, Mrs. Henry Clay Simpson Sr., shared family papers and their own experiences. Mrs. Simpson welcomed me into her home and opened a treasure trove of family papers and artifacts for me to see. Clay Simpson's research has also provided valuable new evidence about family life. Ned Boyajian and Julia McDowell Brock also shared their knowledge. Proud of their heritage, they bring analytical minds and delightful curiosity to their efforts. It bodes well for the future of this family. Dr. William Kenner opened another set of family papers, and, a respected psychiatrist, he encouraged me to explore the issue of mood disorder in the family story and guided me to important literature. I think he, more than anyone else, realized the value of the Clay story to other American families. My friend Bill LaBach has constantly shared his research, his insights, and his family stories. He would prefer that I emphasize the positive aspects of his family, though he has shared information about the tragedies and the eccentricities too. Long, leisurely discussions of the Clay family with Bill LaBach are treasured experiences. To these and other family members, I express my appreciation for their friendship and their support even as they knew Clay idiosyncrasies had to be a part of the story. I hope they know I fervently believe their legacy, as well as that of Henry Clay, is a valuable part of the nation's history. The blessing and the burden of the gift have added to their strength.

I must also thank my family, for I have a greater appreciation for their sustaining grace as a result of this process. I thank my wife, Judy, for sharing my research trips, solving technology problems, preparing family charts, reading portions of the manuscript, and for just being there to encourage me. My children, usually gracefully, agreed to trips to Washington, D.C., Gloucester, Massachusetts, and Rogersville, Tennessee, instead of the beach or Disney World, so that I could do research. They matured significantly when as young teens they were served tea by a gracious Clay host—in china cups brought by Henry Clay from Ghent in 1815. Finally, inspired by the example of the Clay family, I dedicate this book to my grandchildren—Brian, Elizabeth, Andrew, and Gabby—hoping it contributes to their understanding that through thick and thin the concept of family is both important and sustaining.

NOTES

Introduction

1. Merrill D. Peterson, *The Great Triumvirate: Webster, Clay, and Calhoun* (New York: Oxford University Press, 1987), 6.

2. Daniel Walker Howe, *The Political Culture of the American Whigs* (Chicago: University of Chicago Press, 1979), 137.

3. Harriet Martineau to Reverend Samuel Gilman, June 12, 1835, University of Kentucky Special Collections; David Davis, "Some Recent Directions in Cultural History," *American Historical Review* 73 (February 1968): 705.

4. For the importance of family life in the transmission of values in the Victorian era, see Daniel Walker Howe, *Victorian America* (Philadelphia: University of Pennsylvania Press, 1976), 25.

5. Paul C. Nagel, *Descent from Glory: Four Generations of the John Adams Family* (New York: Oxford University Press, 1983); Paul C. Nagel, *The Lees of Virginia: Seven Generations of an American Family* (New York: Oxford University Press, 1990); Jean H. Baker, *The Stevensons: A Biography of an American Family* (New York: W. W. Norton, 1996); Bertram Wyatt-Brown, *The House of Percy: Honor, Melancholy, and Imagination in a Southern Family* (New York: Oxford University Press, 1994); James C. Klotter, *The Breckinridges of Kentucky, 1760–1981* (Lexington: University Press of Kentucky, 1986). See also Peter Collier and David Horowitz, *The Roosevelts: An American Saga* (New York: Touchstone, 1994).

6. Edward Pessen, "Some Critical Reflections on the New Histories," *South Atlantic Quarterly* 78 (Autumn 1979): 482.

7. Henry Clay Jr., Diary, 1840–1841, Folder 3, Box 7, Henry Clay Family Papers, University of Kentucky Special Collections.

8. Elizabeth Stone, *Black Sheep and Kissing Cousins: How Our Family Stories Shape Us* (New York: Penguin Books, 1988), 4–5; Bertram Wyatt-Brown, *Southern Honor: Ethics and Behavior in the Old South* (New York: Oxford University Press, 1982), 123.

9. W. Fitzhugh Brundage, "Contentious and Collected: Memory's Future in Southern History," *Journal of Southern History* 75 (August 2009): 751–52; Alon Confino, "Collective Memory and Cultural History: Problems of Method," *American Historical Review* 102 (December 1997): 1390.

10. After the death of her husband, Mary Webster Anderson put her two sons in military school and traveled—often to the racetracks.

11. Henry Clay to James Clay, January 7, 1851, *The Papers of Henry Clay*, ed. James F. Hopkins et al., 11 vols. (Lexington: University Press of Kentucky, 1959–1993) (hereafter cited as CP), 10:840.

12. The cholera epidemic of 1833 proved the exception to the rule. The family, including the Erwins from the nearby Woodlands, barricaded themselves at Ashland, successfully escaping the fate of a large number of their Lexington neighbors.

13. "Brilliant—but Short-Lived," *Morning* ——, —y 17, 1889, Newspaper Clippings, Thomas J. Clay Papers, Manuscript Division, Library of Congress (hereafter cited as TJC Papers); Henry Clay Memorial Foundation Papers, University of Kentucky Special Collections (hereafter cited as HCMF Papers).

14. Howe, *Political Culture of the American Whigs*, 126–27.

15. J. Raymond DePaulo Jr. and Leslie A. Horvitz, *Understanding Depression: What We Know and What We Can Do about It* (New York: John Wiley and Sons, 2002), 6; Nagel, *Descent from Glory*; Wyatt-Brown, *House of Percy*; Kay Redfield Jamison, *Touched with Fire: Manic-Depressive Illness and Artistic Temperament* (New York: The Free Press, 1993), 7.

1. Marriage

1. Bernard Mayo, *Henry Clay: Spokesman of the New West* (Boston: Houghton Mifflin, 1937), 119–20.

2. Susan M. Clay, "An Heroic Figure of the First Half of the 19th Century," Box 55, TJC Papers. Thomas Hart Clay Jr. in his biography attributed the description to J. O. Harrison, Clay's friend and executor. Thomas Clay apparently agreed with the description. Thomas H. Clay Jr., *Henry Clay*, completed by Ellis Paxton Oberholtzer (New York: George W. Jacobs, 1910), 397.

3. Peterson, 11; Robert V. Remini, *Henry Clay: Statesman for the Union* (New York: W. W. Norton, 1991), 23; Glyndon G. Van Deusen, *The Life of Henry Clay* (Boston: Little, Brown, 1937), 24–25. The story seems apocryphal, if only because few places could contain a table sixty feet in length. All biographers tell the story, but none analyzes it beyond raising the issue of heavy drinking.

4. Cassius M. Clay was the son of General Green Clay. An earlier Henry Clay was the grandfather of General Clay and of Henry Clay the statesman. Zachary F. Smith and Mary Rogers Clay, *The Clay Family* (Louisville, Ky.: Filson Club, 1899), 71.

5. Howe, *Political Culture of the American Whigs,* 125; Harriet Martineau, *Retrospect of Western Travel,* 3 vols. (New York: Harper, 1838), 1:130; Margaret Bayard Smith, *Forty Years of Washington Society,* ed. Gaillard Hunt (London: T. Fisher Unwin, 1906), 276–78, 285–86.

6. Quoted in Howe, *Political Culture of the American Whigs,* 123.

7. Remini, *Henry Clay,* 19.

8. Wyatt-Brown, *Southern Honor,* 339–50.

9. Maurice G. Baxter, *Henry Clay the Lawyer* (Lexington: University Press of Kentucky, 2000), 18–19.

10. Quoted in Van Deusen, 58.

11. David Heidler and Jeanne Heidler, *Henry Clay: The Essential American* (New York: Random House, 2010), 39.

12. Remini, *Henry Clay,* 765; Van Deusen, 23; T. H. Clay, 28. Heidler and Heidler, 41. The Heidlers are somewhat kinder to Lucretia, but they create something of a love story too early in the relationship.

13. Dr. William D. Kenner has placed his portrait of Lucretia on loan at the Henry Clay Estate.

14. Susan M. Clay, "Lucretia Clay: Wife of Henry Clay," Box 57, TJC Papers. Merrill Peterson calls her red haired; Remini says she had dark hair and dark eyes. See Peterson, 10; Remini, *Henry Clay,* 30.

15. Joseph M. Rogers, *The True Henry Clay* (Philadelphia: J. B. Lippincott, 1905), 30, 33; Van Deusen, 69; Remini, *Henry Clay,* 31, 72–73.

16. Van Deusen, 69.

17. James Brown to Henry Clay, September 16, 1804, CP, 1:149–50. Lucretia Clay to Henry Clay, March 10, 1814, *The Private Correspondence of Henry Clay,* ed. Calvin Colton (New York: A. S. Barnes, 1856), 24–25. See also John Morrison Clay to Thomas Clay, June 11, 1841, Kenner Collection [microfilm], Special Collections, Margaret I. King Library, University of Kentucky (original in the possession of the Kenner family; Dr. William D. Kenner provided a CD copy of the papers for my use); Henry Clay to James Clay, December 29, 1849, CP, 10:961; Henry Clay to Susan M. Clay, November 13, 1847, CP, 10:361; Susan M. Clay, "Lucretia Clay," Box 57, TJC Papers; Henry Clay to Anna Mercer, April 5, 1848, CP, 10:424. She would send messages by others who were writing, but Henry was overly kind when he said she hardly wrote to him.

18. The original copy of this letter is not in the collected papers. It was printed in Calvin Colton's edition of Clay's letters, but there is some indication that the letters James and Thomas gave to Colton were not all returned. See James B. Clay to Rev'd Calvin Colton, December 4, 1854, James B. Clay to Thomas B. Stevenson, December 6, 1854, Box 42, TJC Papers. Lucretia Clay to Henry Clay, March 10, 1814, CP, 1:870–71.

19. Note, March 6, 1857, Box 43, TJC Papers; Note, March 1, 1855; Note,

September 1, 1855; Note, March 1, 1856, J. O. Harrison Papers, Library of Congress.

20. An aunt in the McDowell branch often sent letters back with corrections she expected her nieces and nephews to make. Great-grandchildren Thomas and Julia McDowell were probably limited in terms of educational opportunity because of the problem.

21. Van Deusen, 69; M. Smith, 85–86. Ashland, the Henry Clay Estate, has the original of "The Lexington Grand Waltz."

22. Remini, *Henry Clay,* 205; T. H. Clay, 30; J. Rogers, 33. Susan M. Clay, "Lucretia Clay," Box 57, TJC Papers.

23. Henry Clay to James Brown, August 24, 1831, CP, 8:391.

24. Susan M. Clay, "Lucretia Clay," Box 57, TJC Papers.

25. Smith, 86–87, 332; Editor's Note, James C. Johnston, July 24, 1844, CP, 10:89. Johnston compared Lucretia to Martha Washington, lauding their supporting roles that enabled their husbands to serve the country. As I note later, Henry and Lucretia suffered the deaths of a number of their children. In addition to her own children, she raised a number of her grandchildren at Ashland.

26. Thomas H. Clay to Lucretia Clay, May 20, 1852, Thomas H. Clay Papers, Library of Congress (hereafter cited as THC Papers).

27. M. Smith, 85, 130, 207, 332.

28. Ibid., 84–85; Susan M. Clay, "Lucretia Clay," Box 57, TJC Papers; Mary Mentelle Clay to Susan J. Clay, May 5, 1850, Box 42, TJC Papers.

29. M. Smith, 213.

30. Susan M. Clay, "Lucretia Clay," Box 57, TJC Papers; M. Smith, 85, 130, 256, 332, 334.

31. Anne Clay Erwin, the last of six daughters, died in 1835 leaving several grandchildren to be raised by Lucretia.

32. See Aileen Kraditor, ed., *Up from the Pedestal: Selected Writings in the History of American Feminism* (Chicago: HarperCollins, 1968), 9; see also Barbara Welter, "The Cult of True Womanhood: 1820–1860," *American Quarterly* 18 (Summer 1966): 151–74; Christopher Lasch, *Haven in a Heartless World: The Family Besieged* (New York: W. W. Norton, 1979); Carolyn G. Heilbrun, *Reinventing Womanhood* (New York: W. W. Norton, 1979); Anne Firor Scott, *Making the Invisible Woman Visible* (Chicago: University of Illinois Press, 1984).

33. Mary Beth Norton, "The Evolution of White Women's Experience in Early America," *American Historical Review* 89 (June 1984): 606–9.

34. Richard M. Bean, "History of the Henry Clay Family Properties," unpublished manuscript (April 1980), copy at Ashland, the Henry Clay Estate; Jeff Meyer, "Henry Clay's Legacy to Horse Breeding and Racing," *Register of the Kentucky Historical Society* 100 (Autumn 2002): 473; James F. Hopkins, "Henry Clay, Farmer and Stockman," *Journal of Southern History* 15 (February 1949): 89–96;

Richard Laverne Troutman, "Henry Clay and His 'Ashland' Estate," *Filson Club History Quarterly* 30 (April 1956): 159–74. John L. Hervey, *Racing in America: 1665–1865,* 2 vols. (New York: Jockey Club, 1944), 1:227.

35. Henry Clay to Francis T. Brooke, April 19, 1830, Colton, 261.

36. Henry Clay Jr., Diary, Folder 1, Box 7, Henry Clay Family Papers, University of Kentucky Special Collections.

37. The curatorial staff at Ashland believe some of the features were added later by James B. Clay.

38. Some of the legal papers of Nicholas's practice are in the Susan Clay Sawitzky Papers (hereafter cited as SCS Papers).

39. Remini, *Henry Clay,* 133.

40. Lucretia Clay to Henry Clay, March 10, 1814, Henry Clay to Lucretia Clay, July 14, 1815, Colton, 24–25, 45.

2. Parenting

1. John Quincy Adams, *The Memoirs of John Quincy Adams, Comprising Portions of His Diary from 1795 to 1845,* edited by Charles F. Adams, 12 vols. (Philadelphia: J. B. Lippincott, 1874–1877), 5:59.

2. Amos Kendall, *Autobiography of Amos Kendall,* edited by William Stickey (Boston: Lee and Shepard, 1872), 115–24; Harriet Martineau to Reverend Samuel Gilman, June 12, 1835, University of Kentucky Special Collections; Remini, *Henry Clay,* 201.

3. Remini, Van Deusen, Howe, and Peterson have written of his passions.

4. Kendall, 117–24.

5. Howe, *Political Culture of the American Whigs,* 126–27.

6. Lorri Glover, "'Let Us Manufacture Men': Educating Elite Boys in the Early National South," in *Southern Manhood: Perspectives on Masculinity in the Old South,* ed. Craig Thompson Friend and Lorri Glover (Athens: University of Georgia Press, 2004), 35–36; Wyatt-Brown, *Southern Honor,* 127, 142, 152; E. Anthony Rotundo, *American Manhood: Transformations in Masculinity from the Revolution to the Modern Era* (New York: Basic Books, 1993), 26; Robert L. Griswold, *Fatherhood in America: A History* (New York: Basic Books, 1993), 12–13; Stephen M. Frank, *Life with Father: Parenting and Masculinity in the Nineteenth-Century American North* (Baltimore: John Hopkins University Press, 1998), 17–18, 98; Steven Mintz and Susan Kellogg, *Domestic Revolutions: A Social History of American Family Life* (New York: Free Press, 1988), 43–45.

7. Remini, *Henry Clay,* 201.

8. George H. Clay to Maria Pepper Clay, August 9, 1897, SCS Papers. George Clay was a grandson of Henry Clay. See also Wyatt-Brown, *Southern Honor,* 138; Glover, 35. Shawn Johansen, *Family Men: Middle-Class Fatherhood in*

Early Industrializing America (New York: Routledge, 2001), 40, 98. There is little evidence that the Clays used physical punishment to discipline their children, although Amos Kendall apparently did.

9. Johansen, 18.

10. Griswold, 18–19; Glover, 25; Mintz and Kellogg, 49–53.

11. Johansen, 131, 140.

12. Lucretia Clay to Henry Clay, March 10, 1814, CP, 1:870–71; Henry Clay to Horace Holley, February 17, 1820, CP, 2:780–81; Henry Clay to Henry Clay Jr., April 19, 1829, CP, 8:29–30; Henry Clay to Henry Clay Jr., October 31, 1830, CP, 8:285. Clay sent at least four of his grandsons to Transylvania as well. Henry Clay Duralde, Henry Clay Erwin, and James Erwin Jr. were students at the same time. Henry Hart Clay attended Transylvania briefly in the late 1840s. See Student File, Transylvania University.

13. Christopher Hughes Jr. to Henry Clay, September 13, 1816, CP, 2:231–32; Check to John McLeod, November 2, 1825, CP, 4:787; Henry Clay to James Brown, March 22, 1826, CP, 5:187–88. Henry Clay to Henry Clay Jr., October 31, 1830, CP, 8:284–85.

14. Horace Holley to Henry Clay, September 15, 1818, CP, 2:598–99; Henry Clay to Zachary Taylor, May 12, 1849, CP, 10:595–96; Account with Nathaniel Silsbee, CP, 2:619, 864.

15. Henry Clay to Henry Clay Jr., February 6, 1828, CP, 7:80–81; Henry Clay to Enoch Cobb Wines, February 16, 1835, CP, 8:761–62; Henry Clay to Henry Clay Jr., April 2, 1827, CP, 6:385–86; Glover, 31.

16. Johansen, 89, 97; Wyatt-Brown, *Southern Honor,* 168; Glover, 37.

17. Henry Clay to Thomas Dougherty, December 29, 1821, CP, Supplement: 98–99; Henry Clay to Enoch Cobb Wines, February 16, 1835, CP, 8:761–62; Henry Clay to Lucretia Hart Clay, March 4, 1835, CP, 8:767; Enoch Cobb Wines to Henry Clay, April 30, 1836, CP, 8:847–48.

18. Henry Clay to James B. Clay, January 22, 1838, CP, 9:132–33.

19. Henry Clay to Henry Clay Jr., February 9, 1829, CP, 7:616.

20. Henry Clay to Henry Clay Jr., November 14, 1828, CP, 7:538–39.

21. Henry Clay to Henry Clay Jr., April 2, 1827, CP, 6:385–86.

22. Kendall, 115–17, 123–24.

23. Henry Clay to Henry Clay Jr., April 2, 1827, CP, 6:385–86.

24. See Nagel, *Descent from Glory;* Wyatt-Brown, *House of Percy;* see also Frederick K. Goodwin and Kay Redfield Jamison, *Manic Depressive Illness* (New York: Oxford University Press, 1990), 358; Francis Mark Mondimore, *Bipolar Disorder: A Guide for Patients and Families* (Baltimore: Johns Hopkins University Press, 1999), 8, 12, 28–29; DePaulo and Horvitz, 6, 30–31; Jamison, 7.

25. Jamison cites Edgar Alan Poe as saying that his enemies attributed his insanity to drink rather than the drink to insanity; Jamison, 36. Many of Henry

Clay's erratic acts and blunders have been attributed to alcohol, but given the history of the family, perhaps the subject should be revisited. Characteristics attributed by psychiatrists to hypomania—infectious energy, extreme and occasionally irrational confidence, and creativity—can be seen in the personalities of Henry and other family members. Witty and gregarious, the hypomaniac is often charismatic and persuasive, but also prone to making enemies. Hypomania is not a mood disorder, but tension and enthusiasm can often lead to mistakes. Manic and depressive symptoms also frequently exist within the families of such people. See John D. Gartner, *The Hypomanic Edge: The Link between (a Little) Craziness and (a Lot of) Success in America* (New York: Simon and Schuster, 2005), 3–13; Goodwin and Jamison, 358. These authors cite Alexander Hamilton as a classic example of hypomania. See also American Psychiatric Association, *Diagnostic and Statistical Manual of Mental Disorders*, 4th ed. (Washington, D.C.: American Psychiatric Association, 2000), 345, 382.

26. Rudy Nydegger, *Understanding and Treating Depression: Ways to Find Hope and Help* (Westport, Conn.: Praeger, 2008); Susan Nolen-Hoeksema and Lori M. Hilt, "Gender Differences in Depression," in *Handbook of Depression*, ed. Ian H. Gotlib and Constance L. Hammen (New York: Guilford, 2002), 492.

27. Theodore Wythe Clay to Henry Clay, January 16, 1828, CP, 7:38–40.

28. Law Student Catalog, Transylvania University.

29. Henry Clay to Henry Clay Jr., May 24, 1830, CP, 8:213.

30. Henry Clay to John Jamison, April 8, 1828, CP, 7:217–18.

31. Henry Clay to John Jamison, April 8, 1828, CP, 7:217; Henry Clay to Theodore W. Clay, March 15, 1827, CP, 6:307; Henry Clay Jr. to Henry Clay, March 27, 1827, CP, 6:365–66. Jamison, 36, 63ff. Jamison lists alcohol abuse and dissipation as symptoms of illness.

32. See Report on the Estate of John Morrison, September 24, 1829, Henry Clay Papers, Transylvania University; Henry Clay to John Jamison, April 8, 1828, CP, 7:217–18; Henry Clay to Henry Clay Jr., May 4, 1830, CP, 8:213; Henry Clay to Henry Clay Jr., June 30, 1830, CP, 8:231; Henry Clay to Henry Clay Jr., October 21, 1830, CP, 8:284–85.

33. Commonwealth of Kentucky v. Theodore W. Clay, Fayette County Circuit Court, File 745, Kentucky Libraries and Archives; *New York Times*, May 19, 1870. Kenneth W. Noe, *Perryville: This Grand Havoc of Battle* (Lexington: University Press of Kentucky, 2001), 18. Noe describes Braxton Bragg as suffering from narcissistic personality disorder. His description fits Theodore in many respects. The narcissist, he says, swerves from achievement characterized by competence, a desire for power and greatness, and perfectionism to deep depressions with anxiety, panic, and isolation. The disorder often occurs in families that place great demands on children to live up to predetermined plans. As an adult, the narcissistic individual creates a "false self" that is highly competent but that veils self-doubt and a fear

that personal weaknesses will be discovered. See also Mondimore, 200; DePaulo, 9–10, 22–24; Jamison, 18–19, 31.

34. Henry Clay to Thomas Dougherty, December 29, 1821, CP, Supplement: 98–99; U.S. Military Academy, "Staff Records," 1 (1818–1835), West Point, New York, 175, 185.

35. Henry Clay to Thomas Morris, February 25, 1822, CP, Supplement: 100; Henry Clay to Thomas Morris, March 8, 1822, CP, Supplement: 102–3.

36. Henry Clay to Thomas Morris, March 8, 1822, CP, Supplement: 102–3.

37. John Boyle to Henry Clay, January 10, 1825, CP, 5:13.

38. Henry Clay to Henry Clay Jr., April 2, 1827, CP, 6:385–86.

39. John W. Overton to Henry Clay, January 30, 1827, CP, 6:139.

40. Thomas I. Wharton to Henry Clay, March 6, 1829, CP, 8:2–3; Henry Clay to Thomas Morris, March 12, 1829, CP, Supplement: 221–22; Henry Clay to Thomas I. Wharton, March 24, 1829, CP, Supplement: 222. Henry's check is at Ashland, the Henry Clay Estate.

41. Henry Clay to Henry Clay Jr., June 30, 1830, CP, 8:231.

42. Henry Clay to Henry Clay Jr., December 2, 1829, CP, 8:131–32; see also Editor's Note 3, CP, 8:132; Henry Clay to Henry Clay Jr., May 24, June 20, October 31, 1830, CP, 8:213, 231, 284–85. As late as December 1833, Henry Clay Jr. informed his father that Thomas was drinking heavily and was "addicted" to liquor. Henry Clay Jr. to Henry Clay, December 14, 1833, CP, 8:675–76.

43. Henry Clay Jr., Diary, 1840–1845, Henry Clay Family Papers, Folder 3, Box 7, University of Kentucky Special Collections; also quoted in Clement Eaton, *Henry Clay and the Art of American Politics* (Boston: Little, Brown, 1957), 162. Thomas H. Clay, Diary, in the possession of Dr. William D. Kenner. For Henry Clay Jr.'s melancholy and Henry Clay's awareness of it, see Henry Clay to Anne Brown Clay Erwin, December 25, 1831, CP, 8:437–38.

44. Henry Clay to Henry Clay Jr., June 20, 1830, CP, 8:231; Henry Clay to Henry Clay Jr., May 24, 1830, CP, 8:213.

45. Henry Clay Jr. to Henry Clay, December 16, 1828, CP, 7:569–70; Henry Clay Jr. to Henry Clay, July 12, 1830, December 7, 1831, CP, 8:234–35, 426.

46. Harriet Martineau to Reverend Samuel Gilman, June 12, 1835, University of Kentucky Special Collections. Martineau wrote, "His poor son is in a lunatic asylum,—driven there, they think, by the violence of his passions. The second son is a sot, the third so jealous and irritable in his temper that there is no living with him; & the two lads, (fine boys of 17 and 13), give no promise of steadiness. Mrs. Erwin is all that they can desire in a daughter, but she is the only survivor of six daughters. Is it not melancholy?"

47. Henry Clay Jr. to Henry Clay, May 7, 1827, CP, 6:524–25.

48. U.S. Military Academy, "Official Register of the Officers and Cadets of the United States Military Academy," 2 (1828–1837), West Point, New York, 14, 19.

49. Henry Clay to Henry Clay Jr., December 20, 1828, CP, 7:571. See also Henry Clay Jr. to Henry Clay, January 2, 1829, CP, 7:588; Henry Clay to Henry Clay Jr., January 14, 1829, CP, 7:598; Henry Clay Jr. to Henry Clay, January 21, 1829, CP, 7:602.

50. Henry Clay to Henry Clay Jr., January 26, 1829, CP, 7:606.

51. Henry Clay Jr. to Henry Clay, July 12, 1830, CP, 8:234–35; Henry Clay to Henry Clay Jr., August 24, 1830, CP, 8:256.

52. See Henry Clay to Henry Clay Jr., April 2, 1827, CP, 6:385; Henry Clay to Henry Clay Jr., August 24, 1830, CP, 8:256; Henry Clay to Henry Clay Jr., February 21, 1832, CP, 8:465–66; Henry Clay Jr. to Henry Clay, June 7, 1832, CP, 8:529; Henry Clay to Samuel L. Southard, October 23, 1832, CP, 8:587–88. Henry Clay to Anne Clay Erwin, December 25, 1831, CP, 8:437–38; Henry Clay Jr. to Henry Clay, March 26, 1832, CP, 8:480.

53. Henry Clay to James B. Clay, January 22, 1838, CP, 9:132–33.

54. Henry Clay to Henry Clay Jr., May 24, 1830, CP, 8:213; Anne Clay Erwin to Henry Clay, January 7, 1832, CP, 8:441.

55. Thomas H. Clay to Mary Clay, June 4, 1852, THC Papers; John M. Clay Diary, University of Kentucky Special Collections.

56. Henry Clay to James B. Clay, August 22, 1839, CP, 9:318.

57. Henry Clay to James B. Clay, January 22, 1838, CP, 9:132–33.

58. Anne Clay Erwin to Henry Clay, January 7, 1832, CP, 8:440–41; Henry Clay to James B. Clay, January 22, 1838, CP, 9:132–33.

59. Henry Clay to James B. Clay, March 23, 1838, CP, 9:165.

60. The actions of Theodore and John fit DePaulo's definition of several forms of delusion; see DePaulo, 22.

61. Henry Clay to Lucretia Clay, March 3, 1852, CP, 10:957. On July 6, 1850, he wrote to Lucretia, "I am waiting in a state of painful anxiety to hear from home as to John's condition" (CP, 10:763); and again on February 11, 1851, he wrote, "I am all the time uneasy about him" (CP, 10:854).

62. Heidler and Heidler, 480.

63. Henry Clay to Susan J. Clay, February 12, 1852, CP, 10:953.

3. Building Legacies

1. Henry Clay to John M. Clayton, August 8, 1842, CP, 9:753–54.

2. Remini, *Henry Clay,* 19, 24; Wyatt-Brown, *Southern Honor,* 164, 340. Wyatt-Brown argues that it would have been nearly impossible for a male of the southern gentry to have avoided risk taking.

3. Lucius P. Little, *Ben Hardin: His Times and Contemporaries* (Louisville, Ky.: Courier-Journal Printing, 1887), 349; Everett S. Brown, ed., *William Plumer's Memorandum of Proceedings in the United States Senate 1803–1807* (New York, 1923),

608; Remini, *Henry Clay*, 23. Other contemporary accounts can be found in Carol Bleser, ed., *Secret and Sacred: The Diaries of James Henry Hammond, a Southern Slaveholder* (New York: Oxford University Press, 1988), 172; Anna Cora Mowatt, *The Autobiography of an Actress* (Boston: Boston Stereotype Foundry, 1853), 258; Charles Henry Ambler, *Thomas Ritchie: A Study in Virginia Politics* (Richmond, Va.: Bell, Book and Stationery, 1913), 89.

4. Adams, 5:59.

5. Martineau, 1:130.

6. M. Smith, 276–78; Remini, *Henry Clay*, 24; Van Deusen, 152; Eaton, 55; Howe, *Political Culture of the American Whigs*, 125–26.

7. Henry Clay to James B. Clay, March 14, 1852, Colton, 4:629.

8. Henry Clay to Julia Prather Clay, April 14, 1833, March 10, 1834, May 9, 1836, CP, 8:638, 704, 849.

9. Henry Clay to James B. Clay, October 19, 1837, CP, 9:87.

10. Some scholars suggest Charles Wickliffe, a leading landowner and later governor of Kentucky, as the benefactor. Others believe Robert Todd, the father of Mary Todd Lincoln, provided the home. Mary Todd attended a girls' school established by Madame Charlotte Mentelle.

11. Thomas's diary is in the possession of a descendant, Dr. William D. Kenner, Thomas's great-great-grandson. There is a microfilmed copy in the University of Kentucky Special Collections.

12. The Heidler biography suggests that John Jacob was not altogether pleased with his daughter's choice; see Heidler and Heidler, 377. John Morrison Clay did not marry until after Henry's death, but his wife was as iron willed as Julia Prather and Susan Jacob. He married Josephine Russell Erwin in 1865. She was the widow of Eugene Erwin, Henry Clay's grandson, who had died at the Battle of Vicksburg fighting for the Confederacy. A good businesswoman and a keen judge of good horses, she also advanced, and protected, the Clay name aggressively. For example, she brought the remains of Eliza from Lebanon, Ohio, to be placed with other family members in the Lexington Cemetery. See Henry Clay Simpson Jr., *Josephine Clay: Pioneer Horsewoman of the Bluegrass* (Louisville, Ky.: Harmony House, 2005).

13. Paul C. Nagel, *The Adams Women: Abigail and Louisa Adams, Their Sisters and Daughters* (New York: Oxford University Press, 1987), 4.

14. Susan Jacob Clay to Henry Clay, February 2, 1850, CP, 10:658–60; Henry Clay to Susan Jacob Clay, March 10, 1849, CP, 10:583; Henry Clay to James B. Clay, May 14, 1849, CP, 10:596–97.

15. Henry Clay to Mary Mentelle Clay, February 8, 1847, CP, 10:304; Henry Clay to Lucretia Hart Clay, December 26, 1850, CP, 10:836–37; Henry Clay to Mary Mentelle, April 7, 1852, CP, 10:963–64. The April 7 letter is also in Colton, 630.

16. Bean, "History of the Henry Clay Family Properties." Bean suggests that Clay bought the Woodlands for the Erwins.

17. Anne Clay Erwin to Henry Clay, April 1, 1832, CP, 8:486–87; Henry Clay Jr. to Henry Clay, April 15, 1832, CP, 8:493–94; Henry Clay Jr. to Henry Clay, April 22, 1832, CP, 8:496–97.

18. Henry Clay to Henry Clay Jr., July 14, 1833, CP, 8:657–58; Henry Clay to Julia Prather Clay, March 10, 1834, CP, 8:704, Henry Clay Jr. to Henry Clay, April 22, 1832, CP, 8:496–97.

19. Henry Clay, Last Will and Testament, July 10, 1851, CP, 10:900–904; Henry Clay to Richard Graham, September 12, 1835, CP, 8:801; Henry Clay to James B. Clay, October 24, 1837, CP, 9:88; Henry Clay to Henry Clay Jr., April 18, 1845, CP, 10:215.

20. Henry Clay, "The American System," in *The Works of Henry Clay,* ed. Calvin Colton, 6 vols. (New York: A. S. Barnes, 1855–1857), 7:477. See also Charles R. Ritcheson, *Aftermath of the Revolution: British Policy toward the United States, 1783–1795* (New York: W. W. Norton, 1969).

21. Howe, *Political Culture of the American Whigs,* 137.

22. Abraham Lincoln, "Eulogy on Henry Clay," in *Collected Works of Abraham Lincoln,* ed. Roy P. Basler, 8 vols. (New Brunswick, N.J.: Rutgers University Press, 1953), 2:132; Charles Sellers, *The Market Revolution: Jacksonian America, 1815–1846* (New York: Oxford University Press, 1991), 64.

23. Howe, *Political Culture of the American Whigs,* 137. Many of the ideas of the American System were carried out by state governments in the North.

24. Henry Clay to Francis Brooke, April 19, 1830, Colton, 261.

25. Henry Clay to John M. Clayton, Lexington, August 8, 1842, CP, 9:753–54.

26. Hopkins, "Henry Clay, Farmer and Stockman," 89–96; CP, 8:663–64; Henry Clay to Henry Clay Jr., April 11, 1836, CP, 8:841; Henry Clay to Thomas Clay, January 8, 1850, Colton, 4:598; Henry Clay to William Martin, September 20, 1833, CP, 8:663–64; Henry Clay to Lucretia Hart Clay, December 50, 1849, CP, 8:630–31.

27. See Troutman, 170–71; Hopkins, "Henry Clay, Farmer and Stockman," 89–96; Henry Clay to John M. Clayton, August 8, 1842, CP, 9:753–54.

28. Van Deusen, 272–73; Henry Clay to Henry Clay Jr., July 7, 1835, CP, 8:779; Henry Clay to Henry Clay Jr., December 16, 1836, CP, 8:872.

29. Henry Clay to Lucretia Hart Clay, December 5, 1849, CP, 10:630–31; Henry Clay to James B. Clay, November 10, 1837, CP, 9:90; Henry Clay to James Clay, March 23, 1838, Colton, 426.

30. Henry Clay Jr. to Henry Clay, September 17, 1835, Colton, 400.

31. Henry Clay to Adam Beatty and James Byers, December 24, 1835, CP, 8:811–12; Henry Clay to Lucretia Hart Clay, January 19, 1846, CP, 10:257; Henry

Clay to Thomas H. Clay, January 24, 1836, CP, 10:257; Henry Clay to Thomas H. Clay, March 13, 1836, CP, 8:834. Troutman, 169.

32. Henry Clay to James Clay, October 19, 1837, Colton, 419; Henry Clay to James Clay, November 10, 1837, CP, 9:90.

33. Meyer, 479, 495.

34. Henry Clay to Thomas Clay, January 8, 1850, Colton, 598; Henry Clay to John Morrison Clay, March 13, 1852, CP, 10:958; Henry Clay to James B. Clay, February 18, 1851, CP, 10:862.

35. Henry Clay to Henry Clay Jr., December 30, 1832, CP, 8:606; January, Huston, & Co. to Henry Clay, July 17, 1833, TJC Papers. The counting house is also referred to in the papers as Grant and Seaver.

36. Henry Clay to James Brown, April 17, 1830, CP, 8:192.

37. Henry Clay to James Erwin, January 10, 1840, CP, 9:372.

38. Henry Clay to James B. Clay, October 24, 1837, CP, 9:88; Henry Clay to James B. Clay, January 22, 24, 1844, CP, 10:3, 4. James was to sign one note and endorse another for $5,000—no paltry sum in 1844. There were two additional notes sent as well. See also Henry Clay to James B. Clay, December 10, 1841, CP, 9:623; Henry Clay to James Erwin, April 10, 1839, CP, 9:302–3.

39. Henry Clay to Henry Clay Jr., February 19, 1834, CP, 8:699.

40. Henry Clay to James Brown, August 2, 1834, CP, 8:738; Editor's note on James Brown to Henry Clay, August 22, 1834, CP, 8:739; William C. C. Claiborne Jr. to Henry Clay, December 4, 1834, CP, 8:753.

41. Henry Clay Jr. to Henry Clay, May 6, 1834, CP, 8:724; Henry Clay to Thomas T. January, October 6, 1838, CP, 9:238; Henry Clay to Thomas H. Clay, March 6, 1838, CP, 9:155; Henry Clay to James B. Clay, January 22, 24, 1844, CP, 10:3–4. See also Henry Clay to James B. Clay, December 10, 1841, CP, 9:623; Henry Clay to James Erwin, April 10, 1839, CP, 9:302–3; Henry Clay to James B. Clay, January 22, 1847, in Colton, 483–84.

42. Henry Clay to Henry Clay Jr., April 13, 1834, December 16, 1836, CP, 8:714, 872.

43. Henry Clay to James B. Clay, March 7, 1842, CP, 9:672–73.

44. Henry Clay to James B. Clay, March 14, April 28, 1852, CP, 10:959, 966; Henry Clay to James Clay, January 30, 1847, Colton, 538; Wyatt-Brown, *Southern Honor*, 213. Wyatt-Brown argues that it was characteristic of southern fathers and fathers-in-law to provide the capital for the business ventures of the next generation.

45. Henry Clay to Thomas H. Clay, April 3, 1838, May 18, February 12, 1839, May 12, 1840, CP, 9:168–69, 186, 285, 441; Henry Clay to Lucretia Hart Clay, July 7, 1840, CP, 9:430–31; Henry Clay to James B. Clay, December 24, 1841, CP, 9:624–25; Henry Clay to Thomas H. Clay, December 19, 1841, CP, 9:623.

46. Remini, *Henry Clay*, 621; Van Deusen, 359; Eaton, 77; J. Rogers, 45.

47. Henry Clay to Thomas H. Clay, March 6, 1838, CP, 9:155.

48. Henry Clay to Thomas H. Clay, February 12, 1839, CP, 9:285; Henry Clay to Thomas H. Clay, February 2, 1846, CP, 10:259.

49. Henry Clay to James Clay, December 24, 1841, CP, 9:624–25; Henry Clay to Ebenezer Pettigrew, September 24, 1841, CP, 9:610.

50. Henry Clay to James Clay, December 10, 24, 1841, CP, 9:623, 624–25.

51. Henry Clay to Thomas Clay, December 12, 25, 1842, CP, 9:792, 793; Deed of Trust for "Ashland," November 15, 1842, CP, 9:789–90; Bond to John Jacob Astor, August 17, 1843, CP, 9:846; Heidler and Heidler, 396. The Heidlers repeat the traditional interpretation.

52. Henry Clay to James B. Clay, December 24, 1841, CP, 9:624–25.

53. Duncan was careful to include in the contract that he would pay the prevailing price at the time of delivery. He specifically refused to contract for purchase at any stipulated price. See the editor's note on a letter from Stephen Duncan, November 4, 1837, CP, 9:90. See also Benjamin Taylor to Henry Clay, April 21, 1841, Folder 1, Box 4, Henry Clay Papers, Transylvania University. Taylor ordered bagging and rope through Henry, not through Thomas.

54. Henry Clay to Thomas H. Clay, April 3, 1838, CP, 9:168; Henry Clay to Thomas H. Clay, September 11, 1841, CP, 9:606–7; Henry Clay to Thomas H. Clay, May 12, 1840, CP, 9:411, 413; Henry Clay to Thomas H. Clay, March 12, 1840, CP, 9:397.

55. Henry Clay to Lucretia Hart Clay, December 9, 1842, CP, 9:790–91.

56. Henry Clay to Thomas H. Clay, December 12, 1842, CP, 9:792; Henry Clay to Abbott Lawrence, March 20, 1845, CP, 10:209–10.

57. Henry Clay to Henry Clay Jr., April 8, 1845, CP, 10:215; Henry Clay to Thomas H. Clay, May 31, July 1, 1850, CP, 10:736, 759.

58. Henry Clay to Thomas H. Clay, December 27, 1849, CP, 10:637–38.

59. *Lexington Observer & Kentucky Reporter,* October 30, November 7, 1833; *New York Observer,* November 30, 1833. Copies in HCMF Papers. Henry Clay Jr. to Henry Clay, May 6, 1834, CP, 8:724; Henry Clay to Henry Clay Jr., March 2, 1838, CP, 9:152.

60. Henry Clay Jr. to Henry Clay, [late February/early March 1841], CP, 9:507; Henry Clay to Thomas B. Stevenson, June 3, 1849, CP, 10:606; Henry Clay to Reverdy Johnson, March 17, 1849, CP, 10:585–86; Henry Clay to Zachary Taylor, May 13, 1849, CP, 10:595–96.

61. Henry Clay to Henry Clay Jr., March 17, 1845, CP, 10:207–8.

62. Henry Clay to Zachary Taylor, May 12, 1849, CP, 10:595–96; Henry Clay to Susan Clay, March 10, 1849, CP, 10:583.

63. Zachary Taylor to Henry Clay, May 28, 1849, CP, 10:599–600; Henry Clay to John M. Clayton, June 7, 1849, CP, 10:600–601.

64. *U.S. Journal of the Executive Proceedings of the Senate of the United States of America,* 8:111, 127, 160; accessed online at http://www.memory.loc.gov.

65. Sarah B. Bearss, "Henry Clay and the American Claims against Portugal," *Journal of the Early Republic* 7 (Summer 1987): 167–80.

66. James B. Clay to Henry Clay, November 27, 1849, CP, 10:628–29; Henry Clay to Susan Jacob Clay, December 15, 1849, CP, 10:633–34; Heidler and Heidler, 479.

67. Henry Clay to James B. Clay, December 29, 1849, March 17, 1850, Colton, 595–96, 602–3.

68. Henry Clay to James B. Clay, December 29, 1849, January 8, 1850, March 13, 17, 1850, CP, 10:639–40, 645–46, 687–88, 689–90; James B. Clay to Henry Clay, February 18, 1850, CP, 10:677–79.

69. Millard Fillmore to Henry Clay, August 20, 1850, CP, 10:798; Henry Clay to James B. Clay, August 15, 22, 1850, CP, 10:794, 798–99; Henry Clay to Daniel Webster, August 22, 1850, CP, 10:799; James B. Clay to Henry Clay, August 17, 1850, CP, 10:796; Daniel Webster to James B. Clay, November 5, 1850, Box 42, TJC Papers.

70. Daniel Webster to James B. Clay, November 5, 8, 1850, Box 42, TJC Papers. Charles M. Wiltse and Michael J. Birkner, eds., *The Papers of Daniel Webster: Correspondence (1850–52)* (Hanover, N.H.: University Press of New England, 1986), 407–8, 415; Heidler and Heidler, 479–80.

71. Heidler and Heidler, 479; Daniel Webster to the President, n.d., Box 42, TJC Papers, Library of Congress.

72. Modern psychology has discovered some evidence that children of parents who experience depression have a higher risk of developing it themselves. There is also evidence that a mutant gene deprives the brain of serotonin, a mood-balancing agent. See Douglas F. Levinson and Walter E. Nichols, "Major Depression and Genetics," Stanford Medicine website, http://depressiongenetics.stanford.edu/mddandgenes.html.

4. A Deep Acquaintance with Grief

1. M. Smith, 302.

2. Johansen, 29.

3. See Editor's Note, CP, 3:265–66.

4. Heidler and Heidler, 155; Henry Clay to Nicholas Biddle, June 11, 1823, CP, 3:429–30.

5. Henry claimed Lucretia had consumption. See Henry Clay to George W. Jones, June 1, 1823, CP, Supplement: 142–43.

6. Henry Clay to Lucretia Clay, August 24, 1825, CP, 4:589.

7. M. Smith, 286; Susan M. Clay, "An Heroic Figure of the First Half of the 19th Century," Box 55, TJC Papers.

8. Henry Clay to James Brown, April 17, 1830, CP, 8:192.

9. Susan Duralde to Henry and Lucretia Clay, August 8, 1825, CP, 4:570–71.

10. Etienne Mazureau to Henry Clay, September 19, 1825, CP, 4:658–60; George Eustis to Henry Clay, September 20, 1825, CP, 4:665–66.

11. M. Smith, 276; Henry Clay to Charlotte Mentelle, October 24, 1825, CP, 4:755–56.

12. Henry Clay to James Brown, November 14, 1825, CP, 4:822; Henry Clay to Christopher Hughes, November 1, 1825, CP, 4:784.

13. Remini, *Henry Clay*, 283.

14. Commonwealth of Kentucky v. Theodore W. Clay, Fayette County Circuit Court, File 746, Kentucky Libraries and Archives.

15. Henry Clay to Henry Clay Jr., October 31, 1830, CP, 8:2284.

16. Commonwealth of Kentucky v. Theodore W. Clay, Fayette County Circuit Court, File 746; *New York Times*, May 19, 1870.

17. Henry Clay Jr. to Henry Clay, June 23, 1830, CP, 8:227–28.

18. Ronald F. White, "Custodial Care for the Insane at Eastern State Hospital in Lexington, Kentucky, 1824–44," *Filson Club History Quarterly* 62 (July 1988): 308–22; Gerald N. Grob, *Mental Institutions in America: Social Policy to 1875* (New York: The Free Press, 1973), 377.

19. Henry Clay to John Wesley Hunt, February 13, 1832, CP, 8:462; Henry Clay to Henry Clay Jr., May 1, 1832, CP, 8:501–2.

20. Henry Clay Jr. to Henry Clay, December 14, 1833, CP, 8:675–76.

21. Henry Clay Jr. to Henry Clay, November 16, 1830, CP, 8:298; Anne Clay Erwin to Henry Clay, May 16, 1834, CP, 8:725. Interestingly, in this letter, Anne Erwin praised a speech Henry Clay Jr. made and suggested that he would be a successful politician in the future.

22. Henry Clay Jr. to Henry Clay, June 7, 1832, CP, 8:529–31.

23. Henry Clay Jr. to Henry Clay, December 14, 1833, Colton, 373–74.

24. Last Will and Testament of Henry Clay, July 10, 1851, CP, 10:900–904.

25. John A. Joyce, *A Checkered Life* (Chicago: S. P. Rounds, Jr., 1883), 41; White, 326–28; Heidler and Heidler, 234–35.

26. Interviews, Elizabeth Clay Blanford, Bill LaBach. Both Blanford and LaBach are descendants of Henry Clay. Most biographies repeat the story fashioned by the family, although Robert Remini (in *Henry Clay*) does draw a parallel with John Morrison's condition. See Heidler and Heidler, 74–75.

27. Remini, *Henry Clay*, 481; Heidler and Heidler, 269–71; Van Deusen, 273–75. The Heidler biography notes the impact on James and John. Given that Anne had served as a second mother to the two sons the family called the "little boys," her death no doubt affected them greatly.

28. M. Smith, 375–76; Remini, *Henry Clay*, 481–82.

29. Henry Clay to Henry Clay Jr., June 30, 1830, October 31, 1830, CP, 8:231, 284–85; Henry Clay to Daniel Webster, June 13, 1828, CP, 7:350.

30. Henry Clay to Lucretia Clay, November 19, 1835, CP, 8:803; see also Colton, 400–401.

31. Henry Clay to Lucretia Clay, December 9, 1835, CP, 8:805–6. Ironically, Clay expressed his anxiety to James Erwin in a letter written the very day she died. See Henry Clay to James Erwin, December 10, 1835, CP, 8:806.

32. M. Smith, 375–76.

33. Henry Clay to Lucretia Clay, December 19, 1835, CP, 8:808–9.

34. Henry Clay to Lucretia Clay, January 23, 1836, CP, 8:821; Henry Clay to Francis T. Brooke, January 1, 1836, CP, 8:813–14; Henry Clay to Thomas Speed, January 2, 1836, CP, 8:814–15.

35. Henry Clay to Octavia Walton LeVert, [n.d.—1844?], CP, 10:69–70. James F. Hopkins and the other editors of *The Papers of Henry Clay* believe the letter was written in 1844.

36. Henry Clay to George McClellan, September 24, 1846, CP, 10:280–81.

37. Henry Clay to Henry Clay Jr., March 18, April 5, 1845, CP, 10:208, 213.

38. Henry Clay to Henry Clay Jr., April 8, 27, 1845, CP, 10:215, 220.

39. Henry Clay to Lucretia Clay, July 6, 1850, CP, 10:763; Henry Clay to James B. Clay, July 18, 1850, CP, 10:767; Henry Clay to James B. Clay, January 7, 1851, CP, 10:840; Henry Clay to Lucretia Clay, February 11, March 7, 1851, CP, 10:854, 881; Henry Clay to James B. Clay, February 18, 1851, CP, 10:862.

40. Henry Clay to Lucretia Clay, February 20, March 6, April 2, 1840, CP, 9:392, 394–95, 400; Henry Clay to Thomas H. Clay, March 12, 1840, CP, 9:397–98; Henry Clay to Henry Clay Jr., February 20, 1840, CP, 9:391–92.

41. Henry Clay Jr., Diary, February 20, 1840, Henry Clay Family Papers, University of Kentucky Special Collections.

42. Mary R. Block, "'The Stoutest Son': The Mexican-American War Journal of Henry Clay Jr.," *Register of the Kentucky Historical Society* 106 (Winter 2008): 40; Henry Clay to Thomas B. Stevenson, July 23, 1847, CP, 10:341; Zachary Taylor to Henry Clay, March 1, 1847. Copy in SCS Papers.

43. Henry Clay Jr. is the only son whose remains were not interred in the family plots at the Lexington Cemetery.

44. Henry Clay, Speech to Delegations of Citizens from New York City, Trenton, New Haven, and Philadelphia, August 20, 1847, CP, 10:347; Henry Clay to William N. Mercer, April 15, 1847, CP, 10:320; Henry Clay to Robert Morris, May 12, 1847, CP, 10:328; Henry Clay to John M. Clayton, April 16, 1847, CP, 10:322.

45. Henry Clay to Henry Clay Jr., April 11, 1836, CP, 8:841; Henry Clay to Martin Duralde III and Henry Clay Duralde, September 16, 1836, CP, 8:866. See also the editor's notes in CP, 8:848; 9:89.

46. George McClellan to Henry Clay, September 17, 1846, CP, 10:279; Henry Clay to George McClellan, September 24, 1846, CP, 10:280–81; Peter Ferguson

to Henry Clay, November 17, 1846, CP, 10:291–92. Duralde was missing a diamond finger-ring and a breast pin. Ferguson suspected that he had pawned them.

47. Henry Clay to Susan Allibone, July 19, 1848, CP, 10:510–11; Henry Clay to Christopher Hughes, September 30, 1848, CP, 10:548; Henry Clay to Mary Bayard, October 19, 1848, CP, 10:553; R. J. Ward to Henry Clay Erwin, April 10, 1848, Kenner Collection; *New Orleans Picayune,* April 5, 1848; *Maysville Herald,* April 17, 1848; *Lexington Observer & Reporter,* April 12, 22, 1848.

48. H. C. Duralde to Thomas H. Clay, March 17, 1846, Kenner Collection.

49. Henry Clay Duralde to Thomas H. Clay, August 20, 1845, Kenner Collection; Henry Clay Duralde to Henry Clay, November 22, 1849, CP, 10:626–27; Henry Clay to William R. Turner, November 24, 1850, CP, 10:833; Isaac Owen to Henry Clay, September 11, 1850, CP, 10:808–9; Henry Clay to Lucretia Clay, December 26, 1850, CP, 10:836–37.

50. Henry Clay to Susan Clay, March 8, 1847, CP, 10:313; Henry Clay to Henry Hart Clay, November 22, 1847, CP, 10:378; James B. Clay to Henry Clay, November 17, 1849, CP, 10:628; Henry Clay to Reverdy Johnson, March 17, 1849, CP, 10:585–86; Henry Clay to James B. Dodd, April 2, 1849, CP, 10:586; James B. Clay to Henry Clay III, December 20, 1849, Box 42, TJC Papers; Henry Clay to James B. Clay, March 6, 1850, CP, 10:683. Zachary Taylor, who had ten appointments to West Point, did not pick Henry Clay III, so Clay secured a recommendation through Charles Morehead, a Kentucky congressman. See Henry Clay to William C. Brownlow, April 20, 1850, CP, 10:708; Henry Clay to Charles S. Morehead, December 14, 1848, CP, 10:562–63.

51. U.S. Military Academy, "Official Register of the Officers and Cadets of the United States Military Academy," 14 (1848–1857), West Point, New York; U.S. Military Academy, "Delinquencies, 1850–52," West Point, New York, 21–22, 330–31.

52. Henry Clay to Henry Clay III, September 10, 24, November 22, 1850, CP, 10:807, 818, 832–33; Henry Clay to Henry Clay III, October 26, 1851, CP, 10:927; Henry Clay to Henry Clay III, January 18, 1851, CP, 10:843.

53. Interview, Bill LaBach.

54. Henry Clay to Eugene Erwin, September 14, 1851, CP, 10:913; Henry Clay to Seargent S. Prentiss, March 31, 1848, CP, 10:422; Dallas C. Dickey, *Seargent S. Prentiss: Whig Orator of the Old South* (Baton Rouge: Louisiana State University Press, 1946), 387–89.

55. Thomas H. Clay, Diary, September 23, 1858, in the possession of Dr. William D. Kenner; Henry Clay to Eugene Erwin, September 14, 1851, CP, 10:913; Margaret Johnson Erwin to Eugene Erwin, December 6, 1850; Henry Clay Erwin to Eugene Erwin, October 26, 1853, February 8, 1854, Russell-Clay Papers, University of Kentucky Special Collections.

56. Anne Clay Erwin to Henry Clay, January 7, 1832, CP, 8:441; Henry

Clay to Lucretia Clay, May 31, 1828, CP, 9:187; Margaret Erwin to Eugene Erwin, September 27, 1857, December 8, 1851, Russell-Clay Papers, University of Kentucky Special Collections.

57. Henry Clay to Lucretia Erwin, October 27, 1849, CP, 10:625–26.

58. Ibid.

59. John Wallace, Tiffany Schneider, and Peter McGuffin, "Genetics of Depression," in *Handbook of Depression,* ed. Ian H. Gotlib and Constance L. Hammen (New York: Guilford, 2002), 169–88.

60. Remini, *Henry Clay,* 201; Heidler and Heidler, 479–80.

5. Going It Alone

1. Van Deusen, 423.

2. Howe, *Political Culture of the American Whigs,* 137.

3. Peterson, 6.

4. The American delegation consisted of five highly individualistic men from broadly different backgrounds. President Madison appointed John Quincy Adams, the minister to Russia, to head the delegation, largely because the czar had offered to mediate the dispute. Albert Gallatin, Swiss by birth, provided a thorough knowledge of European manners and culture. Clay was chosen partially as a balance for the pro-British James Bayard. Madison named the fifth delegate, Jonathan Russell, when he thought the negotiations would be held in Sweden. He intended to name Russell the ambassador to Sweden.

5. Nagel, *Descent from Glory,* 42–43, 53–54.

6. Adams, 2:657–58, 3:32, 39; Van Deusen, 100; Remini, *Henry Clay,* 109. In an interview with the author, Elizabeth Clay Blanford, a great-granddaughter of Clay, asked with a southern sense of humor why it was more appropriate to rise at 4:00 a.m. than to go to bed at that hour. However, she took the matter very seriously. Living in Gloucester, Massachusetts, she drove to the Boston Public Library to find a particular passage in Adams's memoirs, then sent it to me. The passage concerns a card game in which John Quincy Adams participated. He admitted that "Mr. Clay won from me at a game of all-fours the picture of an old woman that I had drawn as a prize in the lottery." She was extremely proud of her history sleuthing. See Adams, 3:30–31.

7. Adams, 3:101–2; interview, Elizabeth Clay Blanford.

8. Bradford Perkins, *Castlereagh and Adams: England and the United States 1812–1823* (Berkeley: University of California Press, 1964), 63.

9. Remini, *Henry Clay,* 106–7; Perkins, 60–61.

10. Remini, *Henry Clay,* 134.

11. Howe, *Political Culture of the American Whigs,* 120.

12. Ibid., 125.

13. Scaevola (Henry Clay), To the Electors of Fayette County, April 16, 1798, CP, 1:6–7; Van Deusen, 20; Remini, *Henry Clay*, 27. See also Harold D. Tallant, *Evil Necessity: Slavery and Political Culture in Antebellum Kentucky* (Lexington: University Press of Kentucky, 2003), 2–3.

14. An example can be found at http://dbs.ohiohistory.org. Citing the *Cleveland Gazette*, June 27, 1891, it tells the story of an old woman of New Orleans who claimed to have been Henry Clay's mistress. See Remini, *Henry Clay*, 670. Henry Clay to Sydney Howard Gay, December 1, 22, 1847, CP, 10:383–84, 391–92.

15. Remini, *Henry Clay*, 618.

16. Susan M. Clay, "Henry Clay and His Slanderers," TJC Papers. Clay did not free Aaron Dupuy. He believed him too old to care for himself. Charles and Mary Ann left later, but Charlotte remained until after Mrs. Clay's death in 1864.

17. Further evidence of Clay's inconsistency on the issue can be seen in his sale of Lottie's grandson. In 1833 Lottie's daughter, Mary Ann Dupuy, had a son, whom she named Henry. In 1848 Clay abruptly sold him. The fifteen-year-old boy was described as a mulatto, but no reason for his sale was given. See advertisement and sale record dated June 7, 1848, and August 31, 1849, Henry Clay Papers, Transylvania University. As late as the 1990s, at least one family member, Elizabeth Clay Blanford, still referred to "Uncle" Aaron and told warm, engaging stories about him and about Mammy Lottie as if they were family members. She had heard those stories growing up, listening to relatives who had known Lottie when they were children. Interview, Elizabeth Clay Blanford.

18. Remini, *Henry Clay*, 186; Van Deusen, 148.

19. Peterson, 56.

20. Quoted in Remini, *Henry Clay*, 1.

21. Peterson, 225; Van Deusen, 249, 269; Remini, *Henry Clay*, 414.

22. Susan M. Clay, "Henry Clay and His Slanderers," TJC Papers; Remini, *Henry Clay*, 420; Van Deusen, 269; Howe, *Political Culture of the American Whigs*, 139; Henry Clay to Peter B. Porter, February 16, 1833, CP, 8:624.

23. Henry Clay, Speech in Senate, July 22, 1850, CP, 10:782–83; Henry Clay, Remarks in Senate, July 25, 1850, CP, 10:785; Henry Clay to James B. Clay, May 9, 1851, CP, 10:889; Henry Clay to Lucretia Clay, December 18, 1851, CP, 10:938; Thomas M. Daniel, *Captain of Death: The Story of Tuberculosis* (Rochester, N.Y.: University of Rochester Press, 1997), 104, 109. Daniel says physicians frequently refused to call the illness by its name for fear of the psychological impact on the patient. In Clay's case, the Washington physicians claimed his illness was bronchitis. Remini (in *Henry Clay*) says it is uncertain exactly when Clay became tubercular. He had, of course, been subject to numerous nagging illnesses throughout his life. The immune systems in the Clay family were practically nonexistent. However, the bacteria that cause tuberculosis can remain dormant in the body for years. Eleanor Roosevelt, for example, probably contracted the disease as a young

woman while working as a volunteer in a New York City settlement house. She recovered from an early attack and remained free of the disease until the last two years of her life. She died at age seventy-three. See Daniel, 2; Irwin W. Sherman, *The Power of Plagues* (Washington, D.C.: ASM Press, 2006), 274–76; Frank Ryan, *The Forgotten Plague: How the Battle against Tuberculosis Was Won—and Lost* (Boston: Little, Brown, 1992), 4–9.

24. Henry Clay, Comments in the Senate, February 14, 1850, CP, 10:675; Van Deusen, 400; Remini, *Henry Clay*, 739–40.

25. Thomas kept a daily stream of letters flowing toward Lexington with news of Henry's condition. Thomas H. Clay to Mary Clay, May 24, 1852, THC Papers. See also letters of June 16, 18, 19, and 20, 1852, in the same collection.

26. The senators were Joseph R. Underwood of Kentucky, Joseph C. Jones of Tennessee, Robert F. Stockton of New Jersey, Hamilton Fish of New York, Lewis Cass of Michigan, and Sam Houston of Texas. See J. Winston Coleman Jr., *Last Days, Death and Funeral of Henry Clay* (Lexington, Ky.: Winburn, 1951), 8.

27. See U.S. Military Academy, "Official Register of the Officers and Cadets of the United States Military Academy," 14 (1848–1857); U.S. Military Academy, "Delinquencies, 1850–52," 21–22, 330–31.

28. Coleman, 9–12; Remini, *Henry Clay*, 784–85.

29. Henry Clay to Henry Clay, "My Dear Little Namesake," July 7, 1845, CP, 10:230–31. The recipient of this letter is difficult to determine, though it probably went to Henry Hart Clay, who was often called Henry Clay III. Henry's sons and daughters all named a son after him. They were Henry (Harry) Boyle Clay, Henry Clay Duralde, Henry Clay Erwin, Henry Hart Clay, and Henry Independence Clay. Harry Boyle Clay was five years old in 1845, and Henry Hart Clay was twelve years old.

30. James B. Clay to J. O. Harrison, July 19, 1852, Box 40, TJC Papers.

31. Henry Clay to John Morrison Clay, March 13, 1852, CP, 10:958.

32. Henry Clay to James B. Clay, February 18, 1851, CP, 10:862. James may have been correct. Lucretia gave John large sums of money to help build his house in the years after Henry's death. See Ledger Books, J. O. Harrison Papers, Library of Congress.

33. Last Will and Testament of Henry Clay, July 10, 1851, CP, 10:901–2.

34. Henry Clay to Lucretia Clay, January 12, [1852], CP, 10:947; Henry Clay to John M. Clay, April 20, 1852, CP, 10:966–67.

35. Henry Clay to James Clay, May 9, 1851, Colton, 616–17; Henry Clay to James Brown Clay, October 27, 1850, CP, 10:824; James Brown Clay to Henry Clay, November 15, 1850, CP, 10:827–28; Henry Clay to Susan Jacob Clay, November 21, 1850, CP, 10:832.

36. Thomas P. Jacob to James B. Clay, September 24, 1852, Box 42, TJC Papers.

37. James Brown Clay to Henry Clay, November 15, 1850, CP, 10:827–28; Mary Mentelle Clay to Susan J. Clay, May 5, 1850, Box 42, TJC Papers.

38. James B. Clay to J. O. Harrison, July 19, 1852, Box 40, TJC Papers; J. O. Harrison to James B. Clay, September 12, 25, 1852, Box 42, TJC Papers; J. O. Harrison to James B. Clay, February 10, 1853, Box 42, TJC Papers; James B. Clay to J. O. Harrison, July 19, 1852, Box 40, TJC Papers; James B. Clay to J. O. Harrison, September 6, 1852, J. O. Harrison Papers, Library of Congress.

39. James B. Clay to J. O. Harrison, July 19, 1852, Box 40, TJC Papers. Tates Creek lends its name today to a high school and a section of the city of Lexington. John's home, however, was demolished to make way for a housing development.

40. Telegraph, Thomas H. Clay to James B. Clay, June 29, 1852, Box 42, TJC Papers.

41. J. O. Harrison to James B. Clay, November 12, 15, 1852, Box 42, TJC Papers.

42. George W. Anderson to Thomas H. Clay, August 18, 1851 (emphasis original); Thomas Stevenson to Thomas H. Clay, [n.d.]; Millard Fillmore to Thomas Clay, August 4, 1856, Henrietta Clay Papers, Transylvania University.

43. James B. Clay to J. O. Harrison, September 6, October 9, 1852, J. O. Harrison Papers, Library of Congress.

44. James B. Clay to J. O. Harrison, July 19, 1852, Box 40, TJC Papers; J. O. Harrison to James B. Clay, November 15, 1852, Box 42, TJC Papers.

45. Thomas H. Clay to James B. Clay, March 16, 1853, Box 42, TJC Papers.

46. James B. Clay to Thomas H. Clay, March 16, 1853, Box 42, TJC Papers; Thomas H. Clay to James B. Clay, March 16, 1853, Box 42, TJC Papers; James B. Clay to Thomas H. Clay, March 16, 1853, Box 42, TJC Papers; *Kentucky Statesman,* September 23, 1853, 3.

47. J. Rogers, 54.

48. Henry Clay McDowell to Houghton Mifflin Company, March 2, 1898, Letterbook, 330, HCMF Papers; interview, Elizabeth Clay Blanford.

49. Henry Belter created furniture that became extremely popular across the country. Central Kentuckians of the 1850s flocked to New York to purchase his pieces.

50. Henry Clay to Mary S. Bayard, April 16, 1847, CP, 10:321. Ironically, critics generally claim that Henry Jr. and James built fortunes on the money of their wives. Henry Jr. left three children, Henry Hart, Thomas Julian, and Anne. The two sons died in the Civil War, and Anne would take a sizable fortune into her marriage to Henry Clay McDowell.

51. Henry Clay to James B. Clay, February 24, 1852, CP, 10:955; Note, May 27, 1856, Box 54, TJC Papers; Catalogue of Sale, September 14, 1857, Box 54, TJC Papers.

52. John Hervey, *The American Trotter* (New York: Coward-McCann, 1947), 194–95.

53. Meyer, 488.

54. Meyer, 487; Hervey, *American Trotter,* 194–97.

55. See Loan Agreement, June 30, 1860, and Articles of Incorporation, Kentucky River Navigation Company, both in Box 54, TJC Papers.

56. The Thomas J. Clay Papers contain newspaper clippings, cancelled checks, and receipts that illustrate the breadth of interests James and Susan had. See also Auction Plot, S. G. Henry and Co., May 9, 1857; Agreement with E. Katherine Jacob, July 21, 1857, Box 54, TJC Papers.

57. See Bank Books, Box 54, TJC Papers; Financial Book, J. O. Harrison Papers, Library of Congress.

58. See bills of sale and expense log, August 16, September 18, 21, November 5, 18, 1858, July 2, 1859, Box 54, TJC Papers. James B. Clay to J. O. Harrison, October 9, 1852, J. O. Harrison Papers, Library of Congress.

59. Thomas H. Clay, Diary, in the possession of Dr. William D. Kenner.

60. Henry Clay to Thomas Clay, January 18, 1850, Colton, 598; James B. Clay to J. O. Harrison, July 19, 1852; J. O. Harrison to James B. Clay, July 28, 1852, Box 42; J. O. Harrison to James B. Clay, February 10, 1853, Box 40, TJC Papers.

61. Edward Everett to James B. Clay, May 7, 1856, Box 43, TJC Papers; James B. Clay, Memoir, December 14, 1862, Box 44, TJC Papers.

62. Thomas H. Clay, Diary.

63. James B. Clay, Memoir, December 14, 1862, Box 44, TJC Papers; James Clay to Tom Monroe, April 1857, Box 43, TJC Papers. Monroe was the editor of the *Kentucky Statesman.*

64. H. C. Erwin to James Clay, February 8, 1848, Box 44, TJC Papers; D. Provence to Lt. Col. Eugene Erwin, August 18, 1862, Russell-Clay Papers, University of Kentucky Special Collections; George L. Prentiss, ed., *A Memoir of S. S. Prentiss,* 2 vols. (New York: Charles Scribner, 1858), 2:435–44.

65. E. M. Bruce to J. C. Breckinridge, September 14, 1856, Box 43, TJC Papers. Boxes 43 and 61, TJC Papers, contain newspaper clippings critical of James Clay.

66. Newspaper clipping, *Louisville Courier,* September 22, [n.d.], Box 61, TJC Papers.

67. James Clay became involved in two additional altercations that led to challenges. In 1856 an outburst of temper led him to make statements about the American Party platform that offended William H. Russell, a guest in his home. Russell let the matter drop when Clay apologized. See James B. Clay to Col. William H. Russell, June 23, 1856, Box 43, TJC Papers. Two years later a remark to General William Cullum in the bar at the Louisville Brown Hotel led to an exchange of blows between the two men. Cullum issued a challenge. A duel was avoided when a committee found that Cullum had acted under a mistaken inter-

pretation and should apologize to Clay. Cullum agreed, but the affair received national news coverage. See the challenge and the reply, February 18, 1858, and Memorandum of John Mason and Thomas Hawkins, February 20, 1858, Box 44, TJC Papers. There are also numerous press clippings in the Thomas J. Clay Papers.

68. James B. Clay, Memoir, December 14, 1862; James B. Clay, Speech to His Constituents, and newspaper clippings, Box 44, TJC Papers.

69. See Box 43, TJC Papers, for speaking engagements; *Philadelphia Daily Pennsylvanian*, September 11, 1856. On the subject of the Democrats using James Clay, see John Richardson to James Clay, July 31, 1856, Box 43, TJC Papers.

70. James Buchanan to James B. Clay, March 7, 1857, Box 43, TJC Papers; James B. Clay to James Buchanan, March 12, 1857, Box 43, TJC Papers.

71. Thomas B. Stevenson to Clay, March 13, 1857, Box 43, TJC Papers; Box 43 also contains letters requesting his support with the Buchanan administration. Thomas B. Stevenson to James B. Clay, May 13, 1857, Box 43, TJC Papers. See also Thomas to Mary Clay, May 26, 1852, June 1, 1852, THC Papers.

72. Thomas H. Clay to George W. Anderson, February 4, 1856, Anderson Family Papers, Box 1, University of Kentucky Special Collections; Thomas H. Clay, Diary.

73. James Clay to Thomas Clay, March [n.d.], 1856, Box 43, TJC Papers.

74. Thomas H. Clay, Diary, July 4, 1858.

6. Civil War, Family Struggles

1. James B. Clay to Thomas P. Jacob, October 31, 1860, SCS Papers; Eugene Erwin to Josephine Erwin, May 14, 25, 1861, Russell-Clay Papers, University of Kentucky Special Collections.

2. John Fox Jr., *The Little Shepherd of Kingdom Come* (New York: Charles Scribner's Sons, 1903), 234–35. See also Amy Murrell Taylor, *The Divided Family in Civil War America* (Chapel Hill: University of North Carolina Press, 2005).

3. H. Levin, ed., *The Lawyers and Lawmakers of Kentucky* (Chicago: Lewis, n.d.), 432; "Thomas H. Clay Jr. Obituary," *Lexington Morning Herald*, April 9, 1907, 1. Simon Bolivar Buckner (1823–1914) reorganized the Kentucky State Guard as war neared. Refusing a commission as a brigadier general from Abraham Lincoln, he entered the Confederate army at the same rank in 1861.

4. Memorandum, October 18, 1861; Abraham Lincoln to General Meigs, Quartermaster Corps, October 15, 1861; Abraham Lincoln to Simon Cameron, Secretary of War, October 21, 1861, in Basler, 5:555, 557.

5. James B. Clay to Thomas H. Clay, April 6, 1861, Box 45, TJC Papers; United States v. James B. Clay, September 30, 1861, Box 54, TJC Papers; Edward F. Underhill to the Secretary of State, U.S. War Department, *The War*

of the Rebellion: A Compilation of the Official Records of the Union and Confederate Armies (Washington, D.C.: Government Printing Office, 1880–1901) (hereafter cited as OR), ser. 2, 2:733–34.

6. Interview, Elizabeth Clay Blanford. Such praise by a president of the United States later became part of the extended family's sense of contribution.

7. For treaties, see George P. Sanger, ed., *U.S. Statutes at Large, Treaties and Proclamations of the United States of America from December 1863 to December 1865* (Boston: Little, Brown, 1866), 699–710.

8. A. Lincoln to John M. Clay, Letter Book of Mrs. John M. Clay, University of Kentucky Special Collections; see also Basler, 5:363–64.

9. Interview, Elizabeth Clay Blanford. Skedaddle was out of Magnolia and sired by Yorkshire. Day Star, a Kentucky Derby winner that John bred, came from Skedaddle's offspring. See Meyer, 482.

10. Interview, Elizabeth Clay Blanford.

11. John M. Clay to Josephine Russell Erwin, December 27, 1863, Josephine Clay Collection, University of Kentucky Special Collections. Mrs. Louisiana Simpson allowed me to see the correspondence in her possession. In 2007 Henry Clay Simpson placed the papers at the University of Kentucky.

12. Maj. W. A. Coffee to Gen. G. H. Thomas, September 25, 1861; William Seward, Secretary of State, to Gen. Robert Anderson, September 28, 1861; Robert Anderson to William Seward, September 29, 1861; Robert Anderson to Commanding Officer, Department of the Cumberland, October 1, 1861, OR, ser. 1, 2:884–92; "Arrest of James B. Clay," *New York Times*, September 28, 1861.

13. Interview, Elizabeth Clay Blanford. Indeed, the James Clay branch of the family recalled the incident for several generations to justify their pro-South feelings.

14. Interview, Elizabeth Clay Blanford. Mrs. Blanford spoke very emotionally about the treatment of James and Susan during the Civil War. The James Clay branch of the family continued to feel that Lexington's gentry took too much pleasure in the family's difficulties. Her sister Susan refused to move back to Lexington because of it.

15. James B. Clay, Memoir, December 16, 1862, Box 54, TJC Papers.

16. Memorandum, August 28, 1863, Box 54, TJC Papers.

17. G. T. Beauregard to C. J. Villere, February 9, 1863, OR, ser 4, 2:391.

18. At least three grandsons died of tuberculosis or something like it before the Civil War. Martin Duralde died in 1846, Henry Clay Erwin in 1859, and Charles Edward Erwin in 1860. Additionally, Eugene Erwin was suffering from tuberculosis when fatally wounded at Vicksburg in 1863.

19. See fragments in Box 60, TJC Papers. The fragment in question is certainly in the hand of his daughter Lucretia "Teetee" Clay.

20. See Resolution, newspaper clippings, Box 61, TJC Papers; James B. Clay

to James O. Harrison Jr., November 12, 1863, Sarah Agnes Wallace, "Confederate Exiles in Canada: Last Letters of James Brown Clay, 1864, Montreal," *Register of the Kentucky Historical Society* 50 (January 1952): 50–51.

21. Teetee Clay's copies of the letters to Jacob are in Box 57, TJC Papers. There are many examples in the papers of Teetee destroying and copying letters, crossing out sections, and tearing away portions that offended her. More will be said later about the purging of the Clay papers.

22. Susan M. Clay to "My Dear Boys," July 21, 1856, Box 43, TJC Papers. There are other letters to and from both parents in Box 43.

23. Susan M. Clay to Lucy Jacob, January 17, 1857, Box 42, TJC Papers. There are more than twenty letters to James Jr., Harry, Lucy, and Lucretia in the TJC Papers and the SCS Papers.

24. Susan Clay to Gen. Gordon Granger, [n.d.]; Gen. Gordon Granger to Susan Clay, [n.d.], Box 44, TJC Papers.

25. Interview, Elizabeth Clay Blanford.

26. Susan M. Clay to Thomas P. Jacob, August 30, 1863, James B. Clay to James B. Clay Jr., September 9, 1863, S. Wallace, 41–56.

27. Susan Clay to James Clay, March 12, 1863, Box 45, TJC Papers.

28. James Clay to Susan Clay, March 24, 1863, Box 45, TJC Papers.

29. Susan Clay to Thomas J. Clay, March 31, 1863, Box 45, TJC Papers.

30. James B. Clay to Susan M. Clay, March 25, 1863, Susan M. Clay to James B. Clay, June 25, September 3, 1863, Box 45, TJC Papers; Thomas P. Jacob to Susan M. Clay, March 3, 1863, Box 45, TJC Papers; Susan M. Clay to James Clay Jr., October 27, 1863, S. Wallace, 49. Mary Clay rented Thomas's farm, Mansfield, to Mrs. John Todhunter for $500 per year.

31. Susan Clay to Kate Jacob Jones, March 24, 1863, Box 45, TJC Papers; Lucretia Hart Clay, "James B. Clay," Box 57, TJC Papers. Susan left a series of notes regarding the renting of Ashland and the plans for her trip. See Box 56, TJC Papers.

32. Col. J. H. Wilson to Gen. John Rawlins, OR, ser. 1, 49:379. Interview, Elizabeth Clay Blanford. Lucretia Clay, "James Clay, Jr.," an unpublished biographical sketch, Box 42, TJC Papers.

33. Interview, Elizabeth Clay Blanford; James B. Clay Jr. to Susan Clay, October 16, 1864, Box 45, TJC Papers; James B. Clay Jr. to Thomas J. Clay, July 30, 1877, Box 46, TJC Papers.

34. H. Simpson, 6.

35. Eugene Erwin to Josephine Russell Erwin, May 14, 25, 1861, Russell-Clay Papers, University of Kentucky Special Collections.

36. Eugene Erwin to Josephine Erwin, May 14, 1861, Russell-Clay Papers; Kent Masterson Brown, "The Colonel and His Lady: Colonel Eugene Erwin and His Wife Josephine," *Filson Club History Quarterly* 75 (April 2001): 213.

37. Undated note, Russell-Clay Papers.

38. Eugene Erwin had some military training. Henry Clay had sent several of his grandsons, including Eugene, to the Kentucky Military Institute in Frankfort, Kentucky. See CP, 10:377.

39. K. Brown, 221.

40. Eugene Erwin to Josephine Erwin, February 8, 1863, Russell-Clay Papers.

41. K. Brown, 224–25.

42. The passes are dated July 18, 1863. Josephine Clay Collection, University of Kentucky Special Collections. See also H. Simpson, 120n18.

43. Memorandum, August 28, 1863, Box 54, TJC Papers; Fayette County Will Book #13, January 1865–May 1867, 298, Lexington-Fayette County (Ky.) Archives.

44. Thomas Julian Clay to Anne Clay, [n.d.], HCMF Papers. Thomas's letters are in the HCMF Papers. Some accounts have claimed that Thomas Hart Clay fought for the Confederacy. The error probably results from the fact that both Thomas H. and Thomas J. Clay began their military careers in Simon Buckner's command and both reached the rank of captain. Thomas H. Clay left the command, however, when Buckner led it into the rebel army.

45. Henry Clay III to Anne Clay McDowell, October 28, December 2, 1861, HCMF Papers.

46. Simon Bolivar Buckner, General Orders #115, December 23, 1862, OR, ser. 1, 15:905.

47. Thomas Julian Clay to Anne Clay McDowell, March 3, 1862, HCMF Papers.

48. Henry Clay McDowell to Anne Clay McDowell, March 7, 27, 1862, HCMF Papers.

49. Edwin Stanton to the Governor of Ohio, April 19, 1862, OR, ser. 2, 3:465; General Orders #118, August 27, 1862, OR, ser. 2, 4:446.

50. Edwin Stanton to the Governor of Ohio, April 19, 1862, OR, ser. 2, 3:465; General Orders #118, August 27, 1862, ser. 2, 4:446; James B. Clay Jr. to Anne Clay McDowell, October 13, 1863, HCMF Papers.

7. A New Image

1. Harry Boyle Clay to H. C. McDowell, August 7, 1865, HCMF Papers. The legacy of death was inescapable in the American South. See Drew Gilpin Faust, *This Republic of Suffering: Death and the American Civil War* (New York: Knopf, 2008).

2. W. Fitzhugh Brundage, *The Southern Past: A Clash of Race and Memory* (Cambridge, Mass.: Belknap Press of Harvard University Press, 2005), 9.

3. Paul M. Gaston, *The New South Creed: A Study in Southern Mythmaking* (New York: Knopf, 1970), 9; Wyatt-Brown describes legends in a similar fashion. Legends provide a means to repress events and thoughts that a family, or a region, do not wish to explore. See *House of Percy*, 88; see also Brundage, *Southern Past*, 1–11.

4. Thomas L. Connelly, *The Marble Man: Robert E. Lee and His Image in American Society* (Baton Rouge: Louisiana State University Press, 1977), 47; David Anderson, "Down Memory Lane: Nostalgia for the Old South in Post-Civil War Plantation Reminiscences," *Journal of Southern History* 71 (February 2005): 108–9, 135; Christopher Waldrep, "Memory, History, and the Meaning of the Civil War—a Review Essay," *Register of the Kentucky Historical Society* 102 (Summer 2004): 383–402.

5. There are many studies of the Lost Cause. See Gaston, *The New South Creed*; David Goldfield, *Still Fighting the Civil War: The American South and Southern History* (Baton Rouge: Louisiana State University Press, 2002); Gaines M. Foster, *Ghosts of the Confederacy: Defeat, the Lost Cause, and the Emergence of the New South* (New York: Oxford University Press, 1987); Gary W. Gallagher and Alan T. Nolan, eds., *The Myth of the Lost Cause and Civil War History* (Bloomington: Indiana University Press, 2000); David W. Blight, *Race and Reunion: The Civil War in Modern Memory* (Cambridge, Mass.: Harvard University Press, 2001); Laura F. Edwards, "Southern History as U.S. History," *Journal of Southern History* 75 (August 2009): 533–64; Craig Thompson Friend, ed., *Southern Masculinity: Perspectives on Manhood in the South since Reconstruction* (Athens: University of Georgia Press, 2009), xi–xii.

6. Goldfield, 3.

7. See Connelly, *The Marble Man*. The image the family created for Henry Clay and that which the South constructed for Robert E. Lee share much in content and in the causes of their creation.

8. Brundage, "Contentious and Collected," 751–54; David W. Blight notes that "twisted history" had become a "commodity" by the early twentieth century; Blight, 391.

9. Susan M. Clay, Notebook, Box 58, TJC Papers.

10. Connelly, 38; Drew Gilpin Faust, *Mothers of Invention: Women in the Slaveholding South in the American Civil War* (Chapel Hill: University of North Carolina Press, 1996), 251–54. Like members of the Ladies' Memorial Associations described by Caroline E. Janney, it is primarily Susan Clay and other Clay women who are responsible for the Clay family memory. The men of the family had virtually nothing to do with constructing the new image of Henry Clay until the late nineteenth century. See Caroline E. Janney, *Burying the Dead but Not the Past: Ladies' Memorial Associations and the Lost Cause* (Chapel Hill: University of North Carolina Press, 2008), 112–27; William A. Blair, *Cities of the Dead: Contesting the Memory of the Civil War in the South* (Chapel Hill: University of North Carolina Press, 2004), 85.

11. Interview, Elizabeth Clay Blanford. Local legend suggests that elements of the family forced her to sell the estate so they could have their inheritances after the death of Lucretia. Limited evidence to that effect appears in the family papers. Given the tendency to destroy records that might embarrass the family, absence of such evidence is not surprising.

12. Interview, Elizabeth Clay Blanford.

13. Interview, Elizabeth Clay Blanford. Margaret Ripley Wolfe notes the dual role of southern women in *The Daughters of Canaan: A Saga of Southern Women* (Lexington: University Press of Kentucky, 1995), 6–9; Wyatt-Brown, *House of Percy*, 9.

14. Susan M. Clay to Charles D. Clay, December 24, 1901, SCS Papers; Steven Mintz, *Huck's Raft: A History of American Childhood* (Cambridge, Mass.: Belknap Press of Harvard University Press, 2004), 120.

15. Wyatt-Brown, *Southern Honor*, 120–21.

16. Ibid., 120–25, 132. Stone, *Black Sheep and Kissing Cousins*, 7. That was particularly true in Kentucky. Elizabeth Murphey Simpson suggests in *The Enchanted Bluegrass* (Lexington, Ky.: Transylvania Press, 1938) that perhaps Kentuckians were so concerned about pedigree because of the importance of the horse to the region.

17. That did not keep the Clays, Susan included, from destroying items that might be misleading or could be used by those wishing to criticize family members. More will be said later about that family "value."

18. Susan Clay's biography, "Henry Clay and His Slanderers," was never published, but the manuscript is available at the Library of Congress. Thomas H. Clay Jr.'s biography was completed by Ellis Paxton Oberholtzer. A new generation of descendants has added more-reasoned studies of Henry Clay and the family. Henry Clay Simpson has published a small book on Josephine Clay. His branch of the family has also placed a large collection of family papers in the University of Kentucky. Bill LaBach has carefully researched the family genealogy and landownership in Central Kentucky. Ned Boyajian of the James Clay branch has, through laborious research efforts, discovered information that answers nagging questions. And Dr. William D. Kenner, a descendant of the Tennessee Clays, has opened family papers to scholars, shared his own expertise, and cooperated with Ashland to help create a more accurate history of Henry Clay and his descendants. Goldfield, 113.

19. Susan M. Clay, "Henry Clay and His Slanderers," Box 55, TJC Papers.

20. Susan M. Clay to Harry Clay, August 17, 1872, Box 45, TJC Papers.

21. Susan M. Clay, "Henry Clay and His Slanderers," Box 55, TJC Papers; Heidler and Heidler, 179–80.

22. Susan M. Clay, "Henry Clay and His Slanderers," Box 55, TJC Papers.

23. Madeline McDowell, "Recollections of Henry Clay," *Century Magazine*, September 1895, 765.

24. Van Deusen, 6; Remini, *Henry Clay*, 1; Rogers, 21; Heidler and Heidler,

3; Karen J. Blair, *The Torchbearers: Women and Their Amateur Arts Associations in America, 1890–1930* (Bloomington: Indiana University Press, 1994), 2; see Charles Lachman, *The Last Lincolns: The Rise and Fall of a Great American Family* (New York: Union Square Press, 2008).

25. Interview, Robert Clay. A careful genealogist, Robert Clay spent his career in the state archives of Virginia. He is a descendant of a different branch of Clays but a respected authority on the family's genealogy. Z. Smith and Clay, 10–11. Henry's brother, Porter Clay, and Cassius M. Clay, the noted abolitionist, made similar claims long before Susan. Other members of the family told similar stories. See Henrietta Clay, "Bits of Family History, a Paper Read before the John Bradford Club, December 8, 1932," Ashland Collection. Mrs. Minor Simpson, "A Few Memories and a Bit of History," University of Kentucky Special Collections. The Ashland Collection contains newspaper clippings written by Lucretia Clay Simpson and Henrietta Clay. Family members Bill LaBach and Ned Boyajian have conducted useful research on family origins. It is known that Henry Clay wrote a letter of introduction to a member of the British Parliament whom he considered a kinsman.

26. Clay Family Society, Minutes, June 2006. This study is ongoing.

27. Susan M. Clay, "Henry Clay and His Slanderers," Box 55, TJC Papers. See particularly the chapter noted. T. H. Clay Jr., *Henry Clay*, 414.

28. When one of Susan's sons decided to join an expedition to the Arctic, Susan used essays and notes she had saved to prepare fourteen treatises, or sermons, hoping to convince him to be baptized before his trip. See SCS Papers.

29. T. H. Clay Jr., *Henry Clay*, 410–12. On March 30, 1826, John Randolph attacked John Quincy Adams and Henry Clay on the floor of the Senate. It was one in a long line of insults by the eccentric and effeminate senator from Virginia, but it was so pointed that it demanded a challenge. Using literary characters from Henry Fielding's novel *Tom Jones*, Randolph declared Adams and Clay a coalition of Blifil and Black George. Blifil was an overly pious but greedy man, and Black George was a cheat. Clay should have ignored the attack, but losing his temper, he issued a challenge. The men exchanged shots twice. Randolph fired low and then into the air. Honor defended, Clay proclaimed concern that Randolph might be hurt. Randolph responded that Clay owed him a coat because a bullet had torn it. Despite the camaraderie after the fact, the duel hurt Clay politically. Clay and Randolph were generally at odds. When they passed one another on a muddy Washington street, Randolph refused to step off the dry path, saying, "I never step aside for a skunk." Clay quickly jumped aside and said, "I always do." See Remini, 293–95; Heidler and Heidler, 196–99.

30. Elizabeth Clay Blanford told the story of Lizzie Thomas, the daughter of a Presbyterian minister in Frankfort, Kentucky, in the 1890s. The elderly ladies of "the Square," Frankfort's most prominent residential area, all widows or never married, were sitting together at the home of Mrs. Blanford's grandmother,

Elizabeth Pepper. They had been to a funeral and were discussing their own. Miss Thomas, who had remained at home to care for her parents, stated emphatically that when she died she did not want "Rest in Peace" carved on her tombstone. She had rested in peace all her life, she said, and she wanted a decided change. Though it was told as humor, both Mrs. Blanford and her sister recognized the sense of duty and sacrifice involved in the story.

31. McDowell, 765–66.

32. Interview, Elizabeth Clay Blanford.

33. Edward L. Ayres, *The Promise of the New South: Life after Reconstruction* (New York: Oxford University Press, 1993), 21.

34. Clay freed Lottie and her children, Mary Ann and Charles. He believed Aaron too old to take care of himself, so he was not freed.

35. Teetee Clay, untitled piece, TJC Papers.

36. See HCMF Papers.

37. Harry Clay, "The Civil Rights Act," SCS Papers.

38. Susan Clay, "Slavery in Politics: A Plea for the Negro," Box 56, TJC Papers.

39. Howe, *Political Culture of the American Whigs,* 120.

40. See SCS Papers.

41. Edwards, 533–34.

8. Legacy of Family

1. See HCMF Papers.

2. Harry B. Clay to H. C. McDowell, August 7, 1868, HCMF Papers. Harry Clay sent McDowell a blank check for expenses. McDowell did not cash the check, and it remains in the family papers.

3. Harry Boyle Clay to H. C. McDowell, August 7, 1865, HCMF Papers; Harry Boyle Clay to H. C. McDowell, August 22, October 6, 1865, HCMF Papers; Henry Clay McDowell Jr. to Anne Clay McDowell, March 4, 1888, HCMF Papers. Henry Clay McDowell to His Excellency, the President of the United States, August 21, 1899, Letterbook, 289, HCMF Papers; John W. Yerkes to H. C. McDowell, 1899, HCMF Papers. Lexington's elite, always prone to gossip, called the marriage of Henry Clay McDowell Jr. and Elsie Clay incestuous. In fact, McDowell's mother and Clay's father were grandchildren of Henry Clay from different branches. It was a legally and socially acceptable marriage then as it would be now.

4. H. Simpson, 62. See also John M. Clay to Josephine Erwin, August 25, 1864, Josephine Clay Collection, University of Kentucky Special Collections.

5. Teetee Clay to Charley Clay, February 9, 1871, SCS Papers; John M. Clay, Diary, University of Kentucky Special Collections.

6. Wolfe, *Daughters of Canaan,* 108.

7. W. C. P. Breckinridge tried to pit the James Clays and the McDowells against one another to raise the price for the university. McDowell would have none of it. Susan and her children wanted Ashland, but for once, economic reality overcame emotional attachment. Only then did McDowell make an offer for the property. Susan M. Clay to Harry and Charley (Clay), April 29, 1882, TJC Papers.

8. The McDowell papers in the HCMF Papers contain numerous references to these interfamily visits. For example, see Anne Clay McDowell to Madge, April 12, 26, 1891; Magdalen McDowell to Madge, April 19, 1891, HCMF Papers.

9. *Lexington Leader,* July 29, 1894, 5.

10. John M. Clay, Diary, University of Kentucky Special Collections.

11. Colonel Dick Redd was a frequent visitor to the Clay homes, arriving on a spirited horse and sitting for hours with George, Charles, and Tom Clay, spinning tales of Confederate valor and gallantry. Redd was concerned that the youth would forget, so he occasionally rode to the university campus, causing his horse to rear and familiarizing the students with an authentic Rebel yell. Interviews, Elizabeth Clay Blanford, Woodridge Spears.

12. James B. Clay to James B. Clay Jr., March 11, 1858, SCS Papers; Susan M. Clay to President U. S. Grant, September 9, 1876, U.S. National Archives, Records of the Adjutant General's Office, Group 94; Susan M. Clay to President Rutherford B. Hayes, December 15, 1877 (copy), SCS Papers; Susan M. Clay to J. W. Stevenson, April 5, 1876, July 6, 1877, Box 46, TJC Papers.

13. Susan M. Clay to Harry Clay, August 17, 1872, Box 45, TJC Papers; Susan M. Clay to James Clay Jr., February 24, 1865, Box 57, TJC Papers; Henry Clay McDowell Sr. to Anne Clay McDowell, July 30, 1882, HCMF Papers; Harry Clay to Susan M. Clay, August 25, 1873, Box 46, TJC Papers. The importance of Clay blood was evident in other branches of the Clay family. Cassius Marcellus Clay, thanking James for pursuing a measure in Congress for him, wrote in 1855, "I have great faith in the Clay blood and believed if you put your shoulder to the wheel, it would be put through—as our motto is 'never say die.'" Cassius M. Clay to James B. Clay, April 21, 1855, Box 44, TJC Papers.

14. See Harry Clay diaries and papers, SCS Papers.

15. Donald J. Mrozek, "The Habit of Victory: The American Military and the Cult of Manliness," in *Manliness and Morality: Middle-Class Masculinity in Britain and America, 1800–1940,* ed. J. A. Mangan and James Walvin (New York: St. Martin's, 1987), 228.

16. H. C. McDowell to Anne Clay McDowell, February 11, 1882, HCMF Papers; Robert Clay to Mrs. Charles D. Clay, December 7, 1923, SCS Papers; Johansen, 125.

17. L. M. Blackford Jr. to Mrs. Charles D. Clay, December 9, 1913, SCS Papers; Susan M. Clay to Charley Clay, June 25, 1880, Box 46, TJC Papers.

18. Mrozek, 228; *Louisville Ledger,* July 25, 1876; Mrs. Charles Clay to Robert Clay, February 9, 1924, SCS Papers; *Louisville Commercial,* September 22, 1884. L. M. Blackford Jr. to Mrs. Charles Clay, November 9, 1913, SCS Papers. Mrs. Clay related the story of one of Charley's fights in the letter to Bob. Mrs. Hood Harney, the mother of a good friend, rushed out to break up an altercation between Charley and a much larger boy named Tubby Shanklin. She found Charley pinning the bigger boy to the ground. When Mrs. Harney asked Charley to let him up, he allegedly said, "Mrs. Harney, of course, I will do anything you say, but this is a question of honor." Questions of honor would later get him in trouble at West Point and in the regular army.

19. Thomas P. Jacob to James B. Clay, September 24, 1852, SCS Papers; Thomas H. Clay to George W. Anderson, February 4, 1856, Box 1, Anderson Family Papers, University of Kentucky Special Collections; interview, Elizabeth Clay Blanford.

20. Ria Clay to Charles D. Clay, July 24, 1899, SCS Papers; interview, Elizabeth Clay Blanford; Col. Charles D. Clay to Charles D. Clay Jr., June 30, 1918, SCS Papers. When Charley was at West Point, Colonel Clay wrote to him, "I am very proud of you my dear son and feel sure that you will maintain the traditions of our family."

21. Remini, *Henry Clay,* 58–59; Petersen, 11; Van Deusen, 25; Howe, *Political Culture of the American Whigs,* 124–26; J. Rogers, 163.

22. Henry Clay McDowell Jr. to Anne Clay McDowell, Ann Clay McDowell Correspondence, HCMF Papers; Madeline McDowell to H. C. McDowell, n.d., HCMF Papers; interviews, Elizabeth Clay Blanford, Bill LaBach.

23. Interview, Elizabeth Clay Blanford.

24. Margaret Erwin to Eugene Erwin, September 27, 1857, Russell-Clay Papers, University of Kentucky Special Collections; Susan M. Clay to Harry Clay, October 3, 1876, Box 44, TJC Papers.

25. Mrs. Charles Clay to Robert Clay, May 15, 1924, SCS Papers; see also newspaper clippings, 1927, HCMF Papers.

26. Thomas H. Clay, Diary. See SCS and HCMF Papers.

27. Susan M. Clay to Harry Clay, [n.d.], Box 45, TJC Papers.

28. Susan M. Clay to Harry Clay, September 24, 1873, Box 46, TJC Papers; Wyatt-Brown, *Southern Honor,* 122.

29. Draft letters to Lucretia Clay, [n.d.], SCS Papers. Hundreds of pages of notes are located in the SCS Papers and the TJC Papers.

30. Harry Clay, "Speech Notes," SCS Papers; A. W. Greely to H. Clay, August 16, 1881, Box 46, TJC Papers; A. L. Todd, *Abandoned: The Story of the Greely Expedition 1881–1884* (New York: McGraw-Hill, 1961), 21–22.

31. Clay published his plan with the *Louisville Courier-Journal,* May 20, 1883. See Lindsey Apple, "In Search of a Star: A Kentucky Clay Goes to the Arctic," *Filson Club History Quarterly* 71 (January 1997): 25.

32. Bessie Rowland James, ed., *Six Came Back: The Arctic Adventure of David L.*

Brainard (Indianapolis: Bobbs-Merrill, 1940), 23; Todd, 21–22; A. W. Greely to Lucretia Clay, September [n.d.], 1884, SCS Papers; David Brainard to H. Clay, August 11, 1884, Box 46, TJC Papers.

33. *Louisville Commercial,* April 26, 1885; *Louisville Post,* September 22, 1884.

34. Wolfe, *Daughters of Canaan,* 204.

35. Linda K. Kerber, "Separate Spheres, Female Worlds, Woman's Place: The Rhetoric of Women's History," *Journal of American History* 75 (June 1988): 32; Susanne Juhasz, *Naked and Fiery Forms: Modern American Poetry by Women, a New Tradition* (New York: Octagon Books, 1976), 1–2. The dependency of nineteenth-century women on male writers as models is implied in many literary studies; for example, Elaine Showalter implies as much in the title of her work *A Literature of Their Own* (Princeton, N.J.: Princeton University Press, 1977). See also Sandra M. Gilbert and Susan Gubar, *The Madwoman in the Attic: The Woman and the Nineteenth-Century Literary Imagination* (New Haven, Conn.: Yale University Press, 1979) and Carol S. Manning, *The Female Tradition in Southern Literature* (Urbana: University of Illinois Press, 1993), 49. Deposition, sworn in Fayette County Court, Mrs. Charles D. Clay, 1928, SCS Papers.

36. Anne Goodwyn Jones, *Tomorrow Is Another Day: The Woman Writer in the South, 1859–1936* (Baton Rouge: Louisiana State University Press, 1981), 356. Major McDowell warned Madge not to overtax herself—to study only languages, music, and English literature. Henry Clay McDowell Sr. to Madge McDowell, September 13, 1889, HCMF Papers; Susan Clay Sawitzky to Mrs. Charles M. Clay, September 15, October 13, 1927, SCS Papers.

37. The representative of the emperor sent a pair of Japanese vases as a gift to the McDowell family. Busch sent a barrel of Budweiser. See HCMF Papers.

38. Thomas Nelson Page to Anne Clay McDowell, July 14, 1891, HCMF Papers; Program, Once a Week Dancing Club, SCS Papers; photograph of John Fox Jr. and friends at Ashland, HCMF Papers.

39. Kerber, 22; Wolfe, *Daughters of Canaan,* 134; Margaret Ripley Wolfe, "Fallen Leaves and Missing Pages: Women in Kentucky History," *Register of the Kentucky Historical Society* 90 (Bicentennial Issue, 1992): 86. See also Anne Firor Scott, *The Southern Lady: From Pedestal to Politics, 1830–1930* (Chicago: University of Chicago Press, 1970), 169, 180; Wyatt-Brown, *Southern Honor,* 247. For a successful Kentucky woman who struggled with family traditions, see Sallie Bingham, *Passion and Prejudice: A Family Memoir* (New York: Applause Books, 1989), 65–78. See also Lillian Smith, *Killers of the Dream* (New York: W. W. Norton, 1949); Shirley Abbott, *Womenfolks: Growing Up Down South* (New York: Ticknor and Fields, 1983); Sinclair Lewis, *Main Street* (New York: Harcourt, Brace, 1920).

40. Nanette McDowell to Magdalen H. McDowell, May 10, June 17, 1885, Correspondence to Magdalen McDowell, March 30, 1885–December 26, 1885, HCMF Papers; Benjamin H. Bristow to Henry Clay McDowell, December 20, 1889, HCMF Papers.

41. J. David Hacker, Libra Hilde, and James Holland Jones, "The Effect of the Civil War on Southern Marriage Patterns," *Journal of Southern History* 76 (February 2010): 41, 55.

42. K. Blair, 4, 7, 9. Interview, Elizabeth Clay Blanford. According to Mrs. Blanford, Teetee had been sneaking out to the barn to apply a salve used on horses. It was Aunt Matt, the family cook, who told her brothers.

43. Susan Clay Sawitzky, "Mariner," *Poetry: A Magazine of Verse* 57 (February 1941): 306.

44. Gilbert and Gubar, 83.

45. Mrs. Charles D. Clay to Susan Clay, July 12, 1921, SCS Papers.

46. Susan Clay Sawitzky to Mrs. Charles D. Clay, May 5, 1938, SCS Papers.

47. SCS Papers. She wrote the same expressions on several scraps of paper.

48. Interview, James F. Hopkins. Dr. Hopkins, the editor of the early volumes of the Henry Clay papers, met Susan when he was on sabbatical at Yale University. His wife visited her briefly, noting the conditions in which she lived.

49. Quoted in Melba Porter Hay, *Madeline McDowell Breckinridge and the Battle for a New South* (Lexington: University Press of Kentucky, 2009), 184; Sophonisba Preston Breckinridge, *Madeline McDowell Breckinridge: A Leader in the New South* (Chicago: University of Chicago Press, 1921), 212; *Louisville Herald,* November 14, 1915.

50. For the Breckinridge family, see Klotter, *Breckinridges of Kentucky;* interview, Bill LaBach; Madeline Breckinridge to Desha Breckinridge, June 10, 1920, HCMF Papers; Hay, 209–10, 232.

51. Scrapbook, Henrietta Clay Papers, Transylvania University; newspaper clippings can also be found in the TJC Papers, the SCS Papers, and the HCMF Papers. Often, the families independently saved the same articles.

52. E. Simpson, preface; Rebecca Smith Lee, *Mary Austin Holley: A Biography* (Austin: University of Texas Press, 1962), 120–21; Margaret Erwin to Eugene Erwin, May 24, 1852, Russell-Clay Papers, University of Kentucky Special Collections; Harriet Martineau to Rev. Samuel Gilman, June 12, 1835, University of Kentucky Special Collections; Jean H. Baker, *Mary Todd Lincoln: A Biography* (New York: W. W. Norton, 1987), 53–73; see also John Rothenstein, *Summer's Lease: Autobiography, 1901–1938* (London: Hamish Hamilton, 1965). Rothenstein taught at the University of Kentucky and married a Lexington woman, but Lexington's elite found him odd and laughed at his manners and dress.

53. Buddy Thompson, *Madame Belle Brezing* (Lexington: Buggy Whip Press, 1983). Belle Brezing ran a celebrated house of ill repute in Lexington. Interview, Bill LaBach.

54. William Sawitzky to Susan Clay Sawitzky, April 14, 1928, SCS Papers; interview, Jeff Meyer, Curator of Ashland. A docent at Ashland told the story of the shotgun, having experienced it personally as a child.

55. Interviews, William Blanford, Bill LaBach.

56. Susan Clay Sawitzky to Elizabeth Clay Blanford, July 10, 1968, SCS Papers.

57. Interviews, Elizabeth Clay Blanford, Henry Clay Simpson Jr.; Susan Clay Sawitzky to William Sawitzky, April 14, 17, 1928; Susan Clay Sawitzky to Elizabeth Clay, July 23, 1951, SCS Papers.

58. "Defending Henry Clay," *Lexington Herald-Leader,* June 22, 1991, A1, A12.

59. Benjamin H. Bristow to H. C. McDowell, April 21, 1881, HCMF Papers.

60. James Parton, "Henry Clay's Way of Speaking," *Youth's Companion,* January 1, 1880, 3–5; James Parton, "Defeated Presidential Candidates," *Forum,* January 1, 1889, 500–515.

61. Howe, *Victorian America,* 22.

62. James B. Clay to Thomas H. Clay, November 12, 1853, Henrietta Clay Papers, Transylvania University.

63. Carl Schurz to Thomas H. Clay, October 21, 1882, November 23, 1884, May 22, 1885, September 20, 1886, Henrietta Clay Papers, Transylvania University.

64. Van Deusen, vii–viii; George Rawlings Poage, *Henry Clay and the Whig Party* (Chapel Hill: University of North Carolina Press, 1936), 181.

65. See Connelly, 70–76.

66. James O. Harrison to Messrs. Perry Mason & Co, *Youth's Companion,* January 9, 1880; Perry Mason to J. O. Harrison, February 9, 1880. Parton wrote a response that was sent to Harrison. He backed away from some charges and failed to support others, but the editors still refused to print a rebuttal. See Boxes 55 and 56, TJC Papers, for the full correspondence.

67. On a letter to the editor of the *New York Daily Tribune,* December 26, 1891, signed Paul, Teetee Clay circled the name and wrote "Mother" in the margin. See newspaper clippings, Box 61, TJC Papers

68. See TJC Papers.

69. See HCMF Papers.

70. E. Blair Lee to Thomas H. Clay Jr., May 20, 1886; Edward Everett Hale to Thomas H. Clay, October 10, 1891; Joseph Rogers to Thomas H. Clay, December 12, 1904, Henrietta Clay Papers, Transylvania University.

71. There is some correspondence between Henry and John in the papers, but on key issues where written communication can legitimately be expected, no letters are available. See Remini, *Henry Clay,* 709, 765. The Heidlers claim James burned the letter Clay wrote about Crittenden's betrayal. Though credited with some of the information in the notes, I have seen no evidence that the letter was burned. George Rawlings Poage gives a different account. He says that James ripped the letter up, but his wife Susan collected the pieces and copied it. Poage also states that George read the letter to him in 1920. See Heidler and Heidler, 491; Poage, 181.

72. J. B. Clay to Calvin Colton, January 31, 1856, Box 43, TJC Papers. Clay went on to say that John was wounded by his father's reference to him in the letter.

73. "Memorandum for Charley," January 13, 1916, p. 2, Box 48, TJC Papers.

74. Susan M. Clay to Kate Jacob, December 7, 1857, Box 43; Susan M. Clay to Kate Jacob Jones, March 24, 1863, Box 45; Fragment, Box 60; Susan M. Clay to Harry Clay, August 4, 1873, Box 46, TJC Papers.

75. Interview, Elizabeth Clay Blanford. Dunster Foster Pettit, a longtime resident of Lexington and a friend of Susan, Charles, and Robert Clay, knew immediately the woman Susan used as the symbol of the southern belle. Interview, Dunster Foster Pettit. Elizabeth Blanford admitted that she destroyed a letter Susie Clay wrote her father from her deathbed. She told him she thought she might get better if she "could just have an orange." Mrs. Blanford claimed the letter was just too painful. Interview, Elizabeth Clay Blanford. Transcript in Ashland, the Henry Clay Estate Collection.

76. *Rogersville Review,* November 18, 1954, 1, 8; interview, Dr. William D. Kenner.

77. Henry Clay McDowell Jr. to Anne Clay McDowell, January 22, 1893, HCMF Papers; interview, Dr. William D. Kenner; Thomas H. Clay, Diary; Hay, 47–52, 90.

78. George Clay to Lucretia "Teetee" Clay, August 4, 1883, TJC Papers.

79. Susan M. Clay to Charles Clay, October 31, 1882, Box 46, TJC Papers.

80. Robert Clay to Mrs. Charles Clay, May 22, 1922; Robert Clay to Mrs. Charles Clay, October 22, 1923; Robert Clay to Mrs. Clay, December 17, 1923, SCS Papers. See also Mrs. Charles Clay to Robert Clay, May 15, 1924, SCS Papers.

81. Robert P. Clay to Mrs. Charles D. Clay, October 22, 1923, SCS Papers; interview, Elizabeth Clay Blanford.

82. Interviews, Cleo Dawson Smith, Elizabeth Clay Blanford; Robert Clay to Mrs. Charles Clay, June 10, 1927, SCS Papers. Susan Clay Sawitzky to William Sawitzky, April 12, 1928, SCS Papers. The Clays were extremely traditional. Elizabeth Clay Blanford recalled that the installation of a telephone in the Clay home created particular problems. A signal was developed so that when the colonel received a call about the breeding of horses, Mrs. Clay and her daughters would leave the parlor, closing the large oak doors behind them. On one occasion, the colonel became angry and threatened violence when a neighbor kept a bull in a field visible from the Clay house. In an interview in the home of Dunster Foster Pettit, a group of six women who had known the family told stories about the protectiveness of the Clays. All in their eighties at the time of the interview, they considered the family terribly "old fashioned," but unusual in Lexington only by degree.

83. Henry Clay, of course, died of tuberculosis, followed by Lucretia and

James in the second generation, and Martin Duralde, Henry Clay Erwin, Charles Edward Erwin, and Anne Clay McDowell in the third generation. Eugene Erwin had tuberculosis, but he died at the Battle of Vicksburg. In the fourth generation, virtually all the McDowell children and several of the Erwin descendants suffered from the disease at one time or another. Harry Boyle Clay Jr. of the Rogersville Clays died of the disease.

84. *Louisville Commercial,* September 23, 1884; *Louisville Courier-Journal,* September 23, 1884.

85. "Brilliant—but Short-Lived," *Morning* ——, —y 17, 1889, Newspaper Clippings, TJC Papers; HCMF Papers; SCS Papers.

86. Marjorie Spruill Wheeler, *New Women of the New South: The Leaders of the Woman Suffrage Movement in the Southern States* (New York: Oxford University Press, 1993), 46.

87. Interview, Dr. William D. Kenner.

9. Legacy of Risk

1. Gaston, 7, 22. Stanley L. Engerman, "Slavery and Its Consequences for the South in the Nineteenth Century," in *The Cambridge Economic History of the United States,* vol. 2, edited by Stanley L. Engerman and Robert E. Gallman (Cambridge: Cambridge University Press, 2000), 357.

2. Hervey, *Racing in America,* 2:346, 359; Gaston, 22.

3. Henry Clay to Andrew Eugene Erwin, September 14, 1851, CP, 10:912–13.

4. Hervey, *Racing in America,* 2:273–317.

5. Meyer, 481–82.

6. Ibid.; Last Will and Testament of Henry Clay, July 10, 1851, CP, 10:901–2; Henry Clay to John M. Clay, April 30, 1852, CP, 10:966–67. Henry did note that Yorkshire was to be permitted to serve the mares of Thomas and James.

7. The Kentucky Derby winners are Day Star (1878), Riley (1890), Azra (1892), Ben Brush (1896), Alan-a-Dale (1902), Regret (1915), Exterminator (1918), Lawrin (1938), Middle Ground (1950), Venetian Way (1960), Gato del Sol (1982), and Sunny's Halo (1983).

8. Meyer, 482–86; Harriet Fowler, "Politically Gifted: Henry Clay's Horses Have Lasting Influence," *Keeneland* (Fall 2001): 76; H. Simpson, 63–64, 72–79.

9. Charles E. Trevathan, *The American Thoroughbred* (New York: Macmillan, 1905), 322; Meyer, 481.

10. Trevathan, 322.

11. According to Eric Brooks, the curator of Ashland since 2002, the 2010 Kentucky Derby entry, Devil May Care, descended through Maggie B.B., another Clay horse, from Magnolia.

12. Hervey, *Racing in America,* 2:108; H. Simpson, 59; Meyer, 483.

13. "Story of Maggie B.B.," *Spirit of the Times*, March 1, 1884; interview, Elizabeth Clay Blanford; H. Simpson, 61.

14. Meyer, 482; H. Simpson, 58, 61.

15. H. Simpson, 72–73; Meyer, 485–86; *Lexington Herald*, March 30, 1920, June 23, 1901; *New York Morning Telegraph*, March 2, 1896.

16. According to Jeff Meyer, Capt. James B. Clay Jr. bred the leading money-winning three-year-old in the 1902 season. See Meyer, 494.

17. Susan Clay Sawitzky to Mrs. Charles D. Clay, [n.d., but written shortly after George Clay died on June 26, 1834], SCS Papers; George Clay to Harry Clay, March 18, 1879, TJC Papers.

18. George Clay, "On My Phenomenal Success," Box 60, TJC Papers; Charles Clay to Mariah Pepper, March 20, 1896, SCS Papers. See also Indenture George H. Clay and Lucretia H. Clay with Third National Bank, January 16, 1893, Indenture George Clay with William Eastern, April 20, 1894, Box 54, TJC Papers.

19. Meyer, 495.

20. Business Records, Box 54, TJC Papers.

21. *Lexington Herald*, April 13, 1917.

22. Interviews, Elizabeth Clay Blanford, Lucy Clay Boyajian.

23. M. F. Millett to H. C. McDowell, May 23, 1890, HCMF Papers. Millet wrote, "Have you a bay filly two or three years old of the King Rene family that would make a good roadster, and without a fancy price? I mention the King Rene family because of their supposed beauty and style. I would like to have a filly that was handsome and stylish, and could, or promises to trot in about 2.40, with good tail." J. B. Houston to Henry Clay McDowell, June 12, 1889; Earl H. Potter to H. C. McDowell, June 11, 1889, HCMF Papers; B. K. Walker to Henry Clay McDowell, August 16, 1889, K. Fujinami to H. C. McDowell, January 26, 1890, HCMF Papers; S. Niyama to H. C. McDowell, January 20, 1890, HCMF Papers. McDowell sent the horse Vodka among others to the imperial stud farm Shimossa. McDowell and Benjamin Bristow bought horses in the West and sold them to the French at $150 per head. Lt. Col. Baron Feverot de Kerbreck to Henry Clay McDowell, December 20, 1880, HCMF Papers.

24. "Ashland 1888: Thirteenth Annual Catalogue," HCMF Papers. The epithet "Kentucky robber baron" was suggested by Bill Marshall, a historian and archivist at the University of Kentucky.

25. There is a statue of Clay in Venezuela's capital city, Caracas.

26. John H. Wallace, *The Horse in America* (New York: Privately published, 1897), 533; Hervey, *American Trotter*, 277–85.

27. H. C. McDowell to A. C. Hall, December 6, 1890, HCMF Papers. McDowell wrote, "I am sorry that my ancient enemy seems inclined to give us so much trouble."

28. In the 1880s the Kentuckians tried to start a new registry, the *Breeders'* *Trotting Stud Book*. Wallace submitted surreptitiously a fictitious pedigree that the new registry published. He then mocked their qualifications for determining pedigree. Meyer, 490; Hervey, *American Trotter*, 144, 282. Wallace admitted his own fraud in *The Horse in America*, 525–32. N. A. Randall to H. C. McDowell, June 3, 1889, HCMF Papers; for details of purchase of Dictator, see purchase agreement dated August 22, 1883, Box 28, and letter from H. Durkee to Col. R. West, August 22, 1883, HCMF Papers. Jeff Meyer served as curator of Ashland from December 1997 to December 2001.

29. Dwight Akers, *Drivers Up: The Story of American Harness Racing* (New York: G. P. Putnam's Sons, 1938), 192–93.

30. John Dupee to H. C. McDowell, April 25, 1893, Box 39; F. D. Spotswood to H. C. McDowell, November 13, 1893, Box 42; Ashland Stud Book, Box 32; James Hukill to H. C. McDowell, July 20, 1898, Box 41; H. C. McDowell to W. K. Pickens, September 9, 1898, Letterbook, HCMF Papers.

31. "Ashland 1889—Fourteenth Annual Catalogue," HCMF Papers; *Lexington Leader*, March 30, 1890; *Kentucky Farmer and Breeder*, March 3, 1904, HCMF Papers.

32. *New York Telegraph*, HCMF Papers; *Lexington Leader*, [n.d., 1925], HCMF Papers; *Lexington Herald*, June 6, 1914.

33. See HCMF Papers; Meyer, 493. William Adair McDowell and Thomas C. McDowell belonged to the Iroquois Club, and Robert Pepper Clay played polo throughout his career in the U.S. Army. The student annual at West Point noted his skill with horses.

34. Articles of Incorporation, February 18, 1870, Box 54, TJC Papers; Harry Clay to H. C. McDowell, July 1, 11, 1889, December 16, 1889, HCMF Papers.

35. Susan Clay Sawitzky to Elizabeth Clay, November 19, 1932, SCS Papers.

36. Susan M. Clay to J. W. Stevenson, December 18, 1876, Box 46, TJC Papers; Susan M. Clay to J. W. Stevenson, June 20, 1881, Box 46, TJC Papers; J. W. Stevenson to J. Proctor Knott, May 2, 1877, Letterbook, April 18, 1877–July 28, 1878, p. 920, John White Stevenson Collection, University of Kentucky. See also letters on pages 96–99, 555–56, 574, and 636–37. David Davis to Susan M. Clay, May 7, 1881, SCS Papers; Charles D. Clay to Justice John M. Harlan, May 4, 1881, SCS Papers; Susan M. Clay to Charley Clay, June 15, 1877, Box 46, TJC Papers.

37. Susan M. Clay to President Rutherford B. Hayes, December 15, 1877, Military Records of Thomas J. Clay, Records Group 94, National Archives. The letter was placed in Thomas J. Clay's military record and remained there throughout his career.

38. H. C. McDowell to W. A. McDowell, December 6, 1890, January 31, 1891, HCMF Papers; William A. McDowell to Henry Clay McDowell, November

11, 1896, HCMF Papers; Madge to Mamma (Anne Clay McDowell), July 9, 1901, Correspondence of Anne Clay McDowell, HCMF Papers.

39. Harry Boyle Clay to H. C. McDowell, January 7, 1866, HCMF Papers.

40. Harry Boyle Clay to H. C. McDowell, January 7, 1866, HCMF Papers; Thomas P. Jacob to Susan Clay, January 27, 1882; Susan Clay to Charley and George Clay, August 5, 1881, Box 46, TJC Papers. Thomas P. Jacob had partnered with James B. Clay in the years before the war. They had owned a large section of Louisville that they developed as residential and commercial property. See Jacob-Johnson Papers, Filson Club, Louisville, Kentucky.

41. Susan M. Clay to Harry Clay, [n.d.], Box 45, TJC Papers. This letter is quoted at length in chapter 8.

42. Susan M. Clay to Charley Clay, June 25, 1880; Susan M. Clay to Harry Clay, September 24, 1873, Box 46, TJC Papers; Susan M. Clay to Harry Clay, August [n.d.], 1873, Box 46, TJC Papers.

43. James W. Buchanan to Henry Clay McDowell, February 14, 1896, HCMF Papers; "Rental Property," HCMF Papers.

44. Henry Clay McDowell to Buckner, Cummins & Co., November 16, 1897, Letterbook, HCMF Papers; H. C. McDowell to R. A. McDowell, August 20, 1898, Letterbook, HCMF Papers; R. A. McDowell to H. C. McDowell, November 15, 1898, November 18, 1898, Box 24, HCMF Papers. Tax assessment papers indicate that McDowell owned property on Main, Bullitt, Green, Walnut, Jefferson, and Madison—streets in the heart of Louisville's commercial area. See W. A. Kliessendorff to H. C. McDowell, January 16, 1898, HCMF Papers.

45. W. L. Breckinridge to H. C. McDowell, April 27, 1868, HCMF Papers.

46. Charles Blanton Roberts, "The Building of Middlesborough," *Filson Club History Quarterly* 7 (January 1933): 18–33; *Big Stone Gap, Virginia,* HCMF Papers—a pamphlet used to sell prospective investors in the project.

47. The deed and articles of incorporation for the Big Stone Gap Improvement Co. are in HCMF Papers; St. John Boyle to Henry Clay McDowell, May 13, 1887, HCMF Papers; Subscription Flier, HCMF Papers; George Copeland to H. C. McDowell, August 31, 1897, HCMF Papers.

48. G. T. Center to H. C. McDowell, May 13, 1888; Goff Land Co., Notice of Incorporation, May 9, 1887; Dictator Cannel Coal Co., Notice of Incorporation, August 13, 1888, HCMF Papers; G. W. Sewell to H. C. McDowell, May 23, 1892, HCMF Papers; L. T. Rosengarten to H. C. McDowell, November 26, 1888, HCMF Papers; Bullitt and McDowell, Attorneys, to H. C. McDowell, June 11, 1889, Box 21; Agreement, April 1888, Kentucky Coal and Iron Company and Kentucky Union Railway Company; L. T. Rosengarten to H. C. McDowell, April 16, 1889, HCMF Papers.

49. John Ingle to H. C. McDowell, July 2, 1891, HCMF Papers; Bullitt and McDowell to H. C. McDowell, President of South Appalachian Land Co., March

30, 1891, HCMF Papers; H. C. McDowell to H. W. Bruce, May 1, 1891, HCMF Papers. McDowell used his influence to obtain business with the L&N Railroad for his son's law firm.

50. Ross A. Webb, *Benjamin Helm Bristow: Border State Politician* (Lexington: University Press of Kentucky, 1969), 336.

51. Arthur Cary to H. C. McDowell, December 17, 1889; Arthur Cary to H. C. McDowell, September 15, 1892; St. John Boyle to H. C. McDowell, May 13, 1887; C. H. Stoll to H. C. McDowell, February 15, 1889; Arthur Cary to H. C. McDowell, August 7, 1890, HCMF Papers; see Duane Bolin, *Bossism and Reform in a Southern City: Lexington, Kentucky, 1880–1940* (Lexington: University Press of Kentucky, 2000), 21–22.

52. *Big Stone Gap, Virginia,* HCMF Papers. H. C. Brown to H. C. McDowell, October 18, 1892, HCMF Papers.

53. H. Northcote to H. C. McDowell, February 19, 1891; *Lexington Herald* clipping; Subscription Flier, 1890; John R. Proctor to H. C. McDowell, December 5, 1890, HCMF Papers.

54. Meeting of the Directors of the South Appalachian Land Company, April 19, 1889; H. C. McDowell to Stockholders, Big Stone Gap Improvement Company, June 17, 1889, Box 19; J. Stoddard Johnston to H. C. McDowell, October 1, 1891; J. M. Dalton to H. C. McDowell, August 15, 1892; H. C. McDowell to W. J. Lewis, March 20, April 29, 1891, HCMF Papers.

55. J. Kennedy Tod and Company to H. C. McDowell, September 28, 1894; J. Kennedy Tod to H. C. McDowell, October 3, 1894; George W. Davy to H. C. McDowell, June 8, 1896, HCMF Papers; *Lexington Herald,* February 17, 1917.

56. See Business Records, HCMF Papers.

57. *Lexington Herald,* August 6, 1919; *Lexington Leader,* July 6, 1919, July 18, 1925; interview, Bill LaBach.

10. Legacy of Service

1. Henry Clay to "My Dear Little Namesake," July 7, 1845, CP, 10:230–31.

2. Interview, Dr. William D. Kenner.

3. U.S. Military Academy, *Official Register of the Officers and Cadets for the Academic Year Ending 5 June 1963* (West Point, N.Y.: U.S. Army Printing Company, 1963).

4. James B. Clay to Henry Clay, November 17, 1849, CP, 10:628; U.S. Military Academy, "Official Register of the Officers and Cadets of the United States Military Academy," 14 (1848–1857); U.S. Military Academy, "Staff Records," 5 (1851–1854), West Point, New York, 272–73; U.S. Military Academy, "Delinquencies," 21–22.

5. Henry Clay to Lucretia Clay, February 7, 1850, CP, 10:672–73; Henry Clay to Henry Clay III, June 26, September 24, November 22, December 23,

1850, January 18, October 26, 1851, January 25, 1852, CP, 10:818, 832–33, 834–35, 843, 927, 949–50; U.S. Military Academy, "Delinquencies," 22, 330–31.

6. U.S. Military Academy. *Official Register of the Officers and Cadets for the Academic Year Ending 1919* (West Point, N.Y.: U.S. Army Printing Office, 1919); U.S. Military Academy, *Official Register of the Officers and Cadets for the Academic Year Ending 5 June 1963.*

7. L. M. Blackford Jr. to Mrs. Charles Clay, October 13, November 9, 1913; Mrs. Charles Clay to Charley, October 10, 1913; Charles Clay to Charley, October 10, 1913, June 30, 1918; Mrs. Charles Clay to Robert Clay, February 9, 1924; Robert Clay to Colonel and Mrs. Clay, September 20, 1921, SCS Papers. Bob wrote, "The trouble I had about Charley . . ."

8. Henry Clay III to Anne Clay McDowell, October 28, December 2, 1861, Box 115; Henry Clay McDowell to Anne Clay McDowell, March 7, 27, 1862, HCMF Papers.

9. H. Simpson, 49. Josephine occupied a place in family myth because she had bravely rescued the emblems of war. The flag, Eugene's uniform, and a portrait of Erwin hung in a Clay home until very recently. Josephine wrote five novels. *Uncle Phil* tells the story of the Battle of Vicksburg. K. Brown, 222.

10. Thomas J. Clay, "A Synopsis of the Life of Thomas J. Clay, U.S. Army, Retired," p. 2, SCS Papers; Susan M. Clay to President U.S. Grant, September 9, 1876, Records of the Adjutant General's Office, Group 94, U.S. National Archives (emphasis original).

11. Henry Ware Lawton to his wife, July 22, 1886; Captain Thompson to Henry Ware Lawton, August 2, 1886, Correspondence 1886, Box 1, Henry Ware Lawton Papers, Library of Congress; Captain Thompson is probably William A. Thompson, who was on the staff of General Miles. See also Hermann Hagedorn, *Leonard Wood, a Biography,* 2 vols. (New York: Kraus Reprint Co., 1969), 1:54, 77–78, 89.

12. Leonard Wood to Henry Ware Lawton, July 14, 1886, Box 1, Henry Ware Lawton Papers, Library of Congress; Robert M. Utley, *Frontier Regulars: The United States Army and the Indian, 1866–1891* (Lincoln: University of Nebraska Press, 1973), 387–88, 391. See also Nelson A. Miles, *Personal Recollections and Observations of General Nelson A. Miles* (New York: DeCapo, 1969); Jack C. Lane, ed., *Chasing Geronimo: The Journal of Leonard Wood, May–September, 1886* (Albuquerque: University of New Mexico Press, 1970); Lawrence Vinton, "The Geronimo Campaign as Told by a Trooper of 'B' Troop of the 4th U.S. Cavalry," *Journal of the West* 11 (1972): 157–69; Charles B. Gatewood, *Lt. Charles B. Gatewood and His Apache Wars Memoir,* ed. Louis Kraft (Lincoln: University of Nebraska Press, 2005); Britton Davis, *The Truth about Geronimo,* edited by Milo Milton Quaife (Chicago: Lakeside, 1951), 310–32. Odie B. Faulk, *The Geronimo Campaign* (New York: Oxford University Press, 1969).

13. Thomas J. Clay, "A Memoir," SCS Papers; Faulk, 147; M. Doyle to C. B. Gatewood Jr., July 15, 1926, Letter 272, Gatewood Collection, Arizona Historical Society.

14. Diary, Box 2, Leonard Wood Papers, Library of Congress; Thomas J. Clay, "A Memoir," SCS Papers. Years later, in correspondence with Leonard Wood, Clay referred to "that critical experience with General Lawton." T. J. Clay to Leonard Wood, May 25, 1925, Leonard Wood Papers, Library of Congress. See also Faulk, 137. Report of Captain H. W. Lawton, Fourth Cavalry, 1886, Box 15, Hermann Hagedorn Papers, Library of Congress. Victorian values even affected historians. Hagedorn had both Clay's and Wood's accounts of Lawton's behavior toward Clay, but decided that including them would leave the wrong impression of an otherwise noble man. See Leonard Wood: Arizona Years 1885–86, Box 15, Hermann Hagedorn Papers.

15. T. J. Clay to Major Charles Gatewood, September 15, 1925, Letter 122, Gatewood Collection, Arizona Historical Society; T. J. Clay to A. Mazzanovich, May 25, 1930, F 193 Letters 390–92, Gatewood Collection, Arizona Historical Society; Gatewood, 145–48; Thomas J. Clay to Susan M. Clay, August 31, 1886, SCS Papers. Gatewood says he gave Perico's wife a can of condensed milk before the invitation to share their food. Faulk spells the name of Geronimo's brother-in-law Perrico.

16. Letter signed by Geronimo and Naichez, [n.d.], Box 56, TJC Papers; the photograph is in the SCS Papers.

17. T. J. Clay to A. Mazzanovich, April 7, 1930, F 193 Letters 390–92, Gatewood Collection, Arizona Historical Society.

18. Thomas J. Clay, 3176, ACP 1890, #55, Military Records of Thomas J. Clay, Records Group 94, National Archives.

19. For a full account of the early marriage of Charles and Ria Clay, see Lindsey Apple, "The Evolution of a Family: Gendered 'Spheres' and the Spanish-American War," *Register of the Kentucky Historical Society* 94 (Autumn 1996): 363–95.

20. Interview, Elizabeth Clay Blanford.

21. Susan M. Clay to Ria Clay, July 21, 1899, SCS Papers. Interviews, Elizabeth Clay Blanford, Dunster Foster Pettit.

22. James C. Klotter has a strong chapter on suicide from a historical perspective in his book *Kentucky Justice, Southern Honor, and American Manhood: Understanding the Life and Death of Richard Reid* (Baton Rouge: Louisiana State University Press, 2003), 89–102. Klotter suggests a variety of causes, but certainly the Clay sense of honor and the pressures placed on Charley Clay by his family could have led to the sense of hopelessness that contributes to the feeling that death provides the only way out of a situation.

23. Interview, Dunster Foster Pettit; D. T. Spencer to Colonel H. B. Clay, February 11, 1923, SCS Papers. Spencer was writing to C. D. Clay.

24. Telegram, Gen. R. C. Davis to Col. Charles Clay, March 8, 1923; Minutes (copy), U.S. Army Board of Inquiry, Fort Snelling, Minnesota, April 24, 1923, SCS Papers.

25. Bob Clay to Mrs. Clay, January 23, 1923; Susan Clay to William Sawitzky, August 1926; Mrs. Charles Clay to Bob Clay, May 15, 1924; Robert Clay to Mrs. Charles Clay, January 23, 1923, SCS Papers.

26. Robert Clay to Mr. Charles D. Clay, November 21, 1921, September 20, 1921, SCS Papers. Copies of the Robert Clay letters have been given to the library at West Point.

27. Ibid.; Robert Clay to Charles D. Clay, November 17, 1921, SCS Papers. Bob wrote that he was staying at the academy only out of loyalty to his father and family, and that if he was dismissed, it would make him the happiest person on earth.

28. Interview, Elizabeth Clay Blanford.

29. Interview, Bill LaBach.

30. *New York Times,* November 13, 1901; see http://fjc.gov.

31. Henry Clay McDowell Jr. to Anne Clay McDowell, April 5, 1908, March 20, 1910, HCMF Papers.

32. *Louisville Courier-Journal,* September 23, 1884, 6; the *Louisville Post* of August 6, 1883, said Harry "has in him some of the stuff of his grandfather."

33. Louisville Board of Aldermen, Minutes, March 13, 1883, University of Louisville Archives; Cope Snapp v. Commonwealth of Kentucky, Case #15542, Kentucky Court of Appeals, Kentucky Archives and Records Center; *Louisville Courier-Journal,* July 22, 1883.

34. *Louisville Post,* August 6, 1883; *Louisville Courier-Journal,* April 11, 1884; *Louisville Commercial,* August 7, 1883; *Louisville Daily Ledger,* August 8, 1883.

35. *Louisville Courier-Journal,* September 30, 1884; J. Proctor Knott, Executive Journal 1883–1886, March 31, 1886, 472; J. Proctor Knott, Petitions for Pardons, Remissions and Respites, June 1885, Folder 508, Papers of the Governors of Kentucky 1792–1927, Kentucky Archives and Records Center. To Knott's credit, he refused to pardon Wepler. During his trial, however, Wepler remained in his seat on the city council. See Louisville Board of Aldermen, Minutes, November 27, 1884, University of Louisville Archives.

36. That characteristic is not uncommon in the children of political leaders. Although Robert Lincoln served in an appointed office, he avoided public attention. Children of Theodore and Franklin D. Roosevelt felt similar misgivings but, like the Clays, often received public attention for other things.

37. *New York Telegraph,* [n.d.], HCMF Papers; *Lexington Leader,* August 7, 1974, 16; December 19, 1986.

38. Walter I. Trattner, *From Poor Law to Welfare State: A History of Social Welfare in America* (New York: The Free Press, 1984), 1–3; Luke 12:48.

39. For noblesse oblige and charity, see Kathleen D. McCarthy, *Noblesse Oblige: Charity and Cultural Philanthropy in Chicago, 1849–1929* (Chicago: University of Chicago Press, 1982), ix; John Louis Recchiuti, *Civic Engagement: Social Science and Progressive-Era Reform in New York City* (Philadelphia: University of Pennsylvania Press, 2007), 47–64; Helen Lefkowitz Horowitz, *Culture and the City: Cultural Philanthropy in Chicago from the 1880s to 1917* (Lexington: University Press of Kentucky, 1976).

40. Lucretia Clay to Mariah Pepper Clay, January 31, 1899, SCS Papers; Nettie McDowell Bullock to Anne Clay McDowell, December 26, 1904, HCMF Papers.

41. In the McDowell papers in the HCMF Papers, there is a large folder of materials related to McDowell's work at the mental health facility.

42. Henry Clay McDowell Jr. to Anne Clay McDowell, February 6, 1909, HCMF Papers.

43. *Lexington Herald,* March 2, 1930, 1; July 20, 1929, 1.

44. Breckinridge, 15; Hay, 18.

45. Hay, 61–62; Recchiuti, 49–50.

46. Kolan Thomas Morelock, *Taking the Town: Collegiate and Community Culture in the Bluegrass, 1880–1917* (Lexington: University Press of Kentucky, 2008), 222–29.

47. Daniel, 29–30.

48. Ryan, 4–9; Daniel, 2. On Eleanor Roosevelt, see chapter 5, note 23.

49. Irwin W. Sherman, *Twelve Diseases That Changed Our World* (Washington, D.C.: ASM Press, 2007), 125.

50. Hay, 128. For Madge's relationship with Lexington's political boss, Billy Klair, see Bolin, 21–22, 57–58.

51. The 1892 measure gave the right only to women in second-class Kentucky cities. In 1912 the legislature passed a law enacting school suffrage for all women in the state. The Kentucky Equal Rights Association and the Kentucky Federation of Women's Clubs were active in securing the measure.

52. Hay, 235.

53. Robert Clay to Colonel Charles D. Clay, December 4, 1921, SCS Papers. His sister said Harry Clay argued many legal cases for the poor of Louisville. According to a judge in Louisville, Harry had said, "The tears of gratitude from that poor old mother's eyes are better compensation to me than gold." Even if an exaggeration, the account suggests the importance the family placed on such service. Biographical sketch, 57, TJC Papers.

54. Resolution, City of Greenville Mississippi, SCS Papers.

55. Interviews, Dunster Foster Pettit, Henry Clay Simpson Jr., Bill LaBach, Julia McDowell.

56. James B. Clay Jr. to Thomas J. Clay, July 30, 1877, Box 46, TJC Papers;

Ashland Daybook 1884–1885, HCMF Papers; Charles Clay to Ria Clay, May 31, 1898; Susan M. Clay to Charles, [n.d.], SCS Papers; Nannette Bullock to Anne Clay McDowell, February 25, 1894, HCMF Papers.

57. Henry Clay McDowell Jr. to Anne Clay McDowell, May 20, 1894; William C. McDowell to Henry Clay McDowell Jr., October 13, 1913, Letterbook, HCMF Papers.

58. Mrs. Minor Simpson, "A Few Memories and a Bit of History," University of Kentucky Special Collections; newspaper clipping, October 22, 1909, TJC Papers; interview, Elizabeth Clay Blanford; Susan Clay Sawitzky to Thomas J. Clay, July 10, 1935, SCS Papers.

59. Newspaper clipping, *New York Telegraph*, HCMF Papers; interview, Elizabeth Clay Blanford.

60. Elizabeth Clay studied at the University of Kentucky and turned one of the stories into a play called *The Great Freedom*. Frank Fowler, director of the university's Guignol Theater, helped her in her efforts to have it performed nationally, though by the mid-1930s the genre was less popular. Millie's stories included "De Frog Town Spirit," "De Swallah," "De Ahm Er De Lawd," "Liddle Pig," "He Comin'," "Aunt Keziah," and "De Baptisin'." See SCS Papers.

61. Elizabeth Clay Blanford, "Millie," submitted to the *Christian Science Monitor*, copy, SCS Papers.

62. Interviews, Susan Lawson Brown and Elizabeth Clay Blanford. Mrs. Blanford saved the letters that Susan Brown wrote for her mother. Copies are in the SCS Papers.

Conclusion

1. Wyatt-Brown, *Southern Honor*, 386.

2. Interviews, Henry Clay Simpson Jr., Elizabeth Clay Blanford.

3. Wyatt-Brown, *Southern Honor*, 118–23.

4. Interview, Eve Spears. Mrs. Spears taught at the school for years and remembered fondly the flowers Nettie sent regularly to the school in honor of Madge Breckinridge.

5. See HCMF Papers.

6. *New York Times Magazine*, November 14, 1926; *Lexington Leader*, November 17, 1923, HCMF Papers.

7. *Lexington Herald*, July 13, 1948, 1; August 25, 1948, 8; October 9, 1948, 8; October 12, 1948, 10; April 6, 1949; April 2, April 12, 1950.

8. Hay, 99, 214, 247.

BIBLIOGRAPHY

Interviews

Dated interviews cannot reflect the importance of Clay family members to this study. In addition to formal interviews, there have been hundreds of telephone conversations and e-mail exchanges. Elizabeth Clay Blanford, William Blanford, Lucy Boyajian, Ned Boyajian, Julia Brock, Eric Brooks, Harry Jones, Bill Kenner, Bill LaBach, Jeff Meyer, Dunster Foster Pettit, and Cleo Dawson Smith shared the fact and the spirit of the Clay family as they understand it. The dates describe specific interviews or discussions, but cannot encompass the level of contribution. Interviews cited here were with the author unless otherwise noted.

Blanford, Elizabeth Clay. July 17–20, 1984. Cassette tape. In the possession of the author. Notes available at Ashland, the Henry Clay Estate.

———. 1984–1993. Telephone. Notes available at Ashland, the Henry Clay Estate.

———. Interviews with the author and Bettie Kerr, May 18, 19, 21, 22, and 23, 1987. Cassette tape. Special Collections. Margaret I. King Library, University of Kentucky.

Blanford, William. July 17–20, 1984; May 25–28, 1986; May 18–23, 1987; June 3–4, 1990.

Boyajian, Lucy Clay. June 19, 2000; June 19, 2006; June 25, 2010.

Boyajian, Ned. June 19, 2000; June 25, 2010.

Brown, Susan Lawson. September 5, 1988. Telephone.

Clay, Robert. June 19, 2000; June 2002. (Robert Clay also shared copies of his work on Clay family genealogy.)

Hopkins, James F. November 3 and 7, 1984.

Jones, Harry. May 2010.

Kenner, Dr. William D. August 20, 2000; July 1, 2002; April 1, 2007; November 2010; February 2011.

LaBach, Bill. June 1990; March 18, 1998; September 5, 1999; October 15 and December 15, 2004; October 2010.

Martin, Frank. April 17, 1984.

Pettit, Dunster Foster. July 23, 1985.

Simpson, Henry Clay, Jr. October 1, 2001; July 27, 2007; December 2010.

Simpson, Louisiana. October 2001.

Simpson, Wood. October 2001.

Smith, Cleo Dawson. September 23, 1986; May 4, 1987; May 6, 1988.

Spears, Eve. September 3, 1985; November 4, 1993.

Spears, Woodridge. September 3, 1985.

Manuscript Collections

Anderson Family Papers. Special Collections. Margaret I. King Library, University of Kentucky.

Clay Family Papers. In the possession of the Kenner family. Digital copies made available to the author courtesy of Dr. William D. Kenner.

Clay Family Papers. Courtesy of William LaBach.

Clay Family Papers, 1807–1909. Mary Clay Kenner Collection [microfilm], Special Collections. Margaret I. King Library, University of Kentucky. Original in the possession of the Kenner family.

Henrietta Clay Papers. Archives. Transylvania University.

Henry Clay Memorial Foundation Papers. Special Collections. Margaret I. King Library, University of Kentucky. [HCMF Papers]

Henry Clay Papers. Archives. Transylvania University.

Henry Clay Jr. Diary, 1840–1845. Special Collections. Margaret I. King Library, University of Kentucky.

John M. Clay Diary. Special Collections. Margaret I. King Library, University of Kentucky.

Thomas H. Clay Diary. In the possession of Dr. William D. Kenner. Microfilm version in the University of Kentucky Special Collections.

Thomas H. Clay Papers. Manuscript Division. Library of Congress. [THC Papers]

Thomas J. Clay Military Records. Records Group 94. National Archives.

Thomas J. Clay Papers. Manuscript Division. Library of Congress. [TJC Papers]

Commonwealth of Kentucky v. Theodore W. Clay. Fayette County Circuit Court, File 746. Kentucky Libraries and Archives.

Cope Snapp v. Commonwealth of Kentucky. Case #15542, Kentucky Court of Appeals. Kentucky Archives and Records Center.

Gatewood, Charles. Correspondence. Arizona Historical Society.

Papers of the Governors of Kentucky 1792–1927. J. Proctor Knott. Kentucky Archives and Records Center.

Hermann Hagedorn Papers. Manuscript Division. Library of Congress.

J. O. Harrison Papers. Manuscript Division. Library of Congress.

Hunt-Morgan Papers, 1862–1863. Special Collections. Margaret I. King Library, University of Kentucky.

Jacob-Johnson Papers. Filson Club, Louisville, Kentucky.

Law Student Catalog. Archives. Transylvania University.

Henry Ware Lawton Papers. Manuscript Division. Library of Congress.

Louisville Board of Aldermen Minutes. 1883–1884. University of Louisville Archives.

Records of the Adjutant General's Office. Group 94. U.S. National Archives.

Russell-Clay Papers. Special Collections. Margaret I. King Library, University of Kentucky.

Susan Clay Sawitzky Papers. Special Collections. Margaret I. King Library, University of Kentucky. [SCS Papers]

John White Stevenson Papers. Special Collections. Margaret I. King Library, University of Kentucky.

Student File. Archives. Transylvania University.

Leonard Wood Papers. Manuscript Division. Library of Congress.

Books, Articles, and Other Sources

Abbott, Shirley. *Womenfolks: Growing Up Down South.* New York: Ticknor and Fields, 1983.

Adams, John Quincy. *The Memoirs of John Quincy Adams, Comprising Portions of His Diary from 1795 to 1845.* Edited by Charles Francis Adams. 12 vols. Philadelphia: J. B. Lippincott, 1874–1877.

Akers, Dwight. *Drivers Up: The Story of American Harness Racing.* New York: G. P. Putnam's Sons, 1938.

Ambler, Charles Henry. *Thomas Ritchie: A Study in Virginia Politics.* Richmond, Va.: Bell, Book and Stationery, 1913.

American Psychiatric Association. *Diagnostic and Statistical Manual of Mental Disorders.* 4th ed. Washington, D.C.: American Psychiatric Association, 2000.

Anderson, David. "Down Memory Lane: Nostalgia for the Old South in Post-Civil War Plantation Reminiscences." *Journal of Southern History* 71 (February 2005): 105–36.

Apple, Lindsey. "The Evolution of a Family: Gendered 'Spheres' and the Spanish-American War." *Register of the Kentucky Historical Society* 94 (Autumn 1996): 363–95.

———. "In Search of a Star: A Kentucky Clay Goes to the Arctic." *Filson Club History Quarterly* 71 (January 1997): 3–26.

Ayers, Edward L. *The Promise of the New South: Life after Reconstruction.* New York: Oxford University Press, 1993.

Baker, Jean H. *Mary Todd Lincoln: A Biography*. New York: W. W. Norton, 1987.

———. *The Stevensons: A Biography of an American Family*. New York: W. W. Norton, 1996.

Bales, Jacqueline. "The Shaky Pedestal: Southern Ladies Yesterday and Today." *Southern Studies: An Interdisciplinary Journal of the South* 24 (Winter 1985): 398–406.

Basler, Roy P., ed. *Collected Works of Abraham Lincoln*. 8 vols. New Brunswick, N.J.: Rutgers University Press, 1953.

Baxter, Maurice G. *Henry Clay and the American System*. Lexington: University Press of Kentucky, 1995.

———. *Henry Clay the Lawyer*. Lexington: University Press of Kentucky, 2000.

Bean, Richard M. "History of the Henry Clay Family Properties." Unpublished manuscript, April 1980. Copy at Ashland, the Henry Clay Estate.

Bearss, Sarah B. "Henry Clay and the American Claims against Portugal." *Journal of the Early Republic* 7 (Summer 1987): 167–80.

Bednarowski, Mary F. "Outside the Mainstream: Women's Religion and Women Religious Leaders in Nineteenth-Century America." *Journal of the American Academy of Religion* 48 (June 1980): 207–31.

Bingham, Sallie. *Passion and Prejudice: A Family Memoir*. New York: Applause Books, 1989.

Blair, Karen J. *The Torchbearers: Women and Their Amateur Arts Associations in America, 1890–1930*. Bloomington: Indiana University Press, 1994.

Blair, William A. *Cities of the Dead: Contesting the Memory of the Civil War in the South*. Chapel Hill: University of North Carolina Press, 2004.

Bleser, Carol, ed. *Secret and Sacred: The Diaries of James Henry Hammond, a Southern Slaveholder*. New York: Oxford University Press, 1988.

Blight, David W. *Race and Reunion: The Civil War in Modern Memory*. Cambridge, Mass.: Harvard University Press, 2001.

Block, Mary R. "'The Stoutest Son': The Mexican-American War Journal of Henry Clay Jr." *Register of the Kentucky Historical Society* 106 (Winter 2008): 5–42.

Bolin, Duane. *Bossism and Reform in a Southern City: Lexington, Kentucky, 1880–1940*. Lexington: University Press of Kentucky, 2000.

Breckinridge, Sophonisba Preston. *Madeline McDowell Breckinridge: A Leader in the New South*. Chicago: University of Chicago Press, 1921.

Brown, Everett S., ed. *William Plumer's Memorandum of Proceedings in the United States Senate 1803–1807*. New York, 1923.

Brown, Kent Masterson. "The Colonel and His Lady: Colonel Eugene Erwin and His Wife Josephine." *Filson Club History Quarterly* 75 (April 2001): 205–44.

Brundage, W. Fitzhugh. "Contentious and Collected: Memory's Future in Southern History." *Journal of Southern History* 75 (August 2009): 751–66.

————. *The Southern Past: A Clash of Race and Memory.* Cambridge, Mass.: Belknap Press of Harvard University Press, 2005.

Clay, Thomas H., Jr. *Henry Clay.* Completed by Ellis Paxton Oberholtzer. New York: George W. Jacobs, 1910.

Coleman, J. Winston, Jr. *Last Days, Death and Funeral of Henry Clay.* Lexington, Ky.: Winburn, 1951.

Collier, Peter, and David Horowitz. *The Roosevelts: An American Saga.* New York: Touchstone, 1994.

Colton, Calvin, ed. *The Private Correspondence of Henry Clay.* New York: A. S. Barnes, 1856.

————, ed. *The Works of Henry Clay.* 6 vols. New York: A. S. Barnes, 1855–1857.

Confino, Alon. "Collective Memory and Cultural History: Problems of Method." *American Historical Review* 102 (December 1997): 1386–403.

Connelley, William E., and E. Merton Coulter. *History of Kentucky.* Edited by Charles Kerr. 5 vols. Chicago: American Historical Society, 1922.

Connelly, Thomas L. *The Marble Man: Robert E. Lee and His Image in American Society.* Baton Rouge: Louisiana State University Press, 1977.

Daniel, Thomas M. *Captain of Death: The Story of Tuberculosis.* Rochester, N.Y.: University of Rochester Press, 1997.

Davis, Britton. *The Truth about Geronimo.* Edited by Milo Milton Quaife. Chicago: Lakeside, 1951.

Davis, David. "Some Recent Directions in Cultural History." *American Historical Review* 73 (February 1968): 696–707.

Degler, Carl N. *At Odds: Women and the Family in America from the Revolution to the Present.* Oxford: Oxford University Press, 1980.

DePaulo, J. Raymond, Jr., and Leslie A. Horvitz. *Understanding Depression: What We Know and What We Can Do about It.* New York: John Wiley and Sons, 2002.

Dickey, Dallas C. *Seargent S. Prentiss: Whig Orator of the Old South.* Baton Rouge: Louisiana State University Press, 1946.

Eaton, Clement. *Henry Clay and the Art of American Politics.* Boston: Little, Brown, 1957.

Eddy, Mary Baker. *Science and Health with Key to the Scriptures.* Boston: The First Church of Christ, Scientist, 1971.

Edwards, Laura F. "Southern History as U.S. History." *Journal of Southern History* 75 (August 2009): 533–64.

Engerman, Stanley L. "Slavery and Its Consequences for the South in the Nineteenth Century." In *The Cambridge Economic History of the United States,* vol. 2, edited by Stanley L. Engerman and Robert E. Gallman, 329–66. Cambridge: Cambridge University Press, 2000.

Faulk, Odie B. *The Geronimo Campaign.* New York: Oxford University Press, 1969.

Faust, Drew Gilpin. *Mothers of Invention: Women in the Slaveholding South in the American Civil War.* Chapel Hill: University of North Carolina Press, 1996.

————. *This Republic of Suffering: Death and the American Civil War*. New York: Knopf, 2008.

Foster, Gaines M. *Ghosts of the Confederacy: Defeat, the Lost Cause, and the Emergence of the New South*. New York: Oxford University Press, 1987.

Fowler, Harriet. "Politically Gifted: Henry Clay's Horses Have Lasting Influence." *Keeneland* (Fall 2001): 76.

Fox, John, Jr. *The Little Shepherd of Kingdom Come*. New York: Charles Scribner's Sons, 1903.

Frank, Stephen M. *Life with Father: Parenting and Masculinity in the Nineteenth-Century American North*. Baltimore: Johns Hopkins University Press, 1998.

Friend, Craig Thompson, ed. *Southern Masculinity: Perspectives on Manhood in the South since Reconstruction*. Athens: University of Georgia Press, 2009.

Gallagher, Gary W., and Alan T. Nolan, eds. *The Myth of the Lost Cause and Civil War History*. Bloomington: Indiana University Press, 2000.

Gartner, John D. *The Hypomanic Edge: The Link between (a Little) Craziness and (a Lot of) Success in America*. New York: Simon and Schuster, 2005.

Gaston, Paul M. *The New South Creed: A Study of Southern Mythmaking*. New York: Knopf, 1970.

Gatewood, Charles B. *Lt. Charles Gatewood and His Apache Wars Memoir*. Edited by Louis Kraft. Lincoln: University of Nebraska Press, 2005.

Gilbert, Sandra M., and Susan Gubar. *The Madwoman in the Attic: The Woman Writer and the Nineteenth-Century Literary Imagination*. New Haven, Conn.: Yale University Press, 1979.

Glover, Lorri. "'Let Us Manufacture Men': Educating Elite Boys in the Early National South." In *Southern Manhood: Perspectives on Masculinity in the Old South*, ed. Craig Thompson Friend and Lorri Glover, 22–48. Athens: University of Georgia Press, 2004.

Goldfield, David. *Still Fighting the Civil War: The American South and Southern History*. Baton Rouge: Louisiana State University Press, 2002.

Goodwin, Frederick K., and Kay Redfield Jamison. *Manic Depressive Illness*. New York: Oxford University Press, 1990.

Griswold, Robert L. *Fatherhood in America: A History*. New York: Basic Books, 1993.

Grob, Gerald N. *Mental Institutions in America: Social Policy to 1875*. New York: The Free Press, 1973.

Hacker, J. David, Libra Hilde, and James Holland Jones. "The Effect of the Civil War on Southern Marriage Patterns." *Journal of Southern History* 76 (February 2010): 39–70.

Hagedorn, Hermann. *Leonard Wood, a Biography*. 2 vols. New York: Harper and Brothers, 1931. Reprint, New York: Kraus Reprint Co., 1969.

Hay, Melba Porter. *Madeline McDowell Breckinridge and the Battle for a New South*. Lexington: University Press of Kentucky, 2009.

Heidler, David, and Jeanne Heidler. *Henry Clay: The Essential American.* New York: Random House, 2010.

Heilbrun, Carolyn G. *Reinventing Womanhood.* New York: W. W. Norton, 1979.

Hervey, John L. *The American Trotter.* New York: Coward-McCann, 1947.

———. *Racing in America: 1665–1865.* 2 vols. New York: Jockey Club, 1944.

Holt, Michael F. *The Political Crisis of the 1850s.* New York: W. W. Norton, 1978.

Hopkins, James F. "Henry Clay, Farmer and Stockman." *Journal of Southern History* 15 (February 1949): 89–96.

Hopkins, James F., et al., eds. *The Papers of Henry Clay.* 11 vols. Lexington: University Press of Kentucky, 1959–1993. [CP]

Horowitz, Helen Lefkowitz. *Culture and the City: Cultural Philanthropy in Chicago from the 1880s to 1917.* Lexington: University Press of Kentucky, 1976.

Howe, Daniel Walker. *The Political Culture of the American Whigs.* Chicago: University of Chicago Press, 1979.

———. *Victorian America.* Philadelphia: University of Pennsylvania Press, 1976.

James, Bessie Rowland, ed. *Six Came Back: The Arctic Adventure of David L. Brainard.* Indianapolis: Bobbs-Merrill, 1940.

Jamison, Kay Redfield. *Touched with Fire: Manic-Depressive Illness and Artistic Temperament.* New York: The Free Press, 1993.

Janney, Caroline E. *Burying the Dead but Not the Past: Ladies' Memorial Associations and the Lost Cause.* Chapel Hill: University of North Carolina Press, 2008.

Johansen, Shawn. *Family Men: Middle-Class Fatherhood in Early Industrializing America.* New York: Routledge, 2001.

Jones, Anne Goodwyn. "Southern Literary Women as Chroniclers of Southern Life." In *Sex, Race, and the Role of Women in the South,* ed. Joanne V. Hawks and Sheila L. Skemp, 75–93. Jackson: University Press of Mississippi, 1983.

———. *Tomorrow Is Another Day: The Woman Writer in the South, 1859–1936.* Baton Rouge: Louisiana State University Press, 1981.

Joyce, John A. *A Checkered Life.* Chicago: S. P. Rounds, Jr., 1883.

Juhasz, Suzanne. *Naked and Fiery Forms: Modern American Poetry by Women, a New Tradition.* New York: Octagon Books, 1976.

Kendall, Amos. *Autobiography of Amos Kendall.* Edited by William Stickey. Boston: Lee and Shepard, 1872.

Kerber, Linda K. "Separate Spheres, Female Worlds, Woman's Place: The Rhetoric of Women's History." *Journal of American History* 75 (June 1988): 9–39.

Klotter, James C. *The Breckinridges of Kentucky, 1760–1981.* Lexington: University Press of Kentucky, 1986.

———. *Kentucky Justice, Southern Honor, and American Manhood: Understanding the Life and Death of Richard Reid.* Baton Rouge: Louisiana State University Press, 2003.

Kraditor, Aileen, ed. *Up from the Pedestal: Selected Writings in the History of American Feminism.* Chicago: HarperCollins, 1968.

Lachman, Charles. *The Last Lincolns: The Rise and Fall of a Great American Family.* New York: Union Square Press, 2008.

Lane, Jack C., ed. *Chasing Geronimo: The Journal of Leonard Wood, May–September, 1886.* Albuquerque: University of New Mexico Press, 1970.

Lasch, Christopher. *Haven in a Heartless World: The Family Besieged.* New York: W. W. Norton, 1979.

Lee, Rebecca Smith. *Mary Austin Holley: A Biography.* Austin: University of Texas Press, 1962.

Levin, H., ed. *The Lawyers and Lawmakers of Kentucky.* Chicago: Lewis, n.d.

Levinson, Douglas F., and Walter E. Nichols. "Major Depression and Genetics." Stanford Medicine website. http://depressiongenetics.stanford.edu/mddan dgenes.html.

Lewis, Sinclair. *Main Street.* New York: Harcourt, Brace, 1920.

Little, Lucius P. *Ben Hardin: His Times and Contemporaries.* Louisville, Ky.: Courier-Journal Printing, 1887.

Manning, Carol S. *The Female Tradition in Southern Literature.* Urbana: University of Illinois Press, 1993.

Martineau, Harriet. *Retrospect of Western Travel.* 3 vols. New York: Harper, 1838.

Mayo, Bernard. *Henry Clay: Spokesman of the New West.* Boston: Houghton Mifflin, 1937.

McCarthy, Kathleen D. *Noblesse Oblige: Charity and Cultural Philanthropy in Chicago, 1849–1929.* Chicago: University of Chicago Press, 1982.

McDowell, Madeline. "Recollections of Henry Clay." *Century Magazine,* September 1895, 765. Breckinridge Papers. Manuscript Division. Library of Congress.

Meyer, Jeff. "Henry Clay's Legacy to Horse Breeding and Racing." *Register of the Kentucky Historical Society* 100 (Autumn 2002): 473–96.

Miles, Nelson A. *Personal Recollections and Observations of General Nelson A. Miles.* New York: DeCapo, 1969.

Mintz, Steven. *Huck's Raft: A History of American Childhood.* Cambridge, Mass.: Belknap Press of Harvard University Press, 2004.

Mintz, Steven, and Susan Kellogg. *Domestic Revolutions: A Social History of American Family Life.* New York: The Free Press, 1988.

Mondimore, Francis Mark. *Bipolar Disorder: A Guide for Patients and Families.* Baltimore: Johns Hopkins University Press, 1999.

Morelock, Kolan Thomas. *Taking the Town: Collegiate and Community Culture in the Bluegrass, 1880–1917.* Lexington: University Press of Kentucky, 2008.

Mowatt, Anna Cora. *The Autobiography of an Actress.* Boston: Boston Stereotype Foundry, 1853.

Mrozek, Donald J. "The Habit of Victory: The American Military and the Cult of Manliness." In *Manliness and Morality: Middle-Class Masculinity in Britain and*

America, 1800–1940, ed. J. A. Mangan and James Walvin, 220–41. New York: St. Martin's, 1987.

Nagel, Paul C. *The Adams Women: Abigail and Louisa Adams, Their Sisters and Daughters.* New York: Oxford University Press, 1987.

———. *Descent from Glory: Four Generations of the John Adams Family.* Oxford: Oxford University Press, 1983.

———. *The Lees of Virginia: Seven Generations of an American Family.* New York: Oxford University Press, 1990.

Noe, Kenneth W. *Perryville: This Grand Havoc of Battle.* Lexington: University Press of Kentucky, 2001.

Nolen-Hoeksema, Susan, and Lori M. Hilt. "Gender Differences in Depression." In *Handbook of Depression,* ed. Ian H. Gotlib and Constance L. Hammen, 386–404. New York: Guilford, 2002.

Norton, Mary Beth. "The Evolution of White Women's Experience in Early America." *American Historical Review* 89 (June 1984): 593–619.

Nydegger, Rudy. *Understanding and Treating Depression: Ways to Find Hope and Help.* Westport, Conn.: Praeger, 2008.

Parton, James. "Defeated Presidential Candidates." *Forum,* January 1, 1889, 500–515.

———. "Henry Clay's Way of Speaking." *Youth's Companion,* January 1, 1880, 3–5.

Perkins, Bradford. *Castlereagh and Adams: England and the United States 1812–1823.* Berkeley: University of California Press, 1964.

Pessen, Edward. "Some Critical Reflections on the New Histories." *South Atlantic Quarterly* 78 (Autumn 1979): 478–88.

Peterson, Merrill D. *The Great Triumvirate: Webster, Clay, and Calhoun.* New York: Oxford University Press, 1987.

Poage, George Rawlings. *Henry Clay and the Whig Party.* Chapel Hill: University of North Carolina Press, 1936.

Prentiss, George L., ed. *A Memoir of S. S. Prentiss.* 2 vols. New York: Charles Scribner, 1858.

Recchiuti, John Louis. *Civic Engagement: Social Science and Progressive-Era Reform in New York City.* Philadelphia: University of Pennsylvania Press, 2007.

Redd, Richard. *Reminiscences of Richard Menefee Redd, Better Known as Colonel "Dick" Redd, from Childhood to Old Age.* Lexington: Clay Printing, 1929.

Remini, Robert V. *At the Edge of the Precipice: Henry Clay and the Compromise That Saved the Union.* New York: Basic Books, 2010.

———. *Henry Clay: Statesman for the Union.* New York: W. W. Norton, 1991.

Ritcheson, Charles R. *Aftermath of the Revolution: British Policy toward the United States, 1783–1795.* New York: W. W. Norton, 1969.

Roberts, Charles Blanton. "The Building of Middlesborough." *Filson Club History Quarterly* 7 (January 1933): 18–33.

Rogers, Amelia Clay Van Meter. "Ashland, the Home of Henry Clay." Master's thesis, University of Kentucky, 1934.

Rogers, Joseph M. *The True Henry Clay*. Philadelphia: J. B. Lippincott, 1905.

Rothenstein, John. *Summer's Lease: Autobiography, 1901–1938*. London: Hamish Hamilton, 1965.

Rotundo, E. Anthony. *American Manhood: Transformations in Masculinity from the Revolution to the Modern Era*. New York: Basic Books, 1993.

Ryan, Frank. *The Forgotten Plague: How the Battle against Tuberculosis Was Won—and Lost*. Boston: Little, Brown, 1992.

Sanger, George P., ed. *U.S. Statutes at Large, Treaties, and Proclamations of the United States of America from December 1863 to December 1865*. Boston: Little, Brown, 1866.

Sawitzky, Susan Clay. "Abraham Delanoy in New Haven." *New-York Historical Society Quarterly* 41 (April 1957): 193–206.

———. "Mariner." *Poetry: A Magazine of Verse* 57 (February 1941): 306.

Schurz, Carl. *Henry Clay*. New York: Houghton Mifflin, 1899.

Scott, Anne Firor. *Making the Invisible Woman Visible*. Chicago: University of Illinois Press, 1984.

———. *The Southern Lady: From Pedestal to Politics, 1830–1930*. Chicago: University of Chicago Press, 1970.

Sellers, Charles. *The Market Revolution: Jacksonian America, 1815–1846*. New York: Oxford University Press, 1991.

Sherman, Irwin W. *The Power of Plagues*. Washington, D.C.: ASM Press, 2006.

———. *Twelve Diseases That Changed Our World*. Washington, D.C.: ASM Press, 2007.

Showalter, Elaine. *A Literature of Their Own*. Princeton, N.J.: Princeton University Press, 1977.

Simpson, Elizabeth Murphey. *The Enchanted Bluegrass*. Lexington, Ky.: Transylvania Press, 1938.

Simpson, Henry Clay, Jr. *Josephine Clay: Pioneer Horsewoman of the Bluegrass*. Louisville, Ky.: Harmony House, 2005.

Smith, Lillian. *Killers of the Dream*. New York: W. W. Norton, 1949.

Smith, Margaret Bayard. *Forty Years of Washington Society*. Edited by Gaillard Hunt. London: T. Fisher Unwin, 1906.

Smith, Zachary F., and Mary Rogers Clay. *The Clay Family*. Louisville, Ky.: Filson Club, 1899.

Spears, Woodridge, ed. "The Circling Thread: Poems by Susan Clay Sawitzky." *Kentucky Poetry Review* Special Publication (January 1984).

Spiotta, Robert S. "Remembering Father: James Brown Clay, Merchants, Materials, and a New Ashland." Master's thesis, Cooper-Hewitt Museum / Parsons School of Design, 1990.

Stone, Elizabeth. *Black Sheep and Kissing Cousins: How Our Family Stories Shape Us.* New York: Penguin Books, 1988.

Tallant, Harold D. *Evil Necessity: Slavery and Political Culture in Antebellum Kentucky.* Lexington: University Press of Kentucky, 2003.

Tapp, Hambleton, and James C. Klotter. *Kentucky: Decades of Discord 1865–1900.* Frankfort: Kentucky Historical Society, 1977.

Taylor, Amy Murrell. *The Divided Family in Civil War America.* Chapel Hill: University of North Carolina Press, 2005.

Thompson, Buddy. *Madame Belle Brezing.* Lexington: Buggy Whip Press, 1983.

Todd, A. L. *Abandoned: The Story of the Greely Expedition 1881–1884.* New York: McGraw-Hill, 1961.

Trattner, Walter I. *From Poor Law to Welfare State: A History of Social Welfare in America.* New York: The Free Press, 1982.

Trevathan, Charles E. *The American Thoroughbred.* New York: Macmillan, 1905.

Troutman, Richard Laverne. "Henry Clay and His 'Ashland' Estate." *Filson Club History Quarterly* 30 (April 1956): 159–74.

U.S. Military Academy. "Delinquencies, 1850–52." West Point, New York.

———. *Official Register of the Officers and Cadets for the Academic Year Ending 1919.* West Point, N.Y.: U.S. Army Printing Office, 1919.

———. *Official Register of the Officers and Cadets for the Academic Year Ending 5 June 1963.* West Point, N.Y.: U.S. Army Printing Company, 1963.

———. "Official Register of the Officers and Cadets of the United States Military Academy," 2 (1828–1837). West Point, New York.

———. "Official Register of the Officers and Cadets of the United States Military Academy," 14 (1848–1857). West Point, New York.

———. "Staff Records," 1 (1818–1835). West Point, New York.

———. "Staff Records," 5 (1851–1854). West Point, New York.

U.S. War Department. *The War of the Rebellion: A Compilation of the Official Records of the Union and Confederate Armies.* Washington, D.C.: Government Printing Office, 1880–1901.

Utley, Robert M. *Frontier Regulars: The United States Army and the Indian, 1866–1891.* Lincoln: University of Nebraska Press, 1973.

Van Deusen, Glyndon G. *The Life of Henry Clay.* Boston: Little, Brown, 1937.

Vinton, Lawrence. "The Geronimo Campaign as Told by a Trooper of 'B' Troop of the 4th U.S. Cavalry." *Journal of the West* 11 (1972): 157–69.

Waldrep, Christopher. "Memory, History, and the Meaning of the Civil War—a Review Essay." *Register of the Kentucky Historical Society* 102 (Summer 2004): 383–402.

Wallace, John, Tiffany Schneider, and Peter McGuffin. "Genetics of Depression." In *Handbook of Depression,* ed. Ian H. Gotlib and Constance L. Hammen, 169–88. New York: Guilford, 2002.

Wallace, John H. *The Horse in America*. New York: Privately published, 1897.

Wallace, Sarah Agnes. "Confederate Exiles in Canada: Last Letters of James Brown Clay, 1864, Montreal." *Register of the Kentucky Historical Society* 50 (January 1952): 41–56.

Webb, Ross A. *Benjamin Helm Bristow: Border State Politician*. Lexington: University Press of Kentucky, 1969.

Welter, Barbara. "The Cult of True Womanhood: 1820–1860." *American Quarterly* 18 (Summer 1966): 151–74.

Wheeler, Marjorie Spruill. *New Women of the New South: The Leaders of the Woman Suffrage Movement in the Southern States*. New York: Oxford University Press, 1993.

White, Ronald F. "Custodial Care for the Insane at Eastern State Hospital in Lexington, Kentucky, 1824–44." *Filson Club History Quarterly* 62 (July 1988): 308–22.

Wiltse, Charles M., and Michael J. Birkner, eds. *The Papers of Daniel Webster: Correspondence (1850–52)*. Hanover, N.H.: University Press of New England, 1986.

Wolfe, Margaret Ripley. *The Daughters of Canaan: A Saga of Southern Women*. Lexington: University Press of Kentucky, 1995.

———. "Fallen Leaves and Missing Pages: Women in Kentucky History." *Register of the Kentucky Historical Society* 90 (Bicentennial Issue, 1992): 64–89.

Wooster, Robert. *Nelson A. Miles and the Twilight of the Frontier Army*. Lincoln: University of Nebraska Press, 1993.

Wright, John D., Jr. *Lexington: Heart of the Bluegrass*. Lexington: Lexington-Fayette County Historical Commission, 1982.

Wyatt-Brown, Bertram. *The House of Percy: Honor, Melancholy, and Imagination in a Southern Family*. New York: Oxford University Press, 1994.

———. *Southern Honor: Ethics and Behavior in the Old South*. New York: Oxford University Press, 1982.

INDEX

CPSIA information can be obtained at www.ICGtesting.com
Printed in the USA
LVOW062022270911

248156LV00001B/1/P